# A History of
# SWEDEN

INGVAR ANDERSSON

*Translated from the Swedish by*
CAROLYN HANNAY

PRAEGER : NEW YORK

*Published in the United States of America in 1956*
*by Frederick A. Praeger, Inc., Publishers,*
*150 E. 52nd Street,*
*New York 22, N.Y.*

*Library of Congress Catalog Card Number: 55-10489*

MADE AND PRINTED IN GREAT BRITAIN BY
WILLIAM CLOWES AND SONS, LIMITED, LONDON AND BECCLES

# Contents

# List of Illustrations

## ILLUSTRATIONS IN THE TEXT

## MAPS

# Translator's Note

This English version of Dr Ingvar Andersson's History of Sweden has been slightly adapted from the original Swedish text. Certain minor items of solely Scandinavian significance have been omitted, whereas other details needed some amplification. Dr Andersson has been most patient and co-operative in the matter, and made many helpful suggestions.

The translator is primarily indebted to two persons, without whose constant and skilful aid the work could never have been accomplished. Dr Gunnar Ahlström, Director of the Swedish Institute in London, has taken personal charge of all aspects of the work throughout, and has meticulously checked and supervised its progress. Mr Raymond Carr, of New College, Oxford, has given constructive and invaluable help in going through and correcting the preliminary drafts, particularly with regard to technical terminology, and has clarified many difficult points.

Thanks are also due to Mrs Eve Taylor, who thoroughly revised our final manuscript for publication.

C. H.

# Introduction

*by* MICHAEL ROBERTS,

*Professor of History, Queen's University, Belfast*

Few fields of historical research have been more neglected by English scholars than the history of Scandinavia. While our historians have in recent years made notable contributions to the history of most of the smaller countries of Europe, from Holland to Rumania, from Portugal to Poland – to say nothing of Cyprus and Latin America – the Scandinavian countries have attracted the merest handful of enquirers. The majority of English historians derive their ideas of Swedish history either from the austere pages of large-scale co-operative enterprises such as *The Cambridge Modern History*, or from such introductions to the subject – admirable in themselves, but all too short – as Svanström and Palmstierna's *History of Sweden*. At all events, a history of Sweden in English, covering the ground in one volume on a generous scale, and representative of informed contemporary opinion in Sweden, has long been an urgent need. And it has been obvious for more than a decade that what we really wanted was a good translation of Dr Andersson's book. Here at last we have it.

Before 1943, when the first edition of this book appeared, Dr Andersson had been known in Sweden as a distinguished representative of Swedish academic historiography: acute, learned, rigorous in analysis of sources, and with that wide range of *expertise* – in his case from the fourteenth to the eighteenth centuries – which Swedish historians appear to command with such enviable ease. His interests had latterly appeared to be centred on the sixteenth century; and a remarkable series of studies of the middle years of that period had culminated in *Erik XIV*, an acknowledged classic of Swedish historical biography. When the *History of Sweden* made its appearance in 1943, it was seen that the qualities which had made *Erik XIV* so notable a book had not failed on this much wider canvas. It still remains one of his major achievements, and it has been translated into several European languages. In a period when Swedish historians are deeply divided, and academic controversy runs high upon a score of crucial issues, it offers that *juste milieu* of ripe and dispassionate wisdom to which the historians of a later generation may rally, once contemporary tumult has subsided. The Swedes have found in Dr Andersson the judicious interpreter of their history; and they may be happy that his book should go out in translation to interpret that history to other nations.

The late Professor Eli Heckscher somewhere remarked that a small country had no right to demand that its history be studied, merely because it had happened. And it may be that some historians would willingly borrow his dictum to excuse the neglect of Scandinavian history in this country. Yet even the most cursory reading of this book must suggest that there is much in the history of Sweden which is of interest to a non-Swedish public. For Sweden's history is indeed a history unusual and in some respects unique; and though in a number of important respects it may be held to show similarities with the history of England, it differs markedly from that of the general run of Continental countries. We are immediately struck, for instance, by the circumstance that in Sweden so many developments appear to come so late: by western standards the whole history of Sweden seems to be retarded. Man came late to Sweden; the Romans never came at all; Christianity did not finally triumph till half a millennium after St Augustine came to Britain. Lying on the periphery of the world of the western Church, rescued from heathendom only when the renaissance of the twelfth century was in full flower, Sweden escaped those great clashes between *regnum* and *sacerdotium* which provide much of the dynamic of the mediaeval history of the West.

No investiture contest, no statutes of Provisors or Praemunire, mark the history of Church-State relations; and the relatively brief supremacy of Rome is untroubled by a single important heretic. And just as Sweden was late in being incorporated into the unity of western Christendom, so she was late in achieving her own unity – late, at least, by English standards. For a true capital she had to wait till the mid-thirteenth century; for a common law till the middle of the fourteenth. Provincial feeling remained strong for centuries thereafter; and was a political force to be reckoned with perhaps as late as 1743. Indeed, the successive ascendancies of this province or that – now Uppland, now Västergötland, now Dalarna – may almost be said to resemble the rise and decline of Kent and Northumbria, Mercia and Wessex, four or five centuries earlier.

Even more remarkable, to an English observer, is the slowness with which the country emerged from a relatively primitive economic condition. Whatever may have been the case during the Viking period, when that period was over Sweden found herself in a blind-alley, at the end of the trade-routes rather than at their centre. Her commerce came to be conducted, her larger towns to be peopled, mainly by Hanseatic merchants; and the economic life of the rest of the country became less subject to international influences than that of any western state. Even in the sixteenth century, and under a monarch with so sharp an eye to his own advantage as Gustav Vasa, Sweden was content with a 'passive' trade; content that foreign merchants should resort to her, rather than that her own should venture out to engage in commercial enterprises. In a striking comparison, Eli Heckscher once estimated the level of economic development of sixteenth-century Sweden as about equivalent to that of Carolingian France in the year 1000. A barter economy was still dominant. Taxes were collected, salaries assigned, interest upon loans was paid, in commodities (and perishable commodities at that). The fiscal

reforms of Gustavus Adolphus and Axel Oxenstierna temporarily substituted cash for commodities as the main con-
stituent of the revenues of the crown; but fifty years later
Charles XI's *indelningsverk* marked a partial reversion to the
old system. Throughout the eighteenth century a good deal
of this natural economy survived; so that even at the end of
it a Professor at Uppsala might have his emoluments cal-
culated and paid in grain. It was not until the abolition of
*grundskatterna* in 1892 and of the *indelningsverk* in 1901 that
Sweden saw the disappearance of the last traces of a fiscal
system which had probably vanished in England at least six
hundred years earlier. So too with the guilds; which in
Sweden became general only at the end of the sixteenth
century, and flourished mainly in the seventeenth and eighteenth, when their day in England was already over.

The slowness of this progress towards a modern type of
economy is in part to be explained by the social structure of
the country. Sweden has throughout her history been a rural
country; and she remains a rural country to-day, despite her
industries. As Dr Andersson tells us, there were in 1885 only
some 100,000 industrial workers; and even in 1940 only
about 44 per cent. of the population could be reckoned as
urban. And that 44 per cent. was (as to a great part of it, at
least) urban only in a very limited sense. Sweden has still
only two or three really large centres of population; and a
great part of Swedish industry is located in quite small towns.
In Västerås, in Huskvarna, in Borås, in Sundsvall, you feel
the country all around you – the skerries and the forest, the
curve of the river, the broad expanse of the lake, are at your
door, or at least just round the corner. Gällivare and Gusum
are not much more than overgrown villages; Lessebo not
even that. The fathers or grandfathers of a majority of urban
dwellers may probably have worked on the land. This rural
strain colours all Swedish history: Gustav Vasa's letters
put one in mind of Sir Robert Walpole and his bailiff; a
century later, Johan Ekeblad, in waiting at the court of

Christina, is greedy for news from his father of horses and dogs and country matters; even the elegant Tessin sighs to quit Stockholm for the rustic pleasures of Åkerö. Urban society is predominantly the society of the small country town; and the small-town atmosphere is no less characteristic than the rural: it is, indeed, one of the fundamental constituents of Swedish humour.

Swedish history is, in one aspect, the history of the conflicting influences of forest and water. The forests divided and isolated: they ruralized industry, impeded traffic, hindered invasion, preserved provincialism. The waters united: the immense indented coastline offered a highway by sea; the frozen lakes a winter-way through the land; and both, it has been suggested, saved Sweden – as the sea saved England – from those internal barriers of tolls and customs which were the curse of Continental countries. Or to look at it from a slightly different angle: the history of Sweden, until quite recent times, has been a history of internal colonization, of man's gradual subjugation and exploitation of his environment. For the last three centuries Swedish rulers have been forced to hold a nice balance between the enterprise of the colonist, increasing the arable by clearing the woods, and the needs of the settled communities, who looked to the woods for grazing, pannage, timber, and fuel for domestic or industrial purposes. But whichever way you look at it, the central figure in the picture, the man upon whose relationship with his environment the nation's welfare depended, has always been the Swedish peasant.

It may well be that the idealization of the yeoman peasant by such writers as E. G. Geijer has been proved to have but a shaky historical basis; it is certainly true that the earliest Swedish society of which we have a clear picture was not that egalitarian society of peasant proprietors which earlier historians believed in; but it is still safe to say that the peasant in mediaeval Sweden retained his social and political freedom to a greater degree, played a greater part in the

politics of the country, and was altogether a more considerable person, than in any other western European country.
At the close of the Middle Ages the class of free peasant proprietors was still the largest class in the community; it owned
more land than any other; it alone was strong enough to tip
the balance in the swaying constitutional struggle between
monarchy and nobility. And this, it seems, because Sweden
had never been in any true sense a feudal country. Between
a nobility which had already by the close of the Middle Ages
become hereditary and the free tax-paying and landowning
peasantry were no intermediate gradations of any consequence. No tenurial pyramid existed: the distinction was
only between those who paid taxes (the free peasantry) and
those who did not (the nobles, their tenants, and the
crown's tenants). There could be no question of a gentry
class such as existed in England, and no squirearchy. After
the Reformation the clergy either drew their recruits from
the peasantry, or were self-recruiting within their own order.
The towns, always the weakest of the four Estates, never
played a part in Swedish history comparable to that played
by the towns of England, France, and Germany – to say
nothing of Italy and the Netherlands. It was not to them
that the monarchy looked for a counterpoise to aristocratic
faction: even Stockholm was perhaps of less importance to its
possessor than was the capital of any western monarchy. In
Sweden the crown's ally, or its tool, came more and more to
be the peasantry; and from Karl Knutsson to Gustav III
successive rulers turned to it for support when they ran up
against a major difficulty. Hence the demagogic tradition of
Swedish kingship, which crops up again and again: Sten
Sture the younger, Gustav Vasa, Eric XIV, Charles IX,
Gustavus Adolphus – they all had it, in greater or less degree;
all developed a style of oratory which, whatever may have
been its literary merits (and on occasion they were considerable), was essentially popular. Even over-civilized and
over-intellectualized monarchs such as Christina and

Gustav III could strike this note surely and without effort when they chose. When Gustav III spoke to the soldiers in the guard-room on the morning of 19 August, 1772, or stood on the churchyard walls of Dalarna to rally the people, seventeen years later, he was only the last (and not the least eloquent) representative of a tradition which had become part of the stock-in-trade of Swedish kingship.

But even in the nineteenth century, when the tides of politics were setting strongly in favour of the emergent middle class, it was the country, rather than the town, that provided the great issues. The social crisis of nineteenth-century Sweden was mainly a rural crisis; the consolidation of strips in the common field was as great a revolution in rural Sweden as in rural England (though Sweden managed it much more intelligently); and the great emigration of the second half of the century – as in Ireland or Scotland – was the reaction to a rural rather than an urban problem. And though the constitutional reform of 1865 may have resulted from the pressure of those middle classes who had found no representation within the framework of the old system of Estates, it was the peasantry, now organized as a political party, that reaped the main political advantage of the change.

All this is in strong contrast to the course of English history. Yet in some respects the history of Sweden has much in common with our own. And perhaps the most important of these common factors is the long tradition, shared by both countries, of personal and political freedom, and a profound respect for the rule of law. The feeling for law and liberty, the consciousness of having managed to preserve them when most other countries failed to do so, the pride in their un-broken transmission, more or less intact, from a remote past – this is something which, even if at times it verges on mytho-logy rather than history, is nevertheless part of the national ethos of each country. Magnus Eriksson's *landslag* of the mid-fourteenth century was not merely a codification, valid for the whole realm, of criminal and civil law : it was, even more importantly, a statement of the law of the constitution. In a sense it was Sweden's Magna Carta; and it meant much the same to constitutional antiquarians such as Hogenskild Bielke as Magna Carta meant to the contemporaries of Sir Edward Coke. 'The land shall be built upon law' was thus a political tradition handed down from the middle ages, firmly grasped, and never abandoned. Sweden was indeed to experience more than one attempt at absolutism; but such attempts were successful only if they kept within the letter of the law; and the rights of the subject were respected even under such kings as Charles XI and Charles XII. Because it was not until the seventeenth century that Sweden developed a professional class of advocates, the administration of the law, and the custody of the tradition of observance of the law, fell to a great extent upon the nobility; and the mind of the Swedish aristocracy was from an early period soaked in Swedish law. And this in turn strengthened the rule of law, by enlisting among the champions of legality a class which in other countries was sometimes disposed to override it.

Equally ancient is the tradition of self-government. Local self-government, indeed, has roots stretching down to the earliest days of State and Church. The democracy of the *ting*, the co-operation of all classes in the parochial council, are among the fundamental facts of Swedish history; and they proved strong enough in the seventeenth century to resist successfully the contradictory threats of the efficient centralizing officials of the monarchy, on the one hand, and those aristocratic tendencies towards social oppression of the type prevalent in Germany, on the other. Parliamentary self-government is much younger; but it is still of respectable antiquity. Before the end of the fourteenth century the *Riksdag* had begun to take shape; before the end of the fifteenth it had become an important element in the political life of the nation. It was of high significance that the Diet should have included, from an early date, a separate Estate of peasants. As with the English parliament, it was only gradually that the *Riksdag* took over the task of safeguarding the liberties of the nation, and no notion of that sort lay behind its early summonses. The constitutional opposition, the guardianship of the law, the check upon royal aggression, was at first the nobility, in Sweden as in England. They strove to keep the monarchy elective; they made the *råd* the watch-dog of the constitution.

The political accidents which led to the breach of the union with Denmark at the opening of the sixteenth century were utilized by the new monarchy to destroy this constitutional resistance: Gustav Vasa and Eric XIV, reaping where the Stures had sown (much as the early Tudors built on Yorkist foundations) made the monarchy hereditary, stopped the mouth of the nobility with the plunder of the Church, and began the erection of a parliamentary despotism of the Tudor type. Their work was, however, but a half-success. The *Riksdag* in the end did not become the obedient instrument of the monarchy, as the Cortes did in Castile; the crises at the end of the sixteenth century proved that aristocratic constitutionalism was still very much alive; and throughout the whole of the seventeenth century Sweden was engaged in a protracted constitutional struggle between monarchy and aristocracy. In the course of that struggle the *Riksdag* emerged as a truly national representative organ; it crystallized into four Estates; it developed parliamentary procedure. There were times – in 1650, in 1680 – when for reasons social or economic a majority of the Estates was willing to back the monarchy against the aristocracy. But what was important was that the *Riksdag*'s monopoly of legal legislation was established; its control of the executive began to be asserted; its regular meeting was secured; and above all its exclusive right to grant new taxes was successfully maintained. When the death of Charles XII in the trenches of Fredrikshald brought the so-called absolutism to a close, the Estates were ready, with a constitutional tradition, a theory of government, and a long experience, to shoulder the burden of parliamentary rule. This triumphant maintenance of parliamentary constitutionalism, throughout a century which saw the general prevalence of absolutism on the Continent and in Denmark, was a great achievement. It may, perhaps, be related to another peculiarity of Swedish history: the establishment, in 1544, of a truly national army – the first national army of modern times.

However that may be, the eighteenth century saw an extraordinary efflorescence of parliamentary life and habits. The Diets of the Age of Freedom combined a common sense and flexibility in practice which recalls the evolutionary and pragmatic methods of English constitutional advance, with a rigour and logic in political theory reminiscent of revolutionary France. Before that age ended, they had established techniques of parliamentary control far more varied and effective than any that existed in eighteenth-century England; they had grasped the notion of unwritten conventions of the constitution; they had developed true political parties, genuinely divided upon issues of national policy; they had enforced the doctrine of ministerial responsibility to parliament; and they had enunciated the theory of cabinet solidarity. The cumbrous machinery of four Estates had been made to work, if not wholly without friction, still at least with tolerable success. Sweden was the only country in Europe (with the possible exception of Württemberg) in which the old mediaeval Estates were able to transform themselves into something like a modern parliament. The Age of Freedom brought about its own destruction by its vices and its follies, and no retrospective enthusiasm for its constitutional achievements (or, even more, for its constitutional possibilities) can alter the plain fact that the revolution of 1772 was necessary for the health and safety of Sweden; but with all its odiousness the régime of the Hats and Caps had reached a stage of constitutional advance which was unequalled in pre-revolutionary Europe, and which was not attained again in Sweden for many decades after 1772.

The fratricidal strife of Hats and Caps – the political excesses of the one after 1756, and of the other in 1771–2 – suggest a further reflection: that excesses of this kind have been extraordinarily rare in Sweden. The history of modern Sweden shares with the history of modern Britain a quite unusual quality of moderation. There are no great upheavals, no crises which seem to throw the very bases of the state into confusion, no violent outbreaks of lawlessness on a large scale. Unlike most European countries, Sweden has never experienced a *jacquerie*; but neither has she been shaken by great subversive movements of the proletariat. The vision or opportunism of Gustav III enabled her to escape the repercussions of the French Revolution; and in the epidemic of 1848 she came off with the mildest of attacks. Since the Battle of Stångebro in 1598 there has been no civil war in Sweden; nor has there been any really dangerous rebellion. Gustav III provided the only victim of political assassination; and the rabbling of the younger Fersen in 1810 the only serious example of mob-murder. The twin spirits of compromise and conservatism, it would seem, have now presided over Sweden's history for something like three centuries; and they have given it a continuity which has survived many abrupt changes of course. Swedish lawyers have been as reluctant as English to interfere unnecessarily with what has grown venerable by age: it took a century and a quarter of intermittent effort to produce the great recodification of the law which finally appeared in 1734. The revolution of 1809 was as peaceful as the Glorious Revolution in England: James II's nose is said to have bled, Gustav IV certainly vomited; but neither of them otherwise suffered physical discomfort. And the constitution of 1809 had its roots as firmly set in the old order as had the Bill of Rights. No single sharp enactment destroyed the privileges of the Swedish nobility: the process of social levelling went on gradually, with notable accelerations here and there (as for instance in 1789) from 1723 until the Estates themselves came to an end in 1865. The expansion of the electorate after that year proceeded at a pace which would not have appeared unduly hectic to Sir Robert Peel, and might even have seemed sluggish to Disraeli. On all sides there has been a reluctance to draw the uttermost logical consequences from a principle. The absolutism of Charles XI was always bounded by the law; the rule of the Estates after 1718 was carefully declared to be something short of sovereignty. It is noteworthy that as early as 1911 the Social Democrats abandoned the pure dogma of Marxism, as too rigid for Swedish political conditions; while Swedish conservatives have shown a Wellingtonian readiness to swallow reforms which have become inevitable, and even to assist in putting them through.

If we turn now from internal affairs to the part played by Sweden in the general history of Europe, her peculiar contribution is not difficult to isolate. It does not consist in her brief but glorious career as a great power; it does not consist even in Gustavus Adolphus's deliverance of German Protestantism from the threat of the Counter-Reformation: by 1660 Sweden was already struggling to maintain the position which Gustavus Adolphus and Charles X had won, and all that followed was a long-drawn epilogue; while as to Germany, it may be plausibly argued that sooner rather than later much the same result might have been expected by other means. The true international importance of Sweden's part in history is rather that she has always stood, as she still stands, in the gate between East and West. Swedish statesmen have always aimed at keeping open their window to the west, while at the same time establishing some system of security to the east. They have tried on occasion to make Sweden the economic, as well as the political *entrepot* between the two. They have sought – as the elder Sture sought, and Gustavus Adolphus, and Charles XII, and Gustav III – to find security against Russia by a system of outposts in the eastern Baltic, and by driving back the Muscovite from the sea: it is possible to explain the whole history of Sweden's Baltic empire on the ground that it was essentially a defensive policy from first to last. At times they have tried the other tack – Eric XIV tried it, and so did the Caps, and Gustav III at the close of his reign, and the men of 1812 – and made a bid for security by courting Russian friendship. They have even fought to neutralize Russia by putting a Swedish prince on the throne of the Tsars. But whatever the method employed, they have always been conscious of the ultimate importance of the geopolitical problem which they cannot escape: how old, and how unchanging a problem, this book most clearly shows.

These, then, are some of the reflections provoked by a reading of Dr Andersson's account of his country's history. The military historian might well have dwelt on aspects no less interesting and important: on Eric XIV's brilliant anticipation of the military reforms of Maurice of Orange; on Gustavus Adolphus's amendment of what was lacking in those reforms, so that he was able, as Maurice was not, to transform the whole art of war for more than a century; on Charles XII's use of attack in column, transmitted as a direct legacy to the armies of revolutionary France. The naval historian could hardly have failed to advert to Eric XIV's experiments in shipbuilding, and would probably have added a timely warning against over-hasty generalization about the ineffectiveness of galleys, in the light of Baltic experience. The economic historian would have called attention to the close correlation between Sweden's monopoly of the European copper-market and her political ascendancy; to the remarkable experiments in state control by Görtz; to the successful efforts throughout the eighteenth century to ensure a stable price for iron; and to the economic writings of Chydenius. But apart from all such individual facets, which will gleam with varying brightness according to the angle from which we approach them, there remains the general impression produced by the whole story; a story so various, so rich in great moments, so violent in its contrasts. Is it possible to read without excitement the extraordinary epic of Sweden's rise to greatness, or to follow without emotion the story of her last desperate struggles under Charles XII – frantic for righteousness, fatal to his country, and at the end, it would seem, absolutely fey? Extraordinary the transformation of the Sweden of Axel Oxenstierna to the Sweden of Per Albin Hansson! For me, at least, Swedish history has this challenging quality: that it is almost impossible to approach it without taking sides. Gustavus Adolphus or Charles XI? For Charles XII or against? Royalist or aristocrat-constitutionalist? Hat or Cap? And the record is strewn with great actions and peopled with great men. It is not necessary to be a Swede to glory in Breitenfeld, to admire Fraustadt (the perfect victory), to applaud Svensksund. The sixteenth century produced few greater rulers than Gustav Vasa, and none more remarkable than Eric XIV; Gustavus Adolphus has a good claim to be regarded as among the greatest kings of any age, and Oxenstierna as the greatest of his contemporaries; Gustav III is the most baffling, the most fascinating, and perhaps in the long run not the least successful, of the benevolent despots.

But there is no need to prolong the catalogue. There have been moments – not more than two or three, perhaps – when the history of Sweden was also the history of Europe; and at such moments a knowledge of the history of Sweden has always been obligatory upon historians. But between these peaks lie long valleys, secluded from the eye of foreign observation, neglected hitherto by the historical explorer, but crowded with their own peculiar and fascinating forms of life. To the valleys, as to the peaks, this book does justice; and makes it clear that, despite Heckscher's dictum, Swedish history is worth studying for its own sake. The man who finds Swedish history dull had better not read history at all.

# I

# Early History

Before the evidence of geology and prehistory became available, the main source for the study of early Swedish history was the long and adventurous sagas of the Icelander, Snorre Sturlason, which date from the thirteenth century. Sturlason describes the wanderings of Odin and the Ases who travelled from Asia and the River Don right up to the Mälaren region, where the god seized a portion of territory, laid down laws, and established a religion. Other gods followed in Odin's footsteps, and one of them, Frey, also known as Yngve, founded the Ynglinga line of kings in Uppsala. Though Snorre's narrative was partly based on a ninth-century Norwegian epic, the *Ynglingatal*, by Thiodolf of Hvin, much of it was freely invented in the style of the old Icelandic historians.

Towards the end of the Middle Ages, and in the sixteenth century, an even more fantastic version of Sweden's early history was evolved. The Goths (*Götar*) in Östergötland and Västergötland were identified with the famous and mighty Goths of the Teutonic migrations, thus providing an endless series of kings who were believed to have ruled over Swedish tribes. Somewhat presumptuously this line was then linked with that of the Old Testament kings, going right back to the days of the Flood.

Even if these fictitious sources are discounted, the history of Sweden can be traced back to very early times. It is well known that, some tens of thousands of years ago, northern Europe was completely covered with a thick layer of ice, which underwent successive stages of melting and glaciation. The various physical marks left on the earth's surface testify to the course of events, and fairly reliable dates can be given for the different stages by means of the 'geochronological system', which was devised by the Swedish geologist Gerard de Geer and which is based on an examination of the mud and clay strata deposited yearly during the recession of the ice-cap.

This recession did not proceed by even stages, and at times the ice succeeded in resisting the heat of the sun, particularly in central Sweden. Finally, however, the sun won the day. In a sunny year the ice would recede north-ward by as much as 400 yards, ultimately reaching the position which exists to-day. All this, of course, took time; the clay strata show that the great thaw began in southern Skåne (Scania) about 12,000 years before the birth of Christ, and was still going on in central Sweden some 3000 years later.

The southern part of the Scandinavian peninsula had originally been submerged in the Baltic Sea under the enor-mous weight of ice; once freed from this, however, the elastic crust of the earth began to emerge, first in the south, and then, as the ice melted, farther and farther north. The process took longest along the east coast, and for thousands of years Östergötland, Södermanland, and Uppland formed only a small strip or an archipelago in the ice-filled ocean. In the south, on the other hand, the land rose so much that what is now the bed of the Sound of Öresund, and of the Great and Little Belts became exposed, and Sweden was thus connected by Denmark with the Continent. During this period the Baltic became an inland sea, and its waters flowed along great rivers into the Atlantic, which in turn extended over the present-day Lake Vänern in a wide bay. The country bore little resemblance to the Sweden of to-day, so that in any account of the early history of Scandinavia the region should be treated as a whole, rather than according to its divisions.

As soon as the ice disappeared, the willow and the dwarf birch, the reindeer and the Polar fox began to make their appearance in what is now southern Sweden. They were quickly followed by man, prompted by his perpetual search for inhabitable land and food. The climate gradually became drier and more temperate; birch, pine, and, later, hazel forests took root, and the first traces of human settlement, which date from about 6000 B.C., have been found round Lake Ringsjön in Skåne and at Sandarna in the Gothenburg area.

It is not known for certain whether the first settlers came from any other parts of the country. There seems to have been human life on the extreme north-west and north coast of Scandinavia during the whole of the glaciation period; and these tracts appear to have remained free of ice even during the coldest stages. If this is so, the northerly tribes may have survived along the border of the inland ice, rather in the same way as the Eskimos on the coasts of Greenland, in which case settlers may have reached Sweden from these latitudes. Traces of primitive culture have been found as far north as Lappland, though their date is uncertain. Stone Age hunters from the south and south-west also migrated very early as far as Jämtland. Further research, however, is required to confirm these suppositions.

While the ice was still melting and the land was emerging in the north, the most southerly districts began to sink again. The warmer waters of the Atlantic irrupted into the rivers of the Baltic, Skåne was divided from the Danish islands, while the climate became milder and moister. In these more favourable conditions, large numbers of hunting and fishing people migrated to Sweden. They settled with their flint and stone implements, and their hunting and fishing gear, along what is now her south and west coast, i.e. the old Danish and Norwegian provinces; and they also began to learn the important art of pottery. They pressed inland from the coast along small rivers and lakes – not on sporadic hunting expeditions, but with a view to settling. They penetrated right across the country or worked northwards along the east coast, which at that time ran farther to the west than it does to-day, as the whole of what became the Mälaren Valley was still under water. The best known of these tribes were those who settled at Limhamn west of Malmö, and in the south-west corner of the bay of Skälderviken.

A clear picture of the sequence of events in the first millennia of Swedish history has only been arrived at after a great deal of research, both archaeological and geological. One of the techniques used has been a system of typology which was evolved by two Swedes, Hans Hildebrand and Oscar Montelius, and their Danish colleague Sophus Müller. Based on the evolution of one type of tool from another, this has proved very illuminating, even though it has subsequently been found that the different types not infrequently overlapped. Another method is Lennart von Post's pollen analysis, elaborated from the study of the different layers of pollen deposited in bogs through the ages. These two methods of research, reinforcing and checking each other's findings, have also revealed the connection between technical progress and climatic and other natural conditions.

The first Swedish settlements were of a primitive and haphazard nature : life was little more than a brute struggle for existence, and the dead were buried in the precincts of the living without further ceremony. But all this was changed when the settlers began to learn about the different types of grain, and the care of livestock, chiefly cattle and pigs. They no longer needed to be constantly moving about in search of food, as they were assured of the products of their cattle and of supplies of seed for the future. This new culture reached Sweden about 3000 B.C., and it brought about a greater change in the conditions of living than anything before or since.

Our knowledge of this development is based on the discovery of a new type of flint implement, admirably designed for clearing forests, and polished with unprecedented skill. Further light is shed by the impressive burial monuments of these first settlers, which are built in the form of cairns and testify to a new attitude towards after-life, and to new religious conceptions in general. Agriculture was first introduced into those areas of Sweden that were originally Danish, and it is in Skåne and on the west coast that most of the oldest cairns are to be found. Later, when the so-called chamber-tombs became current, settlers can be traced still farther up-country; in Västergötland there is a regular town of about 200 such tombs grouped together, and others have been found on the island of Öland. A primitive farming population was gradually spreading over the land of Sweden and gaining ground on the virgin forests.

It has been suggested that agriculture and cattle-raising were not purely native developments, but were introduced by new tribes who migrated to Sweden through what is now Denmark. However that may be, the practice apparently spread northwards, along rivers and lakes and by the east coast, in the latter part of the Stone Age nearly reaching Södermanland. (Recently remarkable, though disputed, finds have proved the existence in this region of a settlement where wheat and barley were cultivated.) The climate, which was still much more temperate than it is to-day, clearly favoured the new form of livelihood and culture. Nevertheless, it was not the fertile areas cultivated to-day that were then in demand. The husbandmen of the Stone Age had neither the implements nor the draught animals for heavy soils, nor did they know anything about drainage; and it was in districts with light dry earth and good pasture that the first Swedish farmers made their home.

But the claims of these agricultural tribes to the land were by no means uncontested. Fishing and hunting tribes, who still maintained their ancient way of life, were suspicious of this new culture, with its technically improved flint tools and more civilized burial customs. Another rival was to be found in the new civilization which appeared in southern and central Sweden about 2000 B.C., similar to that which developed in Denmark during the later Stone Age. Its representatives had their own burial customs – single tombs just under the surface of the ground, without the enormous blocks and mounds of the cairns – and their own characteristic polished stone weapons in the form of boat-shaped battle-axes. They are believed to have been migrants from central Europe, who came to Sweden from the south-east or east: possibly an equestrian or nomadic race, with an outlook and way of life different from those of the farming population. This race or culture – it is not clear which – spread rapidly, even penetrating the very north of Sweden.

There is little definite information about the various vicissitudes which occurred during these centuries. By the end of the Stone Age, when the cist was the current method of burial, the different elements in the population seem to have fused. A leading position was still maintained by the Danish-Swedish provinces, and particularly by Skåne, whose rich flint resources, lacking in other parts of the country, were eagerly sought after for trading purposes. Primitive flint mines from the Stone Age, bearing actual traces of a rudimentary industry, have been found not far from Malmö, and flint implements of Scanian origin have been discovered even as far north as Norrland. Evidence of European trade relations is also revealed in the south of Sweden in the form of copper and bronze objects; and it was here that craftsmanship in bronze first flourished in a manner similar to that in Denmark proper, though not on such a highly developed scale. These southern provinces, opening on to the Continent, were for long the purveyors of new trends and developments to the remote districts in the north. Nevertheless, even in the most northerly part of what was one day to become the kingdom of Sweden the land was now under cultivation; the central parts of Sweden, too, had emerged from the sea and the settlements there were increasing in number, though they were still little more than isolated patches in the vast waste of forest and bog.

1. Rock carving from Tanum, Bohuslän.

2a. Ornamental Stone Age hammer from Alunda, Uppland.

2b. Bronze Age chieftain's grave, Kivik, Skåne.

During the so-called Bronze Age, flint remained the basic material, though the period gained a certain brilliance from its bronze work. The people became very skilful in casting this new metal into various objects: ornaments, weapons, and even horns. Some of the small bronze images may have been copied from large statues of gods carved in wood.

A new departure is also apparent in such spiritual trends as can be discerned in this period. Here again, most of the evidence is gleaned from the burial customs. The cairns and single tombs disappeared, and were replaced by the practice of laying the dead body, with ornaments and other objects, in a huge mound of earth or stone. And this in turn gave place to the funeral pyre, suggesting a complete revolution in the ideas of life after death. These centuries (1500–500 B.C.) also yield remarkable, if still somewhat obscure, evidence in the enigmatic drawings carved on smooth rock surfaces. Such rock-carvings are particularly common in Bohuslän, Östergötland, and Skåne, but they have also been found in Norrland. Though their exact significance is unknown, they are undoubtedly manifestations of a sun and fertility worship that was adopted and elaborated by the chieftains and farmers of the Bronze Age; and they strike the first personal note in these centuries of hardship, struggle, and discovery.

Many of the primaeval animals had died out, like the terrapin and giant deer; or, like the reindeer, had retreated to the far north. The vegetation, too, had altered appreciably. But man had come to stay, and with the help of flint, clay, fire, the new metals, grain, and cattle was slowly but surely availing himself of what the earth had to offer. The next great step forward was the discovery of iron. This metal, which was produced from bog-ore, revolutionized the position as the old flint settlements were replaced by fresh ones concentrated round the sources of the new material.

There are few archaeological finds dating from the first stages of the Iron Age in Sweden. This new era, which began about 500 B.C., might also be called the age of rye, iron, and

3*

trousers. The climate had become colder and damper, necessitating hardier types of grain and warmer garments; while new tracts, emerging from the sea along the east coast, provided the population with more ground. Agriculture and cattle-raising were adapted to suit the new conditions, and considerable technical progress was made, chiefly in the use of heavier and more efficient ploughs. And for the first time obscure rumours of this land in the north began to reach the races farther south – the Greeks and Romans, whose writings help to give a picture of Scandinavia about the time of the birth of Christ.

A curious conception of the geography of the world prevailed in the Classical Age, when nothing at all was known about the extent and configuration of the northern European coast. About 300 B.C. the Greek Pytheas sailed northwards from Massilia (Marseilles) along the west coast of Europe. It is not known for certain how far he got, but he brought back many strange reports of a place where the sun rose again almost as soon as it had set; of the land of Thule situated near an expanse of sea to the north of Britain, boasting a night that lasted half the year; of fenlands and islands to which the ocean brought costly amber, and of a fabulous island country. The shores of the North Sea were further explored in the time of the Emperor Augustus, and some decades later Pliny the Elder was writing of Scandinavia and other islands in the northern ocean, and of the River Vistula which flows into it. It was the prospect of amber which aroused the interest of the Romans in these remote parts, and a brisk trade in this commodity grew up.

Nor was it long before information about these Swedish tribes reached Rome itself. In his *Germania*, which appeared in A.D. 98, the Latin historian Tacitus tells of the Suiones, a tribe that dwelt beyond those of the Lugii, the Gotones, and Rugii and the Lemovii.

The states of the Suiones [he continues], not on but in the ocean, possess not merely arms and men but powerful fleets: the style of their ships differs in this respect, that there is a prow at each end, with a beak ready to be driven forwards; they neither work it with sails, nor add oars to banks to the side: the gearing of the oars is detached as on certain rivers, and reversible as occasion demands, for movement in either direction. Among these peoples, further, respect is paid to wealth, and one man is accordingly supreme, with no restrictions and with an unchallenged right to obedience; nor is there any general carrying of arms here, as among the other Germans; rather they are locked up in charge of a warder, and that warder a slave. The ocean forbids sudden inroads from enemies; and, besides, bands of armed men, with nothing to do, easily become riotous: it is not to the king's interest to put a noble or a freeman or even a freedman in charge of the arms.

Beyond the Suiones is another sea, sluggish and almost motionless, with which the earth is girdled and bounded: evidence for this is furnished in the brilliance of the last rays of the sun, which remain so bright from his setting to his rising again as to dim the stars: faith adds further that the sound of his emergence is audible and the forms of his horses visible, with the spikes of his crown. So far (and here rumour speaks the truth), and so far only, does Nature reach.[1]

These Suiones, with their huge fleets and honourable warriors, described by Tacitus as living in the ocean itself, have always been identified, not without justification, with the Svear, who inhabited the Mälaren region. It is impossible, of course, to discriminate between fact and fiction in Tacitus's account, but his description of the Suiones' boats has been confirmed by the remains of just such a craft that has been excavated at Hjortspring on the island of Als in Denmark. This boat, which probably dates from the third century before Christ, had a prow at both ends, and a number of light paddles which were found nearby. True, it is not from the land of the Suiones; nevertheless it is from the same cultural region, and is of exactly the same type as those described by Tacitus in the first century A.D.

[1] Sir Wm. Peterson's trans., Loeb Classical Library.

At any rate, it was Tacitus who introduced the Svear into the annals of history, indicating that new regions were beginning to assert themselves alongside the southern provinces which had hitherto dominated the scene. And in about A.D. 150 the Egyptian astrologer and geographer, Ptolemy of Alexandria, drew his first map of the countries on the Baltic Sea, in which Sweden – which he calls Scandia – appears as the largest and most easterly of four islands in the 'Germanic Ocean'. Ptolemy was aware that this island was inhabited by such tribes as the 'Goutai', or the Goths, but he was ignorant of its northern areas and of the fact that it was a peninsula stretching from the north.

Up to the last half-century before the birth of Christ, the Nordic countries had had little contact with the Mediterranean. At this point, however, the Romans and the Germans of the mainland became to an increasing extent involved in common projects both of a peaceable and a warlike nature, and this had an indirect effect on Sweden. Archaeologists have rightly called these centuries the 'Roman Iron Age', when Scandinavia was brought into touch with Roman civilization by means of the trade routes along the great German rivers. Glass goblets and bronze vessels, all made in the Roman Empire, have been dug up from Swedish soil, and the numerous Roman silver coins, particularly from the island of Gotland in the Baltic, provide evidence of economic relations. Runic writing, modelled on Classical script, was introduced, and the Swedes learnt to carve their stones with names and invocations against evil spirits.

The fifth century and the beginning of the sixth was a period of wealth for Sweden, since some of the treasure plundered from the disintegrating Roman Empire fell to her lot. But it was also a period of disquiet and constant feuds. Discoveries of richly decorated weapons of a conquered enemy, or of hoards buried by their owners as a safeguard against war or pillage, all speak of an unrest which was part and parcel of the stormy state of Europe at the time of the great barbarian invasions and the fall of Rome. Other indications of this unrest in Sweden are revealed in the large numbers of primitive fortifications, many of which were clearly intended to accommodate most of the local population, and which were erected at this time in many parts of the country, particularly in the central provinces and on Öland and Gotland in the Baltic.

From about A.D. 500 Sweden had a new centre, Uppland, in the Mälaren region, where the ancient creeks had been turned into productive pastures; this was, moreover, close to the hunting-grounds that yielded what was perhaps the most important export of the time, skins of wild animals. Mounds were raised over the local kings at Old Uppsala and Vendel; and other chieftains were buried in their ships, in the neighbourhood of the River Fyris, with treasure of a magnificence unparalleled anywhere else in the north. It was this period that was portrayed by the Ostrogoth historian Jordanes in his account of Scandinavia and the exploits of the numerous Swedish tribes. Many of these, particularly those of Uppland, had acquired great power and riches. The ship-burial excavated at Sutton Hoo, Suffolk, in 1939, is also significant in this context. The helmet found there bears a striking similarity to one found at Valsgärde in Uppland, suggesting that, even in pre-Viking times, there was some intercourse between eastern England and this Swedish centre.

Further indications are provided by the great English epic, the Song of Beowulf. This poem is mainly concerned with the Danes and the Geats, but mention is also made of battles between Geats and Svear somewhere around the beginning of the sixth century. Scholars differ in their opinion as to whether the Geats meant the Goths or the Jutes, but in either case the poem adds considerably to our knowledge of the early history of Sweden. Thus we read that Beowulf, guardian of the Geatish King Heardred, received at court the banished sons of the Svear King Ohthere, who had

rebelled against their uncle Onela; and when Beowulf subsequently became King of the Geats, he supported Ohthere's
son Eadgils with warriors and arms. Eadgils conquered the
usurper in Sweden and became King in his stead. An older
King of the Svear – Ongentheow, the father of Ohthere and
Onela – is also mentioned as fighting against the Geats and
being killed in battle with them. All this gives but a slight
indication of the Svear rule which is suggested by the mighty
tumuli of the sixth century and the ship burials of the sixth
and seventh. Still, it is here that personalities in Swedish
history are mentioned by name for the first time – Angantyr,
Ale, Ottar, and Adils, to give the Early English names their
Swedish equivalents. It is significant, too, that of these, Ottar,
Adils and Ale are also mentioned in the *Ynglingatal*: Thiodolf
narrates that Ottar fell in battle against Danish chieftains,
while Adils, Ale's adversary, died from a fall from his horse.
These two poems, the Song of Beowulf and the *Ynglingatal*,
are from widely different places, and although they confirm
each other in part, there is absolutely no indication that
either was influenced by the other. Thus for all their legendary character, the existence of these Svear kings has a
strong factual basis.

From about the same period comes the oldest sculptured
stones, which bear reliefs of motifs from heroic saga and
myth. Similar associations can also be dimly discerned on
the Rök stone in Östergötland, the largest and most puzzling
of all Scandinavian runestones; the inscription, however,
probably dates from no earlier than the Viking Age. The
lines, which speak of a great warrior king, Theodrik, on his
Gothic stallion, may be a reference to Theodoric the Great,
in which case they date from the Age of Migrations. Another
reference to the impact of this era on Scandinavia is contained in the work of the sixth-century Byzantine historian,
Procopius; he tells of the Herules, a tribe living north of the
Danube, who were worsted by their neighbours the Longo-
bards and fled to 'Thule', where they settled.

Towards the end of this remarkable epic age an expansion also took place from eastern Sweden and Gotland towards the south-east corner of the Baltic, where the necropolis at Grobin (in present-day Latvia) shows unmistakable Swedish influence. The date of the oldest of the graves has been fixed at the latter part of the seventh century.

Swedish life in the sixth century seems to have been distinguished chiefly by its close contacts with the Europe of the Age of Migrations, its great brilliance and power combined with profound unrest, its trade in costly skins and precious metal, and its piratical raids and colonization on the opposite shore of the Baltic. The foremost tribes in the land were the Svear and the Gotlanders.

Henceforward, a new source of information is to be found in the Swedish place-names which have provided material for scientific research and a comprehensive literature. At one time the existing names were believed to date from the Stone Age, but more critical research attributes the oldest to the Age of Migration. They are of the type Odens*vi*, Gud*hem*, Ull*tuna*, Stig*tomta*, their suffixes denoting different aspects of home or property; and the habit of prefixing them with a pagan name would also be compatible with sixth-century origin. Most striking is the fact that all Swedish place-names were composed in Swedish, proving that the native language, which at that time differed little from the other Scandinavian tongues, had been current in Sweden from the time of the earliest available linguistic evidence. A Danish scholar has remarked that these suffixes testify to the determined struggle made by the peasants for an independent existence.

According to archaeologists and students of place-names, the pattern of life was now evolved which was to prevail in the rural areas of Sweden for more than a thousand years: namely, the village community. A stable organization of this kind was the obvious answer to unrest and economic change. Combined effort and communal labour, besides conducing to greater safety, benefited both cattle-rearing and agriculture, and enabled the farmers to plough the heavier, but ultimately more profitable soil. It was also during this period that even more luxuriant pasture land was made available by the continued recession of the sea. The consolidation and expansion of the farming community combined with the trade, maritime exploits and colonization of the chieftains to make this a notable period of Swedish history, though some of its details are still obscure.

The Viking campaigns of the ninth and tenth centuries followed logically on this process of internal reorganization. With these campaigns, which had been foreshadowed by the expansions towards the south-east, the Swedish tribes make their entry into world history and, as merchants or pirates, penetrate far beyond the limited confines of the Baltic Sea.

# II

# The Swedish Vikings
## 800-1050

---

In the first chapter, Skåne, Halland, Blekinge, and Bohuslän have been included in this account of Sweden's history, although by the time a more advanced political organization becomes apparent in Scandinavia, these provinces belonged to Norway and Denmark. The main reason for dealing with them thus was to preserve the continuity of those cultural features common to all three countries. Gradually, however, the settlements of central Sweden began to assume a character of their own, and during the Viking Age the three Scandinavian kingdoms came to a parting of the ways. Sweden became a separate kingdom, though it was only at a later date that her frontiers took on their present line.

Men from these southern and western provinces accompanied the Danish and Norwegian Vikings in their expeditions to the islands in the North Sea and the Atlantic, to the Frankish Empire and to even more remote seas and territories. Sometimes they were joined by the more adventurous members of the Swedish settlements; but generally the Swedes, influenced by already existing trade relations, preferred to follow up the earlier eastward expansion. These great enterprises took place against a background of the consolidation of power by the chieftains and more effective local organization. Extensive trading expeditions were also undertaken, and as slaves constituted one of the main commodities there was naturally a good deal of plundering.

In the centuries after the birth of Christ the vast domains on the other side of the Baltic were inhabited by scattered and primitive Finno-Ugrian and Slavonic tribes. They were

bounded on the south and south-east by the great kingdoms
of the Kazars on the Volga, the Byzantine Empire, and the
Baghdad Caliphs; and through these empires ran the chief
trade routes to the Orient. In between them and Scandinavia
lay Russia, where Scandinavian and Russian furs, slaves, and
other commodities could be traded for the silver, spices, and
silks of the East.

The Swedes were already experienced traders, and now
bent all their energies towards expansion in these trans-
Baltic markets. The ancient Slavonic *Nestor's Chronicle* contains a crude but illuminating account of their arrival, telling
how the Rus (Swedes) brought law and order into Russia.
The big towns were placed under the control of powerful
representatives, and, as time went on, more and more centres
came to be held by Swedes. The chronicle is naïve in tone
and often chronologically inaccurate; but it brings out very
clearly the immense trading advantages which these Swedish
Vikings had obtained. Many of the conquered towns were
situated in key positions on rivers or lakes; experience at
home had taught the Vikings how to construct their boats
so that they could be dragged on rollers between stretches
of navigable lake and river or navigated in shallows;
and they knew how to unload and reload their cargoes
at difficult landing-places. *Nestor's Chronicle* puts the arrival
of the Swedish Vikings in Russia at A.D. 862, but there
is no doubt that it actually took place earlier in the
century.[1]

The progress of these Swedish warrior merchants down the
Dnieper on their way to the Black Sea and Constantinople
is described in detail in a book on the Byzantine constitution,

---

[1] The name Nestor gives the Swedes, 'Rus', which is also embodied in
the name 'Russia', derives from the settlement on the Swedish east
coast whence most of the Viking expeditions set out, namely, Roden or,
nowadays, Roslagen. The Finnish name for Sweden, namely 'Ruotsi',
undoubtedly has the same derivation. The most common name for
Sweden in Icelandic literature, *Svithiod*, is found in the Nordic name for
those parts of Russia ruled by the Rus – the great Svithiod.

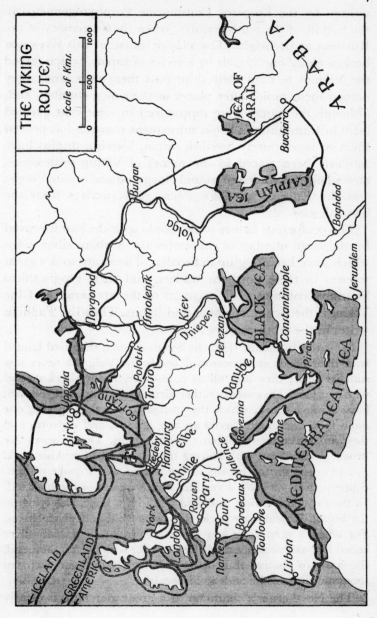

THE VIKING
ROUTES
Scale of Kms.

0   500   1000

ARABIA

SEA OF
ARAL

Bughara

CASPIAN SEA

Baghdad

Bulgar

Volga

BLACK SEA

Constantinople

Jerusalem

Novgorod

Smolenk

Kiev

Dnieper

Berezan

Piraeus

Polotsk

Truso

Danube

MEDITERRANEAN SEA

Uppsala

Birka

GOTLAND

Hedeby

Hamburg

Elbe

Ravenna

Rome

Rhine

Rouen

Paris

Valence

York

London

Nantes

Tours

Bordeaux

Toulouse

Lisbon

ICELAND

GREENLAND

AMERICA

written by the Emperor Constantine Porphyrogennetos in the middle of the tenth century, when the supremacy of the Rus was at its height. The placid course of this river was broken along one stretch by a series of rapids, which forced the Vikings to haul their ships past them over land; they named these rapids after places in their own country, and, although the names were reproduced in somewhat garbled form in Constantine's book, subsequent research has proved them to be of purely Swedish origin. Swedish origins have similarly been traced in the names of Viking settlements, now wholly Slavonicized, round Novgorod and on the Volga; and the Russian word for town, *gorod*, derives from the Swedish *gård*.

The prosperous nature of this trade with the east is proved by the large number of contemporary Arabian silver coins which have been dug up in Sweden. The Arabs took a great interest in these northern traders, and their geographical literature contains vivid accounts of the appearance of the Vikings, their characteristics and habits. Thus Ibn Fadhlan writes in the tenth century:

I saw the 'Russians' [i.e. the Swedes] when they had landed with their goods and encamped beside the Volga. I never saw statelier men; they are tall as palm-trees, ruddy-cheeked, and with red hair. They wear neither kirtle nor caftan, but the men have a rough cloak, which they throw to one side, leaving one hand free. Each man carries an axe, a knife, and a sword, and they are never seen without these weapons. Their swords are broad, pranked out with flowing tracery, and of Frankish work. . . . Fastened on the breasts of the women is a capsule of iron, copper, silver, or gold, according to the wealth of the husband. In the capsule is a ring, and attached to it a knife, also lying on the breast. Round their necks they wear gold and silver chains. For when a man owns ten thousand dirhems (Arabian silver coins) he has a necklace made for his wife; with twenty thousand, she has two chains; thus, a new chain is added for each ten thousand dirhems he adds to his wealth.

The Northerner's character as a great merchant is clearly

revealed in this description of the rich man amassing his dirhems. The picture is completed by that of another, somewhat earlier Arab writer, Ibn Dustah:

They have neither settled property, nor towns, nor fields; their sole occupation is trade with sable, squirrel, and other skins, which they sell to all who will buy. The money they receive in exchange is kept by them in their belts. . . . They are brave and valiant. When they go forth against another people, they do not cease until they have utterly annihilated them; they plunder the vanquished, and make them slaves. They are well grown, fair to look upon, and bold in attack; but their boldness is not displayed on horseback, for all their warlike enterprises are performed in ships.

Both chroniclers add that this race were exceptionally unclean in their habits.

As a result of the trade in costly skins and slaves from Scandinavia and the Russian region, the 'Rus' acquired great wealth and brought large quantities of Oriental silver to Russia and their homeland. Economic historians have maintained that Sweden's mastery of the main trade routes to the east actually enabled her to restore the Frankish kingdom as the trade link between Orient and Occident. Moreover, in addition to the coins that have been dug up on Gotland and in Sweden, further evidence of her economic predominance is provided in the growth of the remarkable town of Birka on an island in Lake Mälaren. This town, which was visited by Friesians and other seafarers from western Europe, was to become a centre of northern European trade during the ninth and tenth centuries. Birka seems to have already fallen into decay some time during the eleventh century and has now entirely disappeared, but much of its former character can be gleaned from archaeological finds, including the remains of houses, coins, ornaments, and every kind of human requisite and luxury. The town was protected by a great wall and a special fortress, and relics of palings on the shore show where harbours once stood. A whole world, which still awaits full investigation, lies buried there.

The next inevitable step towards Swedish mastery of the route between east and west was to acquire control of the south Jutland trading town of Hedeby, on the Bay of Slien. At that time the merchants from the south were unwilling to embark on a risky voyage carrying costly goods round the north of Jutland; they preferred to reload in the inner part of the Slien bay where Hedeby grew up, and follow the safe land route over southern Jutland. The Swedish Vikings accordingly took the offensive, with the same success that the 'Rus' had earlier experienced in Russia; and this strengthens the impression that these enterprises for trade and conquest were characterized by great energy and singleness of purpose – even if it is not yet fully established that the various expeditions were based on a unified direction, common to the whole country.

The dynasty set up by the Swedish Vikings in Hedeby on Danish soil is commemorated by two runestones raised to commemorate King Gnupa and his consort and son; it is also mentioned by Adam of Bremen, who wrote a history of Denmark in the 1070's. This dynasty flourished during the first half of the tenth century. It was of short duration, however; a Danish state was forming to the north, and the east Frankish kingdom threatened it from the south. Swedish rule in south Jutland probably ended some time during the 930's; but a runestone from Sædinge on Låland bears further witness to the extent it attained during its brief heyday.

In addition to those who helped to establish this Viking dynasty, many individual Swedish warriors took part in the campaigns in the west – particularly from the end of the tenth century onwards – and they generally chose to serve with the Danish and Norwegian chieftains who were then systematically plundering and levying tribute in England. Runestones were beginning to be raised more frequently, and the exploits in the west were commemorated by a large number in various parts of Sweden – including, for example, the Swedish Viking from Uppland, who served under three different leaders, and received the Danegeld each time; the eastern provinces provide many examples of this participation in the Viking campaigns against England. Nevertheless, this was not the first time that Swedes had directed their energies towards the west, for they had been among the first Nordic colonists of Iceland, though they had gone there via the British Isles. Indeed, the whole of northern Europe and the territories to the west and east of it lay open to these Swedish Vikings, who made full use of their opportunities. Many thousand silver coins from the English Danegeld have been found in Swedish soil.

While these Vikings were accompanying the Danish kings to England, conditions in Russia had changed considerably. Nearly two hundred years had elapsed since the 'Rus' had first set foot there, and by this time their little colonies had been incorporated in the vast Russian population; and contact with the homeland had either been lost or weakened. Moreover, changed conditions in the Orient had affected the trading prospects of the 'Rus' organizations: Europe's trade with the east now passed through more southerly countries, and Sweden had lost her supremacy. Nevertheless, men from the north continued to make their way to the Russian kingdoms and to Constantinople; here they took service in the Emperor's bodyguard, as is shown by the famous rune carved by one of these Swedish warriors on a marble lion in the Athenian seaport of Piraeus some time during the eleventh century. By this time, however, the 'Rus' in Russia had been entirely absorbed into their surroundings, though the ruling families continued for a little while longer to maintain contact with Sweden. Our knowledge of the changes taking place in Russia at this period, however, is very limited.

As late as 1040, or thereabouts, the Swedes made a raid in the east, and, judging from the runestones raised in

Sweden, many of those who took part lost their lives. Many other aspects of Swedish life in the tenth and eleventh centuries are condensed into these terse, stoical inscriptions, as, for example, those on the Turinge stone that was raised in Södermanland to a band of brothers, one of whom fell in Russia. In their brief statement of the respective characteristics and fates of the brothers, the lines express the threefold ideal of the Viking Age: the landowner who commands respect, the gallant fighter, and the generous master and leader of men. The inscription on another stone from Östergötland might almost be a catalogue of Viking voyages, the five brothers whom it commemorates having fallen in widely different quarters of the earth. Other achievements of a less warlike nature were similarly recorded – as, for example, on the stone that tells of a man who had roads cleared and bridges built in memory of his father. The wealth acquired by Sweden as a result of the armed trade with Russia unquestionably helped to further peaceable pursuits at home, and gave rise to striking developments. Roads were made, agriculture improved, and the village community system was stabilized and developed, all of which constituted the domestic aspect of the Viking expeditions.

Very little is known of the political organization of the country at this time. There was a king in Birka at the beginning of the ninth century, but the size of his kingdom is unknown; it is certain, on the other hand, that his subjects had considerable influence in the *Ting*. Towards the end of the century, however, when the 'Rus' were at the height of their power in Russia, a Norwegian named Wulfstan recounted to Alfred the Great his impressions of a voyage through the Baltic Sea. From this it transpires that large parts of what is now eastern Sweden, together with Gotland and Öland, at all events belonged to the Svear; and thus, an eastern realm extending over the Baltic islands – so important for navigation – makes its first appearance in the records. While the merchants and warriors were at sea

3. Boat-shaped graves of the Iron Age, Badelunda, Västmanland.

4. Helmet and sword from a ship-grave, Vendel,
Uppland.

5a. The Sparlösa Stone,
Västergötland, *c.* 800.

5b. The Rök Stone, Öster-
götland, 9th century.

6a. Sculptured stone from Hablingbo, Gotland, 6th century.

6b. Sculptured stone from Lärbro, Gotland, *c.* 700.

amassing riches and honour, the settlements were gradually being merged into one another.

There is no definite proof that the Svear also ruled in western Sweden at this time, though a Västergötland rune-stone of about 800 (the Sparlösa stone) can probably be interpreted to mean that a King Alrik, son of King Eric in Uppsala, was then King in that province. This would indicate that the separate provinces were already beginning to draw together a hundred years before Wulfstan made his Baltic voyage. The next problem, therefore, is to decide at what date the remaining parts of the country were finally incorporated with the central and eastern Swedish kingdom. It is dangerous to set a definite date, but some point in the early eleventh century would probably be a reasonable estimate. The first Swedish monarch about whom anything very much is known is Olof Skötkonung (c. 1000); a king who is described at some length in the Icelandic sagas.

Denmark and Norway were the main external enemies of this newly-integrated Swedish kingdom, while Olof Skötkonung and his sons were ruling in Sweden (c. 995–1060); during the same period Denmark was ruled by Sweyn Forkbeard, Canute the Great, and finally Sven Estridsen, and Norway by Olav Haraldsson and his successors. It was also at about this time that the frontiers between the three Scandinavian countries were first formally drawn.

After his victory over the Norwegians and Swedes near the Helgeå river in 1026, Canute the Great of Denmark had for a short time ruled simultaneously over Denmark, Norway, 'some of the Svear' and England – the first attempt to unite the three newly formed and as yet undeveloped Scandinavian countries. The attempt was ephemeral, however; incompatibilities proved too strong and the experiment was soon abandoned. Sweden was thus to remain a separate kingdom.

4*

# III

# The Coming of Christianity
## 830-1100

In 829 a Frankish monk named Ansgar was travelling from
Hedeby to the well-known trading town of Birka on Lake
Mälaren. Ansgar came from the Carolingian Empire, and,
moved by his loyalty to the Frankish Empire and the Church
of Rome, he intended to try and convert pagan Sweden to
Christianity. He also hoped to provide spiritual comfort for
the Christian merchants who visited Birka, and for the many
Christian slaves whom the Scandinavians had taken in
battle. The suggestion that a missionary should be sent to
Birka had been made by the King himself.

By this time some knowledge of Scandinavia had spread
to others besides the seafaring merchants. The age of the
Teutonic migrations and the Viking raids had provided
contact between the Christian world and the north, and a
constant flow of reports from the Baltic countries had per-
meated southwards. At the court of Charlemagne and Louis
the Pious, the chronicler Einhart was trying to localize
these countries in relation to more familiar lands. But Ansgar
can only have got his information from vague hearsay, and his
was a courageous enterprise. It also demanded vision: the
ability to see that the Church could help to counteract the
effects of the Viking raids and could bring the Scandinavian
countries within her universal rule.

Ansgar's voyage to this unknown land of pirates has been
vividly described by his biographer, friend, and successor,
Rimbert. In its dual aim of spiritual conversion and material
colonization it might be compared with Livingstone's East
African expeditions into the regions of the Arabian slave
dealers. Rimbert describes how, while crossing the Baltic in

merchant ships, Ansgar and another monk called Vithmar fell in with pirates – or, more accurately, Vikings:

and the merchants who travelled with them defended themselves manfully, and in the first encounter they proved superior, and in another battle with the same pirates they were conquered and overcome, and the robbers took from them both ship and cargo, and they were scarce able to flee to land and escape on foot. Thus they lost even the royal gifts they should bring to the Svears, besides all they had, save that little they could snatch up when they leapt from the ships. . . . [Yet they would not give up.] And so they walked a long and laborious way, crossing the seas that lay between in boats, and came duly to the harbour of the realm, that is called Birka. And here they were received with kindness by the King, whose name was Björn.

They told him what their errand was, and after taking counsel with his men he allowed them to proceed freely. The bailiff of the town having received their message with enthusiasm, made a donation of land and built a church, and the mission continued to prosper until 831.

After leaving Sweden, Ansgar became bishop of a new diocese in Hamburg, and a fresh mission to Sweden was undertaken by the Frankish bishop Gauzbert, who, however, was soon driven out of Birka as a result of a pagan reaction. Ansgar suffered from similar resistance in Hamburg: in 845 the town was attacked and burnt by Vikings, and the see was temporarily transferred to the more secure environment of Bremen. Twenty years after his first perilous journey to Sweden, Ansgar again sailed north, since no one else was willing to do so: all that was known of the intermediate period was that one missionary had been driven out and another murdered; while a third, formerly a missionary hermit, had returned to his solitary existence on the death of the last of his scanty flock. Ansgar again assembled a congregation, which lasted for a few years, but in view of the common preoccupation with Russian trade, the new doctrines stood little chance of success.

These are the main episodes described in this account of Ansgar's life. Much of it has been influenced by the prevailing conception of the perpetual struggle between good and evil; nevertheless, this rather rigid outlook cannot conceal Ansgar's unique personality, and he is shown to have possessed great visionary powers, an indefatigable urge for discovering new countries, a gift for organization, and great strength of will. Ansgar, the first really distinct figure in Swedish history, was unquestionably a remarkable person, even if he was not the saint that his successors and disciples would have us believe.

At that time Sweden's attention was concentrated exclusively on her interests in the east and south-east, however, and Ansgar's mission was doomed to failure. It remained an episode, chiefly memorable for the glimpses it gives of life in the trading centre of the Mälaren region, and of his own fascinating personality. A mission undertaken by Archbishop Unni of Hamburg in the 930's was equally short-lived, and was terminated by Unni's death from some disease in Birka.

These setbacks, together with their aftermath, provide the first indication of the stubborn nature of the paganism with which the Christian missionaries were faced. The obscure prehistoric rites and cults of sun, thunder, and fertility gods had to some extent crystallized into fixed forms and an incipient mythology reminiscent of the mythical world of the Edda poems. A number of place-names in Sweden – as elsewhere in Scandinavia – commemorate the chief pagan deities, e.g. *Odens*vi, *Tors*harg, *Frigger*åker. The names of Nordic gods are also incorporated in the names of the days of the week, which were based on Roman models and taken over by the Swedes from more southerly Germanic tribes. Other objects of belief included various elemental spirits, both good and evil, and both these and the old fertility myths retained a hold on the imagination of the country peasants long after the introduction of Christianity – and, indeed, down to the period of industrialization a thousand years later.

The Ansgar legend makes little mention of the pagan gods, however, merely stating that a Swedish king called Eric had been admitted to their ranks after his death. The first person to provide a more concrete picture of Swedish paganism was the famous German canon, Adam of Bremen, who wrote the Latin history of the first Hamburg archbishops. He seems to have gained considerable information about Sweden from an anonymous Christian narrator, from the Danish King, Sven Estridsen, who had spent a long time in the country, and from Hamburg travellers. When he was writing in the 1070's, Sweden's great centre of pagan worship was the celebrated Uppsala temple, situated in what was then Sweden's leading province, the country round Lake Mälaren; moreover, it was not far from Sigtuna, which had replaced Birka as a trading centre. Of this temple Adam of Bremen writes:

This shrine is adorned all over with gold and here the people worship the images of three gods: Thor, the mightiest, has his throne in the centre of the hall, with Odin and Frey on either side. These gods have the following characters: Thor, they say, is god of the air; he rules over the thunder and the lightning, the tempest and the rain, and the fair harvesting weather. Odin (which means madness) is the god of war and makes a man bold to face his enemy. Frey bestows on the peaceful peace and sensual pleasures; he is depicted with an enormous phallus. But Odin is shown in armour, as Mars in our country; while Thor with his sceptre (plainly the hammer of the thunder god) seems to resemble Jupiter. All these gods have their own priests, who offer the sacrifices of the people. If disease or famine threaten, sacrifices are made to Thor; if war, to Odin; if marriage is to be solemnized, to Frey. Moreover, every ninth year a solemn celebration encompassing all the provinces of Sweden is held in Uppsala, and it is incumbent on all to attend. The kings and the people all send each their own gifts to Uppsala . . . and those who have already embraced Christianity must buy themselves off these ceremonies. . . .

The sacrifice proceeds thus: Nine of all living males are sacrificed, and it is the custom that the gods are propitiated by their
blood. The bodies are suspended in a grove near to the shrine.
So hallowed do the pagans hold this shrine that they regard each
separate tree to be divine by virtue of the death and putrefaction
of the victims hanging there. As well as men, dogs and horses are
strung up in that place, and one of the Christians has told me that
he has seen seventy-two such bodies hanging side by side in the
trees of the sacrificial grove.

This temple, of which probable relics are still standing,
was a centre not only for the Mälaren region but also for
other Swedish chieftains and tribes, who had a bond of
union in the famous shrine and in the common cult. It also
formed the core of resistance to the attempts at conversion,
which from the beginning of the eleventh century became
increasingly persistent and gradually came to threaten the
main strongholds of paganism. Though the documentary
evidence is slight, there is no doubt that the eleventh century
was marked throughout by a struggle between the two rival
creeds; there is, however, no satisfactory explanations as to
why the older beliefs persisted more obstinately in Sweden
than in the rest of Scandinavia. Did this resistance have its
roots solely in political and geographical conditions, or did it
spring from the psychological make-up of the inhabitants?

Developments abroad seem to have played a certain part,
however, in the history of this period. Sweden began to turn
her attention from the east to the south, a movement which
helped to further the cause of Christianity; the Hamburg
mission was reinforced by the stabilization and ever-increasing
influence of the German Empire, and the Hamburg-Bremen
archbishopric was held by strong personalities; while the
conversion of her neighbours had significant repercussions in
Sweden. The Swedish King, Olof Skötkonung, had become
a Christian, though he was not able to counteract the influence of the Uppsala temple. Coins marked with a cross
were struck for him by his English mintmaster in Sigtuna,

where English influence can also be traced in the architecture of its most ancient churches. Missionaries also came from Norway, where the kings had wholeheartedly embraced the new faith, and from Denmark, already a Christian country. It appears that they came too from Russia, where the Greek Orthodox Church was later established, and, towards the end of the century, even from France. But it was the Hamburg mission which did most to decide the issue by organizing strong Christian centres in Skara, in Västergötland, and in Sigtuna, not far from the Uppsala temple. The mission was joined by Olof Skötkonung's son Anund Jakob, who had fought with Canute by the Helgeå river in 1026, and an increasing number of clearly Christian runestones dating from this time bear witness to the advance of the new doctrines, as their inscriptions invoke the Christian God instead of the heathen Thor.

The victory was not yet won, however. The Uppsala temple still maintained its sway, and the nine-yearly sacrifice provided a rallying-point for pagan resistance. The internecine strife and feuds between the various pretenders to the throne were also influenced by religious differences. Most of Olof Skötkonung's successors had been converted, thus gaining the support of Västergötland, the earliest Christian province, though paganism too had its royal adherents. Mass resistance and even counter-attacks occurred fairly frequently; the bishop of Sigtuna, for example, was driven out during the 1060's, at a time when the see at Skara was also empty.

Apart from Ansgar, no individual king, chieftain, or missionary emerges very clearly from this period of bitter struggle. Church legends of a much later date mention such saints as Sigfrid, Botvid, Eskil, and David, but give no very exact information. Eskil, however, also makes his appearance in the writings of the Anglo-Danish monk Aelnoth about the beginning of the twelfth century, though the account merely states that he was an English missionary who preached to the savage Swedish tribes and was finally

martyred. Aelnoth himself had heard something of the conflicts between Christianity and paganism in Sweden. His
interpretation was that the Swedish people paid lip-service
to the Christian faith as long as things were going well with
them, but in times of need they denounced it both in word
and deed, turning on the true Christians and seeking to
drive them out of the country. This view of the situation,
artless though it is, provides a glimpse of yet another facet of
this obscure, though important, phase in Swedish history.

Finally, however, the pagan resistance was broken,
probably some time towards the end of the eleventh century.
The Uppsala temple fell, its images were torn down and
destroyed, and a church was erected on the foundations of the
old shrine. Shortly afterwards, the see of Hamburg ceased to
hold sway over Scandinavia, and Sweden came under the
new archbishopric that had been founded in the then Danish
Lund about 1103.

The full effect of these changes was naturally not apparent
for some time, and paganism probably lingered on in remote
parts of Sweden until well into the twelfth century. But the
country had now become a member of the vast organization
of the Church of Rome. As time went on, many new churches
were built, most of them still probably of wood; priests
were ordained, and parishes of a more integrated type grew
up round each church; the seats of the bishops became fixed,
and Christian communities, comprising a new type of town,
formed round them. Six such sees are known to have existed
about 1120: Skara, Linköping, Eskilstuna, Strängnäs,
Västerås, and Sigtuna; and the last-named also contains
ruins of early stone churches in the Romanesque style. It
should be noted that the main southern provinces of Väster-
and Östergötland only had one see each, Skara and Linköping, while the old unruly Svear regions round the Mälaren
had no less than four. In the 1130's the Sigtuna see was
transferred to Old Uppsala, where the famous pagan temple
had once stood, and the missionary era came to an end. It

was now the task of the organized Church to refashion the hitherto pagan kingdom according to new standards and new ideals, far removed from those of the Vikings. Influences from the south did much to shape Sweden's further development, and, after the period of expansion in the east, the country began to assume a new and very different position in the fabric of Europe.

# IV

# First Steps towards Uniformity
## 1050-1250

In the time of the Vikings and during the period of the conversion the basis of the social order was the kin. The family feuds in the Icelandic sagas had their counterpart within the Swedish provinces, and violent disputes over property and questions of honour raged among chieftains and peasants alike. Treachery, murder, revenge, and reprisal are often implicit in contemporary runic inscriptions; the Rök stone, for example, which is the longest and most puzzling of its kind, is believed by some to provide a single magic formula to protect the honour of the family and promote its revenge. The primitive law by which personal and family disputes were regulated can be discerned in the oldest legal fragment to have been preserved in Sweden; this was the 'pagan law' which related to single combat. But while honour had to be defended at all costs, murder had to be expiated as well, and a rune from Östergötland recounts how a man called Gunnar demanded sanctuary from the kinsfolk of his murdered victim in a sacrificial grove, where a reconciliation was ratified by the officiating priest.

The current instrument of summary retribution by the individual and his kin was thus subject to certain regulations. These rules were administered by the *Ting*, the assembly of the freemen who were entitled to bear arms, where, under the direction of the *lagman* (literally 'lawman'), new laws were created according to the requirements of the various provinces; the smaller district known as a *härad* (hundred), which probably came into existence during this period, also had its local *Ting*. Snorre Sturlason was long believed to have given an authentic picture of these assemblies in a

chapter of his saga *Heimskringla*, in which the lawman Torgny
was the spokesman of the people against Olof Skötkonung;
but later research has shown that Snorre was merely
interpreting history in the light of his own Icelandic times.
Though the *Tings* are also mentioned in the Ansgar legend
and by Adam of Bremen, the only authentic information
about them is to be found in the later records of the provincial
codes of law. It is interesting to note that, though they were
by then committed to writing, the oath formulae invoking
'the gods' were handed down into the Christian era – a direct
link with pagan customs.

It is difficult to form a complete picture of the magnates
and the peasant communities of this period; the Viking
expeditions reveal only the outward aspect of the country,
and the rich trading centres, foreshadowing the towns of a
later period, were forgotten and only rediscovered by
archaeologists in the nineteenth century. In all essentials
each province led an isolated existence and was linked with
others only by the Viking and trade expeditions, a common
military organization, and by the Uppsala sacrifice, until it
was abolished after the spread of Christianity. A few additional details of this period of transition are given in two contemporary accounts. Adam of Bremen, whose main source of
information was the Danish King Sven Estridsen, describes
the fertility and wealth of the land, the Swedes' contempt of
ostentation, and their moderation in all matters save that of
their numerous wives; and he praises, too, their lavish
hospitality and the sacred laws by which it was governed.
Still using the Danish King as his source, he goes on to speak
of the small but belligerent mountain tribes somewhere in
the north, who occasionally came and wreaked great havoc
in the south, implying that a large part of Norrland, which
bordered on the even more primitive Lapps in the north, had
not yet been incorporated with the Swedish provinces. The
second account comes from an eleventh-century eye-witness.
the Norse court poet and diplomat, Sigvat, who described in

verse form a journey made for political reasons across
Sweden. He tells how one evening he came to a homestead;
the door was closed; and in answer to his questions the
people within roughly bade him begone, for they were busy
with holy things, a sacrifice to their household gods. 'I fear
the wrath of Odin,' said the wicked woman. 'We worship the
old gods!'

It was into this primitive and fierce community that new
ideas were introduced by the Catholic Church, which
preached peace as one of the main virtues and relegated
retribution to the world to come. This new doctrine contained much more that was not immediately acceptable, and
at the same time the organization of the Church came into
direct collision with the old traditions. The uncompromising
family loyalty that was revealed in the legal order was
applied not only to questions of honour but also to property;
and now the Church was preaching that one of the most
effective ways of winning salvation was to endow her with
legacies. Marriage, too, which had long been concerned with
the kin, was also to come under the regulation of the Church;
and since priests and churches were to be maintained by the
parishes, the Church demanded a uniform taxation in
accordance with the new unity which it imposed. It took time
for these unaccustomed ideas to find acceptance in communities and overcome the primitive desire for independence and
the family traditions; nevertheless, they ultimately proved to
be an important influence in furthering the fusion of the
organized communities with the more scattered settlements.

At the beginning of the twelfth century there was a temporary respite from religious and dynastic strife; and in the
1130's Sverker, a member of a tribe of Östergötland magnates, was acknowledged as King. He lived on the most
important royal manor in his home region near Lake Vättern, and this district thus took over the supremacy which had
formerly been wielded by the Mälaren region.

Sverker kept on good terms with the Church and, in

consultation with Archbishop Eskil of Lund, supported the
founding of the Cistercian monasteries in Sweden. But the
throne was not yet secure. Somewhere around 1156 a Danish
prince, Magnus Henriksson, effected the murder of Sverker;
and a little-known claimant, who later became the legendary
'Eric the Saint', then made his appearance, though he was
soon put to death. He was succeeded by Sverker's son Karl,
who was killed in 1167 by Knut, the son of Eric the Saint.
Knut seems to have been a forceful monarch who made
short work of other claimants; and a period of calm ensued.
In order to protect Lake Mälaren against pirates he founded
a stronghold on the site of modern Stockholm; the coinage
was regulated, and, with the King's co-operation, the Church
was organized on a more systematic basis. After 1196, however, the throne was the object of a series of confused struggles
whose true significance has never been fathomed. The
descendants of Sverker and Eric were in constant conflict
right up to the middle of the thirteenth century, with sometimes one line in power, sometimes the other; and these conflicts extended beyond the frontiers of the country, for in this
period Danish kings and magnates often took part in the
domestic feuds of Sweden. At the beginning of the thirteenth
century, the Zealand family of Sunesson supported the
claims of Sverker the younger, grandson of the first Sverker,
and soon afterwards the Danish kings rallied to the support
of the rival dynasty.

In the midst of this confusion new and significant trends
were becoming apparent. In 1164 the first Swedish archbishop was installed in the see of Old Uppsala, where the
founder of the Eric dynasty became first the local saint and
later the patron saint of the whole country. The boundaries
of the dioceses were now fixed: apart from that of the archbishop, the five sees were Linköping, Skara, Strängnäs,
Västerås, and Växjö, and in Finland there was Åbo. In the
middle of the century the Cistercian monks arrived in Sweden
and founded monasteries in fertile valleys on the pattern of

Clairvaux. The Church acquired her own canon law and her own courts, and she also secured a separate system of taxation by royal privilege. The kings began to seek ecclesiastical sanction for their coronation, a practice which, so far as is known, was employed for the first time in Eric Knutsson's coronation by the archbishop in 1210.

A class of magnates now emerged, recruited from the old 'great peasants', or families of more prosperous peasantry. This class at first gave the kings a great deal of trouble, but was later to become a characteristic feature of the country as a whole. Its contribution to the government of the kingdom was made through a Council (*Råd*) composed of magnates and churchmen; and it was this Council that acted as Regent during the minority of the last of the Erics. These former peasant proprietors were, ultimately, in conjunction with the King's personal retainers, to form the nucleus of a new Estate: the secular *frälse*,[1] or nobles. These nobles and their Council, assisted by the Church organization, played an important part in welding together the various Swedish provinces.

This period also saw the emergence of a political figure, second only in importance to the crown, whose office similarly embraced the whole kingdom. This was the *Jarl*, who was chosen from among the leading noble families. The most outstanding *Jarls* of the first half of the thirteenth century, such as Birger Brosa and his younger kinsman (known in Swedish history as Birger Jarl), belonged to a family that has since often been wrongly given the name of 'Folkung'. The chief function of the *Jarl*, it seems, was to organize and

---

[1] There is no exact English equivalent of this term. It denoted the total or partial exemption of both persons and, by extension, the land they owned from taxes and services owed to the crown. Since the nobles chiefly enjoyed this exemption in return for knight service (although it could also be enjoyed by some others, e.g. mine-owners), the word '*frälse*' generally means the 'free' noble Estate and its members. The Church was also 'free' (*andligt frälse*). Those who were not 'free' were called *ofrälse*.

command the *ledung*, i.e. the traditional levy of armed men and ships from the eastern provinces. At a given order this force would be assembled early in the summer for campaigns across the sea, with the object of renewing the attempt, not always with success, to gain control of the old and profitable trade routes in the east. Echoes of the Viking era are to be heard in these later expeditions; on the other hand, the *ledung* was sanctioned by the Church provided its attacks were directed against pagan tribes, and these expeditions thus became 'crusades' against Finns, Estonians, and Russians.

These battles in the east are distinct landmarks in an otherwise obscure period, and Finland now begins to assume the prominent place in Swedish annals that she was to retain for seven centuries. Russian chroniclers describe how Sverker, sailing towards the east with sixty ships, fought against Russia; while a much later legend states that St Eric led a crusade against Finland, though the background of this narrative is obscure. At all events, by the beginning of the thirteenth century the south-west region of Finland was part of the Swedish Church and possessed its own bishop in Åbo. There is also evidence of Swedish campaigns round Lake Ladoga in 1164, while in 1220 a *ledung* fleet sailed against Estonia, clearly in order to forestall Danish expansion in the same area. This 'crusade', however, ended in disaster. It was becoming increasingly evident that the aim of these campaigns, and also of the colonization of Finland which was going on at the same time, was to gain control of the old trade route to Russia, which was at that time being used by the inhabitants of Gotland and by the German merchants who travelled between Lübeck and Novgorod. The chief men of the country – King, *Jarl*, magnates, and churchmen – were all variously concerned in this policy of expansion, and this provided a common interest which further helped to consolidate the kingdom. Internal strife during the reign of the last of the Erics, Eric Ericsson (1226–50), temporarily

damped their interest, but it had revived again by the
1240's.

The leading figure in Swedish politics at this time was
Birger Jarl, a member of the so-called Folkung dynasty. He
had married the sister of the childless King Eric; and consequently, according to current practice, his sons were next
in succession to the throne. In his capacity of *Jarl* he had led
a successful 'crusade' against Tavastland in Finland, as a
result of which this part of the kingdom had been consolidated and enlarged. This exploit was celebrated seventy-
five years later in the famous *Chronicle of Eric*, and though the
anonymous poet has written the episode in the heroic style
of the period, his account is based on actual events which
occurred in the course of the traditional expansion towards
the east.

Meanwhile another factor was emerging which was to be
the core both of the new constitution and of the future unity
of the country; the farming-peasant community. Place-
names provide no more than an indeterminate guide to its
development; as in the Viking era, however, a considerable
number of new villages seem to have sprung up during the
early Middle Ages, with name-endings such as *-torp* (croft),
*-säter* (shieling), and *-hult* (copse); and it is interesting that
certain names of these types are also to be found in Swedish
Finland. That a fair degree of economic prosperity prevailed
at that time is confirmed by the many hundreds of country
churches which began to be erected in stone, a building
enterprise unparalleled in scope until the rapid expansion of
urban communities towards the end of the nineteenth century. Thus the settlements began to grow, spreading
along valleys and watercourses even farther into the great
forests.

Life in these expanding Swedish communities can be
studied most easily in the provincial codes which give detailed
regulations for all aspects of daily life and work, and which
were without doubt already in force, although they were not

7. Round church at Hagby, Småland, 11th century.

8. Wooden font from Alnö Church, Medelpad,
12th century.

written down until the next period. Despite conflicts between kings and nobles, the villager was guaranteed protection by both the Church and the embryonic State, and in return for this security he was prepared to accept the new taxes which were gradually imposed on him. In their turn, these taxes provided the State with fresh resources and opportunities.

It is not known at what date the various field systems were introduced into Swedish agriculture; it is certain, however, that the farming-peasant community constituted by this time an economic unit, and that all the great annual agricultural operations were carried out in common. The peasants had drawn up rules for the settlement of all the disputes that inevitably arise in the everyday life of a farming village. The earliest of these provincial codes, the Law of Västergötland, is full of detailed instructions, revealing the anxiety of the peasants to live in harmony at all costs according to the new Christian ideals of peace and justice: 'Christ is first in our community. Then comes our Christian doctrine and all Christians: king, peasants, and all propertied men, bishops and all learned men.'

This Västergötland Law, which dates from the first half of the thirteenth century, also contains the oldest decrees in existence which deal with the political constitution of the country. Its nature is made clear in the opening words: 'The Swedes may take a king but may also depose him.' Much of what it then says is obscure, but one thing is obvious: Sweden was a country with an elected monarchy, and it was the will of the country – the folk – expressed first at the *Ting* of the Svear and subsequently in the other provinces, which determined who was to rule. Another fact that emerges is that the provinces had not yet been wholly absorbed into the kingdom of Sweden; the King who was chosen by the Svear was a stranger to the other regions which he visited on his *Eriksgata* – a tour of the realm after his coronation to receive their allegiance. This ancient division is also illustrated in those parts of the Västergötland Law which deal

5

with murder and its penalties, which varied according to the home province of the victim.

In the middle of the thirteenth century the Swedish Church was far from being a closely-knit part of the universal Roman Church. The parish and its church were far more real to the Swedish peasant than was the diocese, to say nothing of Rome. A change was not long in coming, however. Towards the end of the reign of the last Eric, Sweden was finally incorporated as a province in the Universal Church at a meeting in Skänninge in 1248, attended by the Papal Legate, Cardinal William of Sabina. A papal bull in 1250 gave this meeting particular significance. The rule of celibacy was laid down, the cathedral chapter was organized on stricter lines, and the study of canon law was prescribed. The mendicant orders had also obtained a firm footing in the country by this time. The first stage of the development which Ansgar had initiated had now been concluded and the Church was henceforth to make a significant contribution, both as a force working for the unity of the kingdom and as an important economic factor.

All these new social, political, and ecclesiastical trends combined to produce, towards the middle of the thirteenth century, a Swedish kingdom which, if not so far advanced, possessed a standing similar to that of the other Scandinavian countries. The loosely linked provinces had become a State which already revealed that homogeneity in tradition, language, and culture that was to mark the whole of its subsequent development, a homogeneity which is unparalleled outside Northern Europe.

# V

# The Age of the Folkungs
## 1250-1363

On the death of Eric Ericsson in 1250, his nephew Valdemar, Birger Jarl's eldest son, was elected King of Sweden, and the first of the dynasty later known as the Folkungs ascended the throne. Valdemar ruled jointly with his father until the latter's death in 1266, after which he ruled alone. Soon afterwards, however, he was overthrown as a result of a quarrel with his younger brother Magnus Ladulås, who now held a duchy and the title of Duke, according to the *Jarl* tradition; and with the support of Denmark Magnus was elected to the throne, which he retained until his death in 1290. The quarrel was dramatized in the *Chronicle of Eric*, in which particular stress was laid on King Valdemar's questionable liaison with his wife's sister, Jutta of Denmark. The epoch owes its historical significance, however, to other events; and indeed, the four decades between Valdemar's accession and the death of Magnus Ladulås constitute a remarkable period. Though more is known of the reign of Magnus Ladulås there is evidence that even in Valdemar's time the King managed to increase the power of the central government, both by keeping down the nobles and by better organization. In foreign policy close contact, manifested in fluctuating alliances and frequent inter-marriages, was maintained between Sweden and the two other Scandinavian kingdoms. The most important of the intermarriages were those between King Magnus's son Birger and the sister of the Danish King Eric Menved, and between Eric Menved himself and Magnus's daughter Ingeborg – the latter union was a clear dynastic alliance against Norway and the obstreperous Danish lords. Apart from King Magnus's desire to maintain

Swedish rule on the island of Gotland, projects of eastern expansion were temporarily abandoned. Yet in spite of this active foreign policy the most interesting developments, which had their origins in the preceding period, took place at home.

In these years the Church, whose power was steadily increasing, had become an important ally of the crown in the work of stabilizing the monarchy. This was particularly true in the case of Magnus Ladulås, and he showed his gratitude by extending the privileges of the Church and granting more extensive immunities from taxation to Church land. A proof of the Church's growing power can be found in the large number of cathedral buildings which were either completed or begun from this time onwards. Of these by far the most important was Uppsala Cathedral, which was founded in the 1280's. It was from this cathedral that St Eric was proclaimed patron saint of the realm, and his remains were transferred from Old Uppsala to the new archiepiscopal see. By this time the bishops were powerful lords with large armed retinues.

The result was a new and more powerful monarchy, in which the King was more than just a figurehead and a war lord. The taxation system was organized and expanded to meet the increased needs of a centralized government, as the King could no longer 'live of his own' on the proceeds of the royal estates. A system of dues replaced such services as the *ledung* and the enforced provision of hospitality for the King's troops, and customs duties furnished the government with a new source of income. New laws and ordinances, which had formerly grown spontaneously out of the day-to-day life of the community, were enacted by the central government to meet specific needs, exemplified particularly by the laws for the preservation of the King's peace.

The rise of the monarchy was interwoven in a peculiar way with the growth of the secular nobility. Reference has already been made to the way in which this class, forming as it did a unifying factor in the different provinces, helped to weld the kingdom together, and it continued to develop, sometimes in opposition to the monarchy and sometimes with its co-operation. King Magnus's rule provides a good illustration of this interplay, for the close co-operation which plainly existed between King and Church was paralleled by equally obvious persistent differences between the sovereign and certain noble families – the famous Algotsson brothers from Västergötland, for example, who had thrown in their lot with Norway and the unruly Danish lords. It is clear that Magnus gathered round him men who did not belong to the old families, though the old first Estate of the 'great men' simultaneously acquired an organization which came to include the King's immediate servants and the vassals of temporal and spiritual lords – the *frälse* or privileged noble class mentioned in the preceding chapter. Their greatest privilege was freedom from taxation (by the Statutes of Alsnö), and on the basis of this exemption an army of mounted knights was formed, similar to those which existed in other parts of Europe. The co-operation between these nobles and the King is illustrated by the emergence of the great offices of the kingdom: the old-established post of *Kansler* (Chancellor) was supplemented by those of *Marsk* (Marshal) and *Drots* (Lord High Steward),[1] and the appointment of a *Jarl* was discontinued.

The combination of conflict and co-operation which characterized this period merely constitute two sides of the same picture. In all essentials feudalism – not the Continental form, however, as this never existed in Sweden – went hand in hand with the monarchy, despite all apparent signs to the contrary. As the Norwegian historian Halvdan Koht puts it: William the Conqueror and Charlemagne were both great and powerful rulers and yet they both furthered feudalism; and it was therefore perfectly natural that feudalism in

[1] These translations are only approximate. The titles have no exact equivalent in English.

Scandinavia should have been founded by a new and powerful monarchy in each country: the Valdemars in Denmark, the Sverre house in Norway, and the Folkungs in Sweden.

Another significant development during the last part of the thirteenth century was the increasing importance of Swedish towns and mining districts. Birger Jarl, like former rulers, co-operated with the German trading towns, and German immigrants obtained a recognized civil status in Sweden. Stockholm, which could boast not only the Royal Castle and a number of churches and religious houses but also an enterprising class of merchants and artisans, was soon to become the capital of the kingdom. Magnus Ladulås himself often held his court on the island of Visingsö in Lake Vättern, where a royal hall had been built in the new Gothic style; the *Chronicle of Eric* also states that Magnus Ladulås was responsible for the erection and embellishment of the Riddarholmen Church, the main sanctuary of the Franciscan monks in Stockholm. Foreign trade flourished, much to the government's satisfaction, as the customs duties made a significant contribution to its coffers. The European market was eager to receive Swedish goods, including butter, skins, and furs, and, above all, silver, iron, and copper from the mines. New methods of working the mines were introduced, mainly from Germany, and fresh abundant sources of ore were found in the central Swedish district of Bergslagen to supplement the older bog and lake ores. These rich assets were exploited with the help of capital and techniques imported from Germany, particularly from Lübeck, and thus was born the oldest real mining industry of Sweden. King, Church, and nobles each took an interest in the new concerns, and crown taxes from the mines undoubtedly helped to stabilize the monarchy at this period.

As a result, new types of communities and settlements began to emerge: the coastal towns which, since they were centres of a flourishing foreign trade, differed in character from the old markets and cathedral towns; the foundries in Bergslagen; the solid castles and new types of manor houses which the King and his nobles built in towns along the coast and elsewhere. There was also an active cultural life. New laws were passed and old ones revised, the newly-organized nobility began to be influenced by conceptions of chivalry, and Swedish students made their way to the University of Paris. One of the most important changes was the gradual disappearance of slavery, which was finally abolished in 1335, and the slave trade of the Viking Age was superseded by better and more profitable methods of obtaining labour.

Hitherto, a balance had been maintained between monarchy, Church, and nobles. After the death of Magnus Ladulås in 1290, however, the position of the nobles was considerably strengthened by the fact that the late King's oldest son Birger was still a minor. The government was taken over by the Council, which, having begun as an informal gathering, was now a well-organized assembly of the foremost men of the kingdom. The Churchmen moreover soon found themselves opposed by the temporal lords led by the *Marsk*, Torgils Knutsson. His importance is clear, despite the meagre records; at home he was the leader of a powerful group of nobles in opposition to the Church, and abroad he vigorously pursued and developed the policy of expansion towards the east which had been in abeyance since the time of Birger Jarl. From 1293 Torgils Knutsson undertook various 'crusades'; he built the fortress of Viborg near the important Russian trade route through the inner part of the Gulf of Finland; his troops pushed forward to Lake Ladoga and the Neva, and the Hansa merchants revealed in their active diplomacy how seriously they regarded this threat to their lucrative Russian trade. Indeed, Torgils Knutsson unconsciously perpetuated in his foreign policy the traditions of the Swedish Vikings. These 'crusades' have been described in glowing terms in the *Chronicle of Eric*, which dwells with considerable pathos on the beleaguering of the

Swedish outpost on the Neva. Nevertheless, though the stronghold eventually fell, the greater part of Torgils's conquests were retained for centuries to come.

Torgils Knutsson continued to exert considerable influence, though of a rather different nature, even after the coronation of Birger Magnusson in 1302, and at first no very significant changes appear to have been made in the government. The first signs of unrest appeared with the attempt of the King's younger brothers, Dukes Eric and Valdemar, to introduce a policy of their own with the help of a group of nobles. In the subsequent quarrel with Birger, the Dukes were forced to flee to Norway (1304), where the Norwegian King presented them with the fief (*län*)[1] of Kungahälla on the west coast (the southern part of what is now Bohuslän). The Dukes were soon reconciled with their brothers, however; they returned to Sweden, where Duke Eric's position was further consolidated as a result of the gift of the Danish fief of Northern Halland together with Varberg; and thenceforward the complex inter-relations between Sweden, Denmark, and Norway, all concentrated round the mouth of the Göta river, tended to centre to an increasing extent on the person of Duke Eric.

Soon after the return of the Dukes a new faction obtained political supremacy in Sweden. The leading Churchmen, who had long been kept down by Torgils Knutsson, gained the support of a group of nobles, including the Dukes, and proceeded to challenge the *Marsk*. He was overthrown, imprisoned, and executed – ostensibly as an enemy of the Church, for to begin with his dead body was not allowed to be buried in consecrated ground – while King Birger, conforming to his father's policy, granted the Church another comprehensive charter. By now, however, Duke Eric had prepared a fresh coup, and in the autumn of 1306 he and his brother Valdemar took the King prisoner at Håtuna. Thus

---

[1] The Swedish *län* was not a heritable fief but a temporary enjoyment of the incomes and administration of the district concerned.

Duke Eric, whom the *Chronicle of Eric* depicts as possessing all the virtues of the knight, but who in fact was a singularly ruthless and unscrupulous opportunist, became the leading figure in the land.

Birger was liberated soon afterwards, however, and naturally made an attempt to recover what he had lost. It would be impossible to follow all the vicissitudes of the next ten years. Duke Eric sometimes co-operated with Denmark and Norway, and on other occasions fought against them both – though Eric Menved remained loyal on the whole to his brother-in-law Birger – and treaties, negotiations, and campaigns followed in rapid succession. The Duke's possessions on both sides of the Göta river became the nucleus of a feudal state extending within the frontiers of all three kingdoms and forming what might be called the rough draft, geographically, of a Scandinavian union. In 1310 the kingdom of Sweden was divided between the claimants; Birger received large areas of eastern Sweden, Gotland, and Viborg in Finland, while the Dukes took the western provinces of Värmland and Västergötland. In addition, they claimed the key defensive and trading bases in the east: the Castles of Stockholm, Kalmar, and Borgholm, with their adjoining fiefs, and most of Finland. The Dukes subsequently divided their share into two portions, and Eric was to rule over western Sweden, northern Halland, southern Bohuslän, and Kalmar. His 'Scandinavian' kingdom seemed within sight, and his dynastic aims were further revealed by his marriage with the Norwegian Princess, Ingeborg.

This was without question a critical point in Swedish history. Was the unity of the kingdom to be preserved or was it to be split up into feudal states? A gruesome family tragedy provided the answer. In December 1317, both Dukes were invited by the King to the Castle of Nyköping in Södermanland. After a banquet had taken place, the Dukes were taken unawares in their sleep and thrown into prison, where they subsequently died – either from starvation or ill-treatment, according to contemporary report. King Birger made an immediate attempt to conquer the entire kingdom; the Dukes' adherents had already taken up arms against him, however, and their rising was soon joined by most of the Swedish nobility. Notwithstanding the support of the Danish King, Birger was forced to flee the country in 1318, while his son Magnus was taken prisoner and subsequently executed. King Birger died in exile in Denmark, where his grave now lies, and with considerable help from the widows of the Dukes and the *Drots*, Mats Kettilmundsson, the nobles seized power.

Those who took control did not, however, intend to abolish the monarchy. Their aim was to ensure their own power and make clear their view that the King of Sweden obtained his throne by election and not by hereditary right. The next candidate was an obvious one; the infant son of Duke Eric and his Norwegian consort Ingeborg. In July 1319 the gentry and peasants of the kingdom assembled in Uppsala from the different provinces; and, shortly after he had become, in his own right, King of Norway, the young Magnus Ericsson was elected King of the Swedes. A significant document, embodying an attempt to establish a Swedish constitution, was drawn up, which endorsed the privileges of the nobility and of the Church, confirmed in certain respects the status of the Council, and, in order to prevent the King from imposing arbitrary taxation, gave the Council and people the right to consent to new taxation. Much stress was laid on the election of the King, as opposed to the tendencies of certain Folkungs to establish a hereditary monarchy.

Power was then assumed by the nobles, who had plenty of opportunity to consolidate their position during the thirteen-year Regency, which, indeed, formed one of their most notable periods. Their qualifications were certainly of the highest. They had acquired political training in the Council and in the work of administration; moreover, from a very early date, members of the great peasant families had acted as 'lawmen' in the administration of justice, and they carried on this tradition by revising the laws of Sweden; the Uppland Law was accomplished by the middle of the 1290's, and the Södermanland law in 1327. It is largely thanks to this work of compilation and revision that a coherent picture can be obtained of the Swedish community in the Folkung era, and linguistically these documents are among the most valuable of Swedish records. The nobles had also learnt a good deal about complicated problems of foreign policy during this period of fraternal strife, and the *Chronicle of Eric*, which was actually written at the time of this Regency, bears witness to a thorough familiarity with the life and ideals of the Age of Chivalry.

This ruling class managed affairs with considerable success during the following decade. Sweden's interests in Finland were asserted in opposition to Russia by the *Drots*, Mats Kettilmundsson, who held the castle fief of Viborg; and the Peace of Nöteborg in 1323 established the frontiers between the two countries for many years to come. On one occasion the Regency government intervened to prevent Duke Eric's widow, Ingeborg, and her Danish-born second husband, Knut Porse, from embarking on a policy of their own, thus saving the country from an awkward situation. Nevertheless, the Duchess Ingeborg had been making the most of the great confusion in Denmark, where she had managed to obtain a footing. She and Knut Porse had designs on Skåne and had already succeeded in annexing southern Halland and parts of Zealand. The Swedish government finally took over the province of Skåne, where Magnus Ericsson was proclaimed as ruler in 1332. On payment of a ransom his title was formally recognized by Count John of Holstein, to whom the province had been pledged by Denmark, then in a state of disintegration. In 1335, when King Magnus made his 'Eriksgata' – the traditional tour made by the King to receive the homage of his people – he

ruled over the largest combination of nationalities that
Scandinavia had yet known: Sweden and Finland, Skåne,
Blekinge, northern Halland, and Norway. His realm was
further extended at the beginning of the 1340's when he
purchased southern Halland from Valdemar Atterdag of
Denmark and became the unconditional ruler of Skåne.

A significant step towards national unity was taken during
the reign of Magnus Ericsson with the preparation of a body
of law ('*landslag*', literally: law of the land), which, in contrast to the old provincial codes, was to apply to the whole
of Sweden. This task was completed in 1350, and the new
law embodied Sweden's earliest form of constitution. It
defined the position and scope of the monarchy, incorporating ideas that had been formulated at the election of the
King in 1319, and stated explicitly that it should be elective;
the only qualification was that the King should be chosen
whenever possible from among the previous King's sons.
The old custom by which he rode round the country to
receive homage, the 'Eriksgata', was retained, and the
mutual relationship between King and subject was established in solemn oaths to be sworn by both parties, each
undertaking to accept and honour his rightful obligations.
These principles, stated in powerful terms, were to form the
basis of the Swedish constitution for many centuries. And the
towns subsequently obtained a new municipal law, which
regulated their life and gave extensive rights to their strong
German element.

Foreign policy during Magnus Ericsson's reign was dictated to some extent by the projects for eastern expansion.
The King tried to carry them out, though with little success,
by war with Russia, and also by the personal union with
Norway, which was later modified by his sharing the rule of
this kingdom with his youngest son Håkon. But the most
important factor that had to be taken into account was Denmark, where Valdemar Atterdag's energetic attempts to
restore the country soon brought him into conflict with

Sweden. Valdemar made some concessions at the beginning of the 1340's, but these were only in the nature of a temporary compromise.

Internal conflicts came to be linked up in a curious way with this Danish problem. It was not long before Magnus Ericsson's attempts to expand his power in accordance with earlier Folkung traditions produced a clash with his nobles. He had already caused his oldest son Eric to be recognized as heir to the throne – another step towards the hereditary monarchy. The King's foremost supporter in his efforts to establish a stronger centralized monarchy was Bengt Algotsson, who had been raised to a dukedom and who was bitterly hated by the nobles on account of his intimacy with the King. These nobles won the sympathies of the young King Eric, and also of King Magnus's brother-in-law, Albrecht of Mecklenburg, who skilfully exploited the unrest in Scandinavia for his own ends; and Magnus was forced to get rid of Bengt Algotsson and share the kingdom with his son. In spite of these setbacks, however, he refused to give up. He leagued himself with Valdemar Atterdag, an alliance that was sealed in 1359 by the betrothal of Magnus's son, Håkon of Norway, with Valdemar's daughter Margaret – the most ambitious dynastic union in the history of Scandinavia. Events now moved fast. The young King Eric died the same year, 1359, and Magnus again became the uncontested ruler. He proceeded to take the significant step of summoning to Kalmar a parliament, a *Riksdag*, in which all four Estates[1] were represented. It is not known whether this meeting ever took place; but the principle of a parliament of the Estates was clearly implicit in the summons, and this principle was ultimately to be followed up with momentous results.

While everything appeared to be proceeding smoothly

---

[1] The four Estates of the fully developed *Riksdag* were the nobles, the clergy, the burgesses and the peasants. The last three of these were collectively the " unfree " commons (*ofrälse*).

Valdemar Atterdag, suddenly changing his tactics, seized
Skåne in 1360 and Gotland shortly afterwards (see Chapter
VII). This did not prevent Magnus from resuming his
alliance with Valdemar, however, as the lords were again
proving a source of anxiety, and the marriage between Håkon
and Margaret was duly solemnized. Just then another
character made his appearance in Swedish politics. Albrecht
of Mecklenburg, who was married to Magnus's sister, had a
son, also called Albrecht; and in the autumn of 1363 Albrecht
the younger set off with ships and troops to conquer Stockholm. He was supported by the Swedish nobles, who hoped
to find in him a pliant ruler, and Magnus Ericsson was driven
out. His son Håkon was still King of Norway, and he himself
retained western Sweden for a time; but they were never
able to win back the whole of Sweden either with or without
the occasional support of Valdemar Atterdag. The strong
north German influence which coloured Swedish economic
and cultural life during the Folkung era was thus extended
to the sphere of politics; and the Vadstena monks were later
to write in their annals: 'Then the birds of prey alighted on
the mountain-tops.'

And so the Folkung era came to an end. In many ways it
forms a very gloomy chapter in Swedish history. The first
half was characterized by violent internal strife, and it concluded in defeat and humiliation. In the middle of the
fourteenth century, Sweden, like the rest of Europe, had been
scourged by the terrible Black Death, which was interpreted
by the mediaeval mind as a punishment from God. In foreign
affairs the country met with many setbacks. Yet, in spite of
everything, the Swedish communities grew and flourished,
strenuously restoring that which had been destroyed by war
and pestilence. The areas of settlement and cultivation continued to spread; many new 'crofter-villages' grew up in
Västergötland, Småland, and other provinces, and cattle-
rearing prospered in these newly-settled areas. Internal
colonization had been begun both in Norrland and in the

waste tracts in the interior of Finland. A diverse community was developing, similar in many respects to that which existed in continental Europe, and butter and metals were exported in considerable quantities. The violent clashes between constitutional and absolutist ideas were to have repercussions in the centuries to come. Yet at the same time, and despite German influence, a Swedish mediaeval culture had emerged and was destined to survive the Mecklenburg rule. Few centuries have left behind them such magnificent legacies as the fourteenth, which saw the birth of the *Chronicle of Eric*, the greatest Swedish mediaeval poem, and of the national laws. Moreover, it was this century that produced Saint Birgitta, one of the most exceptional and fascinating personalities of Swedish history, who was herself a typical child of one of the great families of the Folkung dynasty.

# VI

# Saint Birgitta

## c 1300-1373

Saint Birgitta of Sweden has left her mark on the whole of Scandinavia, where the religious houses founded by her Order formed important centres of devotional life in all its aspects. Birgittine houses were also established in many other European countries, where some of them still exist. But their real home has always been in the north, where they constituted an inner Nordic circle of study, authorship, and the exercise of piety during the last centuries of the Middle Ages.

Ever since the time of Sverker the Elder, monasteries and nunneries had done much to establish Christianity in Sweden, the best of them exemplifying the new and at first confusing ideal of life preached by the Church. Many of their inmates were skilled in the arts of husbandry, simples, and the care of the sick, all of which they were able to impart to others; certain of the institutions served as asylums and hospitals, while others were seats of learning and study. It was not uncommon for men and women from the most exalted families to take religious vows, either withdrawing completely from the world or becoming prominent figures in their new sphere. In about 1280 Ingrid, the daughter of an old magnate family, had received Papal sanction to found a nunnery in Skänninge on the Östergötland plain, and daughters of King Valdemar and Magnus Ladulås had also taken the veil.

The virgin and the widow have always been favourite types of female saint in devotional literature, and it was in the latter capacity that Birgitta was to become a figure of international fame. The Swedes acquired in her a saint of their own. She was born on a big estate in Uppland at the

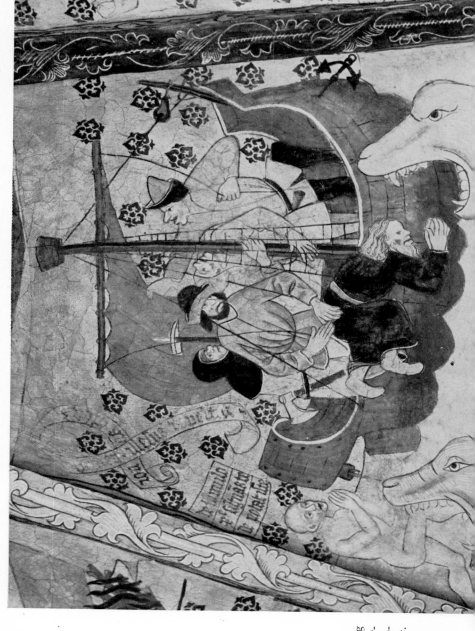

9. Detail of wall painting by Albertus Pictor, Härkeberga Church, Uppland, end of 15th century.

10. St Birgitta, wooden statue in Vadstena Chapel,
*c.* 1435.

beginning of the fourteenth century, just when the disagreements between the second generation of Folkungs were starting. Her father was the lawman Birger Persson, well versed in both law and politics – he helped to revise the Uppland law – and a great landowner; on her mother's side she was related to the royal house. As a child she shared in the workaday life of the estate and in the great family feasts, where the new chivalric mode of life was given free rein; but according to the legend she began very early on to have visions of the Virgin Mary and of Christ upon the Cross. In the fashion of the time she was married very young – at the age of thirteen, according to her daughter – to a young man from one of the leading magnate families, Ulf Gudmarsson of Närke, who was both a knight and a lawman. To him she bore eight children on their estate Ulvåsa in Östergötland. Long after his death she vividly described his shortcomings, and revealed his addiction to the material pleasures of life; obviously, Birgitta was the stronger character of the two. She did not allow her preoccupation with practical matters to interfere with her studies and devotions, in which she sought whenever possible to include her husband; as, for example, in their joint pilgrimage to the shrine of the Apostle James in Compostella. She also found time to visit the court of the young King Magnus Ericsson to propagate her particular form of piety; and there is no doubt that she took a lively interest in her husband's legal business. She appears, indeed, to have influenced everyone she met.

The years Birgitta spent on a big estate, first as a child and then as a housewife, provided a realistic basis for her imaginative mind. She took an active part in every aspect of life: work in the fields, the mills and the smithy, the stables, hencoops, and kitchens; hunting, tournaments, and festivities; the *Ting*, administration of justice, and the political discussions of the magnates; pilgrimages over land and sea. All these activities set their stamp on her subsequent literary work and are implicit in the metaphors she uses, Biblical

6*

concepts being intermingled with scenes from her own daily round. She recalls the estate in times of unrest when she describes in a vision the bowman who is wont to look about him through the windows and shoot those who take no heed for themselves; and when she speaks of 'pulling up mossy and barren stumps and casting them into the fire, setting fruitful plants in their place', she draws on her experience of swithening in the forests, or maybe work in the herb-garden in early spring. Even at this time she was able to discuss religious questions with her domestic chaplain Nils Hermansson, afterwards Bishop of Linköping, and with the canon of the same town, Magister Mattias, a learned man who had studied abroad.

When Birgitta was about forty her husband died, and henceforward she could express more freely her true inclinations. She sought to exchange an active existence for one of contemplation, although a passive life was ruled out by her enormous vitality and masterful nature. She now had the opportunity to realize the great Catholic ideal of the widow-saint, and she bent all her ambition and energy to its achievement. With this in view, authorship, activity in the Church, the foundation of religious houses, pilgrimages, asceticism, and charity were all undertaken with astonishing perseverance and zeal, and in addition she gave free rein to the visionary side of her character.

Before long she began systematically to record all her visions. She, or one of her confessors, tells how 'her bodily powers were taken away or rendered impotent, but all the powers of her soul were supremely quickened to see, hear, utter, and feel those things that are of the spirit'. Not all of her visions were of this kind, however. In addition to her power of ecstasy or mystic communion with God, she gradually became convinced that her will and her wishes were divinely inspired, and many of her prophecies on topical matters are of this nature. Others, again, were purely devotional literature. These three groups constitute a noteworthy collection, the largest of its kind in mediaeval Swedish literature.

It would not have occurred to any mediaeval man or woman to doubt the authenticity of these visions. As in the case of Joan of Arc and her 'voices', the only question was whether they came from God or the Devil; and it was the authority of the theologian Magister Mattias that finally vouched for their divine origin. These hours of doubt and the subsequent confirmation of her vocation unquestionably proved the turning-point in Birgitta's life. She went to the Alvastra monastery where her husband was buried, finding in the subprior Petrus Olai a suitable amanuensis to translate her visions into Latin. She now had a working knowledge of this language, the tongue of the Church and the learned world, and the work was carried on under her stringent supervision. Petrus and a namesake of his, who was also Birgitta's helper, describe such hours: 'The words imparted to her she wrote down, when in health, with her own hand in her own tongue, and then caused us her scribes to render them with utmost precision into Latin, whereupon she compared the rendering with her own manuscript, so that no single word therein should fail or exceed that she had heard or seen in her vision'.

It must have been during this period that she was divinely inspired to produce her greatest work. Christ revealed Himself to her in a vision in which He laid down the rules of the Order which she was to found in Vadstena; and she immediately brought her remarkable will-power to bear on the task of carrying out these commands, which she considered as coming direct from God. Her first step was to enlist the support of her kinsman, the King; and in 1346 Magnus and his consort Blanche of Namur bestowed on her the royal estate of Vadstena for her purpose. The next, more precarious, step was to obtain Papal sanction. She resolved to seek this in person, and a vision gave divine confirmation to her will. Destined never to return, Birgitta left Sweden to plunge into the Europe of the Hundred Years War and the 'Babylonian captivity' of the Popes. Her relations with Magnus Ericsson were no longer the same as they had been, and she felt the need of a wider arena for her prophecies and her calling – one is tempted to call it her spiritual ambition.

But, though Rome was her goal, no Pope had lived in the city since the beginning of the fourteenth century. The head of the Church had long been under the influence of France, and at this period resided in Avignon; and, though it was hoped that he would return to Italy for the Holy Year of 1350, he did not actually come until nearly twenty years later. Birgitta spent more than twenty years in Rome awaiting his advent, and soon became a notable figure there. Her visions still centred round the homeland, her own circle, and the foundation in Vadstena; but they also began to encompass the entire affairs of the Church, as well as the great political topics of Europe. This was characteristic of Birgitta. Unlike so many of the mediaeval female visionaries, who were content with wholly mystical experiences, she was eager to intervene in a practical way in the burning questions of the day, proving herself a true scion of her energetic ancestors.

'My hour is nearly come' – thus Birgitta proclaims the words of God to Pope Clement VI in Avignon at the approach of the Holy Year – 'when I shall visit upon thee all thy forgetfulness and sin. And as I raised thee above all others, so shall thy soul be plunged into terrible torment, which shall sorely afflict thy body and thy spirit, if thou obeyest not my Word. And thy unruly tongue shall be silent within thy mouth; that title which thou sanctifiest on earth shall be forgotten and dishonoured in the sight of me and my saints.' But if the Pope would only follow the commands of God to make peace in the Hundred Years War between England and France and then betake himself to Rome, he should receive the eternal reward. Long and earnestly did Birgitta plead with Pope Clement VI and his successors Innocent VI and Urban V, but for many years it was in vain.

Meanwhile she had ample opportunity to study conditions in Rome and to make many pilgrimages throughout Italy. It was a curious environment for the Swedish noblewoman; but, just as her childhood had done, it provided her with vivid material for her writings, and inspired many prophetic visions embodying the commands, wishes, and wrath of God.

In Birgitta's Italian revelations Rome and its surroundings are represented as a new Sodom and Gomorrah. 'Many altars are left desolate,' she writes, 'the sacraments exposed in taverns, and those who offer them serve mammon rather than God.' Elsewhere she declares that five profanations have taken root: few people attend confession or mass, there is much loose living, Lent is not observed, the rich men force their servants to work on the Sabbath, and Christians practise usury more avariciously than the Jews themselves. But she still hoped that in spite of all this iniquity the city was not beyond the redemption for which she was working so zealously. She also visited the court at Naples, where Boccaccio had acquired much of his worldly wisdom, and where now her tongue spared neither man nor woman. Meanwhile she was making firm friendships throughout Italy and in other countries; the Birgittine circle included such personalities as the former Spanish bishop Alfonso of Jaen, who had given up his office in order to serve God better; in due course he was to have a great influence on Birgitta's visions and on the manner in which she ultimately recorded them.

All this time Birgitta was awaiting the return of the Pope, for not until then could her Order be approved, and as the years went by this had become almost an obsession with her. And it was not until 1367 that Urban V came back to Rome, spending only three years in the Papal city before setting out again for Avignon. Birgitta followed him to Montefiascone, where in scathing terms she revealed to him a vision in which God sternly called the Pope to account. As a result of this encounter Urban ratified her new Order as a part of the Augustinian Order, and gave his sanction to the command

which Birgitta had received in a vision more than twenty
years earlier. Meanwhile work on Vadstena Convent had been
proceeding, and Birgitta must have felt that she had at last
been granted final proof of the divine source of her inspiration. Step by step she was accomplishing, with admirable
devotion and perseverance, the task which she had set herself. But one thing remained, and that one of the most important – the great pilgrimage to the Holy Land, which was
to crown her saintly life. She knew that there she would be
vouchsafed a vision of the birth of Christ; and she did not
wish to die until she had had this supreme experience.

She began her journey in 1372, when she was nearly
seventy years old, accompanied by several of her closest
friends and relations.    In Naples, where she was received
with all ceremony by Queen Johanna, her son Karl fell ill
and died. The story goes that while the Queen, accompanied
by her husband King John and the great men of Apulia, followed the dead knight to the tomb with weeping  lamenta-
tion, Birgitta walked dry-eyed behind the bier, thanking God
that His will had been done. This episode was later worked
up into the familiar tale of how Karl had found favour in
the eyes of the Queen of Naples, who wished to have him for
her husband, and how Birgitta's prayers for divine interces-
sion were answered by the illness and death of her son. This
mixture of the family saga, hagiography, and Renaissance
story brings out, notwithstanding its historical inaccuracy,
the fundamental divergence between Birgitta and the Boc-
caccian Italy in which she moved.

After Karl's death Birgitta's pilgrimage proceeded over
the Mediterranean Sea to Cyprus, where the prevailing conditions conduced to a series of visions on sin, punishment, and
years of grace. Thence from Jaffa to Jerusalem, where the
pilgrims spent some months. They returned home by the
same route, arriving in Rome in the spring of 1373. In the
summer of the same year Birgitta died. A short while before
her death she had been informed in a vision that her dead

body was to be brought back to Vadstena, and that her soul
should, in the words recorded at the time, 'enter into her
house, into the joy of Christ'. Her remains were carried north
towards the end of the year, where they were laid to rest in
the land she had quitted nearly a quarter of a century
earlier.

Birgitta had never lost her contact with Sweden during her
stay in Italy, and many travellers to Rome brought her news
from home. She was particularly interested in the political
developments both of her own time and during the preceding period. An older Swedish King, who can probably be
identified with Magnus Ladulås, is shown in everlasting torment in a powerful vision of the Day of Judgment, Birgitta's
counterpart to Dante's Divine Comedy – and she strongly
objected to Magnus Ladulås being worshipped as a saint.

In his youth Magnus Ericsson had tried to keep in step
with Birgitta's advice and rules of piety, which as time went
on swelled into what might almost be called a Mirror for
Princes. But their relations became increasingly strained, and
when Magnus clashed with the magnates Birgitta's sympathies were all with the latter. She never forsook the political
views of her father and kinsmen, who favoured an aristocratic government based on constitutional principles and
were strongly opposed to the constant attempts on the part of
Magnus to strengthen the monarchy. These views were
expressed both in the election of the King in 1319 and in the
composition of the *kungabalken* of the *landslag* (p. 50).
Birgitta's theories on the true function of the state are a
curious blend of the religious and the political. Lacking a
closer knowledge of the real state of affairs in Sweden, she
visualized Magnus Ericsson as a typical tyrant, a servant of
the Devil. She approved the acquisition of Skåne in 1332;
but when Valdemar Atterdag, with the help of the army,
regained the province in 1360 and, in the next year, made the
famous attack on Visby she laid all the blame for these
reverses on the Swedish King, and her reproaches became

increasingly bitter and abusive. One vision which she had during this period even gives counsel for an organized rebellion against Magnus. Nor was Magnus the only one to suffer from her political prophecies. Valdemar Atterdag was compared to a fox, which in its turn resembles the Evil One; and Magnus Ericsson's successor, Albrecht of Mecklenburg, fared no better. Many of the sins attributed to the Scandinavian monarchs of this period originated in Birgitta's grim and threatening visions, and the view which later generations were to take of the history of this period was strongly influenced by her powerful personality.

Some years after Birgitta's death an official investigation was started of her claims to canonization. The evidence collected from those who had been in direct touch with her reveals many vivid aspects of contemporary Swedish and Italian life, and gives a full and detailed picture of Birgitta and her associates. All this, coupled with the visions compiled and edited by her followers, form a collection unsurpassed in Swedish records. It was a long time before the object was achieved, however, for the investigation coincided with the great schism in the mediaeval Church. Nevertheless, it was finally attained, thanks to the efforts of powerful supporters, Queen Margaret of Denmark and Sweden among them, and the canonization ceremony took place in 1391. Birgitta had achieved the goal which she had set herself.

# VII

# Visby and Valdemar Atterdag
## 1361

The most famous town of Scandinavia in the Middle Ages was Visby, on the island of Gotland. The numerous mediaeval houses which still stand, the magnificent church ruins, and the great city wall with its gates and turrets give some idea of its vanished glory, which equalled that of any other mediaeval town in northern Europe, and far exceeded that of the early Swedish towns of Birka, Sigtuna, and Stockholm. Gotland had preserved a strategic and economic significance ever since the eventful era of the Migrations and the Vikings; and when this phase of history came to an end the Gotlanders still continued to navigate the trade routes to Russia and the south and west coasts of the Baltic Sea. This is proved by later Swedish finds of Arabic, Anglo-Saxon, and German coins dating from 800–1000, more than half of which were dug up on Gotland. The important trade route by which Russian furs and other commodities were brought to the world market ran from Novgorod down to Hedeby; and, at a time when it was considered necessary not to lose sight of land, the peasant skippers and merchants who carried on the older Baltic trade found a natural and valuable base in the series of harbours along the Gotland coast; the town of Visby did not exist at this time, though the present site shows traces of early settlement. During the twelfth century German colonists from the west settled all the way along the southern coast of the Baltic, previously inhabited by the Wends and other Slavonic tribes. This expansion also gave new opportunities to the German merchants whose only access to the Baltic trade routes of the coveted Russian region had hitherto been across Denmark or Slavonic territory; and the new mercantile town of Lübeck came into being on the lower reaches of the Trave in the 1140's. Having thus established a firm footing on the Baltic, the German traders were now able to sail to Novgorod in their own ships, instead of using Danish or Gotland fleets, as they had done before. They made good use of their improved position, and the result was that Gotlanders and Germans were both competing for the Russian trade. The Germans were not slow to realize the advantages of the island as a base for the trade organizations which had been formed in Lübeck and in the hinterland of western Germany. The present site of Visby was chosen for their centre, and a town gradually grew up similar to Lübeck, though not without protest from the native trading strongholds on the island.

The Germans in Visby comprised both permanent residents and merchants from northern and western Germany, who made it their base for trading expeditions into Russia. Thus the town had a stable German population and contained also the storehouses and offices of those who, though residing in their own country, had acquired economic interests in Visby and Novgorod. These merchants naturally appointed their own agents in the new town, and Visby in effect provided a link on foreign soil between traders from different parts of Germany.

These enterprising Germans gained considerable prosperity from their trade with Russia and northern Europe, a prosperity which was reflected in the growth of the new town. From the end of the twelfth century Visby's remarkable rise is revealed in its buildings, some of which can still be seen to-day, either in ruins or much altered. The German Church of Saint Mary (now the cathedral) was consecrated in 1225, and the city wall was probably completed during the same century. Thus Visby became the most important of the Baltic towns, its population drawn largely from northern and western Germany and particularly from Westphalia. Nevertheless there was also a native community, and the two elements constituted what was later described as 'the two tongues' of the city. This gave Visby a peculiar dual character, and it possessed a further unusual feature in that, although a Hansa town, it acknowledged the King of Sweden and, like the island on which it stood, formed part of the Swedish kingdom.

A somewhat fanciful account of the rise of Gotland is given in the so-called *Guta Saga*, which in its present form dates from the thirteenth century – that is, from the time when the Icelandic sagas were at their finest. It begins by describing the way in which the island sank each day into the sea and was forced to remain static by the magic agency of fire, and goes on to define the island's relations with Sweden. Naturally, a tale of this kind does not aim chiefly at achieving historical accuracy. Nevertheless the *Guta Saga* is of great literary interest. Evidence of a more complete and reliable nature can be found in documentary and archaeological sources. Needless to say, the rise and progress of the island owed much to its extremely favourable position. Yet its history is full of violent conflicts. At the beginning of the thirteenth century its progress inevitably aroused widespread envy and resentment. The old Gotland peasants, who were still trading in Russian squirrel and wax with the English court, regarded the innovations of the intruders with disfavour. It was a plain clash between the rural traditions of the Vikings and the urban civilization of the Middle Ages. An open feud broke out in the 1280's. The citizens of Visby, safe behind their impregnable wall, were victorious. The Swedish King Magnus Ladulås supported them, demanding in return the payment of taxes and the recognition of his royal authority. Thus the city became supreme on the island. New developments, however, were threatening Visby's dominant position in the Baltic. From the beginning of the thirteenth century the North Sea merchants abandoned the difficult route across the narrow neck of the Jutland peninsula and the route which ran between the Elbe and Lübeck in favour of the direct route north of Jutland. They also found an important source of trade at the entrance to the Baltic: salted herrings from the Scanian fisheries were much in demand; and the German Hansa towns, Lübeck in particular, wielded a good deal of influence over Skanör and Falsterbo. Moreover, the Hansa ships were now navigating the North Sea direct. The result was that, by fair means or foul, Visby was gradually superseded in importance by Lübeck. The latter, together with its Hansa associates, was better placed for uniting the North Sea and the Baltic into one trading area, since Visby was situated rather on the periphery. This change in the relative importance of the northern European trade routes was confirmed by the decision in 1299 that the seal of the Hanseatic merchants should no longer be used in Visby.

But Visby's period of greatness was by no means over. The town was still to act as an important local trading centre in the great Hanseatic scheme, and was of particular value to the Novgorod traders. The trade of the late Middle Ages has been rightly called a world trade; though small in quantity it comprised a large variety of goods. Accounts from the funeral feast of St Birgitta's father in 1328 include such items as ginger, cinnamon, pepper, and other spices from India and West Africa; almonds, rice and sugar from Spain; saffron from Spain or Italy; wines from the Rhineland and Bordeaux. Visby was still drawing considerable profits from this trade and also from that in raw materials from Sweden and Russia, and in broadcloth, salt, and ale from western Europe and Germany. A fourteenth-century Lübeck chronicle has exemplified the wealth which accrued from this commerce in the statement that in Visby the swine ate from troughs of silver. It was at this time too that interest was centred on Visby and Gotland as a result of the part they played in the great feud between Denmark on the one hand and Sweden and the Hanseatic League on the other.

The relations between Sweden and Denmark in about

1360 are obscure. The Kings Valdemar Atterdag and Magnus Ericsson were alternately at war with each other and in alliance. As we have seen, Skåne reverted to Denmark in 1360, and at the same time Valdemar was involved in quarrels with the Hansa towns, particularly over the question of trading privileges. He wanted to persuade the rich peasants to pay a high price for the renewal of these privileges, but his clients proved refractory. He therefore decided to subdue them by force, believing that in this way he could at the same time strike a blow at Sweden, provide occupation for his very fine mercenary army, and win booty for himself. In the early summer of 1361 he planned a campaign of which the ultimate goal was known only to a few people. The most dramatic episode in Visby's early history was under way.

Valdemar's fleet first embarked for Öland, where the Castle of Borgholm was taken. The next objective was the west coast of Gotland, where the King landed at the end of July. Here, however, his well-equipped army met with hastily organized resistance on the part of the peasant population. Three battles are mentioned in contemporary records; the last was a desperate struggle which took place just outside the walls of Visby. The spot is marked by a memorial cross, whose brief and pathetic Latin inscription can be translated thus: 'In the year 1361 on the Tuesday after St James's day (27th July) the men of Gotland fell into Danish hands at the gates of Visby. They lie here. Pray for them.' Contemporary sources estimate the peasant losses at 1,800–2,000 men; Lübeck refers merely to an overwhelming defeat suffered by the peasants who lacked both training and arms.

At the beginning of the twentieth century, excavators discovered by chance the mass graves into which the dead were unceremoniously bundled after the battle; and these led to other finds of a somewhat macabre nature. Curious rusty weapons, mangled limbs, skulls transfixed by arrows

from a cross-bow, grinning crania still in their chain-mail
helmets – these, in addition to a mass of bones which were
impossible to identify, constitute one of the most fearsome
revelations of a mediaeval battle that has ever been known.
Detailed investigations of this material enable us to follow the
course of the bitter struggle. The Gotlanders fought to the
last man; the remains include the bones of men of all ages,
of boys and cripples, and even of women. But these pathetic
amateurs stood no chance against Valdemar and his professional soldiers. And after that the island was his.

It is not known what part the citizens of Visby played in
this struggle, though some indication is given by subsequent
events. Shortly after the catastrophe the city opened its
gates to the conqueror; a record which dates from about the
same time states that this was a voluntary act, while the
Franciscan monks in Visby describe it in their account as a
formal capitulation. Two days after the battle Valdemar
drew up a charter for the city, promising that it should retain
all its ancient rights and privileges. A portion of the wall has
been associated on account of its peculiar character with the
mediaeval custom by which an armed conqueror entered a
vanquished town through a breach in its wall, and Valdemar
may have entered Visby in this manner. However that may
be, the city had surrendered, and the inmates were prepared
to make concessions in return for the renewal of their trade
privileges. It is clear from this that they did not share the
attitude of the countryfolk towards Valdemar Atterdag, and
they thus afford another instance of the divergent interests
of town and countryside which characterize the mediaeval
history of Gotland.

The walled city had opportunities of negotiation with
Valdemar which were denied to the open country, and it
must have been obvious to the citizens that capitulation was
preferable to a siege with all its attendant horrors and of
which the outcome was in any case uncertain. They may
have been moved by the bloodshed among the peasants,

which they could witness from the wall, or prompted by the inadequacy of their own fortifications and strength; a mediaeval town needed citizens who were also soldiers. At all events Valdemar entered the town in triumph, and Visby had to pay the price he demanded for a treaty. A good deal of legend has grown up around the tributes which the city had to pay to escape destruction. Nevertheless, evidence of what Valdemar may have received for taking the city under his protection is provided by a quantity of wares which had been deposited in Visby by merchants from the other Hansa towns; later, the citizens of Visby informed these men that they had had to safeguard this property by relinquishing part of their own, probably hoping by this means to induce the Germans to share the burden. In any case, they themselves had to yield up part of their accumulated treasures.

Gold, silver, Russian furs and other costly wares had to be delivered over to the conqueror. There was no question of wholesale pillage, however, and Visby continued to hold its own as a trading town. There is a natural temptation to interpret a decline in fortune as the immediate consequence of dramatic events, and some later historians have tried to trace the decline of Visby from Valdemar's campaign, but there is little ground for the popular view that the Danish King stripped it of all its wealth. Visby had already lost its earlier position as the centre of Baltic and Hanseatic trade, and the effect of the disastrous days of July 1361 may well have been no more than incidental. On the other hand, they had far-reaching consequences for the peasant population, and it was long before they recovered from the blow.

Valdemar's campaign against Gotland and the conquest of Visby was a dual manœuvre directed equally against Sweden and the recalcitrant Hanseatic merchants. With regard to the former, Valdemar had now conquered a favourable position in the Baltic, which brought about a change in the relations between Sweden and Denmark; and Gotland was to become a bone of contention in Scandinavian politics right up to the middle of the seventeenth century. We must pass over its chequered career in the years that followed ; but its early history and particularly its subjugation by Valdemar Atterdag throws considerable light on trade in the Baltic during the early Middle Ages, and also gives a comprehensive picture of the bitter feuds of the fourteenth century.

11. Visby. 17th century print.

12a. Part of the city wall, Visby.

12b. Ruins of St Nicholas' Church, Visby.

13. The Valdemar Cross, end of 14th century. The inscription reads: 'Anno Domini MCCLXI, feria III post Jacobi ante portas Wisby in manibus danorum ceciderunt gutenses. Hic sepulti. Orate pro eis'.

14. Mass grave at Kors-
betningen: photograph
taken during excavation.

# VIII

# The Union of Kalmar
## 1363-1434

After the overthrow of the Folkungs by Albrecht of Mecklenburg's German troops it seemed as though the German exploitation of Sweden was about to begin in earnest. The traditional picture of Albrecht as a weak and incapable ruler derives from later hostile propaganda. In fact, he succeeded in his foreign policy, in seizing Skåne from Denmark and holding it for some years; and at home it was only by constant exertion that the Swedish Council was able to keep him in check.

This restraint was at first exercised by the leader of the Council, Bo Jonsson Grip, the *Drots*, who was the highest official under the crown and held a large number of important fiefs. After Grip's death in 1386 the King's obvious plans for a revolutionary change began to cause the nobles some uneasiness. His Mecklenburg-Swedish empire began to appear threatening both to them and also to other groups of society. Once again a war seemed to be brewing between a king who desired absolute power – this time with effective foreign support – and those who wished to uphold the freedom of the constitution.

During the fourteenth century the Swedish military system had been rapidly developing along lines already discernible at the beginning of the Folkung era. Fortified castles were built, many of them under the auspices of Albrecht, who had had experience at home of their military importance. These castles also became administrative centres. The surrounding fiefs were leased out on varying conditions (in return for services rendered by the holders, or as a security and pledge for loans to the crown) to the great nobles, who

7

undertook the responsibility for their defence and maintenance. It seems likely that foreign servants of the crown
under Albrecht had already introduced new methods of
administering these fiefs, and the polemical literature later
directed against Albrecht makes repeated references to their
brutal levies. During his rule many of the important castles
and fiefs were held by his father and other Mecklenburgers,
and it was therefore inevitable that the clash between King
and magnates at the end of the 1380's should centre round
these possessions. Only a small portion of the country was
under the direct control of Albrecht, but he planned to
recover the fiefs which had been pawned to Bo Jonsson Grip
and others.

In 1388 the Swedish lords appealed for help to Queen
Margaret of Denmark and Norway, who was Valdemar
Atterdag's daughter and widow of Magnus Ericsson's son,
King Håkon of Norway. Her troops defeated Albrecht at
Åsle in Västergötland in February 1389 – and she herself was
acclaimed Sweden's legal ruler. She recovered for the crown
some of the castles and fiefs held by the nobles. But this was
not the end of the struggle. In Stockholm loyal Germans
massacred a number of their Swedish fellow-citizens in the
so-called 'Käpplinge murders' of the summer of 1392;
Albrecht's adherents, nicknamed the Vitalians, made the
Baltic Sea unsafe for navigation, and Margaret did not gain
complete control of Stockholm until 1398, nor of Gotland
until 1408 – while Bo Jonsson Grip's son Knut Bosson, who
was formerly employed by Albrecht, retained an independent
position in Finland up to 1399. To all intents and purposes,
however, all three Scandinavian countries now had the same
ruler. In this they followed the pattern of Poland and
Lithuania, which had been united three years before by
marriages between members of their leading families, and
also of the Burgundian Dukes, who at that time were en-
deavouring to fuse together the scattered regions on the
north-east frontier of France. But though Margaret's policy

had always been influenced by dynastic considerations, the Scandinavian races were far more closely related to each other than those of the Polish or the Burgundian realms; and Sweden and Denmark had a further link in that they were both involved in the struggle against German influence.

This union of the three kingdoms was a new and remarkable development in Scandinavian politics. Yet it was not entirely without precedent. Even if we disregard the attempts in the eleventh century or the struggles of the twelfth and thirteenth, the union had already been foreshadowed earlier in the fourteenth century. Duke Eric had tried to consolidate his territories round the mouth of the Göta river; Magnus Ericsson had reigned simultaneously over Sweden, Norway, and the Scanian provinces for nearly thirty years, and had also, with his son Håkon, united parts of western Sweden with Norway during the conflicts which followed the overthrow of the Folkungs; and Albrecht of Mecklenburg had tried to regain Skåne. Though admittedly these were temporary phases, they are nevertheless significant. Moreover, some of the natural trade routes of southern Sweden passed through coastal provinces, which at that time belonged to Denmark; and members of the Scandinavian nobility, which had become a distinct group during the fourteenth century, had formed family and economic connections beyond their respective frontiers.

If her dynastic alliance was to become permanent, Queen Margaret would have to make plans for the future. Her only son Olof had died, but she found a possible successor in her great-nephew, Eric of Pomerania. He had already been elected heir to the Norwegian throne in 1388 and to those of Sweden and Denmark eight years later. He was then to be acclaimed and crowned at Midsummer of the following year by leading representatives of the three Scandinavian kingdoms in Kalmar, the most important town in southern Sweden, not far from the Danish frontier.

There is no eye-witness account of the proceedings at

Kalmar in 1397, but they can be gathered from documents connected with the various negotiations involved. Eric was crowned King of Denmark, Sweden, and Norway on Trinity Sunday in the presence of the Scandinavian deputies, who swore allegiance to him in the name of their respective countries. This was endorsed in a deed written on parchment, with attached seals in token of the agreement of the participants. This document gives only the bare outlines; a second document which is preserved in the Danish archives is more complicated and contains the draft of a joint Scandinavian constitution. The three countries were to have Eric as their king during his lifetime, and thereafter were always to be ruled jointly by *one* king. This king was to be chosen from Eric's direct descendants; should this line die out, counsellors of the three kingdoms should elect a king acceptable to all. The three were also to make common cause in certain matters of foreign policy; any one who attacked one of them was to be regarded as an aggressor by the others; regulations were laid down for negotiations with other powers; an outlaw from one country was to be similarly banished from the other two; and all feuds which had hitherto prevailed between them were to be buried and forgotten. Each kingdom, however, was to keep its own laws and its own form of administration.

This is a remarkable attempt to ensure close political co-operation under joint leadership – a union which yet makes allowance for each kingdom's political tradition and its laws. It would be difficult to express such a conception unequivocally, nor did the authors wholly succeed, despite the maturity of thought which the document displayed. Enlightened and even inspired as it is acknowledged to be, historians are not agreed as to its true purport. Was it a valid Act of Union or only a preliminary? And who was responsible for its ideas – the Queen or her opponents?

For the fact is that the document shows some striking inconsistencies. It was not written on the regulation parchment but on paper, and it reads almost like a draft. The seals, which in the Middle Ages served the same purpose as a signature to-day, have in this case been stamped directly on to the paper, so that it has been extremely difficult to identify the jumbled and damaged wax fragments. Nor does their number tally with the list of seven Swedes, six Danes, and four Norwegians who are quoted as its authors; there is not a single Norwegian seal, and there are only three Danish ones. The six parchment copies which it prescribes were never made. Obviously, then, this was not an inviolable decree; the document as preserved testifies only to the workings of a great idea, to discussions and plans.

Nevertheless, the Union existed, albeit only during Margaret's and Eric's lives. It had supporters in all three kingdoms. It could not but be approved by those nobles – and they were many – who had inherited or purchased estates in more than one of the Scandinavian countries. The question was whether the coalition could endure in face of the individual interests of the three kingdoms and their different traditions in foreign policy – Denmark leaning towards the south, Sweden towards the east. Co-operation had been feasible and even essential during the heavy German pressure on Sweden at the end of the fourteenth century, but this pressure had now been eased. Further, could the old struggle between monarchy and aristocracy abate, let alone disappear in this new setting? Much depended on the course chosen by the joint heirs to the Folkungs and the Valdemars.

The main aim of Queen Margaret's foreign policy was to drive back the Germans and expand Denmark's frontier southwards. At home she sought with equal consistency to create efficient government and financial order by appointing royal bailiffs, directly dependent on the crown, to carry on the administration of the country – and in this she succeeded where Magnus Ericsson and Albrecht had failed. Her careful diplomacy prevented any clashes with the Swedish nobles, who moreover had made important concessions to the Queen

at the assembly at Nyköping in 1396, when the danger from
Mecklenburg still threatened. These concessions enabled her
to restore some of their estates to the Swedish crown, a process called in Swedish 'reduction'.[1] The effects of this
achievement, for which Magnus Ericsson had striven in vain,
fell most heavily on the churchmen, who were therefore less
kindly disposed towards the Queen than were the nobles.
But she had an amazing gift for avoiding friction during her
rule. She refrained from placing Swedish castle-fiefs in the
hands of foreigners, and she spent a great deal of her time
in Sweden – more, probably, between 1398 and 1412 than in
Denmark; King Eric also visited Finland on two occasions.
She was adept at winning over public opinion, shrewdly
exploiting the religious foundation in Vadstena and the
Birgittine tradition generally to this end. Not only did she
promote the canonization of Birgitta and patronize the
Birgittine houses in Denmark but she also paid frequent
visits to Vadstena, where she would spend some days in the
foundation. Her sojourn there over the Christmas of 1403 has
been sympathetically recorded by the otherwise hostile
monks, revealing a curious facet of life in this age. Margaret
had demanded to be received as a 'Sister' in Vadstena, and
was solemnly permitted to do so. The chronicler describes
the scene when she kisses the hands of the inmates in farewell,
and chides a lay-brother for his humility in wrapping his
hand in his mantle before offering it to her. This intensely
human side of the Queen was later to be reflected in her will,
for her beneficiaries included many of those who had suffered
humiliation or material loss during and after the war with
Albrecht, and the souls of those on both sides who had been
killed on land or at sea.

[1] The term 'reduction' is applied to the resumption by the crown of
any kind of land, i.e. fiefs, hereditary estates, Church lands. This reduction could be made under various pretexts. The greatest of these reductions was that of Charles XI, to which the term 'reduction' is almost
exclusively attached in English. We shall use it in its more general
Swedish sense.

Margaret died in 1412, and Eric of Pomerania became sole monarch. He possessed neither her popular appeal nor the unflinching authority born of her remarkable triumphs. He zealously pursued and expanded her programme of administration and foreign policy; but he lacked both charm and tact, and he soon stirred up antagonism, which his consort Philippa, sister of Henry V of England, was powerless to conciliate, though she often came to Sweden and held meetings with the Council there. There were more Danes and Germans among the royal bailiffs than had been the case in Margaret's time, and the Swedish nobles, who by now held only a small number of fiefs, felt increasingly slighted; furthermore, they were allowed very little political influence, and it was clear that Eric was aiming to establish an absolute monarchy. The churchmen found in him a ruler who encroached on their rights by interfering in clerical appointments, and there was a particularly violent clash over the election of an archbishop in Uppsala in 1432. The King's costly foreign policy, directed towards the south, made financial and military demands on Sweden, while his attempts to increase the state revenues by reorganizing the taxation system alienated the sympathies of the peasants. Moreover, not only did Eric's deliberate attempts to establish over the three countries an absolute monarchy, similar to those that were being formed by rulers elsewhere in contemporary Europe, arouse opposition in Sweden but his ambitious foreign policy involved him in long and expensive wars with Holstein, which had important if indirect consequences.

At this time Sweden's main exports were the iron and copper from the Bergslagen mines. These were shipped by Hanseatic merchants, who had a long-standing interest in the industry. In 1426 Eric's war against Holstein induced the League to support his enemies with the time-honoured weapon of an economic blockade. This meant that Eric's kingdoms were cut off from the supply of salt and other essentials, and Bergslagen was particularly hard hit, since it had no market for its products. The position grew steadily worse, and at the beginning of the 1430's there was an uprising among the miners which struck at the foundations of Eric's Union. Once again a new Swedish province enters the limelight, illustrating afresh the strong regional individuality which gives Sweden's history its peculiar character, revealed most clearly during the last century of the Middle Ages and the beginning of the modern era. The people of Västmanland and Dalarna now enter Swedish annals with explosive force.

Bergslagen, Sweden's only 'industrial' area at this time, was naturally more advanced economically than the other provinces, and reacted more quickly than the purely agricultural areas to violent economic changes; its special organization and the 'free' status of the more prominent mine-owners (bergsfrälse) gave it some of the characteristics of contemporary urban communities. In this particular crisis the men of Bergslagen chose their leader from among their own ranks. His name was Engelbrekt Engelbrektsson, and he was one of the 'free' miners, bore the title of 'squire', and came originally of German family which had settled in Sweden some generations earlier. Little is known of his earlier life; even his date of birth is uncertain.

This was not the first time that Bergslagen had murmured against Eric's bailiffs and the principles of centralization they represented. The royal bailiff in Västerås, who had jurisdiction over Västmanland and Dalarna and whose ruthless methods seem to have been based on feudal tradition, had already been forced to resign. Nevertheless he continued to act as a convenient scapegoat for all the unpopular features of Eric's rule; he has even come to be regarded as the main cause of Engelbrekt's rising. Actually his removal would not have prevented it; as we have seen above, it had other more complex roots.

Eric had made a truce with the Hansa towns in 1432, but

the unrest in Sweden still continued, and the rising in Bergslagen broke out in the early summer of 1434. One after another the manors of the bailiffs were captured by the peasants. At Västerås, the heart of Bergslagen, Engelbrekt assumed leadership of the rising. Men of all classes joined his ranks, Västerås was taken, and the lawman of Uppland, who was socially the most important man among the rebels, was installed in the castle. The rebels pressed on through Uppland towards Uppsala and Stockholm, and there were also risings in the coastal settlements of Norrland, on Åland, and in Finland. The first account of Engelbrekt's rising that has come down to us is contained in a letter written home on 1st August by a Danzig merchant then in Stockholm:

Here is a man called Engelbrekt Engelbrektsson; he is Swedish, born in Dalarna, where copper and iron are quarried. He has gathered about him a good forty or fifty thousand men and can surely muster more, if he wishes; they have conquered and burnt many towns, castles and villages in the realm. When they came to Stockholm and there encamped on the one side, as the Hussites in Danzig, the castle and the town went manfully to the defence; there was no storming. . . . The chief demands of the men of Dalarna centre round their desire to have one King in Sweden and to drive out the King of Denmark from the three kingdoms; they themselves will be rulers. They therefore wish Sweden to return to her state under King Eric, whom the country now worships as a saint. In his time no customs duties or taxes existed and no burdens were laid upon the peasants, and they will therefore have back the same rights as in former days.

Engelbrekt's men failed to take Stockholm, but a truce was made with King Eric's castellan which was to last until November. Engelbrekt himself proceeded with the bulk of his army to Örebro. Here it was agreed that the castle should capitulate to Engelbrekt if it was not relieved within six weeks. Nyköping was his next goal, where a similar agreement was made, and then Engelbrekt marched into Östergötland. The purpose of the campaign was undoubtedly to

establish contact with the Council of the State, which was at
that time assembled at Vadstena. The proposal of the rebels
to abolish taxation, among other things, was a strong induce-
ment to take up arms; but if there was to be any lasting
result, the rebels would have to make an alliance with those
in Sweden who were politically experienced. The disagreements over the Uppsala archbishopric must have shown
Engelbrekt that not all the great lords of the kingdom
approved of Eric's absolutist tendencies. It is true that the
opposition of the Church had been broken; the previous
year three Swedish bishops on a visit to Denmark had been
forced to express their support of Eric in a letter to the Pope,
though they afterwards revoked what they had written.
The clergy had at first condemned the rising as 'a fire of evil
and desolation' comparable to the Hussite movement, but
this could easily be modified or reversed in the common
cause. The lords of the Council also had reason enough to
ally themselves with Engelbrekt, and awaited his coming in
Vadstena.

This meeting resulted in an alliance between the Council
and Engelbrekt. The members of the Council blamed the
rising itself for the subsequent violent measures against the
King, and claimed that Engelbrekt had forced the alliance
on them under duress – just as the bishops had been forced
to support the King in the previous year. Before long, however, they had drawn up a comprehensive indictment
couched in legal terms, accusing the King of infringing
Sweden's fundamental law contained in the *kungabalken*. The
Church and the nobles thus joined with Engelbrekt and his
armed forces in opposing the principles of absolutism, and
Eric found himself in a very awkward position, since he was
checkmated also in his conflict with Holstein and the Hansa.
Meanwhile, the rising continued to spread; one by one the
strongholds fell before the attacks of Engelbrekt and other
leaders. In addition to the peasants, the bishops' soldiers and
a large number of Swedish nobles took part in these sieges,

reinforcing with their lances and iron armour the clubs, axes, and arrows of the peasants. Even cannon were used on both sides in these Engelbrekt feuds, though the noise of this mediaeval artillery still exceeded its effectiveness.

In September Engelbrekt, who was then in Västergötland, urged Bishop Thomas of Strängnäs and the lords of Uppland to be responsible for the naval defence against King Eric's anticipated counter-attack, while he would undertake 'with the help of God and St Eric to answer for the defence on land as far as to the Sound'. The rising was now in its third month and had made enormous strides. How was the King of the Union going to react?

It is a curious coincidence that some months after these events the future Swedish archbishop, Nicolaus Ragvaldi, made a speech at the Council of Basle in which, following up certain earlier ideas, he identified the Goths of the Teutonic migrations with the Swedish *Götar*; thereby laying the foundations for an interpretation of Swedish history which would ultimately far outweigh the one offered by Snorre Sturlason.

# IX

# The Settlement with
# Eric of Pomerania
## 1434-1448

Eric of Pomerania was not unaware of the Swedish rising, but he was involved during the summer in negotiations with Holstein and the Hansa. In October 1434, however, he led his fleet against Stockholm, ready to match his absolutist programme against the Swedish demands for a constitution. Parleys took place, and by the middle of November the two sides had agreed on a truce of one year; the following September a court, composed of members of the Council from all three kingdoms, was to pass judgment on the great dispute between King Eric and his subjects. Royal troops were quartered in the Castle of Stockholm and Eric returned with his navy to Denmark.

In January 1435 a great Council meeting was held at Arboga, and Engelbrekt was among its members. Here the future government of the country was decided upon, particular stress being laid on the immediate military arrangements. Engelbrekt was to be the commander, assisted by six local commanders chosen from the aristocracy. Everything in the kingdom was thus kept in readiness; only the castle of Stockholm and a few other castles remained under Eric's control. Mediation between the two sides was undertaken shortly afterwards by Eric's castellan in Stockholm and a representative of the Teutonic Knights who was at that time visiting Sweden. An agreement was reached in the spring, at Halmstad, and was followed by a formal treaty after the return of the King to Stockholm in the autumn of 1435. The trial ordained the previous year was no longer to take place, and apart from some revisions in Eric's earlier policy the *status quo* was to prevail. Eric was to appoint a *Drots* and a *Marsk* – leading state offices which had long remained vacant – and to guarantee the Council a voice in the appointment of royal bailiffs (except in Stockholm, Nyköping, and Kalmar). Engelbrekt was to receive the important fief of Örebro, and Eric also undertook to reduce taxation. The agreement also provided for the payment of compensation on account of Engelbrekt's campaign in Halland and for the restoration of the King's authority. As a result of this the Council gained some control over the King, and Engelbrekt became one of the leading men in the kingdom. But it was questionable whether the original dispute had in fact been settled.

Interpreting somewhat freely the terms of the agreement, the King appointed his own bailiffs in Stäkeborg and Stäkeholm, on the east coast of Sweden. And when Eric left the country the new *Marsk*, Karl Knutsson Bonde, found himself in a delicate position as the highest officer of the realm. Both he and Engelbrekt were to play an important part in the events which followed.

Once again unrest began to reveal itself. The rank and file regarded the reconciliation with Eric as a defeat, despite the constitutional guarantees made to the Council. Their dream of reverting to the Utopian state of affairs in the days of St Eric had not been fulfilled. Nor were the Council and the *Marsk* slow to notice the discrepancy between the terms of the agreement of October 1435 and actual practice. The country was particularly opposed to the presence of the King's bailiffs in a number of important castles, and the general feeling was bluntly expressed by Engelbrekt and his right-hand man, Erik Puke, in their dealings with the *Marsk*.

In January 1436, exactly one year after the Arboga meeting, another great assembly was held in the same place, and from it the nobles conveyed to the King the grievances which had been aired. Again Erik was threatened with deposition

if he did not mend his ways; and Karl Knutsson and Engelbrekt went straight from the meeting to the capital and took
it by surprise, though Eric's castellan still held the castle. It
was almost the Vadstena episode over again, though there
were certain important differences. A leader for the new
rising was the first essential, and a commission of thirty
lords met in the Dominican monastery in Stockholm to elect
him. Of the three candidates, Engelbrekt received only three
votes, Erik Puke two, and Karl Knutsson was victorious with
twenty-five. This revealed a change in the situation since the
days of Vadstena, due chiefly to the hostility which had
grown up between Engelbrekt and some of the lords, and
which was later to have disastrous results. The position was
not yet too serious, however, and the results of the election
were soon modified; Engelbrekt, as Commander, took his
place by the side of the *Marsk* and launched his second
campaign. During the spring of 1436 he swiftly marched
along the south coast, past Kalmar (where the Danish castellan
Jens Grim resisted his attack), and on to Laholm in southern
Halland; then towards north-west Skåne, where a fresh
truce was made, and finally along the Halland coast. A
deliberate purpose underlay this campaign: to gain control
of those rivers which rose and had their longest reaches
within Sweden, but which ran out into the sea from the
Danish coastal provinces. It was this same idea which had
prompted Eric of Pomerania to build up his strongholds
guarding the Sound, and to try to control the east coast of
Sweden by the appointment of loyal castellans. Both parties
were fully aware of the internal communications and the
coastlines.

Engelbrekt never completed this campaign. He fell ill – it
is thought with a rheumatic disorder – and retired to his
castle in Örebro. In this district lived two of his bitterest
enemies, the lawman of Närke, Bengt Stensson Natt och Dag,
and his son, Magnus Bengtsson. The original cause of their
quarrel is obscure; but whatever it was the two parties were

at daggers drawn, and it was decided that the Council should arbitrate between them in the spring.

About the beginning of May Engelbrekt, though still a sick man, left Örebro for Stockholm. He spent the first night on a small island in Lake Hjälmaren, not far from Bengt Stensson's estate. Englebrekt's followers lighted a camp-fire, as the night was cold. Suddenly they saw Magnus Bengtsson rowing over the lake with his retinue. Seizing his axe, he sprang ashore and fell on Engelbrekt, who, according to the rhymed chronicle, had hobbled down on his crutches to meet him. Engelbrekt fell, and Magnus's armed band shot his body full of arrows. The position in Sweden was greatly changed by the assassination of her national hero, since he had been the only man capable of organizing the peasants into anything resembling an army. Popular resistance to royal absolutism therefore declined, and Karl Knutsson regained his supremacy.

Some of the events in the ensuing months are very significant. In October the Council issued letters of safe-conduct for the murderer of Engelbrekt and for the murderer's father, Bengt Stensson. And when some months later Erik Puke, Engelbrekt's brother-in-arms, quarrelled with Karl Knutsson and placed himself at the head of the disturbances still going on in Västmanland, Närke, and Dalarna, Karl Knutsson caused him to be seized, sentenced, and executed; some of his adherents had already suffered such punishments as being burnt at the stake for high treason. The conditions for genuine co-operation between the popular movement and the Council had now disappeared. The leader was gone who had been able to control provincial discontent and guide it into a channel where its energy could be used most effectively.

Engelbrekt's name lived on in the minds of his friends and followers; he became to them a man through whom God wrought His miracles, comparable to the heroes of Biblical legend. His pierced body recalled the martyrdom of St Sebastian. In Lübeck, where interest was naturally taken in a man with a German name from a well-known province, the chronicler Hermann Korner wrote of him thus:

A Swedish-born gentleman called Engelbrekt, a man of great insight and resource, rose against King Eric, for he would not suffer the overweening indignity to which knights, citizens, peasants, and the whole Swedish nation were subjected by King Eric's bailiffs and captains; peradventure he was chosen by the Lord and given strength, as Saul, to preserve his people and put down the adversaries of righteousness. Of a certainty, Engelbrekt began his war not from vainglory or lust for power, but from compassion to the oppressed.

Before long the countryfolk and even the townspeople of central Sweden came to regard him as a saint. His grave in Örebro became a pilgrim's shrine, like that of St Eric in Uppsala and St Birgitta in Vadstena, and it was even said that miracles occurred there.

The Swedish Council and its leader Karl Knutsson were now faced with the task of coming to terms with Eric of Pomerania. In the middle of the summer the two opposing parties – the King and the Council – met in Kalmar, where the Danish and Norwegian Councils and representatives from the Hansa towns were to act as mediators. The dispute boiled down to the question as to whether the King should appoint his own representatives in the Swedish castles or whether he should comply with the Swedish demand that the appointment should be made according to their own national law. There were long deliberations on the matter. The King had clearly realized that his absolutist policy favoured his Danish and German retainers, and with this bait he sought to enlist the support of the Danish Council. But the Swedes also had something to offer: if their demands were accepted and the Union perpetuated, they would allow the Danish lords uncontested right to their property in Sweden, whether it comprised their hereditary lands or those held in security from the crown; these lords would also recover the hereditary estates which they had lost during the

Kon CARL VIII K...

15. Karl Knutsson, wooden figure by Bernt Notke,
*c.* 1485.

16. St George, statue of wood and elk's horn, by Bernt
Notke. Erected in the Great Church, Stockholm, in 1489
to commemorate the Brunkeberg victory.

Engelbrekt feuds. This was a major concession in view of the
'Scandinavian' distribution of noble holdings at this time.
In other words, the King held out prospects of *fiefs* in
Sweden, while the Swedish government proposed to give
complete *possession* of existing property. The Danish Council
chose the latter, and a treaty was drawn up in September
1436 embodying the constitutional programme of the
Swedish Council. The King had been forced to yield. The
point that emerges most clearly from these negotiations is
that they did not represent a battle between Sweden on the
one hand and Denmark or the Union on the other, but constituted rather an assertion by the Swedish Council of its
ancient political traditions against the form of personal and
absolutist government favoured by King Eric – a form which
he considered essential if his great Scandinavian state were
to be really effective. Thus it seemed that for the third time
the balance had been restored. Swedes were now in control
of the main Swedish castles, while Karl Knutsson and the
*Drots*, Krister Nilsson Vasa, were responsible for the government. Disturbances among the peasants continued, but they
were ruthlessly suppressed with the help of new laws and
ordinances. But unity depended on the attitude of the
opposing parties to the Kalmar treaty of 1436. In spite of his
apparent meekness, Eric of Pomerania was reluctant to give
up his ideas. Once again he set to work, and within two years
was ready for action. In 1438 he installed his Pomeranian
kinsfolk in Danish fiefs, and tried to carry out his former plan
by which one of them should be recognized as Regent. He
took up his own quarters on Gotland, a particularly strategic
position, and demanded the restoration of his former status in
Sweden. The Swedish and Danish Councils merely ignored
him, and confirmed the Union between themselves. They
believed that the bonds between their kingdoms were strong
enough in themselves to survive the collapse of the original
unifying factor – the dynasty. At the next election the pleni-
potentiaries of the two kingdoms would consider whether it

8

would be preferable to have one king, or more than one. Eric was now out of the running.

In the autumn of 1438 Karl Knutsson was appointed Regent in Sweden, pending the election of a king. The proposed candidate in Denmark was Eric's nephew, Duke Christopher of Bavaria, who had already offered his services to the Swedish Council, promising to be a 'just ruler' if he were chosen. In July 1439 the Danes abjured all allegiance to Eric of Pomerania, and Duke Christopher became the King of Denmark; and, since he had promised to conform to the constitutional programme which the Swedes had drawn up, there was every chance that he might also become King of Sweden.

Meanwhile Eric from his base on Gotland had made a bid to reconquer Sweden. The country was in a state of great unrest; the peasants were discontented and there were frequent feuds among the lords temporal and spiritual. Karl Knutsson had caused the *Drots* to be taken unawares and imprisoned, later consigning him to his fief in Finland on the condition that he would not create any more opposition. Three brothers of the Natt och Dag family – Bengt Stensson, father of Engelbrekt's assassinator, Nils and Bo Stensson – were among Karl Knutsson's main adversaries, and in March 1439 King Eric and Nils Stensson joined forces. Eric bestowed on Nils the office of *Marsk*, and placed him in command of the royal troops in Sweden under the Danish banner. At the same time he drew up a skilfully-worded accusation against Karl Knutsson. Thus one party, or rather one family group was now fighting in Sweden for Eric against the Regent. It was a curious situation, which throws considerable light on the confusion which reigned when the country was governed by an aristocratic Council.

The Council now had to counter Eric's propaganda and drive back both his troops and those led by Nils Stensson. It found a symbol of unity in the national hero and popular saint Engelbrekt, who thus played a significant rôle in

Swedish politics even after his death. The story of Engelbrekt, Karl Knutsson, and liberty inspired Bishop Thomas of Strängnäs to write a poem which is one of the finest of its period, and is still deeply rooted in the Swedish mind. Thomas describes Eric's tyranny, and compares the sufferings of his subjects to those of the Children of Israel under Pharaoh. Then, says Thomas, God raised up in Engelbrekt a saviour of the people, and after his death Karl Knutsson carried on his work, using every possible means to achieve this end. The climax of the poem consists of a stirring challenge to the people of Sweden to stake everything in the fight against King Eric and in the vindications of freedom, which is 'the best thing in the world'.

Thus the tyrant was defeated and freedom secured. Nevertheless the goal was freedom from Eric's absolutism, not from the Union: freedom, as conceived by the Council and Bishop Thomas, could perfectly well exist within the framework of the Union. And this view triumphed after Eric's deposition in the autumn of 1439.

The new King was not, it is true, elected by the joint methods which had been agreed upon, for the Danes had anticipated them and chosen Duke Christopher as their sovereign in 1440. In 1441, however, the Swedish Regent Karl Knutsson laid down his office, and the Swedish Council endorsed the Danish choice. The ex-Regent retired to his large holdings in Finland, where he awaited developments in the castle of Viborg – an indication of the importance which began to be attached to the Russian frontier in the mid-fifteenth century.

According to the rhymed chronicle King Christopher was regarded in many circles as a poor substitute for Karl Knutsson. Nevertheless the Union was established, and the constitutional freedom demanded by the Council was granted; Christopher's oath represented the triumph of this aristocratic constitutionalism. A new version of the national laws, 'Christopher's law', appeared during this reign, and the

King ruled in peace and amity with the Council and his subjects until 1448, when he died without leaving an heir. The ensuing election resulted in a conflict which was to have a radical effect not only on Sweden but on the whole of Scandinavia. For the second time Karl Knutsson stepped into prominence, a man familiar to all, rich, noble, and of great political experience; moreover his years of idleness had done nothing to abate his zest for action. At this point trends begin to emerge which were ultimately to lead, through the Stures, to Gustav Vasa.

# X

# Karl Knutsson and Sten Sture
## 1448-1471

There were a number of possible candidates to the Swedish throne after Christopher's death. Eric of Pomerania, who was still living from well-organized piracy on Gotland, had his champions. Two brothers of the Oxenstierna family, Bengt and Nils Jönsson, had been appointed Regents, and it may be that this powerful Uppland family favoured a son of Nils as claimant. A possible rival was Karl Knutsson, chief among the Swedish nobility. There was no one candidate equally acceptable to all three kingdoms, and the advantage would therefore be with the country which first accomplished an election.

Karl Knutsson, who was favoured both by circumstances and by his own prominent position, was the successful candidate in Sweden; for Jöns Bengtsson, son of the Regent Bengt Jönsson Oxenstierna, had already been elected Archbishop of Uppsala shortly after Christopher's death, and it was thought wiser not to choose the temporal Head of the State from the same family. Soon after his election in Stockholm Karl Knutsson despatched an army to Gotland to overthrow Eric of Pomerania. Visby was conquered, but Eric maintained the stronghold of Visborg. Meanwhile the Danish Council had elected Christian of Oldenburg as their King Christian I, while in Norway each of the two chief rivals – Christian and Karl Knutsson – was elected by his respective party. Christian had already seized Gotland, and the rivalry between the two kings brought the Union to the verge of war. However, representatives of the three Councils met in Halmstad and drew up a treaty which laid down that the first throne to be left empty should pass to the surviving monarch, *provided* that

agreement was unanimous; otherwise the Union was to be
restored after the death of the second king. Regulations
were drawn up for this future Union, and the Swedish
Council handed over Karl Knutsson's rights in Norway to
Christian.

The success of this compromise depended on Karl Knutsson. He had no mind to give up any of his newly won power
for long, however, and the meeting in Halmstad led not to
the restoration of the Union but to war between the Swedish
and the Danish kings. Once again hostilities began with a
Danish attack in 1451, and the following year Karl Knutsson
retaliated by ravaging Skåne. Christian then attacked
Västergötland, the traditional battleground of the two
neighbouring countries right from the Battle of Lena in 1208
to the Battle of Åsunden in 1520; but despite initial successes
he did not reach the centre of the kingdom, for Sweden possessed the advantage of size, and her stretches of uninhabited
land, almost impenetrable as they were, formed a natural
defence against the numerous onslaughts. The war was in-
conclusive; the diplomatic victory, however, lay with King
Christian and the Danes. There were other reasons too for
Karl Knutsson's defeat; to consolidate his monarchy he had
resorted to the same tactics as Eric of Pomerania: heavy
taxation and the practice of choosing bailiffs and castellans
from among his personal servants; and to these were added
his arbitrary measures against the Church. In 1457 the lords
under Archbishop Jöns Bengtsson, supported by the discontented peasantry, had risen in revolt against him; and he had
been forced to flee to Danzig, where he remained for several
years. The Archbishop and Erik Axelsson, a member of the
Danish noble family of Tott, became Regents, and the
leaders of the rising acclaimed Christian I as King in
Sweden. But, although the Union was temporarily restored,
the events of the last few years had considerably modified its
original conception, and civil war had intensified party
differences. During the early 1460's Sweden was ruled by

different noble factions who followed each other in rapid succession and rent the country with their feuds. The Council's clashes with the two Kings resulted in general chaos of an almost feudal character, since the policies of the various factions tended to be dictated by family connection or interest. One of the most remarkable episodes during the prevailing confusion took place in 1464, when a Swedish peasant levy under Bishop Kettil Karlsson Vasa overthrew King Christian's trained troops at the Battle of Haraker in Västmanland.

Karl Knutsson is one of the first notable mediaeval figures in Sweden whose personality can be fairly easily deduced from contemporary sources. He achieved a great deal by his forceful propaganda. A series of political pamphlets were issued from his Chancery intended for different sections of the public: politico-legal arguments for the Hansa and, even more important, popular writings for the common people. The best of these documents still in existence is the rhymed *Chronicle of Karl*, to which several of his professional household poets contributed. The King was not overscrupulous about truth in his propaganda; and his numerous enemies, from Erik Puke and Krister Nilsson Vasa to King Christian and Jöns Bengtsson Oxenstierna, are portrayed in the darkest colours. He himself appeared as an open-handed and dignified gentleman with a taste for pomp, striving to incorporate in his own person the current fashions of the time. In so doing he was patterning himself on the best chivalric models of the Middle Ages, similar to those adopted in the English, French, and, above all, Burgundian courts. In fact he came no nearer to the original ideal than did his European counterparts; times had changed, and the knightly aspect could be no more than a veneer. Shorn of all his own propaganda and judged purely by his actions, Karl Knutsson emerges as a power politician who, although bold, quick-witted, indefatigable and unscrupulous, nevertheless endowed his office with lofty ideals, as did his contemporaries elsewhere in

Europe. A contemporary wooden carving by the Lübeck sculptor Bernt Notke, reputed to be a portrait of Karl Knutsson, shows a gnarled, almost brutal, face with a strong jaw and a prominent nose: a countenance well in accordance with his character as revealed in his deeds and his writings.

Further personal details are given by his historian Ericus Olai in his Latin Chronicle. It is a biased description, since the writer's ecclesiastical sympathies caused him to regard the King as the enemy of the Church and of the Archbishop; but it gives credit where credit is due, praising Karl's appearance, understanding and wisdom, while deprecating his inadequate military experience and his greed for money and possessions. This latter trait, writes the historian, made him reluctant to yield up strongholds or fiefs for purposes of defence, an attitude which not only alienated the nobles but encouraged the Danes and his other enemies to wage constant war with the aim of overthrowing him.

Once more Karl Knutsson was to plunge from triumph to disaster, as though in illustration of the mediaeval symbol of Fortune's wheel. Overthrown in 1464, he again returned to Finland just as he had done after his regency; but even now he continued to lay fresh plans and to look around for suitable alliances. Conditions among the Scandinavian nobility gave him yet another chance to try his luck, though he would never be able fully to regain the royal dignity which he had striven for during the 1450's.

At this time in the Union's history many of the noble families owned property on both sides of the old frontiers. Moreover, long tradition had given them a strong political influence, which tended to be expressed in a form of 'family politics'. These features are clearly illustrated in the powerful Axelsson brothers of the Tott family; originally of Danish extraction, they had managed in the 1460's to amass estates and fiefs both in Sweden and Denmark. One of these 'Scandinavian' nobles, Ivar Axelsson, held Gotland, Western Blekinge, and two hundreds in Eastern Skåne, thus taking on the aspect of a semi-independent feudal prince. His brother Erik was mainly concerned in the affairs of Sweden and Finland, and had even at times acted as Swedish Regent. In 1466 Karl Knutsson married his daughter Magdalena to Ivar Axelsson, and the same year saw a break between Erik Axelsson and Jöns Bengtsson, the representatives of the two most powerful groups in the Swedish Council. A new political relationship began to emerge, and the position was clarified when the disharmony which had for some time existed between Ivar Axelsson and King Christian broke out into open conflict. Supported by the Axelssons and certain Swedish lords, chiefly Nils Bosson Sture, Karl Knutsson was acclaimed King of Sweden for the third time with the help of Ivar Axelsson. His power was, of course, completely illusory, and his third and last period of government from 1467–70 was thus a mere parody of the ideal for which he had fought during his first period as king.

Nevertheless, throughout all these years he had embodied and kept alive the conception, which he himself had created, of a strong national monarchy; and it was always possible that his ideas might be adopted by someone else. His clashes with the Danish King, in which his motives had not been altogether disinterested, had also given a nationalist and anti-Danish colour to fifteenth-century Swedish politics. The hostility towards Denmark, suspected but never actually demonstrated when the Union was first formed, was to some extent a creation of Karl Knutsson and those who drafted his propagandist literature. One of the first and most effective examples was the *Song of Gotland*, which describes how Christian seized Gotland from under the nose of his Swedish rival, and in which the Danish invaders are compared to scorpions, with smooth tongues but with stings in their tails.

Few could have prophesied what would happen after Karl Knutsson's death in 1470. The Oxenstiernas and their allies of the Vasa line held many of the most important castles and fiefs in the country, but the Axelssons and their kinsfolk still retained a powerful position; and the plan was that Ivar should govern the country until a king had been chosen – even that he might himself become King. This was not to be, however. Karl Knutsson had appointed as executor of his will Sten Sture, who, though he did not afterwards fulfil his commitments as executor, contracted to support the King's widow and his bastard but legitimized son. This meant that Sten entered into possession of various important castle-fiefs, and before long became the Regent. Ivar Axelsson accepted the situation; Sten Sture was, after all, married to his niece. But Christian of Denmark, who had once been elected King of Sweden, was prepared to uphold Sweden's 'laws and privileges' in return for the restitution of what he considered his God-given right. He mustered a considerable army to back up his offer to the Swedish Council: he would certainly need it, for Sten Sture's Regency was flourishing and neither he nor the Axelssons, who were not yet reconciled with the Danish King, wished for another Union. The Danish navy anchored outside Stockholm in the summer of 1471, and negotiations were set on foot. A truce was made, but Christian continued to press his claim. Meanwhile Sten Sture and Karl Knutsson's assistant Nils Bosson Sture (the two were in fact unrelated) proceeded to assemble troops in different parts of Sweden with a view to driving Christian out of the country. The chief member of the Council, Archbishop Jakob Ulfsson, did his utmost to bring about a peaceable solution on the lines of the Council's previous programme, and predicted a dire issue to any bloodshed.

But a bloodless settlement no longer seemed possible, for neither the Stures nor Christian would yield an inch. A powerful Danish army was stationed in strategic positions north of the present site of Stockholm, and particularly on the hill of Brunkeberg; it included, in addition to native and German soldiers, a large number of Swedish nobles who had supported the policy of Christian – as their own personal lord – during the feuds of the previous decade. Several of the leading Oxenstiernas and Vasas also fought on the Danish side, besides some of the bellicose peasants from Western Uppland, called in by the Swedish nobles. Behind the Stures stood those Swedish nobles who belonged to the Axelsson faction, soldiers from the towns and from Bergslagen, and Dalarna archers who had won a military reputation in the previous feuds. The citizens of Stockholm were also wholeheartedly on the side of the Stures. Thus, as the Archbishop said, there were 'good Swedish men' on both sides.

There have been various accounts of the Battle of Brunkeberg, and as they do not always tally it is difficult to describe its course in detail. Certain features are clear, however. According to the rhymed chronicle, the Sture army advanced bravely, singing an old Crusader song and the song of St George. But Christian's troops, who were divided into two sections, held a strong position, and a long and bitter struggle ensued. The Stures finally won the day as a result of their well co-ordinated attacks, and the Danish troops were forced to flee. The citizens of Stockholm had watched the fighting from the city walls and they were able to add to the confusion of their enemies by hewing down the bridge which they must cross to reach their boats; many of the routed troops fell into the water and were drowned, thereby increasing their already heavy losses. According to a subsequent legend St Eric's burning sword had that day appeared in the heavens above the Swedish army. At all events, King Christian returned home discomfited, and Sten Sture proceeded to win over the castles still held by his adversaries. The supporters of the Council's original programme, led by the Archbishop, were reduced to begging for mercy on behalf of the Uppland peasants who had fought for King Christian at Brunkeberg.

A clear picture of contemporary Swedish society is provided by the social content of the two armies. There had been various changes since the secular *frälse* or privileged nobility had first been formed, and its influence had greatly increased. The disturbances during the fourteenth and fifteenth centuries had enabled enterprising lords to add to their possessions and power. They had acquired a great deal of land, although it was often in different parts of the country, and their position was made even stronger by their possession of lucrative fiefs from the crown.

The revenues from the ecclesiastical estates had greatly increased since they were first established in the thirteenth century, and the Church had now become the largest land-owner in the country. The cathedrals had been embellished by outstanding contemporary artists, the country churches too had been enriched by coloured wall-paintings and imported altar-pieces, and the bishops had built castles. Cathedral chapters, churches, and monasteries owned home-steads throughout the country, and the Church property was often administered more meticulously and effectively than that of any other body.

The towns had continued to expand. Some of them, such as Stockholm, Söderköping, Kalmar, and Lödöse, had become important centres of foreign trade; most of them, however, were small, and the inhabitants lived by handicraft and trade on a small scale, strictly regulated by guilds and privileges, which forced the country-dwellers to deal solely in the town. Several of the towns were fortified by royal strongholds but their right to self-government was uncontested, and their various court rolls are among the most interesting of the contemporary records. The mining district of Bergslagen had attained a status which in some respects was similar to that of the towns.

At this time the population of Sweden consisted mainly of peasants who, unlike their counterparts in most other parts of Europe, did not lose their freedom during the Middle Ages. The village community, dating from about A.D. 500, remained basically unchanged. Its main surplus product was butter; fourteenth-century records of Sweden's trade with Lübeck show that the export of butter gradually came to comprise a quarter of the total exports, almost rivalling that of the metal trade. The founding of new villages and the colonization of uninhabited areas in Norrland and Finland continued apace. But the peasant of the fourteenth and fifteenth centuries also had his difficulties. Both the value of agrarian products and the value of the soil seem to have declined during the period of the Union; taxes were oppressive, and the wars left their mark on the countryside. There was sometimes a shortage of labour, and forced labour had to be introduced by law among the landless peasantry. The nobles and the Church appropriated more and more homesteads, and the holders of crown fiefs were not always easy masters. Still, the Swedish peasants kept their freedom and even had a voice, with the burgesses and miners, in the political struggles, particularly after Engelbrekt's time. Their home-made weapons and their familiarity with the country made them desirable allies for any party. Their main strength lay in the traditional organization of the village community, for it was this which, though it retarded the development of new techniques in agriculture, gave to the country-dwellers their solidarity and unity.

# XI

# The Regency of the Stures
## 1471-1515

The Battle of Brunkeberg, won as it was by a coalition of Swedish nobles, burgesses and peasants, was followed by a tremendous surge of national feeling. On October 14th, 1471, the Council revised certain of the municipal laws, declaring that henceforth the town councils should consist exclusively of 'native Swedish men' and not as hitherto 'half of Germans', and the triumph was also commemorated in concrete form by a monument erected in Stockholm's *Storkyrka* (the Great Church) to St George, whose song had been sung by the Sture army while they marched against Christian of Denmark. Six years later the Church Council and the Pope gave permission for a *studium generale* – a University similar to that of Bologna – to be founded in Uppsala. It was the first university in Scandinavia, and its establishment had an undoubted association with the victory at Brunkeberg. But it was a long time before this national feeling found full expression in Swedish culture. Swedish civilization in the late Middle Ages is paradoxical: while the Swedes were doing all they could to achieve national independence their literature, art, and indeed whole way of life revealed predominantly German and Danish influence. This is perhaps most noticeable in the language, which had changed considerably since the era of the early laws and the *Chronicle of Eric*. The Latin and Greek words which had been lent by the international culture of the early Middle Ages were now supplemented by words and phrases of Danish and Low German origin, introduced by foreign merchants, scribes and others; while the literary language took on a more complicated syntax based on that of mediaeval Latin. Yet these influences, though they expanded the range of the Swedish language, also distorted it – temporarily, at any rate.

Nevertheless, the Battle of Brunkeberg marked the beginning of a new period in Swedish history. King Christian and his supporters in Sweden had unquestionably been worsted. But it was more doubtful who had actually won the battle. Was it the inter-Scandinavian family alliance of the Axelssons, or the Swedish national movement that had rallied round the Stures? The answer was to depend on Sten Sture's ability to maintain his position and co-operate with his various supporters.

For the moment it seemed as if the Axelssons had come off best, for during the negotiations of the next few years they practically regained their former position in Denmark. Their 'realm' extended from the Scanian provinces through Gotland, held by Ivar, to the Finnish fiefs of Eric and his brother Laurens. The alliance between this powerful family and the national peasants and burgesses held together by the person of Sten Sture had obvious weaknesses, arising largely from the state of affairs after Karl Knutsson's death. But the Axelssons strengthened the Swedish government by their connections and possessions on both sides of the frontier, and Christian's plans to regain Sweden never came to fruition.

When Christian died, however, the question of the Union was again revived, and the Councils of the Scandinavian kingdoms began new negotiations for its restoration. A draft programme was drawn up which contained constitutional and administrative guarantees of a far-reaching nature. This was the Halmstad Recess of 1483, one of the most remarkable attempts ever made to provide a definite Union constitution; and it was accepted by the Swedes in Kalmar, with certain provisos, in the following year. For the moment, however, it remained a paper programme. Sten Sture followed the negotiations with the Danish King Hans very carefully, though he pleaded eye trouble when he did not consider it expedient to attend the Council's meetings on the question of Union, while he was working for the goal he had set himself: the consolidation of the central government. To this end he sought to gain direct control over more and more fiefs,[1] and to create a personal army, though a small one, of foreign mercenaries in his own pay. In 1481 Eric Axelsson died in Finland, and Sten considered the time had come for action. He confiscated Eric's Finnish fiefs and compensated his brother Ivar with Öland; thus the latter now ruled over a regular island kingdom in the Baltic Sea. But his rule was short-lived; by 1487 his position had proved to be so weak a link between the various territories that his Swedish fiefs were reclaimed. This was the last round in the contest which had started in 1470 between Ivar Axelsson and Sten Sture. Ivar, however, delivered Gotland into Denmark's hands, thereby thwarting the Regent's hopes of regaining the coveted island. The fall of the Axelssons, whose feudal 'buffer state' now no longer existed, had a tremendous effect on affairs in Scandinavia. Nevertheless, for the time being there was peace between the countries and both the members of the Swedish Council and Christian I's son and successor King Hans bided their time. The Regent appeared to be nearing his goal.

But the position in Sweden during the 1480's and 1490's was also complicated by external problems. Mention has already been made of the traditional policy of eastward expansion from the time of Sverker onwards. Sometimes it took the form of onslaughts on the south coast of the Gulf of Finland, with a special eye to the important trade route to the interior of Russia. Karl Knutsson's command in Viborg led to a revival of this interest, which was revealed during the 1440's in the feuds with Novgorod. While he was in Finland, the former Regent had had opportunities to study the position, and he had found a successor in Eric Axelsson Tott; it was this Danish-born Swedish-Finnish nobleman who built

---

[1] The Swedish term is *län*, i.e. a non-heritable fief granted to a noble for a specific period; it was thus different from the usual feudal fief.

the great fortress of Olofsborg – called after the canonised Norwegian king – on a rocky eyot in the Kyrönsalmisund Sound at the junction of several river systems near the Russian frontier. Early in Sten Sture's regency, there were clear indications of continued interest in affairs east of the Baltic. It was further evidenced in Sten's deliberate appropriations of the Axelsson Tott's Finnish fiefs and by a number of rather hazardous attempts to intervene in the internal affairs of the Baltic province of Livonia, which at that time belonged to the Teutonic Knights. However, at the end of the 1470's a decisive change took place in Russia's policy which from Sweden's point of view was disastrous, when the advancing Muscovite State annexed Novgorod, hitherto Sweden's main base in Russia. The Muscovite Empire was now beginning to take shape, and from the second half of the 1480's Sten Sture became increasingly preoccupied with the Russian question. He tried to extricate himself from his Livonian complications, and placed capable commanders in Viborg. Russian forays over the frontier had already taken place, and the Regent sought an alliance with the Teutonic Knights. There was strong reason for such measures, for at the beginning of the 1490's a new development of lasting significance occurred in the politics of northern Europe: an alliance between Denmark and Russia against Sweden. King Hans of Denmark, who now considered the time opportune for the conquest of Sweden, made common cause with Ivan III against Sten Sture.

Sten himself already had enough to do in maintaining his provisional regency. He was well qualified for this task; he had proved his military capacity in the 1460's, and as time went on his diplomatic gifts, his powers of popular appeal, and his utter tirelessness became increasingly apparent – one might even say that he and Karl Knutsson between them made this last quality part of the tradition of Swedish government. When necessary, he could be 'as bright and mild as an angel' in his public appearances. By his constant

9

journeys throughout Sweden he maintained contact with the countryfolk and ensured their support, most of all in Dalarna. There were a number of weapons he could use against the opposition in the Council led by Archbishop Jakob Ulfsson. If he threatened to resign – a device used later by Gustav Vasa – he was invariably entreated to remain in office. He might even threaten, either openly or with ironic intent, to resort to arms. The Archbishop himself gave an example of these tactics. The Regent, he declared, had boasted that 'in the twinkling of an eye we could raise up twenty or thirty thousand peasants to bring forth a new Engelbrekt to take the realm by the throat' (here the great popular leader becomes a new political symbol). To this charge Sten protested 'that he had not mentioned more than seven or eight thousand peasants'. The utterance illustrates one aspect of the Regent's nature; the other side is shown in his talents as a popular agitator. So far, his various tactics had answered well; and when Nils Sture died in 1494 Sten was strong enough to dispose of the dead man's fiefs as he liked, to the disappointment of Nils's son Svante Sture. He favoured the towns and kept strict control over economic policy. His followers, who included the Stockholm clergy and burgesses, supported him faithfully; his bailiffs were carefully supervised, and the accounts and tax rolls which have survived bear witness to his scrupulous administration.

The development on the Russian front, however, provoked a domestic crisis which struck at the roots of the power which Sten had consolidated with such perseverance. In 1495 the Russians invaded Sweden through Karelia and besieged Viborg. A bitter struggle ensued. In October Knut Posse, commander of Viborg, revealed in a letter to Sten Sture that he was being hard pressed by the Russians but promised that he and his men 'would stand out as long as we are able'.

It was not until nearly the end of the year that Sten himself went over to Finland, carrying to the 'crusade' the banner of St Eric. But by that time Knut Posse had beaten back the assailants, notwithstanding their arrogant boast that they 'would not return until they had sighted Stockholm'. The Regent was by this time on very bad terms with the Council, whom he suspected of welcoming his absence in Finland as an opportunity to pursue their own policy. The members of the Council accused him of being reluctant to employ his own troops in the Russian war, while the churchmen resented the taxes he imposed on them for the defence of the country and charged him with avarice. In the following year Svante Sture conquered and sacked the Russian fortress Ivangorod opposite Narva (both places were to play a prominent part in Swedish history more than two centuries later), and he was then involved in a serious rupture with the Regent. Peace with Russia was concluded at the beginning of 1497, but meanwhile the internal crisis was coming to a head. Sten's growing power and independent administration caused increasing dissatisfaction in the Council, and at the same time King Hans of Denmark was preparing to invade the country. By the time open hostility had broken out between the Archbishop – as leader of the Council – and the Regent, King Hans and his army had reached Stockholm. Sten Sture's auxiliary troops from Dalarna were defeated by King Hans's German mercenaries at Rotebro north of the capital, and his own attack from Stockholm was unsuccessful. He agreed to negotiate, and the result was that King Hans was acclaimed King of Sweden according to the decision of 1483. In return Sten Sture received Finland and certain fiefs in Sweden. The Council's constitutional principles had again triumphed, this time over the centralized government as conceived by Sten. In 1499 Hans's son Christian was appointed heir to the Swedish throne.

This apparent victory of the King and the Council in fact turned out to be ephemeral. This Danish King's policy towards Russia proved incompatible with the interests of his new kingdom, and in 1500 he suffered a heavy defeat during his campaign against Dithmarschen which gave his opponents fresh courage; his supporters in Sweden had already been alienated by his unsatisfactory methods of government. A revolt was planned by Sten Sture and his friends, and Sten himself went to Dalarna to prove that he was actuated not by personal ambition but by the desire for an independent Sweden. Supported by his former enemy Svante Nilsson Sture, he was again appointed Regent.

Sten retained his position until 1503, when his death occurred after he had escorted the captive consort of King Hans to the Halland frontier. There was some doubt as to who should succeed him, for neither his immediate supporters nor his widow Ingeborg, whom he used to call his 'dear stable-companion', could be expected to favour the chief candidate, Svante Nilsson. Nevertheless Svante won the day, his success being largely due to the cunning of the Bishop elect of Linköping, Hemming Gadh, who was travelling in Sten's train at the time of his death. To give Svante a longer breathing-space, Gadh arranged to have Sten's body conveyed in a merchant's load of skins, while one of the dead Regent's pages disguised himself in Sten's regalia and travelled in a covered sleigh, pretending to be the sick man. Svante was elected Regent by a group of Council members, and was soon following in Sten's footsteps.

He took over the office at a particularly difficult time, when Sweden was involved in almost continuous war with Denmark. It is true that Svante had amassed considerable power, but national solidarity was sometimes weak and the countryfolk were weary of war and of the heavy taxes with which they were burdened. Moreover, by confiscating the hereditary estates owned by the Swedish nobles in Denmark, King Hans effectively revealed to them the advantage of a Union. Despite the vacillations of the Council, however, Svante succeeded in preventing Hans from again being proclaimed King, and he also gained the support of Lübeck on account of its fear of Danish commercial policy. Many bitter struggles were fought during this period on the frontiers between Swedes and Danes. Yet it was in the middle of all this unrest that a new source of wealth – silver – was discovered in Sweden and began to be mined at Sala.

Svante's chief helper was undoubtedly the versatile Bishop Hemming Gadh. It was he who led the siege of Kalmar Castle which, like that of Borgholm, was in Danish hands. Here he shared the life and used the language of the ordinary soldier; he used Church phraseology only in his urgent prayers to the Regent for ships and armaments. For some time he acted as Sweden's envoy in Lübeck, where he gave the town council a vivid picture of the evil designs of the Danes. He had spent many years in Rome and employed his own lute player, whereas Sten and Svante were content with court minstrels. He could quote classical authors and mediaeval Roman lawyers, while at other times his speech was that of the coarsest soldier. He was perhaps most useful to the Regent in inciting the common people in their assemblies to support Svante's anti-Danish policy. This method of presenting official policy, which had been developed since Sten's time, is an important feature of the period and one of the main bases of the Regent's government. On one occasion Gadh quotes the peasants of Östergötland as having declared that they could neither judge of the Danish King's right to the kingdom nor say whether he had offended them in any way, since no one had either written or spoken about it. It was therefore up to Gadh to enlighten them, a task which, appreciating as he did the significance of public opinion, he accomplished most effectively. And though his interpretation of events was frequently biased, his speeches introduced a new element into Swedish politics: the common man was to be told the reason for his risking his life and his property. The meetings of Sten Sture and Hemming Gadh with the country-people prepared the ground for a remarkable tradition of rhetoric in Sweden which was to culminate in Gustav Vasa's letters to the commons and Gustavus Adolphus's speeches to the *Riksdag*.

The death of Svante Sture early in 1512 freed the hands
of the Swedish Council for a reconciliation with Denmark.
Though Svante had generally tried to co-operate with the
Council, the nobles had already been anxious to depose him
shortly before his death and replace him by a Småland nobleman, Erik Trolle, whose family owned large estates in the
Danish-controlled Scanian provinces and who was therefore
well disposed towards Denmark. By appointing him as Regent
the Council achieved a temporary truce with Denmark.

But they reckoned without the son of the dead Regent,
Sten Sture the Younger, who at this time was about twenty
years of age. He was already known in some parts of the
country; Svante's partisans in Dalarna had urged on the
Regent the importance of introducing his son to the country-
people in good time, and this advice had not gone unheeded.
Immediately after his father's death, the young Sten threw
himself into the struggle in a manner which suggested that
he was both courageous and talented. He seized the castles,
mines and fiefs held by his father's bailiffs and by his step-
mother – whom he always treated very ruthlessly – and
roused public opinion in his favour. His coup d'état was
resolutely opposed by the Council, whose members united
against those men who sought to remove its right 'since
heathen times' to rule the country according to 'the law of
Sweden and the good old customs'. They were forced to
comply with Sten's bold demands, however, and he was
appointed Regent. He continued to strengthen his position
by a number of skilful manœuvres, particularly with regard
to the distribution of fiefs in Finland.

Like his father, Sten Sture the Younger had powerful
assistants – a twenty-year-old youth could hardly have
achieved such a success without them. They included Hemming Gadh, who was still in Lübeck at the time of Svante's
death, but it has been suggested with some justification that
his chief supporter was the pastor in Stockholm, Peder
Jakobsson Sunnanväder. From the outset Sten seems to have

aimed at the ruthless destruction of the power of the mediaeval Council. Again like his father, he concentrated on bringing as much land as possible under his own administration, which was centred on Stockholm. At the same time, he devised a legal basis for his policy. His court was organized on typically mediaeval lines and consisted of confidential advisers – who were later to be called 'secretaries' – trusted supporters and mercenary captains; intellectual interests were represented mainly by the fashionable science of astrology, which was cultivated by the Regent's wife, Christina Gyllenstierna. A vigorous propaganda emanated from this court which was fostered by Sten himself, his secretaries, and his agents throughout the country. Young Sten's ultimate objective was the throne. It was to this end that he directed his unremitting efforts to strengthen his government, and meanwhile his envoys in Rome were working to obtain the sanction of the Pope.

There were many who advised him against so blatantly absolutist a policy. Nevertheless, Sten took advantage of the peace with Denmark, which lasted until 1517, to intensify his policy. In the Council, opposition again began to form around a young and capable leader, the new Archbishop Gustav Trolle, who succeeded Jakob Ulfsson. The stage was set for a prolonged and bitter clash between conflicting principles of council rule and popular dictatorship of Church and of State; and by no means the least striking feature lay in the vivid personalities of the main protagonists – the Regent and the Archbishop.

# XII

# Sten Sture and Gustav Trolle.
# The Rising in Dalarna
## 1515-1523

---

At the end of 1514 the old Archbishop Jakob Ulfsson resigned his office, and Gustav Trolle, who had studied at German universities and was then in Rome, was elected to succeed him. Although little is known of the intrigues surrounding his election and its confirmation, it was not long before he and the Regent crossed swords. When the new Archbishop returned to Sweden in 1515 he found that Sten's resumption of fiefs threatened him with the loss of the castle and fief of Stäket, one of the strategic demesnes by Lake Mälaren which had long been held by the archbishops. In the time of Karl Knutsson and the elder Stures, it had been common enough for the Regent to be opposed by the Archbishop as principal spokesman of the Council, and now that the Archbishop was attacked in his capacity as leader of the Church his opposition was intensified.

Sten leapt into the fray with an energy which shows that he intended to bring about a speedy decision. His propaganda, which took the form of letters, addresses to the Council, and popular harangues at fairs and meetings, exploited particularly the opposition's threats of conspiracy and rebellion. The Archbishop's father was taken prisoner; Gustav Trolle himself, who had occupied Stäket, was surrounded and besieged. Civil war broke out in full force, and the Regent sought to bolster up his cause by summoning a genuinely representative assembly which had the power to take binding decisions – a new departure in the development of Sture policy.

A representative body, which was later to be known as the

*Riksdag* (Parliament), was no innovation. Its beginnings can be traced from various sources. The old assembly which had elected the King had included deputies from each province. Magnus Eriksson, in this, as in other things, a man of enlightened ideas, had summoned a different kind of representative assembly in 1359. The more important business of the realm had usually been dealt with at afforced meetings of the Council, representing the specific groups – the later Estates – as set forth in the letters of the Council. There had been many such meetings during Engelbrekt's time, and the idea of the representation of the Estates had been further developed in the occasional presence of the armed peasants and the burgesses. But they were still in the nature of informal meetings summoned for specific purposes. During the last half of the fifteenth century, and particularly under the Stures, popular meetings of various kinds (the *Ting* and fairs) had played an increasing part in the politics of the country, and the next logical step was therefore the regular inclusion of peasants and burgesses, thus creating an assembly apart from – and sometimes in opposition to – the traditional Council. These tactics had even been used by Sten Sture the Elder, but it was under the younger Sten that they were brought to fruition, in accordance with his slogan that 'what concerns all should have the approval of all' – an expression taken from canon law. It was during the struggle against Gustav Trolle that the *Riksdag* made its great advance, in large measure owing to the tireless and well-organized propaganda of the Regent and his local agents.

An assembly representing the whole kingdom was held in Arboga early in 1517, and Sten presented his view of the present conflict to the Council, the nobles, and to 'the merchants, mine-owners, men of Dalarna and other commoners'. Having won their support, and backed now by the authority of the *Riksdag*, he continued the siege of Stäket. Both he and his allies were excommunicated, and the Danish King Christian II thereupon attacked Sweden. Gustav Trolle, by this time hard-pressed, hoped for relief from this action, but the Danes were defeated by Sten Sture outside Stockholm. In November of the same year the *Riksdag* met in the capital, the Archbishop attending under a safe-conduct. The proceedings almost resolved themselves into his trial, and a verdict was passed by all those present, led by the Council (which included the bishops) 'representing themselves and those at home'. The verdict, which was solemnly confirmed on pain of heavy penalties, was that Stäket, which had caused so much trouble ever since the days of Jöns Bengtsson Oxenstierna, should be razed to the ground, so that it should never again afford sanctuary to traitors. In addition, all swore solemnly 'with "Aye" and upraised hands' never again to acknowledge Gustav Trolle as Sweden's Archbishop. State and Church were now in violent conflict. The siege was completed, and Stäket with all its sacred relics was captured and demolished. The Archbishop himself was maltreated and imprisoned, and many of his supporters were beheaded or broken on the wheel. Church property was confiscated – this, incidentally, coincided with the beginning of an attack on the Catholic Church by a young and hitherto unknown German theologian, Martin Luther. Public feeling ran high. The Regent proclaimed in rousing terms that he would always further the interests of the Church to the best of his ability, but would not succour those of her members who allied themselves to traitors of the realm.

Meanwhile, in 1518, King Christian of Denmark had made another attack on Stockholm, but had been thrown back at Brännkyrka. As a result of the ensuing armistice negotiations he acquired as hostages six Swedish nobles. These he took to Denmark as prisoners, and once there disclaimed the armistice. Sten retaliated against both Denmark and Gustav Trolle by obtaining the support of a Papal Legate, Gian Angelo Arcimboldi, who was organizing the sale of indulgences in Sweden. The two countries were bitterly hostile to each other, and the war was fought in a violent and ruthless manner. Christian's perfidy afforded excellent matter for Sten's propaganda, for the abducted hostages included Hemming Gadh himself, and of the other five young noblemen, one, Gustav Eriksson, was a member of the renowned Vasa family.

King Christian now made extensive preparations for the conquest of Sweden. This country admittedly possessed numerous attractions, of which the most significant were the mines of Bergslagen, while there are indications that the Fuggers of Augsburg, who controlled most of Europe's copper trade, were interested in the Swedish copper mines. Some of the funds for the enterprise came from the proceeds of the sale of indulgences in Sweden which the King had seized from Arcimboldi on his way to Rome. Moreover, the Pope had put Sweden under an interdict for the treatment meted out to Gustav Trolle, and King Christian could now act as its executor. At the beginning of 1520 a huge army of mercenaries from Germany, France, and Scotland broke over the Halland frontier into Västergötland, where, on the frozen surface of Lake Åsunden, it joined issue with Sten's army of knights and peasant levies. At the outset of the battle the Regent was severely wounded in the leg by a cannon ball. The Swedish army was defeated and retreated towards the north, while the inhabitants of Västergötland surrendered to Christian and paid him a ransom. The Swedish army suffered another defeat in the forests of Tiveden, and thereafter the Danes had a free passage to the main provinces of central Sweden. Two days later Sten died on his journey by sledge to Stockholm across the Mälaren.

The peasants and miners were now without a leader, since there was no one to replace the dead Regent, and the leading nobles and commanders of the Danish army made contact with Gustav Trolle, who had by this time regained his freedom, and a truce was made. The Council acknowledged Christian as King of Sweden, and in return they were promised pardon and, equally important, a constitutional government, conditions which seemed reasonable enough. But the position of Gustav Trolle and Christian was not yet absolutely secure. Sten's widow, Christina Gyllenstierna, was still in Stockholm Castle with a few faithful followers and, calling upon the aid of Poland and Danzig, they refused to give in. The issue was for long undecided; however, on Good Friday the burgesses of Stockholm, the miners, and the peasants were at last defeated by the Danes after a hard-fought battle at Uppsala. Nevertheless, resistance among the peasants continued throughout the summer. In May the King's fleet surrounded Stockholm on all sides; but it was not until the beginning of September that Christina Gyllenstierna, lacking a leader to organize her cause in country districts, was forced to capitulate.

It was as a hereditary, not an elected, King that Christian received homage, thus completely ignoring the Council's former design; and the ceremony took place, in the presence of his army, on the heights of Brunkeberg, where his grandfather had been defeated half a century earlier. On 4th November he was crowned by Gustav Trolle in Stockholm, where he ratified the promises of a general amnesty. The coronation was observed with banquets and solemnities, and many nobles (including the Swedish lords) were dubbed knights. But Gustav Trolle and his adherents still demanded a settlement with their enemies, the Sture party. With the support of the King they could legally circumvent the amnesty by a charge of heresy, which the Stures had incurred by their treatment of the Archbishop and the Church; it was not necessary, they declared, to keep faith with heretics.

On 7th November the King and his counsellors in Stockholm Castle were presented with an appeal drawn up in the name of Gustav Trolle, which craved the sovereign's help in obtaining redress from the dead heretic Sten Sture and his supporters for the sins they had committed against the Church. In their defence the accused pleaded the agreements which had been made at the Stockholm *Riksdag* in 1517; but this, on the contrary, was found to be a proof of their guilt. On the next day they were tried before an ecclesiastical court presided over by the Archbishop, in the presence of the King. The accused were pronounced guilty of heresy on the ground that they had defied the Papal interdict and sworn that the Archbishop should never regain his freedom and his cathedral – a clear case of disobedience towards the Church. Under canon law this verdict was applicable also to those who had aided and abetted the accused.

But it was the function of the secular power, King Christian, not the Church, to determine the punishment; and it was ruthless in the extreme. According to the executioner eighty-two persons were put to death; even the churchmen were not spared for, contrary to the legal forms which had so far been strictly observed, two bishops were among the victims. These included also several noble members of the Council and a large number of the Stures' supporters among the lower nobility and the Stockholm merchants, all of whose property was confiscated. Christina Gyllenstierna was thrown into prison and declared by Christian to be 'dead to the world'. On the following Saturday the King ordered a fire to be built in the open space in the southern part of the town, whither the dead bodies were dragged and burnt. And, not content with this, he caused the body of Sten the Younger to be dug up and burnt with the rest. The punishment of a heretic was burning at the stake; and even a man long dead was still liable to such retribution. The Sture party seemed to have been completely wiped out.

It is difficult to assess the exact responsibility for these events of the various groups concerned. Historians are divided as to whether it was King Christian himself, the King's counsellors, or Gustav Trolle and his Swedish party who were the prime movers. One feature which emerges quite clearly, however, is the steady intensification of the desire for revenge between the time of Sten's clash with

Gustav Trolle in 1517 and the Stockholm massacre three years later. A great Scandinavian empire now seemed possible. King Christian had already established absolute monarchy in Sweden, where he took strong legal measures to suppress the belligerent peasantry. Moreover, his plans included the formation of a Scandinavian commercial league which, with the help of the Dutch, would drive out the Hansa. Believing that all real resistance had been crushed, the King now crossed over to Denmark through Östergötland and Småland, where more trials and executions took place at Christmas and the New Year.

Nevertheless, despite his efforts, the Sture party had been by no means eliminated. Local risings continued to break out in Småland and Dalarna, and the Stockholm blood-bath had added fresh fuel to the agitation. The legal contraventions which marked the trials and sentences meant nothing to the commons, whereas the subsequent behaviour of the victors roused general apprehension and panic. The difficulty was to find a leader. Earlier in the year Christina Gyllenstierna had received a letter from the people of Dalarna in which they complained that 'no one of noble blood would take upon himself to help the commons of Sweden' against their enemies, the King's troops who 'burn, murder, and pillage'. But Christina and her sons were now prisoners; her chief supporters among the lower nobility and burgesses had been killed or had fled, and the aristocracy had given its homage to Christian. Was there anyone left?

Christina Gyllenstierna's nearest adult relative was Gustav Eriksson Vasa, her sister's son, who had been among the hostages whom Christian had taken to Denmark in 1518 and who was also related to the older Stures. Disguised as a cowherd he had escaped in 1519 to Lübeck, where he found protection from the Danish demands for his extradition. In 1520 he managed to make his way to Sweden, where he witnessed the defeat and massacre of the Sture party. His father and brother-in-law were among the victims; his mother and sister were in Danish captivity; and he himself was too young to have made any mark in Swedish politics. Stealthily he made his way to the province of Dalarna, where the Stures had always found their staunchest supporters. His only assets were a burning thirst for revenge, a gift for oratory, an attractive appearance, and his connection with the Stures; perhaps, too, his sojourn in Lübeck had given him a hint that King Christian was beginning to overreach himself. No one could have foreseen that this young man was to become one of the most brilliant politicians in Swedish history.

Little is known of his first visit to Dalarna, though his adventures there were later embodied in a heroic saga similar to those which were woven round so many national heroes. The young fugitive, disguised in his round hat and his peasant clothes, has become one of the most popular figures in Swedish history, but reality and legend have become almost indistinguishable. At a later date he himself instructed his chroniclers to relate how he first stayed with an old friend from his student days, but was discovered and advised to flee farther afield; how he later reached the regions round Lake Siljan and negotiated with the peasants in Rättvik and Mora; and how he was here pursued by the agents of the government and forced to proceed towards the Norwegian frontier. But when the men of Dalarna heard of King Christian's actions they changed their minds and sent messages after the young fugitive, whom they found at Lima in the western part of the province. They appointed him as their commander, and by January 1521 his name had reached the ears of King Christian, who was then in Småland on his return journey to Denmark.

The rising in Dalarna was soon in full swing. It was joined by the men from the Kopparberg mining district, and those in other areas were called upon to unite in the attempt to liberate Sweden, to 'free yourselves and your children, as faithful Swedish men have done before'. The successes of the young rebel aroused concern in the Stockholm government. He soon had the support of a large northern part of central Sweden, and he had also made contact with the Sture privateers who were plundering the Danes in the Baltic Sea. Fighting took place around Västerås and Uppsala, and by the spring of 1521 the liberating army had reached Stockholm. Meanwhile a rising had broken out in Värmland under the leadership of the lawman Nils Olofsson, and the Smålanders too were playing their part. Ture Jönsson Tre Rosor of Västergötland, one of the leading men in the kingdom and a relation of Gustav Eriksson, joined his kinsman in the early summer, with the significant words: 'A man does better to follow with the best in his fatherland than to beg his bread on foreign soil.' He was followed within a few months by Bishop Hans Brask of Linköping, and shortly afterwards Gustav was elected Regent of Sweden at Vadstena. King Christian's Stockholm government was transferred to Denmark, and soon only the capital and the important stronghold of Kalmar remained in the hands of the Danish commander. The young leader seemed favoured by fortune, and his position grew stronger every day. In 1522 he persuaded Lübeck to come to Sweden's assistance with ships, troops, and money; the town had long been hostile to King Christian, and Gustav had retained its goodwill since his sojourn there in 1519–20. Developments in Denmark also played into the hands of the Swedish rebels, and in the spring of 1523 Christian was forced to leave the country. Before he did so the Swedish Regent had issued a manifesto printed in German denouncing the Danish King – the first time that the Swedish State had used the power of the printing-press for political ends.

The emergence of Gustav Eriksson of Rydboholm (as he called himself) into power in Sweden coincided with equally remarkable developments elsewhere. America had recently been discovered, Magellan was making the first circumnavigation of the world, and in Germany controversy was raging round the new doctrines of Martin Luther. The ideas of the mediaeval world were in the melting-pot. In Scandinavia the dream of a great Nordic kingdom had been shattered; on the other hand the visions that Karl Knutsson and the Stures had cherished of a unified national State under a strong ruler had been fulfilled.

# XIII

# Gustav Vasa: The Triumph of the Kingdom
## 1523-1538

The Regent, Gustav Eriksson Vasa, was now in a fair way to accomplishing what the Stures had so often attempted but only partially achieved. Taking advantage of the circumstances, notably Denmark's internal crisis and Lübeck's firm support, he had succeeded in detaching Sweden from the Union. Moreover, like Engelbrekt before him, Gustav looked beyond the old frontiers and undertook the conquest of Bohuslän, Blekinge, and Skåne, ruling for a period over the first two. So far, however, three of the most important Swedish strongholds, Stockholm, Kalmar, and Älvsborg, were still in the hands of the Danes, and Finland too was largely controlled by Christian's supporters. Nevertheless it was anticipated that the ships and money from Lübeck would soon enable the Regent to win the rest of the kingdom.

The help given by Lübeck had certain important consequences. The 'honourable council' which governed the town was naturally anxious that the capital it had invested in Scandinavian politics should be firmly guaranteed. This was impossible, however, until Sweden possessed a settled and recognized government, and that meant, in effect, a king. A *Riksdag*, attended by delegates from Lübeck, met in Strängnäs at Whitsuntide 1523, and Gustav Eriksson Vasa was elected King of Sweden. The Lübeck counsellors were placed at the right hand of the new King during the ceremony in the Cathedral and shortly afterwards Gustav Vasa and his Council (which had now been reconstructed) granted certain very favourable trading rights to Lübeck and its allies. The Hansa merchants had thus proved successful in their speculation, and they no doubt hoped that they would find in the young King a willing tool.

The Danes had already evacuated Älvsborg before the election of Gustav Vasa, and within a few weeks he controlled the capital. On Midsummer Day he rode through the south gate into the sorely ravaged Stockholm, where 'he was received and admitted with great ceremony, with pomp and circumstance, as was meet'. At the beginning of July Kalmar Castle surrendered to one of Gustav Vasa's principal commanders, the German nobleman Berend von Melen, and in due course Finland, too, was conquered. Relations of a kind were established with Denmark and her new ruler, Frederick I; Sweden was repulsed in her attempt to conquer Gotland, and by degrees Denmark recovered the frontier provinces that Sweden had annexed; the last to go was Bohuslän, which Gustav Vasa retained until the beginning of the 1530's.

Notwithstanding all that had been achieved, however, the security of the throne was more apparent than real. The strength of Gustav Vasa's position in Sweden depended primarily on the willing support of the various localities, and this could not always be relied upon. The policy of the Stures had favoured licence and brutality in the countryside, and the forces which had supported Gustav Vasa might easily be deflected by a change of circumstances or mood. Again, the King had achieved his position with the support of the Sture party, and that party might well hold the view that, in ascending the throne and accepting the help of Lübeck, he had usurped the place which belonged by right to one of Sten Sture's young sons. Equally unpredictable was the attitude of the nobles and the Church, both of them forces over and above the provincial authorities. Nor was the King's task made any easier by the fact that both he and the kingdom were indebted to Lübeck, especially as he had inherited from his predecessors in the late Middle Ages the problem of making both ends meet in his treasury. Consequently the first few decades of Gustav Vasa's rule were a period of recurring crises which, with their intrigues, their violence, and their trickery vividly illustrated the methods of the Renaissance era.

The first crisis was precipitated by discontent among the old adherents of the Sture party. Peder Jakobsson Sunnanväder, possibly Sten Sture's chief adviser, was again in Sweden, and it was not long before he had fallen foul of the King. Early in 1524 Sten's widow, Christina Gyllenstierna, returned from captivity in Denmark, eager to re-enter the political arena. Supported by the Admiral Sören Norby, Christian II's last faithful follower in Scandinavia, she intrigued against the man who had ousted her sons from the position she had hoped would be theirs. The fractious population of Dalarna were complaining of the high cost of living and the shortage of salt, and these grievances were fully exploited by Peder Sunnanväder, Christina Gyllenstierna, and several of Sten's former retainers. The King was also causing dissatisfaction by his apparent interest, exaggerated by rumour, in the new and disturbing doctrines preached by the Lutheran reformers, principally the Swede Olaus Petri. Norby was campaigning in the south to reinstate Christian II, while the King chose just this moment to quarrel with his commander Berend von Melen. Nevertheless he weathered the storm. Sören Norby was defeated in Skåne, Christina Gyllenstierna was forced to surrender, and Peder Sunnanväder fled to Norway; Berend von Melen retired to Germany, and many of the soldiers he left behind were executed. A skilful blend of threats and cajolery temporarily restored order in Dalarna, and the King later won a symbolic victory over the Sture party by capturing Peder Sunnanväder and his ally Master Knut. His chronicler, Peder Svart, relates how they were led into Stockholm, 'clad in old, threadbare tattered cloaks, riding backwards on famished horses, Peder Sunnanväder with a coronet of straw on his head and a broken wooden sword by his side, Master Knut with a crosier of birch-bark'. Both men were sentenced to death and executed.

Meanwhile, a fresh rising was threatening in Dalarna and Värmland, led by an enigmatic figure who is known in Swedish history as the *Daljunkare*. He claimed that he was Sten Sture's son Nils, who died about this time, but Gustav Vasa declared that he was a farmhand and an impostor.[1] Whatever his real identity, he was supported by the Norwegian aristocracy, with whom he was on intimate terms, and by members of the old Sture party. The grievances of his adherents in Dalarna centred on the taxes imposed by the King, the new 'Lutheranism', and the recent fashion for 'slashed and scalloped garments'; and although Gustav Vasa replied in his plausible way that the taxation was to defray the debts of the country, that he had ordained nothing but the preaching of God's word and the Gospel, and that the new fashions harmed none but those who adopted them, the disturbances continued, and the time-honoured name of Sture proved well able to hold its own against the new name of Vasa. The King had simultaneously to cope with the uncurbed defiance of the peasants, the demands of Lübeck for a speedy repayment, and an unstable situation in the field of foreign affairs. Yet he did not lose heart. During these critical years he and his followers undertook an extensive reorganization of administration and finances, revealing in the process both his undaunted optimism and his remarkable foresight. Harassed though he was by risings and conspiracies, Gustav Vasa strove to put into practice the system of centralization which had been conceived by the Stures, aiming first and foremost at freeing himself from his dependence on Lübeck and secondly at the provision of loyal troops. He found support among the burgesses of the towns, whom he in his turn treated favourably, and also among the reforming clergy and certain groups of the nobility. Moreover, not all

---

[1] A recent suggestion is that he was an illegitimate son of Sten Sture the Younger. In *Lady Inger of Östråt* Henrik Ibsen depicts him as such.

the provinces were as fractious as Dalarna – provided, at least, that the King would grant some of their economic demands and ensure supplies of salt.

Sten Sture the Younger, who had been in a similar position, had already fallen foul of the leaders of the Church ten years earlier. If clashes were easy enough then, they were still more so now, when Lutheranism was being preached by Olaus Petri and other Swedish theologians who had been trained at Wittenberg. Gustav Vasa, as a practical man, soon saw the possible connection between the new teaching and the political concepts he had inherited from the Stures. The Catholic Church was the only rich corporate body in the country, and if the King was to subdue the *Daljunkare* and stabilize the finances, he must have its property at his disposal. It was calculated that by the end of the Middle Ages the Church owned 21·3 per cent. of the Swedish homesteads (as against 20·7 per cent. held by the nobles, 5·6 per cent. by the crown, and 52·4 per cent. by the tax peasants[1]; it should, however, be noted that in Finland, where nobility and Church had not achieved so strong a position, tax peasants' land amounted to over 96 per cent. of the whole). Although the leading churchman, Bishop Hans Brask of Linköping, had been a supporter of Gustav Vasa, it was not long before the two were on bad terms. The King irritated the bishops and the monasteries by his demands for loans and the maintenance of soldiers; and his Chancellor, Laurentius Andreae, who held Lutheran views, prophesied the speedy downfall of those who had previously held great power. It was evident that a crisis was at hand; and in 1527, while the rising of the *Daljunkare* was going on, the representatives of the four Estates were summoned to a *Riksdag* in Västerås.

The meeting was attended by delegates from Lübeck, who

---

[1] Tax peasants (*skattebönder*) *owned* the land they farmed and paid a *public* tax, not a private rent, to the crown. Crown peasants (*kronobönder*) who *rented* their land from the crown were similar in status and rights to those who rented their lands from lords (*frälsebönder*) or from the Church; they could not be said to own the homesteads they cultivated.

endorsed the King's pronouncement that discontented members could themselves negotiate with the Lübeck creditors and see 'whether they wished to be paid with rebellion'. In the royal proclamations which were read before the Estates, Gustav Vasa affirmed that *he* had fulfilled all his obligations to the people, but that the *people* had not responded in kind. The revenues, he declared, were insufficient for the country's needs. The nobles had been weakened as a result of the loss of most of their estates, either by will or donation, to the Church and the monasteries, and they were demanding compensation in the form of crown fiefs. The King in turn pointed out that since the revenue was already inadequate, he was unable to meet their demands. His statement culminated in a request that he should be allowed to abdicate, leaving the Estates to overcome the difficulties as best they could.

The King argued his case with a skill which was well calculated to sway the opinions of the nobles. The fault was (though he did not reveal it at the time) that his project for a centralized administration under his direct control was incompatible with the mediaeval system under which large fiefs were bestowed on the nobles, though he admitted that they were justified in asking aid or fiefs of the crown. He concluded his statement with a clear hint as to where the solution was to be found – namely in the Church – thereby putting into the nobles' mouths the answer he desired. With irrefutable logic he had linked together the new administrative system, the crown's need for increased income, and the demands of the nobles. Let the Church meet the crown's demands for money and the nobles' demands for fiefs and estates.

The nobles responded precisely in the manner he had intended. They made detailed proposals as to how the property and income of the Church should best be used for the benefit of the crown and the nobility, and they promised to support the King against all rebels. The other Estates – apart from the clergy, who had no voice in the matter – agreed with the nobles in all essentials, and the decisions were enacted in the famous *Riksdag* decree known as the Västerås *Recess*. The castles owned by the bishops were to be handed over to the King, who was also to determine the number of soldiers they should maintain. The surplus revenues of the bishops, the cathedrals, and the canons were to be regularly paid to the King in cash. The monasteries were to be handed over intact as fiefs to the nobles. Moreover the nobles were to be permitted on certain conditions to reclaim the estates which they had given to the Church since the middle of the fifteenth century. In a later statute, the Västerås *Ordinantia*, the power of the State over the Church was established in a manner which paved the way for further progress along the lines laid down in the Västerås *Recess*.

Gustav Vasa had thus shrewdly got the Estates exactly where he wanted them. The representatives of the Church were powerless against the unanimity of the nobles, burgesses, and peasants; and in the following years the acquisition by the State of Church revenues brought about a reduction in ecclesiastical property which affected even the parishes. Having achieved this great victory over the Church's powerful 'State within a State' – a victory which he did not fail ruthlessly to exploit – Gustav Vasa was able to press on towards his great goal: the replacement of the existing loose federation of families, parishes, and provinces by a centralized administration. The nobility's demand for fiefs had been satisfied for the moment at the expense of the Church, and the administrative reforms could be undertaken with little fear of opposition from the aristocracy.

Moreover the King was now certain of the unconditional support of the Estates for any step he might take against the *Daljunkare*. Having summoned the rebels to him at Tuna, he treated them without mercy. The *Daljunkare's* chief agents were executed, and 'when the others saw the blood begin to flow, then they changed their tune; they were sorely afraid,

lifted up their voices and wept, fell on their knees, praying
and beseeching mercy of the King, in God's name'. Thus did
Gustav Vasa himself persuade his chronicler Peder Svart to
describe the great reckoning which followed the Västerås
decisions. Finally the *Daljunkare* himself, who had fled to
Germany, was captured and executed.

It had also been decreed at the Västerås *Riksdag* that God's
word should purely and plainly be proclaimed in the kingdom – a somewhat vague formulation, which left open for the
present the spiritual aspect of the Church question but
which allowed full scope for the propagation of Lutheran
doctrine. There was as yet no question of a final break with
the Pope. But even before the Västerås meeting Olaus Petri
had published in Swedish a book of sacred songs which were
strongly Lutheran in tone (several of them, incidentally, sung
to-day in J. O. Wallin's revised versions); and five years
later, in 1531, he drew up some of the fundamental doctrines
of Lutheranism which summarize the finest features of the
early Swedish Reformation: 'We in Sweden also belong to
God, as do other nations, and the tongue we have has been
given to us by God. . . .' Mass should therefore be celebrated
in Swedish. But he also urged another fundamental principle,
that of toleration: 'Let none be constrained or forced to
attend the Swedish service . . . in the same way as none can
be forced to God's word; freely and unconstrainedly must it
be accepted, if it is to bear fruit.' After the Västerås *Riksdag* it
became clear that there was an impassable gulf between the
members of the old Church and the young and ruthless
State-builder, and Gustav Vasa's erstwhile faithful counsellor, Bishop Hans Brask, soon left the country, never to
return.

But all was not yet plain sailing for the King and the new
monarchy. The peasants, conservative by nature, were
suspicious of the innovations in the Church and, if they found
the right leaders, were still capable of breaking out. And
although the Sture party was defeated, leaders might still be

found. Some bold churchman might try and retrieve the losses of Västerås; and although a large number of the nobility had supported the King's policy on account of the advantages they were offered, there were still representatives of the old aristocracy who, realizing what the outcome must be, preferred to join forces with the Church. After all, the demagogic methods which Gustav Vasa had inherited from the Stures could equally well be used against him. The most prominent of these lords was Ture Jönsson Tre Rosor, who had had many years of political experience. In 1529, with the assistance of Bishop Magnus of Skara, he incited the peasantry of Småland and, more particularly, Västergötland to rise against the King; and the rebellion threatened to spread to Östergötland and Hälsingland. The state of affairs in the Church offered suitable material for propaganda, and for a time Gustav Vasa was really anxious. Once again fortune smiled on him, however, and the rising was put down by a combination of violence, subterfuge, and persuasion. Some of the leaders were executed, others fled the country. The victory of Västerås was now complete.

Shortly after this, in 1530, the King decreed that one bell in every church should be sacrificed to the exchequer. At first the decree applied only to the towns and monasteries, but the following year it was extended to include the country churches. This constituted a heartless attack on ancient beliefs; the bells, which called the congregation to worship and purified the air of evil spirits, had played a significant part in the religious life of the people ever since the time when they had first pealed forth from steeple and belfry during the great period of church-building in the early Middle Ages. In Bergslagen and Dalarna the King's agents were received with sledge-hammers, and driven away. To add to his difficulties, in 1531–2 Christian II launched an expedition to Norway in an attempt to recover his kingdoms; his retinue included both Gustav Trolle, an exile for the past ten years, and the leaders who had escaped from the Västergötland rising. The fourth crisis, 'the Bell Rebellion', was under way – Gustav Vasa had to face such situations with curious regularity during this first period of his reign. However, King Christian was taken prisoner; and at Kopparberget, in February 1533, Gustav Vasa settled his accounts with the unruly men of Dalarna for the third and last time. His reprisals were more ruthless than ever before. Among the spokesmen of the malcontents were men who had supported him at the beginning of his career. They, like the other leaders, were condemned to death. Gustav Vasa's feelings at being forced to demand the blood of his old friends were never revealed. At all events, the sentences were duly carried out, and thus the most recalcitrant province in the country was completely subdued. The King's path was certainly bloody; but it led him to his goal.

By this time Gustav Vasa had completed in all essentials the reorganization of the administration. Many of the mediaeval fiefs, which had been used by the aristocracy to further their individual interests, had already been largely incorporated into the new system, which was closely supervised by the King, his Chancery and Treasury. The nobles who had controlled those fiefs which contained royal castles were replaced by bailiffs, dependent on the central government. Gustav Vasa had throughout been favoured by circumstances, and many of the chief nobles had died during the early years of his reign; this social class had been further undermined by the failure of the Västergötland rising. There was no younger generation equipped to safeguard the interests of the higher aristocracy, and the remaining members had been placated by the decline in the power of the Church. The reform of the administration could thus proceed without any very serious opposition. Gustav Vasa was certainly the right man for the task. His own upbringing as a landowner stood him in good stead, and he had also learnt much from the Stures, from the excellent estate management of the Church and from Lübeck. He reformed the assessment and collection of the land taxes, and reorganized the various uses to which the natural products they yielded could be put. Further, a comprehensive survey was made of the entire revenues of the crown in ready money and in kind for the years 1530 and 1533 – an unprecedented achievement. The King personally supervised all the work of the government, carrying on a profitable trade with the crown's levies of oxen, butter, and grain, and using them to ensure supplies to different parts of the country. In this he was able to anticipate local shortage and famine, thereby removing one of the standard grievances. The increasing appropriation of the Church's property and revenue lightened the burden of taxation and helped to improve the crown's financial position; and the King was now able to attract capable men into his service by the offer of good rewards. By these means a centralized state was being established on modern lines; and the increased power of the King was further manifested in the success of his policy of emancipating the Swedish Church from Rome, a process which was completed during the 1530's.

On many occasions during the first fifteen years of his reign it had seemed as though the King must give up. He had constantly been forced to use the threat of abdication as a weapon against the intractable peasantry with whom he treated in market place and assembly – above all at the Västerås *Riksdag*, where the prospect hung over the proceedings like a sword of Damocles. But in fact he had no intention of surrendering. He had already identified himself with his kingdom, which he ruled as to the manner born. The weakening of Lübeck's hold on him, however, he owed partly to external circumstances. The end of the first phase of his reign had seen the origin in Denmark of a domestic crisis known as the *Greve* (Count's )Feud – so called after the Count of Oldenburg, who had commanded a strong army of mercenaries from Lübeck and elsewhere against Duke Christian, subsequently Christian III of Denmark. The Swedish King saw in this feud his chance of settling with Lübeck, and he intervened on Christian's side (they were brothers-in-law married to two sisters). He did not win all he had hoped for, but the reverses suffered by Lübeck considerably strengthened Sweden's position against the town which, by virtue of the 1523 privileges, dominated her foreign trade. Lübeck still retained a powerful control over Swedish trade, but her political decline was in Sweden's favour.

Thus Gustav Vasa had swept aside the three main obstacles to his goal – the Church, provincial self-government, and Lübeck. Unrest in the country had been stamped out and the administration was being given its last touches. The King was putting into practice the system which the Stures had envisaged for Sweden. The question now was : should he stop at this point, or could he – dare he, indeed – go further?

# XIV

# Gustav Vasa: The Final Crisis
## 1539-1560

The years 1539–42 were a period of experiment by the government. A Treasury was formed for the first time, new legal ideas, derived from Roman Law, were introduced, and at the same time the King's power was extended to embrace all spheres of life.

These developments were only to be expected. Gustav Vasa, after all, had devoted the first fifteen years of his reign to building up his position. Moreover, a similar process was going on elsewhere in Europe. Some years after the Count's Feud had ended the King had procured counsellors from Germany who were well versed in contemporary ideas of the all-powerful centralized State, as exemplified particularly in the form of the Lutheran State Church which had been set up in the small German territories. Chief among these advisers were Konrad von Pyhy, a learned jurist who had once been in the service of the Hapsburgs, and the theologian Georg Norman, who had been recommended by Luther and Melanchton as a tutor for the King's children but who soon became absorbed in church politics. The careers of the two men may possibly have been advanced at this time as a result of the King's severe illness. Nevertheless, a man of Gustav Vasa's temperament could not fail to welcome their assistance in realizing his desire for absolute power, a desire which von Pyhy merely defined for him.

In a manifesto to the inhabitants of Uppland in December 1539 the King compared himself to Moses, and his people to the Children of Israel. His subjects were no longer oppressed, they no longer suffered from enforced idleness, as they had done under King Christian; yet still they are discontented, shutting their eyes to the fact that the country's progress is due solely to the King. It has since been suggested that this letter was a typical example of the King's style, though the original draft, which is still in existence, was actually made in German by Konrad von Pyhy. Henceforward many edicts, couched in similar terms, were issued from the Chancery. The peasants of Öland were instructed, under threat of a fine, that their hay must be in by St Olaf's day and their corn by St Bartholomew's; the hiring of labour was regulated with a view to preventing vagrancy; the crown established its rights over the tax peasants and controlled both internal and foreign trade; and the long-standing export of cattle and other commodities from the southern Swedish provinces through the Danish ports in Skåne was prohibited. The kingdom was to be regarded as the property of the crown – or, in personal terms, of the King himself.

Similar tendencies were at work in ecclesiastical policy. In the 1530's Sweden finally severed herself from Rome, and her last Catholic Archbishop, Johannes Magnus, retired to Italy, where he composed his famous history of the Kings of the Goths and the Svear: *Historia de omnibus Gothorum Sveonumque regibus*. Laurentius Petri, brother of Olaus, was enthroned as Sweden's first Protestant Archbishop, and the Reformers won a great victory for their programme at the Church assembly at Uppsala in 1536. The King, however, considered that this weakened his own control of the Church, and he therefore requested his German advisers to draw up a different form of organization. Early in 1540 Olaus Petri and Laurentius Andreae were tried for treason, but, though sentenced to death, they were subsequently reprieved. Nevertheless the principles which they represented had been defeated, and the Church was reorganized in such a way as to place it under the virtual control of the State; and with the appointment of Georg Norman as Superintendent (a position almost equivalent to that of a Minister for Ecclesiastical Affairs), the State Church was born. The change was

further emphasized in 1540 when Norman visited the provinces with the aim of transferring to the crown all the
movable property of the Church which he considered super-
fluous. As in the case of the church bells in the 1530's, this
spoliation aroused considerable resentment, and it was not
without protest that many sacred vessels were handed over.
Nevertheless, the silver continued to pour into the King's
coffers to the increasing enrichment of the crown. The
reduction of Church property had assumed far greater proportions than had ever been anticipated.

As before, such high-handedness on the part of the King
was regarded by the community as an intolerable infringe-
ment of its rights and freedom. The unruly province of
Dalarna had been subdued, however, and the King does not
seem to have expected any violent reaction to his policy,
while his new counsellors were unaware of the risks involved.
Yet the risks were very real ones. The war-like Småland
peasantry were particularly aggrieved at the new decrees,
above all at the ban on trade over the Danish frontier; and
in May and June of 1542 Gustav Vasa learnt that one Nils
Dacke had organized a rebellion in the province and was
putting to death nobles and bailiffs. The movement spread
rapidly, and the King hastened to strike back with both
troops and propaganda. But Dacke's forces steadily increased,
and in the autumn they defeated the royal troops at Kisa in
Östergötland. As in the Dalarna risings, the rebels took the
name of Sture as their emblem, offering to Svante Sture (the
son of Sten Sture the Younger) the position of Commander
of the Kingdom. Notwithstanding Svante's refusal, however,
Nils Dacke won a notable success in November 1542 when he
came to terms with the King's representatives on the basis of
the *status quo*, thereby achieving a formal armistice between
the rebels and the sovereign.

The King spent the winter in enlisting the support of the
commons in the loyal Swedish provinces, defining his aims
in popular manifestos which, for sheer vigour, equalled

17. Gustav Vasa. Painting by an unknown artist, *c.* 1555.

18. Stockholm in 1535: detail of a contemporary
painting

anything he had yet produced. Nils Dacke had accused the King of abolishing all that was 'old and traditional'. In a demagogic manifesto, addressed to the most troublesome provinces at the end of 1542, Gustav Vasa explained exactly what the term involved. The peasants, he wrote, appeared to believe that these concepts were synonymous with reduced taxation and other reliefs. But were they in fact? If the old customs meant that only a few soldiers were kept in readiness, then the country would soon be overrun by her enemies. But the peasants seemed to forget that defence costs money; they were as those who wanted a warm cottage without breaking into their store of logs. Warming to his theme, the King reminded them that in former days foreign invasion and pillage had been common occurrences, and the merchants who brought the necessities of life were attacked by privateers and drowned like dogs. 'We ask every reasonable Swede to ponder whether these old traditions were to the advantage of our country,' he concluded. In such terms he outlined his great scheme for reform, and promised redress to the commons against nobles or bailiffs.

Gustav Vasa laid particular stress on the fact that so long as his government had remained unmolested it had maintained peace both at home and abroad, and pointed out that these peaceful conditions were now in jeopardy. He realized, in the winter of 1542–3, that the worst was yet to come, and in moments of depression he even feared that he might be forced to retire with a few loyal supporters to the Mälaren district, where, on the island of Gripsholm, he was erecting a strongly fortified castle. Twenty years of personal rule had given him an unrivalled knowledge of the resources of the country, however, and he was able to send reinforcements to Småland and cut off the rebels. The first move came from Nils Dacke, who, in the New Year, engaged the King's troops not far from Skänninge, in Östergötland. But he was unable to penetrate farther, and had to retreat south. Two royal armies marched into Småland and inflicted a heavy defeat on the rebels, Dacke being wounded in battle; the victors pressed home their advantage, forcing the Smålanders to beg for mercy. Dacke made one more attempt, which was equally unsuccessful, and he was probably killed while fleeing towards the forests on the frontier of Blekinge, where he had lived as an outlaw before the rising. The rebels were either executed or deported and heavy fines were extorted from the province. The last great conflict between the State and the provinces was over.

It had been a hard contest for the King, who now got to work to remove all possible incentive for further local opposition. He allowed his most unpopular German counsellor, Konrad von Pyhy, to fall from power; and though Norman for long remained one of the King's most trusted servants, he became more moderate in his policy. For the rest of his reign Gustav Vasa took care to avoid ruffling local susceptibilities, for his recent struggle, though ultimately successful, had taught him to treat his people in a less autocratic manner; his speeches and manifestos took on a milder note; his sole aim, he affirmed, was to serve his country.

It now remained to stabilize his position. The first step was to strengthen the country's defences, a task which the King pursued conscientiously from 1544 until the end of his reign. He further tightened up the administration and continued, though less stringently than before, to confiscate church property. The King's main concern, however, was with posterity; he wanted to ensure for his descendants the advantages that he had won for himself. He was still regarded by many people as a usurper, and a consort of royal blood had not been easy to find. His overtures to Poland having failed, he finally married Catherine of Sachsen-Lauenburg, sister-in-law to Christian III of Denmark. A son was born in 1533, and was christened Eric after Gustav Vasa's father, who had lost his life in the Stockholm blood-bath. Queen Catherine died shortly after his birth, however, and Gustav Vasa then married Margaret Eriksdotter, a member of the Swedish noble family of Leijonhuvud; she bore him many children, of whom the eldest was a son named John. Gustav Vasa had already caused his sons to receive homage as hereditary princes of the realm before his conflict with Dacke, and, after its successful issue, he formally established the principle of hereditary succession. This was an innovation in the Swedish constitution, though the idea had been broached as long ago as the Folkung era. Several European countries had already adopted it. The King was able to obtain information from Norman as to the procedure adopted in France and in the German States – Brunswick, for example.

In 1544 the first complete *Riksdag* for fourteen years was summoned in Västerås. The King made a statement of policy which culminated in the suggestion that the crown should become hereditary with a view to forestalling feud and unrest. The Estates solemnly swore to acknowledge Gustav Vasa's eldest son, Eric, as their king; Eric was to be succeeded by his male heirs or, if he died without male issue, by Duke John and his descendants. The communities throughout the country set their seals to this decision, and thus the new dynasty was ratified.

By establishing a hereditary monarchy Gustav Vasa had safeguarded himself both against the possible claims to the Swedish crown by the heirs of Christian II, and against the danger of conspiracy. He was well aware that he had many enemies on the Continent, including the Lübeck Council and such of his former servants as Berend von Melen, who was now in exile in Germany; and the fact that these antagonists had been involved in intrigues against his throne had caused him considerable anxiety. All his foreign ventures were prompted either by fear of these threats to his security or by commercial considerations. Although he followed events in Europe with close interest, he avoided any extensive commitments. His attitude to Denmark was one of caution and suspicion, based on the experiences of his youth; nevertheless, the two countries had certain interests in common, since neither was altogether safe from the designs of Christian II's heirs and their Hapsburg patrons. The two brothers-in-law, Kings of Sweden and Denmark, therefore maintained peaceful relations, and even concluded a treaty between their respective countries at Brömsebro in 1541. Gustav Vasa encouraged foreign trade by means both of the products of crown taxation and those of his own estates; and since he had already learnt the importance of safeguarding against sudden shortages of essential food, he was careful to make his plans on a long-term basis.

By the time Gustav Vasa died in 1560 his reforms were virtually complete. More than two-thirds of the country was directly controlled by the royal Treasury; large duchies were administered by the King's sons; the great fiefs, formerly held by noblemen, had been distributed amongst those who were related to the King, who was able by these means to keep on good terms with the higher aristocracy. Stock-breeding on modern lines was extensively carried on in the royal farms under the King's personal supervision, and internal colonization was under way in the north and also in Finland. The King also took a close personal interest in mining – the only industry in his peasant kingdom – and new methods in the manufacture of bar iron were introduced by German smiths. No detail escaped his notice, whether it be a bailiff's overaddiction to ale or a peasant's neglect of his land to the detriment of the King's revenue. Gustav Vasa has been described as tending his kingdom as though it were his own estate; and it was in this practical sphere that his most effective work was accomplished. He revealed another side to his character where spiritual matters were concerned, however. Culturally the Catholic Church in Sweden had been totally disrupted by the Reformation. Ecclesiastical works of art had been appropriated for the use of the State and the King, parchments from the libraries had gone to bind the reckonings of the bailiffs, and no effective substitute had been found for the former Catholic

# S. Johannis första Epistel. CXLI.

## Första Capitel.

Thet som war aff begynnelsen / thet wij haffue hördt / thet wij haffue seedt medh wår öghon / thet wij haffue beskodhat / och wåra hender handterat haffua aff lijffsens ord / Och lijffuet är uppenbarat / och wij haffue seedt / och witnom / och kungörom idher thet ewigha lijffuet / hwilket war när Fadhren / och är oss uppenbarat. Hwadh wij haffue seedt och hördt / thet förkunnom wij idher / på thet ock j skolen haffua selskap medh oss / och wårt selskap skal wara med Fadhrenom och hans Son Jesu Christo. Och thetta scriffue wij idher / på thet idhor glädhe skal wara fulkommen.

Och thet är bebodhelsen / som wij haffue hördt aff honom / och förkunnom idher / at Gudh är itt Liws / och intet mörker är j honom. Om wij säye oss haffua selskap medh honom / och wandrom j mörkret / tå liughom wij / och görom icke sanningen. Men wandrom wij j Liuset / såsom han är j liuset / tå haffue wij selskap inbyrdes / och Jesu Christi hans Sons blodh / renar oss aff alla synder. Säye wij at wij haffue ingen synd / tå bedraghe wij oss sielffua / och sanningen är icke j oss. Men om wij bekenne wåra synder / han är trofast och rettwijs / at han förlåter oss wåra synder / och renar oss aff alla orettferdigheet. Men säye wij at wij haffuom intet syndat / tå göre wij honom til liughare / och hans ord är icke j oss.

## II. Capitel.

Ijn barn / Thetta scriffuar iagh idher / at j skole icke synda. Och om någhor syndar / tå haffue wij en Förswarare när Fadhrenom / Jesum Christum / then retferdigh är / Och han är försoningen för wåra synder / Icke allenast för wåra / uthan ock för hela werldennes. Och ther på wete wij / at wij kennom honom / om wij hålle hans bodh. Then ther sägher / Jagh kenner honom / och håller icke hans bodh / han är en liughare / och j honom är icke sanningen. Men then som håller hans ord / j honom är sannerligha Gudz kärleek fulkomlighen / Och ther på wete wij / at wij ärom j honom. Then ther sägher sigh bliffua j honom / han skal ock wandra såsom han wandradhe.
Aa iij     Brödher

A page from Gustav Vasa's Bible

schools. Gustav Vasa himself was only interested in these
matters from a practical standpoint; nevertheless a great deal
was accomplished by others. Foremost among the achievements of the reformers were their devotional writings and the
Swedish translation of the Bible, which appeared in 1541.
The influence of the Bible was felt not only in the religious
life of the community, but also in the Swedish language,
where it laid the foundation for the 'Earlier New Swedish'.
The translators had shaken off some of the Danish influences of the late Middle Ages and, assisted partly by the
literary tradition of the Vadstena foundation, had endowed
the language with a new firmness and clarity. Another outstanding literary work was the Swedish chronicle of Olaus
Petri, who had tried conscientiously to give an account of
early Scandinavian history – and to pick his way through the
controversies which had arisen over the national versions
which had been put forward respectively by Sweden and
Denmark.

Yet notwithstanding all this, the period will be remembered primarily for the personality of the King, as portrayed
by his chronicler Peder Svart, and revealed in his speech to
his last *Riksdag* in 1560. Here he represented himself as the
instrument of God, comparing himself to David in the Old
Testament. His favourite rôles were those of the young hero
in the days of the war of liberation, and the patriarchal
father of his country; and in both cases King David of Judea
could be used as a prototype. Peder Svart related that he was
born with a caul, symbolizing victory, and that all his early
exploits were accompanied by a northerly wind, signifying
that God would send good fortune. His nephew Per Brahe
describes him as a man of great skill, wide understanding,
and many princely virtues. When his mind was at peace he
was a 'gay, charming, and witty companion, with a word for
all present, however many they might be'; and he possessed
besides a phenomenal memory. As for his appearance, Brahe
says that he had a round head, tow-coloured hair, a fair long

beard, piercing eyes, a small straight nose, a well-cut mouth with red lips, a healthy complexion, and a shapely body without a single flaw. He loved fine clothes, as was meet in a King, and he graced everything that he wore.

These pictures, drawn at the end of his career, were for long those which were adopted by subsequent generations; yet they do little justice either to the recurring crises which threatened the King's work, or to his dynamic personality. He was quick tempered, suspicious, crafty, and unscrupulous. Added to this, he was a brilliant demagogue, with considerable insight into human nature, and the violence of his temperament was offset, when he wished to exert it, by an irresistible charm. His astounding memory and prodigious capacity for work, his practical talents, his energy – which, however, was not proof against occasional fits of black depression – all these qualities seen against the background of his eventful career, his sayings and his writings, combine to produce one of the most vivid personalities in Swedish history.

# XV

# Eric XIV and John III
## 1560-1592

Johannes Magnus in his exaggerated history of the Swedish Kings had adhered to the interpretation put forward by Nicolaus Ragvaldi in 1434 and identified the Goths of the Teutonic migrations with the Götar, or Goths. The fact that most of the material had been invented was not revealed, and consequently this view of Swedish history was accepted by all – including even Gustav Vasa, except in so far as it repiesented a veiled attack on himself. Nevertheless, though he referred to it in a manifesto to his subjects, he did not really sympathize with the aggressive spirit which lay behind these tales of Gothic prowess in war. His whole policy was directed towards solving the problems of Sweden's position in the European world from *within* the confines of the State. His successors took a different line.

It cannot be explained too often that Sweden's politico-geographical structure in the middle of the sixteenth century bears no comparison with the situation to-day, and after the dissolution of the Scandinavian Union the threats to her existence became even more sharply defined. Her only contact with the North Sea was by a narrow strip of land between the Danish and Norwegian coastal provinces; the route to western Europe through the Baltic Sea was controlled by Denmark, who dominated what was perhaps the chief waterway of northern Europe, the Sound, and drew large profits from the customs duties she imposed. Thus Sweden could easily be isolated from western Europe, and in addition her southern routes to northern Germany were controlled by Lübeck, so long as the town retained its naval power. Sweden was also more closely connected with eastern

Europe than she is to-day; Finland bordered on Russia, and the northern coast of the Gulf of Finland belonged to Sweden. In the north, the Russian frontier stretched farther west, and the waste tracts in the far north were divided between Finland, Norway, and Russia in a rather haphazard fashion which gave rise to frequent conflicts. Sweden was therefore as vulnerable in the east as in the west, due to the vicinity of Russia and the State of the Teutonic Knights in Livonia, with Reval, the chief mercantile centre there, and its claim for a monopoly of Russian trade. That the confused situation in the east presented innumerable problems had already become apparent at the time of the Stures.

It was natural that Gustav Vasa should try to overcome Sweden's geographical weakness as far as possible by peaceful means. His sons, on the other hand, had already considered the alternative solution of an aggressive foreign policy. Duke John, from his favourable position in his duchy of Finland, had followed with close attention the incipient collapse of the Teutonic Order at the end of the 1550's and the conquest of Narva by Russia in 1558 which gave her access to the Baltic. He now proposed to cross the Gulf of Finland and establish strong bases on its southern coast. Meanwhile in Kalmar the heir Duke Eric was watching Danish politics with disquiet and suspicion; his plan was to win a foothold in western Europe by marrying Queen Elizabeth I of England, and with this in view he undertook frequent missions to the English court. The project failed, but it was typical of his attitude. However, though Gustav Vasa was able to prevent his sons from carrying out their schemes during his lifetime there was nothing to stop the new King Eric XIV from proceeding with them after his death.

Swedish foreign policy now became marked by a spirit of aggression and hazard, exemplifying Machiavelli's conception that the main purpose of the State lay in territorial expansion and war; and in its main features it set a precedent which was to be followed for a long time to come.

It was the political and geographical situation in the Baltic area rather than the specific quarrels over coats-of-arms and sovereignty which was the basic cause of the inter-Scandinavian conflict of the reigns of Eric XIV and Frederick II of Denmark. Denmark first provoked hostility by her attempt to rival Sweden in acquiring a firm footing in the former territories of the Teutonic Order on the Baltic, since this would complete her chain of strategic bases from the Sound, through the Scanian provinces and Gotland, to the mouth of the Gulf of Finland. Eric countered with an equally ambitious plan. Realizing that it would be greatly to Sweden's disadvantage for either Poland or Russia to have so excellent a harbour as Reval so near the Finnish border he took over his brother John's designs on the south coast of the Gulf; for if Sweden held the Gulf she would be able to control Russian trade from Finnish ports – Viborg in particular – and profit from the customs duties just as Denmark did in the Sound. This, of course, depended on his maintaining good relations with Russia, not to mention the fact that in the south Poland too was a rival for the territories of the Teutonic Order.

Eric began to put his plans into practice in 1561, when he induced Reval, together with adjacent parts of Esthonia, to acknowledge Swedish rule; and since Lübeck, the rival of Reval, was immediately up in arms at this Swedish threat to its important trade routes to Russia, Sweden's new policy soon had wide repercussions. She must therefore be prepared against possible attack, and with this in view Eric continued and expanded his father's work in building up both army and navy, basing it to a large extent on the recruitment of native Swedes. There seemed little doubt that war was brewing.

Eric's position was complicated, however, by the reluctance of his brother John to relinquish, in the King's interests, his designs on the Baltic provinces. Early in his reign the King had made a vain attempt to limit the Duke's power by strong measures (the Arboga articles, 1561). Having appealed to Poland for support, and married the sister of the Polish King, Catherine Jagellonica, John subsequently gained control of fortified castles to the south of Eric's new possessions in Esthonia. The schemes of the half-brothers had thus, quite literally, crossed, and reconciliation was rendered impossible by the ambition which was a characteristic of the Vasas. In the ensuing clash Eric proved the stronger; by 1563 John was a prisoner in Gripsholm Castle and his adherents were executed. It was at this point that Sweden found herself at war with Denmark and Lübeck.

Frederick II of Denmark had not been slow to take advantage of the civil war in Sweden; in the very first month, September 1563, he had conquered Älvsborg, thus cutting Sweden off from the North Sea and threatening her with a blockade. The Seven Years War of the North, as the struggle between Sweden and Denmark has been called, was a brutal episode marked by savage destruction and bitter hatred on both sides of the frontier and setting the seal on the enmity which had been engendered by a century of disagreement and propaganda. Yet for all the havoc which was effected each country had the same logical aim: to destroy her enemy's operational base, while the Swedes, in addition, wanted to break through the Danish ring of strategic strongholds. But although the young Swedish army acquitted itself well against Frederick's professional troops, the Danes possessed in Daniel Rantzau an outstanding commander who won for them a number of tactical successes. Little was achieved by them, however, and the issue remained undecided until Rantzau broke into Östergötland in the winter of 1567–8. The Swedes were more successful at sea, where their new fleet not only succeeded in keeping open the routes to northern Germany and ensuring supplies but, under a new ensign – a golden cross on a blue ground – and commanded by Klas Kristersson Horn, won a glorious victory over those of Denmark and Lübeck. King Eric was a capable organizer and chief of staff, though his nerves tended to go to pieces at

the approach of the enemy; nevertheless, Denmark ultimately won the day. Moreover her victory coincided with a
fresh outbreak of civil war in Sweden, where in 1568 Eric
was deposed by his half-brothers John and Charles in alliance
with the nobility. Two years later the war with Denmark
came to an end with the peace of Stettin, under which
Sweden was compelled at great sacrifice to pay a heavy ransom for the restoration of the important stronghold of Älvsborg. Eric's hopes of expanding to the North Sea and of controlling the Russian trade route had both failed; the problem
of Sweden's relationships to her neighbours still remained to
be solved. The struggle had exhausted both Sweden and
Denmark; and forty years were to elapse before either was
again challenged by the other.

All the same, Eric's successor, John III, was unwilling to
give up his plans for controlling Russian trade. The Stettin
peace had stipulated that the route to Narva should be open.
Conforming to his brother's ideas, however, John again
blockaded the city, and pursued a policy of expansion to the
east, the only difference being that it was now directed
against Russia. The ruler of the country, Ivan the Terrible,
had personal reasons for regarding John as his enemy; the
two monarchs exchanged insulting letters and were soon
involved in bitter warfare. From 1580 onwards the Swedes
were commanded with great skill by a talented southern
Frenchman, Pontus de la Gardie. During these years his
forces carried out daring surprise attacks, engaged in battles
against vastly superior Russian forces, and accomplished bold
marches over the frozen sea. De la Gardie himself became
almost a mythical hero. His greatest achievement was the
conquest of Narva in 1581, which effectively put an end to
the dispute over the blockade; 'according to the custom'
(to quote de la Gardie) men, women, and children in the
town were murdered in their thousands. The commercial
effects were not as great as had been anticipated, however,
partly because John III had failed at the same time to gain

control of a new route to Russia through the White Sea which had been in use since the end of the 1550's. Still, Sweden's ambitions in the Baltic were by no means satisfied, and were ultimately to prove disastrous. John III's next manœuvre was an attempt to gain Catholic support by exploiting his marriage with the Polish Princess Catherine. Their son Sigismund had had a Catholic upbringing, and on the death of the Polish King Stephen Báthori, John put him forward as a candidate for the Polish throne. In 1587 the Swedish nobles who represented him at the meeting of the Polish Estates brought about his election by promising that Sweden's Esthonian possessions should be incorporated into the Polish province of Livonia. Whether or not the promise was made in good faith – and it seems hardly likely – it certainly was not kept. Nevertheless the election held out prospects of a personal union between Sweden and Poland, and revealed even more plainly Sweden's leanings towards the east. Soon after Sigismund's accession to the Polish throne, however, other complications emerged which were to produce unexpected developments in Swedish policy.

The aggressive schemes of Gustav Vasa's sons, prompted as they were by a desire to control the Russian trade routes, formed the basis of the next hundred and fifty years of Swedish history. But no less important were the conflicts between the Vasa monarchy and the nobles at home, and also between Eric XIV and John III themselves. Indeed it was a period enlivened both by incident and by the exceptional personalities of the characters involved.

Eric XIV, depicted now as an effete romantic, now as a tragic artist of genius, and now as a man who did not know his own mind, is one of the most fascinating of the long line of Swedish kings. He was a man of great talent who had acquired a depth of European culture at that time unique in Sweden. He composed music, and was also well versed in astrology, a science which was particularly popular in Tycho Brahe's time. From his father he inherited diligence and an interest in administrative affairs, to which he added a vivid imagination which often distorted his sense of reality, and a theoretical mind which frequently prevented him from realizing that politics is the art of the possible – a defect which was revealed in his ingenious but unrealistic foreign policy. The family tendency to mistrust others was developed in him to the point of persecution mania, and he was capable of violent changes of mood which ranged from wild exultation to black melancholia. It was this combination of traits which helped to bring about the revival of the former conflicts between monarchy and aristocracy and between Stures and Vasa, culminating in a brutal episode generally known as the Sture murders.

For Eric XIV, with the support of his secretary Jöran Persson (the son of a priest) and others who held a modern outlook, ruthlessly used the power of the central government as an instrument against the nobility.[1] To this end a Royal High Court was established, in which not even the most prominent nobles were spared if the King suspected them of disloyalty. One of his victims was Nils Sture – grandson of Sten Sture the Younger, and son of the Svante Sture whom Nils Dacke had tried to win over – who was forced to ride into the capital under humiliating circumstances, similar to those imposed on Peder Sunnanväder some forty years earlier; while Duke John's uncle, Sten Eriksson Leijonhuvud, having returned from captivity in Denmark was virtually imprisoned in Stockholm. Actions such as these generated among the aristocracy an intense hatred of the King and his lowborn counsellors, and the King began to suspect a conspiracy. Indiscreet remarks reached his ears, and in 1567 the nobles in question were arraigned for high treason before the High Court, a decision which the *Riksdag* was expected to ratify in Uppsala. Eric seems to have been convinced of their guilt, and after much vacillation he had them put to death in

[1] When Eric XIV introduced the new titles of counts and barons it was primarily for the purposes of diplomatic representation.

May 1567. Among them were Nils Sture, his father Svante, and other prominent men, and the King himself participated in their murder – or execution, according to one's view. It was discovered shortly afterwards that the King's mind was affected. He gradually returned to normal and was fully aware of the nature of his malady. But although a formal reconciliation took place, his break with the aristocracy was irreparable.

The nobles were further antagonized by the King's subsequent marriage with Karin Månsdotter, a lowborn girl with whom he had long had a liaison and who had borne him a son and daughter. Duke John had been released from captivity at the time of his brother's insanity, and in 1568, in the middle of the Danish war, he and his younger brother Duke Charles placed themselves at the head of a rebellion against the King. Eric was seized in Stockholm, deposed, and condemned to imprisonment for life, being confined for some of the time in the same Gripsholm where he in turn had held John a prisoner; while Duke John and the nobles proceeded to defame his character with a consistency rarely equalled in Swedish history. Eric died in 1577, and although John undoubtedly welcomed his death, his complicity in it has never been fully established. Many aspects of the bitter strife between the brothers are reminiscent of the Folkung era, a parallel which Eric himself did not fail to see.

With Eric's deposition the nobles emerged as the real victors, and John III confirmed the privileges which had already been promised by him during Eric XIV's insanity. Special exemptions were to be enjoyed by the peasants who rented their farms from the nobles (as opposed to tax peasants, who were virtually freeholders with an obligation to pay taxes to the crown); and these exemptions (from crown taxation, conscription, and labour dues to crown castles, etc.) were a source of profit to the lords in that they demanded compensation for the burdens which their peasants escaped. The nobles were also granted exemption from customs dues and market tolls, the right to be judged by their peers, and the right to hold most of the important posts in the countryside – the hundred judgeships, for example. Gustav Vasa's direct line of succession had now been broken for the first – but not the last – time, and the fact that the change had to be sanctioned by the *Riksdag* introduced a new alignment into the constitution. The nobility as an Estate and the *Riksdag* as an institution could together counterbalance the strong monarchy created by the first Vasa kings. The monarchy still persisted, but with certain modifications. Though the *Riksdag* itself was not yet capable of assuming all the prerogatives implicit in the changes at the beginning of John III's reign, the nobles were becoming increasingly powerful. A new generation of the chief families – Brahe, Bielke, Banér, Sparre, Leijonhuvud – had grown up, and its members were rapidly acquiring education and political experience. The younger nobles made the Grand Tour; at home they would write to each other in Italian so as to ensure that their letters could not be understood by anyone but the recipient. They studied theology, jurisprudence, and political theory, and they were well versed in current political questions; deeply conscious of their status, moreover, they never failed to further the claims of the nobility. They took full advantage of their new privileges, and those who owned large estates were particularly favoured by the rising prices of agricultural products. In opposition to the Vasa monarchy and the rule of secretaries they set up the banner of a constitutional oligarchy, claiming that the nobility had a right to share in the government of the country – their frequent interest in mediaeval history was assuredly no mere accident! In the face of their desire for political power, the alliance which the nobles had made with John III in 1569 was bound to weaken. Incidentally, the talented and cultured Erik Sparre was already a prominent figure in their ranks.

In 1589 John met Sigismund in Reval, with a view to inducing his son to leave Poland and return to Sweden; and

19. Eric XIV. Painting by an unknown artist, *c.* 1560.

20a. The old royal castle 'Three Crowns', Stockholm.
Painting by G. Camphuysen, 1661.

20b. Vadstena Castle, completed 1620.

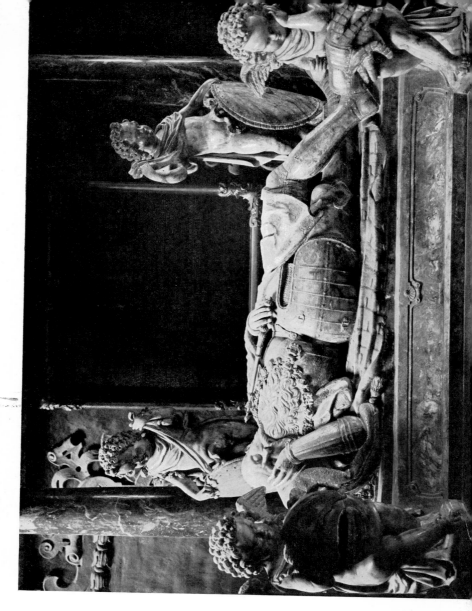

21. Tomb of John III in
Uppsala Cathedral.

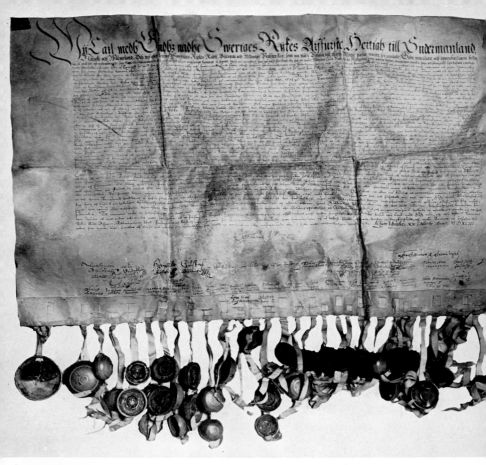

22. Document from the Uppsala Assembly, 1593.

it was the Council's vigorous and, in the King's opinion, un-
warranted objection to this Polish policy that inaugurated
the long conflict between them. The imprisonment by John
of some of the chief nobles aroused apprehensions of an outcome similar to the Sture murders; but with all his suspicion
and irascibility, John was not violent by nature. However, the
clash was serious enough, and John had the support of his
brother Duke Charles in his opposition to the lords of the
Council. A grudging reconciliation was achieved before the
King's death, but it could not remove the essential conflict
between the nobility and the monarchy. Eric's hatred of the
nobility, culminating in the Sture murders, had been merely
a more personal aspect of a division that went very deep.

This fundamental tension is one of the main features of
John III's reign. Like his elder half-brother, the King was an
intellectual, with a predominant interest in theology; and
his intervention in ecclesiastical affairs created considerable
uneasiness. His strong aesthetic and historical bias was
revealed in the way in which he called in foreign architects
to beautify the unwieldy strongholds which Gustav Vasa had
built or rebuilt, such as the castles of Gripsholm, Vadstena,
and Kalmar. Behind this action lay his desire to transfer the
aesthetic values and traditions of Catholicism to the new
Lutheranism, which had been officially adopted in Sweden
by the Church Ordinance of 1571. In 1576 he incorporated
his ideas in a liturgy which had strong Catholic leanings; and
he was consumed with a desire that the priests should use it.
Some of the Swedish clergy had already accepted unconditionally the orthodox tenets of German Lutheranism, however, and John's 'Red Book', as the new liturgy was called,
encountered strong opposition; even the reputedly Cal-
vinistic Duke Charles threw in his lot with the clergy. Several
churchmen were banished, and the King harshly condemned
the 'dirty, unkempt, and quarrelsome' priests. For a number
of years he was closely associated with members of the
counter-Reformation, one of whom issued a vehement

12

polemic in the form of a letter from Satan to the Lutheran clergy. The Protestants responded in kind. Orthodox Lutheranism, which had been consolidated by these events, viewed with aversion the prospect of a Catholic heir in Poland, and it now fought with all its might to protect its own. This conflict in the Church was to have remarkable consequences during the subsequent years.

When John III died there were several factions ready to exploit the confused situation which would undoubtedly follow. The new Swedish King in Poland represented the old Vasa claims of absolute power, though they were modified to some extent by his experiences in Poland. The Swedish aristocracy, anxious to defend their country and their class against the demands which they anticipated from Sigismund, mustered their resources in the Council, and formulated arguments to support their cause. The Swedish clergy, whose strength depended on their firm organization and their influence over public opinion, stood ready to oppose the Liturgy and Catholicism. As for the *Riksdag*, no one could predict what part it was to play. Still somewhat shapeless in form, it was nevertheless increasing in importance, and since 1569 had been a factor to reckon with. Would it succeed in combining the demands of the various Estates, or would it be exploited by a clever demagogue, as it had been at the beginning of the sixteenth century? Behind these expectant groups was Duke Charles. Whether on his brother's side or in opposition, he had been keenly following the developments in foreign affairs; and, moreover, with an administrative talent worthy of his father, he had consolidated his duchy, Södermanland, Närke, and Värmland into a firm and well-governed whole. He certainly would not be content with the rôle of onlooker.

# XVI

# Charles IX and Gustavus Adolphus
## 1592-1617

In September 1593, ten months after John III's death, the new King's ships reached the Stockholm archipelago from Poland. During the interim the situation in Sweden had begun to clarify, and political and religious parties took on a more definite shape. Sigismund was firmly resolved to maintain a strong monarchy – the more so as he had had in Poland a glimpse of the more disagreeable aspects of a constitution dominated by the nobility. Moreover, he and his Catholic counsellors – chief of whom was the Papal nuncio Malaspina, a typical representative of the counter-Reformation – were anxious to reintroduce Catholicism into Sweden. Poland had returned to the faith in the middle of the sixteenth century, despite a strong Protestant faction, and a similar movement seemed feasible in Sweden, where the traditional rites were still observed in isolated provinces. Nevertheless, though some royalist opinion existed both among the common people and the nobles, particularly in Finland, Sigismund met with considerable opposition, and even the King's friends began to waver.

The opposition was diverse in character. Duke Charles and the Council had temporarily made up their quarrel, and were determined to consolidate their position – a policy for which the beginning of a new reign offers particularly favourable circumstances. In anticipation of Catholic pressure more than three hundred Lutheran clergy had attended a Church assembly at Uppsala in March 1593, when they had organized their resistance on the basis of orthodox Lutheranism. They had also rejected John III's Liturgy as 'superstitious' and 'the root of much unrest'; and denounced all divergent doctrines as 'lamentable delusions'. Papists, Calvinists, and others were to be allowed to remain in the kingdom only on condition that they held no public services – a startling decision in view of the expected arrival of the King and his Polish retinue. The spirit of the meeting was summed up in the classic words of the chairman, Nicolaus Botniensis: 'Now is Sweden become one man, and we have all one Lord and one God.' Copies of the decision were circulated for confirmation by the Council, nobility, clergy, towns, provinces, and hundreds.

Sigismund, reserved and melancholy by nature, was hardly the man to deal effectively with this militant mood. He had many of the intellectual interests of the Vasas, particularly in the arts (he was a painter); but he seems to have had no trace of Gustav Vasa's charm. His first clash with his subjects on a constitutional issue took place at his coronation in Uppsala, in February 1594, which was attended by Duke Charles with an armed following. Though it was ostensibly a battle between Sigismund's Catholicism and the uncompromising Lutheranism of the Estates, it symbolized also the conflict between royal absolutism and constitutional monarchy. Would the King succeed in obtaining the right of public worship for non-Lutherans – including his own Polish following – or would the Estates force him to conform to their own religious outlook? This linking up of the political and the ecclesiastical was typical of the time, the two being regarded merely as different aspects of the same problem. In the event the King had to yield, after the Estates had angrily threatened to disinherit anyone who lapsed from the pure doctrine. The nobles were unrestrained in their criticism of the absolutism of the Vasas, and the Council's chief spokesman, Erik Sparre, formulated the demands of the nobility and emphasized its importance in maintaining order and good government. Once again the old aristocratic constitutionalism had proved its political maturity.

Somewhat aggrieved, the King shortly afterwards returned

to Poland, and during his absence Duke Charles and the
Council – that is to say the higher aristocracy – together
assumed the government of Sweden. This was no more than
an improvised solution, for, although a number of proposals
had been put forward by Erik Sparre and others, no precise
form of government had yet been adopted. However, for the
moment, the Duke and the Council agreed to defend jointly
their constitutional rights both against any designs which
Sigismund might harbour of assisting the development of
absolutism in the State and the counter-Reformation in the
Church, and against Polish influences.

Such an alliance, formed to deal with a specific emergency,
could hardly be expected to last. In the very next year, at
the *Riksdag* of 1595, it showed signs of cracking. The Duke
was even more eager than the Council to assert the independence of the home government against the King; and he
managed to win over the commons – the priests, burgesses,
and peasants of the three lower Estates – to his views. Having
been acknowledged by them as Regent he carried out his
immediate aims, exhorting the peasants not to be constrained
by 'intimidation, overbearingness, fear or favour' to retract
their decision. It was ironic that the first signs of this clash
in Sweden should have coincided with a gain which sprang
from her personal union with Poland – the peace concluded
with Russia at Täysinä in May 1595, by which Esthonia and
Narva were ceded to Sweden. But while Finland at last
gained some respite from the ravages of frontier warfare, the
position inside Sweden deteriorated. The Governor of Finland, Klas Fleming, was one of Sigismund's most faithful adherents, and he had refused to accept the Duke's decision
concerning the form of government. The Duke demanded
action against him, but the Council hesitated; and the disagreement came to a head in 1596–7 when the peasants of
Österbotten, with the approval of Duke Charles, rose against
Klas Fleming. This struggle, known as the 'Club war', soon
spread to other areas of Finland. The King's party was

victorious; but the Duke, staking everything on one throw, challenged the Council and appealed to the Estates, summoning them to Arboga in February and March 1597. Only one lord of the Council attended the meeting, and henceforward the Duke and the lower Estates formed a unit against both Sigismund and the higher aristocracy. The nobles took a long time to decide whether to renounce the obedience due to their lawful king. In a spirit reminiscent of the Kalmar Union they thought their political ambitions might well be expressed more freely under a king who lived in Poland.

Duke Charles, however – or 'Charles Crooknose' as he was called – found their views as distasteful as those of Sigismund himself, and he proceeded to concentrate all his powers of persuasion on the peasants, both inside and outside the *Riksdag*. His policy reveals no hard-and-fast line between personal ambition and a desire to preserve the Vasa monarchy intact. His propaganda, which was both ruthless and effective, was marked by a bitter contempt for and a dispassionate exploitation of his fellow men. Like Gustav Vasa, he was skilful at swaying his followers, though he lacked his father's charm; and he was capable of being offensive in argument, much to the delight of the commons among the audience.

Meanwhile, the Duke's relations with the Council had steadily worsened, so much so that several of its members took refuge with Sigismund, thereby promoting open hostilities. In 1598 Sigismund responded by bringing an army to Sweden; while his faithful commander in Finland – Arvid Stålarm, who had succeeded Klas Fleming on the latter's death – attacked the Uppland coast. Sigismund engaged his uncle's forces in Östergötland, again the scene of battle between members of the Vasa family. But after two indecisive skirmishes Sigismund unexpectedly gave up the struggle and handed over to his uncle the councillors who had fled to him. It was agreed that hostilities should cease, and that a settlement should be drawn up at a meeting of the *Riksdag*; Sigismund broke this agreement, however, and returned to Poland, leaving his fortresses and his adherents (many of whom were put to death, mainly in Finland) to the mercy of his enemies.

The councillors who had deserted to Sigismund were tried at the *Riksdag* held in Linköping in 1600. Four of them, having refused to confess themselves in the wrong, were found guilty of perjury, slander, and high treason by an extraordinary court of the four Estates, in which the Duke himself acted as prosecutor. Among them was Erik Sparre, whose execution, with that of several of his associates, later became known as the Linköping massacre.

The struggle was over, and aristocratic constitutionalism had, for the moment, been defeated. Duke Charles was all-powerful; no further resistance need be expected inside the country, while Sigismund was fully occupied by Polish affairs and therefore unable to prolong the fight. Moreover, the Union with Poland had been irrevocably broken. A number of Charles's former opponents among the Swedish aristocracy were still living there, and they spread lurid reports of what they called his 'slaughter-bench', denouncing him as an offspring of Machiavelli, the main object of dislike at the time. But Charles was now safely established, and in due course he assumed the title of King. The Council was reconstructed in 1602, and two years later the new dynasty was confirmed by the Pact of Succession in Norrköping, whereby in certain circumstances women too were to be allowed to inherit the throne.

Charles IX had thus followed in his father's footsteps and was animated in many ways by the same ideals. He had innumerable projects, though few of them were ever realized, for his activities were marked by a certain restlessness. His main achievements lay in the sphere of legal reform and the administration of justice, though he also took an interest in the mining industry. Following the break with Sigismund and

Poland it was foreign policy, however, which absorbed most of his energies.

Sweden had never yet lacked an adversary in the east: under Eric XIV it had been Poland, under John III, Russia. Peace had been made with the latter in 1595, so it was once more Poland's turn. Charles determined to take Poland by surprise and be the first to attack: 'better to wage war on the territories of your enemy than on your own' was to be the guiding rule of Swedish military politics during the next century. But the Polish cavalry appeared invincible, and Charles's campaign in Livonia did not prosper; more effective was his attempted blockade of the Polish ports. Soon, however, the theatre of war was transferred to Russia, which was at that time experiencing the so-called 'Time of troubles'; the old dynasty had died out, and the country appeared to be in a state of disintegration. A pro-Polish party was already in existence, and Charles, true to type, decided to exploit the situation in his war with Poland. He entered into alliance with a powerful Russian faction, and Swedish troops marched into the country. Led by Jakob de la Gardie, son of the victor of Narva, they entered Moscow in 1610, and there were even plans to make one of Charles's sons – Gustavus Adolphus or Charles Philip – Czar of Russia. A bitter struggle ensued, during which the Swedes suffered a number of reverses. But if they could only conquer Novgorod and northern Russia they might yet fulfil, though in a slightly different form, the designs of Eric XIV, and Sweden would gain control of the coveted trade routes. If this plan failed, she would instead find that both Russia and Poland were her enemies.

This combined strategical and commercial policy depended for success on further expansion. The route to Archangel round the coast of Norway was thought to pass through Danish waters; but Sweden too was eager for a say in the matter. Charles himself was particularly desirous of acquiring part of Finland's Arctic Sea coast, whence Sweden could control the northern route to Russia. Assisted by Dutch immigrants he built Göteborg (Gothenburg) on the narrow strip of land in the west, and granted its citizens the right to trade with Lappland, to sail to Russia through the White Sea, and to fish in the North Sea. Since the Narva route had proved less profitable than had been hoped, this control of the White Sea water was a logical development. Though Charles's concern in Lappland and the northern waters was primarily determined by political considerations, it was combined oddly enough with an interest in reindeer-breeding. This curiosity about other lands, largely engen-dered by Olaus Magnus's ethnographical work on Sweden, *Historia de gentibus septentrionalibus* (1555), had also been evinced by Eric XIV, whose coronation celebrations had included a display of Lapps and reindeer.

Charles IX's foreign policy had the same dynamic quality as that of his elder brother, though with the addition of new elements. For his designs in the Arctic, together with more traditional disputes, also prevented cordial relations with Denmark. Christian IV wanted war, and he saw his chance when Charles started to tie up his military forces in the east. A Dano-Norwegian chain of fortresses had already been forged in the Scanian provinces, and in 1611 Christian IV went into action. Charles, exhausted and suffering from a stroke, was pessimistic as to the outcome; and in an atavistic outburst of mediaeval chivalry and ancient 'Gothicism' he impetuously challenged Christian to single combat; the chal-lenge was rejected with withering scorn, and shortly after-wards the Danes conquered the important stronghold of Kalmar.

At the *Riksdag* of 1610 the effects of his stroke had prevented Charles from speaking more than a few slurred pathetic words: 'Could I speak, I should speak, I should pronounce freely; but now I have not the power. Know ye, good men, God hath chastised me.' He was accompanied by his oldest son, the sixteen-year-old Duke Gustavus Adolphus, who was shortly to assume the command in the Danish war. But none could tell whether the young man was to prove capable of overcoming three enemies; and when the King died in October 1611 the Swedish aristocracy bided its time – unbroken, if subdued, by the impositions of the last few years, and filled with rancour against the dead King and the rule of 'lowborn' secretaries which had originated with Eric XIV and was now exemplified in Charles's Chancellor, Dr Nils Chesnecopherus. There is no doubt that Charles himself favoured a reconciliation with the nobles, but the obstacles proved too great. Though Erik Sparre's generation had disappeared, men twenty years younger were now old enough to take up the struggle; and the time was particularly favourable for enforcing their demands in that, according to the law then in force, Gustavus Adolphus would not come of age for seven years. It became apparent during the proceedings of the *Riksdag* in 1611 that the aristocracy were determined to submit no longer to the frustrations imposed on them by the all-powerful Vasa monarchy over the past ten years.

The youth on whom the fate of the monarchy now hung had been carefully trained with a view to his subsequent task. His tutor, Johan Schroderus (subsequently ennobled with the surname Skytte), was a learned man who had travelled extensively, and from him the young Duke could learn at second hand the kind of things that his contemporaries absorbed on their foreign tours. Theology and Latin had been the main subjects in his education; followed by rhetoric and dialectic, arithmetic and geometry, politics, history, law, modern languages, and – last but by no means least – the art of war; his favourite hero was Maurice of Nassau, the most celebrated general of his time. Travels with his father, attendance at the Council meetings, and the management of his own duchy had early given Gustavus Adolphus experience of the different aspects of his calling; and while still a boy he had been expected to follow the negotiations with foreign powers.

Although Gustavus Adolphus at once assumed the full powers of government, he was at the same time compelled to register an oath which gave the Council and the higher aristocracy considerable influence in the government. This was a reaction to Charles IX's ruthless despotism, and was an appreciable victory for the aristocracy, the more so as the twenty-eight-year-old leader of the Council, the Chancellor Axel Oxenstierna, was, despite his comparative youth, both talented and experienced. In 1612 the position of the nobles was further strengthened by an extension of the privileges which they had acquired in 1569.

The new government was faced with a desperate situation. The Danes had followed up their successes, and in May 1612 had again severed Sweden's connection with western Europe by the conquest of Älvsborg. At the same time the Danish fleet attacked the Swedish east coast and reached the Stockholm archipelago. All that Sweden could do was to request a speedy settlement in the hope that the conditions would not be too crippling. In fact, under the terms of the peace, which was concluded at Knäred in the same year, she was forced to redeem Älvsborg by a sum which proved a severe drain on the national exchequer, while Denmark retained the stronghold with its adjacent territory until the ransom was paid. At the same time, the war in Russia had to be continued. De la Gardie was fighting against heavy odds: the Muscovites had united against the invaders, and the Swedes were no longer allies of a Russian party but the enemies of the Russian kingdom. From 1614 onwards Gustavus Adolphus took part in the campaign, thereby acquiring considerable insight into Baltic problems. Sweden was eventually victorious, and a favourable peace was concluded at Stolbova in 1617, which finally embodied Eric XIV's dream of controlling Russia's commercial outlets into the Baltic and protecting the Finnish frontier; though Charles IX's plan of controlling the route to northern Russia had to be given up. Sweden had won this important victory partly with the assistance of her

new ally, the Netherlands, whose support had put an end to
her dangerous isolation after the Kalmar war. To the Estates,
the Swedish King summed up the gains of the Russian war –
the entire territory round the innermost parts of the Gulf of
Finland to Lake Ladoga – with the characteristic and oft-
quoted words : 'I trust to God that it shall hereafter be hard
for the Russians to cross or leap over that stream' – having
also in mind Finland's increased security against frontier
raids.

During these years of struggle the monarchy in Sweden –
limited by the oath of 1611 – had acquired considerable
stability and authority. This may have been partly due to the
young King's exceptional military prowess, a prowess rarely
shown to such a degree by the earlier Vasas. Raw adolescent
though he still was in some ways, his attractive, and at times
overwhelming, personality was bringing him to the forefront
of Swedish politics. He had already begun quite early in his
reign to make innovations and follow up the tentative
schemes put forward by Charles IX. Foremost among them
was the institution in 1614 of the Court of Appeal (*Svea
hovrätt*), which discarded many of the more clumsy mediaeval
practices and helped to establish a uniform judicial procedure; and the King's progressive ideas were also revealed
in the Chancellor's draft of a *Riksdag* Ordinance in 1617.

When, at the age of twenty-three, Gustavus Adolphus was
formally crowned, he made an eloquent speech which clearly
pointed the contrast between his former and his present relations with the Estates. He enquired of them what resources a
seventeen-year-old stripling could possibly have possessed to
force a country to submit to him, and he disclaimed using
any means whatsoever save 'trust in God, and that power
which derives from the loyalty of Swedish men'. Herein,
perhaps, lies the explanation as to why the oath of 1611 did
not ultimately give the aristocracy that supremacy to which
it had aspired; for the young King's words betokened a
remarkable personality which augured strongly the re-

establishment of the Vasa monarchy. Curiously enough, the new generation of nobles showed little bitterness towards the dynasty, despite the voices still raised against it by those in exile. The extensive privileges which had been granted to them may have encouraged a tolerant attitude, but it is obvious that Gustavus Adolphus himself possessed an unusual capacity for smoothing away former differences.

Meanwhile, other developments had been taking place. Sweden was still largely an agricultural country, only about 5 per cent. of the population as yet living in towns. Rural life was dominated by the seasons and the village community, and the techniques employed continued to be those of the past. The peasant farm was virtually self-sufficient, the only commodity it lacked being salt for the preservation of food stuffs. Barley and rye were the main crops, and coarse black bread, salt meat, and fish the staple diet, washed down with water, milk, or ale; only in the summer and at slaughter-time was there fresh meat to relieve the monotony. With few exceptions the life of the nobleman differed little from that of the peasant farmer. On the other hand, in the mining in- dustry, which had its roots in mediaeval Sweden, great changes were foreshadowed by the introduction of such im- proved methods as, for example, the 'French furnaces', which replaced wooden and earth ones, and the German and Walloon forges for the more efficient production of bar iron, which spread from the iron districts of Central Sweden. But although these developments were to have tremendous in- fluence on economic life, the most important change resulted from the increased demand for Swedish copper, and its appreciable rise in price; one of the reasons for this was Spain's adoption of a copper currency in 1599. It was largely due to her resources in copper that Sweden was enabled for the second time to redeem Älvsborg from Denmark. She had Holland to thank for bringing the commodity into the market, the headquarters of which was in Amsterdam; and businessmen in the Netherlands kept a close eye on Sweden,

with her wealth of unexploited mineral deposits and unlimited supplies of wood.

The strength of a nation is in proportion to its numbers,
and painstaking efforts have been made to estimate Sweden's
population at this juncture, based on records relating to the
levies for the Älvsborg ransom. Excluding Finland, they vary
between 427,000 and 830,000 for the period round 1570, and
suggest that the population had grown to about 850,000
(with 350,000 for Finland) by the end of Gustavus Adolphus's
reign. None of the figures are exact, and they are probably
on the low side.

Such was the background to the unexpectedly strong position which the Swedish State acquired during the following
years as a result of the labours of Gustavus Adolphus and his
helpers. Slowly Sweden emerges from the former isolation
which had first been reversed as a result of her Baltic policy.
The administrative machine which the early Vasa Kings had
built up, already a source of strength, was to be systematized
and developed; and there followed a period of expansion and
progress unparalleled in Swedish history.

# XVII

# Sweden becomes a Great Power
## 1618-1632

The Swedish government had not finished with Poland despite the truce between the two countries. During the Russian war the King had begun to realize what tremendous prospects were offered in the east and south-east. In his mind and those of his counsellors the dynastic, the political, the strategic, and the religious questions were all linked together in a manner typical of contemporary thought. Sweden lived in constant fear of Polish and Catholic intrigue, an attitude which manifested itself in ruthless trials for treason and violent suspicion. With all its rigid orthodoxy, the Swedish Church had an apocalyptic streak. The *Riksdag* which met in Örebro in 1617, preceding the coronation *Riksdag* in the same year, still exuded some of the heat which characterized Duke Charles's assemblies; the famous statute of Örebro prohibited any relations with Poland on pain of severe punishment, and further decreed that neither Catholics nor apostates should be allowed to remain in the country. The possibility of a Polish attack was magnified into a positive bogey: 'What have we to expect of King Sigismund,' cried Gustavus Adolphus at the Örebro *Riksdag*, 'who is not only evil himself, but allows himself to be governed by that Devil's party the Jesuits, the authors of the grievous tyranny in Spain, France, and elsewhere?' When the Thirty Years War broke out shortly afterwards the Swedish King, with his usual acumen where foreign affairs were concerned, was not slow to realize how the traditional enmity of Poland could be exploited; indeed she was the victim of preliminary, though minor, attacks by Sweden in 1617–18 quite soon after the end of the Russian war.

But before Sweden turned her attention to Poland in earnest, she herself was the scene of important innovations based on plans which had been drawn up while the Russian war was still in progress. The nobles played a prominent part in these developments; for the 'rule of secretaries' had been replaced, at all events for some years, by an aristocratic bureaucracy. The landowners, great and small, which the upper classes had formerly comprised, were now transformed into civil and military officials, and the seeds sown by Erik Sparre and his generation were at last bearing fruit. A nobleman no longer held his position by knight service. The basis of nobility was now birth or royal patent, and its task 'the service of the kingdom' in all its aspects.

The central government was largely recruited from the higher aristocracy, and the remodelled Council became a closely knit nucleus in sharp contrast to the personal and shapeless government of the sixteenth century. The administrative machinery had become so complicated that one man could not possibly keep track of its ramifications; the personal direction of Gustav Vasa's era had therefore to give way to an ordered system. Already the Court of Appeal had a 'collegial' organization, and later the Chancery and Treasury were modernized on the basis of Dutch models.[1] Though many of the essential features of the earlier Vasa period were preserved, they were expanded and developed. Uppsala University received a generous royal donation for the purpose of training potential government officials; Courts of Appeal were set up in Åbo and Dorpat; new towns were built and were granted charters; and the ecclesiastical system took on its final shape. The bishops, foremost among whom was Johannes Rudbeckius in Västerås, vigorously fulfilled the wide functions they had acquired in their dioceses, and besides organizing the educational system yet found time

[1] The collegial system was the organization of government offices under a board on which the principal officials sat, presided over by the head of the department concerned.

23. Gustavus Adolphus. Drawing by L. Strauch, 1632.

Kön. Mayt: in Schweden Gustavi
Adolphi Ankunfft in Pommern
Anno 1630.

24. Gustavus Adolphus landing in Germany.
17th century painting.

25. A Swedish cavalry charge.
Detail of engraving by J. v.d. Heyden, 1632.

*Illustrissimus D.D Axelius*
*...ntierna fait le vendredy*
*...may 1633 en moins*
*...ne demie heure devant*
*...le naturel*
*par Dumonstier*

26. Axel Oxenstierna.
Pastel portrait by D. Dumonstier, 1633.

to pursue their own theological studies. The driving power behind all these reforms, apart from the King, was Axel Oxenstierna. Thus the aristocracy assumed in a peaceful manner and in co-operation with the King those powers for which Erik Sparre had fought; the constitutional conflict seemed over, and for the time being a balance was achieved. The privileges granted to them in 1617, controversial though they were, had already predisposed the nobles to co-operate, and in 1626 their position was further confirmed by the Order of the House of Nobility which, by organizing the Estate of the nobility, influenced the development of the *Riksdag* itself.

The army too, one of the obvious bases of Sweden's position as a great power, was reorganized between the time of the Stolbova peace and the middle of the 1620's. Even in the sixteenth century the Vasa Kings – Eric XIV particularly – had had in mind an army composed exclusively of Swedish nationals, and this aim, though ahead of contemporary ideas, was now put into practice. A small proportion of mercenaries, both Swedish and foreign, still remained, but the bulk of the army, and especially the infantry, was mustered by a form of conscription which enrolled, according to necessity, a proportion of the male population between the ages of fifteen and forty-four – though those in the lower-age ranges might sometimes be deferred on the plea of youth. Units were generally formed according to provinces, each bearing its local name. It was this army, unique of its kind during the seventeenth century, which was the mainspring of Sweden's ultimate expansion. It was, of course, a heavy burden for the country folk to bear, and conscription levies caused several local risings during the 1620's. Nevertheless, the government took care that the levies should be regularly approved by the *Riksdags*; and in spite of all difficulties an army of exceptional quality was raised, provoking a tribute even from the Danish envoy Peter Galt, one of the most critical observers.

In 1621 Gustavus Adolphus and his troops invaded Livonia

13

and besieged Riga, the capital of the province. Here the King was informed that the Russian frontier had been finally staked out according to the terms of the peace of Stolbova, Sweden thereby acquiring Ingermanland and eastern Karelia, including the route which ran beside the Neva from the Ladoga to the Gulf of Finland. Riga capitulated shortly afterwards, and in September the King made his solemn entry into the town. Riga had long been one of the chief trading towns on the Baltic, and the rich grain districts of

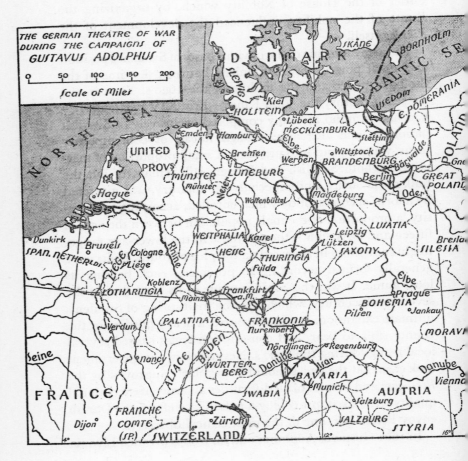

THE GERMAN THEATRE OF WAR DURING THE CAMPAIGNS OF GUSTAVUS ADOLPHUS

Polish Lithuania had hitherto exported their produce down
the river Dvina. Sweden now held the mouth of this river,
and Gustavus Adolphus was not slow to realize its advantages. The route to the west had again been freed by the
ransom of Älvsborg in 1619, and Sweden's position in the
Baltic was considerably improved by her successes in Poland.
Moreover, Riga also possessed an importance for commerce
in the countries of the west, and Sweden was soon in a position to expand her outworks in the Baltic.

Gustavus Adolphus's new peasant army was now ready,
and after a truce of two years he again marched into Livonia.
For the first time the Polish cavalry, which had been feared
since Charles IX's heavy defeat, was overwhelmed, at
Wallhof, by the Swedish troops. The victory greatly stiffened
their morale, and the King decided to continue the war,
though on a new front and a wider basis.

The Thirty Years War had by this time reached northern
Europe. Denmark's intervention in 1626 had proved unsuccessful, and Wallenstein's troops were moving up methodi-
cally towards the Baltic Sea. It was in the light of this that
Gustavus Adolphus formulated his plan of attack. The Protestant princes were anxious that he should enter the war on
their side, but he refused to submit to their proposals. For the
moment he was still conducting a war of his own, and in 1626
he directed his attack against Prussia, the country which
linked Poland proper to the sea. The Prussian ports were the
great attraction for Sweden, even though the King lamented
in 1624 that he was 'suspected of wanting to drink up the
entire Baltic, just because he'd been constrained to take one
pail of water from it'; and, moreover, Prussia would provide
an excellent base from which to observe the German war.
Here Sweden waged a successful campaign against Poland
from 1626–9, while the European conflict continued to
spread on all sides. From 1627 onwards, Poland was supported by the Hapsburg Emperor, whose troops attacked
Jutland and proceeded to establish themselves along the

south Baltic coast. It became increasingly clear that Wallenstein aimed to extend the Hapsburg Empire to the Baltic and
create a fleet there. He had early noted the Swedish King's
designs on the Baltic ports from the Neva to the Memel; and
the Swedish commanders anticipated that he would attack
Sweden as soon as he had defeated Denmark. Thus, both
sides foresaw a clash. In 1628 Gustavus wrote to inform
Oxenstierna that all the various wars in Europe had now
converged, and that the Swedes must sooner or later be prepared to measure swords with 'that Wallenstein'; and in the
same year he sent six hundred men from his Norrland troops
to relieve Stralsund, which was being besieged by Wallenstein, proclaiming that it was necessary for him to uphold
Stralsund's position as a free imperial city in order to counteract enemy preparations in the Baltic. In making this gesture,
Sweden for once co-operated effectively with Denmark.

In 1629 an armistice was concluded between Sweden and
Poland, with France, England, and Brandenburg acting as
mediators. Sweden was to keep Livonia and most of her
Prussian gains; she was also, for the six-year duration of
the truce, to continue to receive customs dues in the form of
'licences' from the Prussian ports – a revenue amounting to
about 30 per cent. of her total income. Sweden, as Oxenstierna proudly claimed, now held all the Baltic ports from
Kalmar, through Livonia and Prussia, to Danzig; and since
these ports played a vital part in the commerce of the Baltic
she had become a significant factor in European politics.
In addition, the balance between Denmark and Sweden had
been perceptibly altered in the latter's favour as a result both
of her Baltic conquests and the reorganization of her army,
especially after Christian IV's unsuccessful intervention in
the German war.

Despite her profits, both from the Prussian duties and from
her own exports of copper and iron, Sweden had been hard
put to it to support the campaigns of these last four years.
Over forty thousand men had been conscripted in Finland

and Sweden – an impressive proportion of the total population. Camp fever had partly accounted for the heavy losses in the field – while at home the burden of the regular 'yearly taxes' had been augmented by fresh demands which were originally dictated by the exigencies of the time, but which gradually took a permanent place alongside the older taxes. Though in theory he upheld the right of the Swedish people to tax themselves, Gustavus Adolphus in fact showed considerable inventiveness in his taxation policy.

Having achieved so much, would Sweden be content to stop at this point? At the end of 1629 Gustavus, despite his preoccupation with the German war, seemed undecided as to his next move, although in a letter to Axel Oxenstierna he suggests that there is strong reason for entering the German war, which, since 1618, had concerned not only Germany but the fate of the whole world. To this war there were three main facets: the struggle between Catholics and Protestants, between the territorial princes and the Emperor, and between the Hapsburg Empire and the France of Richelieu. The Netherlands were directly engaged in the war, and Scandinavia could hardly remain outside it; Denmark indeed had already been involved. To Gustavus Adolphus and several of his advisers, Swedish participation appeared inevitable, particularly in view of the Emperor's Baltic plans. This being so, it would be wiser to engage in fighting as far away from Sweden as possible. The matter was repeatedly debated by the Council and the Estates, Gustavus Adolphus bringing into play all his well-known powers of persuasion. It was obvious to all that a war on the scale suggested would cause serious suffering to the commons, since it was they who would have to bear the heaviest burden; nevertheless, as Gustavus had correctly assumed, their representatives in the *Riksdag* and at other assemblies merely echoed the strategic conceptions of their leaders: 'It is better', they declared, 'that we tether our horses to our enemy's fence, than he to ours.'

The important question was finally put in the spring of
1630 at a special meeting – a so-called 'committee *Riksdag*' –
in Stockholm; there, despite the risks involved, the King's
view of the political situation was accepted as it stood, as also
was his expressed intention to negotiate with the Emperor
only at the point of the sword. Thus the decision had been
taken; and incidentally it is characteristic of the relations
between Sweden and Denmark that the two countries proved
as unable to co-operate now as they had been when Denmark
had entered the German conflict five years before. Gustavus
Adolphus once declared that there was no potentate with
whom he would rather be at one than Christian IV: 'the
only obstacle being that he is my neighbour'.

For the Swedish State the new war was a financial gamble.
Various expedients had been tried during the last few years
to finance the large-scale wars, including the experiment,
which had already been made elsewhere on the Continent,
of farming out taxes to rich capitalists; this relieved the
crown of the laborious task of collecting dues paid in kind,
and yielded ready money for the upkeep of the army. This
need for ready money also led to the sale of crown lands, in
the place of money wages, for cash or donation. Taxes in kind
had served their purpose under the rural economy of Gustav
Vasa's regime, but recent developments demanded ready
money and a money economy. The government consequently
favoured a comprehensive system of indirect taxation,
including customs duties, internal tolls, and dues on manufactures and mines, which were believed to be the securest
sources of income. The tolls from Livonia and Prussia were
thus deliberately treated as spoils of war, and the government
developed a warm interest in the towns and their commerce.
Finally, the Swedish copper trade was diligently fostered.
Large quantities of the metal were coined in order to diminish
supply and maintain a high price for it on the European
export market, and the copper-producing area of Sieben-
bürgen was requested to guarantee Sweden an effective copper

monopoly in Europe, a special company being set up for this purpose. A lesser, but still perceptible, contribution was made to the war effort by timber and tar, of which the latter was third only to iron and copper among Sweden's exports.

During this period Dutch capital and Dutch skill were playing an increasingly important part in Sweden. Further improvements had been introduced by Walloon smiths into the manufacture of bar-iron, and both mining in general and the iron industries in particular were assuming larger and more modern organization. In all this the leading pioneer was the Dutchman Louis de Geer, who was to become one of the chief personalities of Sweden's period of greatness. It was thanks to the iron-works run by De Geer and his colleagues in Östergötland and other provinces that the Swedish army which invaded Germany was equipped with Swedish weapons. Significantly enough, the armament industry was the first large-scale industry to be developed in Sweden.

This, then, constituted the economic background to Sweden's participation in the German war. Having completed his military preparations on an extensive scale, Gustavus Adolphus decided, after much deliberation and on the basis of his earlier experiences, to make a concentrated attack on the mouth of the Oder. Shortly after midsummer 1630 his troops landed on the island of Usedom off the Pomeranian coast. Stralsund had been a sure ally since 1628, and moreover the manœuvre was happily timed. During the first critical months of the campaign there was a split in the Catholic camp, and in the late summer Wallenstein was forced to resign from his command. Slowly but surely Gustavus Adolphus began to occupy the line of the Oder. Diplomacy went hand in hand with military progress; an alliance with Pomerania was effected in July, and in January 1631 an important treaty was made with France at Bärwalde, by which French subsidies were guaranteed to the Swedish King. The main achievement on the part of the enemy was the storming of the Protestant town of Magdeburg in May 1631 ; but this was neutralized shortly afterwards by Gustavus Adolphus's pact with the Elector of Brandenburg, enabling him to advance his front over the Havel line towards the Elbe. Having reached Werben he succeeded in keeping at bay the famous Catholic general, Tilly, while Swedish troops penetrated to the far north-west of Germany. Finally, the Swedish King entered into an alliance with the Elector of Saxony. For long this powerful Protestant prince had prudently held his hand ; now, however, faced with an Imperial ultimatum, he had to seek support where best he could. His army joined forces with that of Gustavus Adolphus in September 1631, and together they marched on Leipzig, which had shortly before been taken by Tilly. A crisis had been reached.

Gustavus Adolphus's army consisted partly of Swedish regiments and partly of mercenary troops, mainly German and Scottish. Even professional soldiers flocked to join him, despite the strict discipline he maintained among his men, whose high standards began to arouse universal admiration. During the preceding months they had been drilled in an art of warfare evolved by the King himself. His army at this point numbered about 23,000 men ; the Saxon army comprised 17,000, while Tilly's forces have been estimated at about 32,000 strong. It was the first time that the King's new military organization and tactics, developed during the Polish campaigns but as yet unfamiliar in Central Europe, were to be tried out in full force against the recognized methods of the old school of warfare ; and his carefully trained formations, built for flexibility, were drawn up facing Tilly's compact squares of well-tried pikemen and musketeers, with their enormous potentiality for frontal attack.

On 7th September the Battle of Breitenfeld took place. The greater part of the Elector's army was soon borne down and dispersed by the tremendous onrush of Tilly's foot-soldiers, and for a moment the battle seemed over. But the combination of infantry and artillery, cavalry and musketeers, and the carefully drilled firepower in combat and bold generalship of the Swedish army turned defeat into an overwhelming victory: within six hours Tilly's army was destroyed. All Europe marvelled at the result. An account of the contrast between the opposing parties is given in a letter from one of the King's diplomats. The Swedes and their horses had appeared ragged, dirty, and of little account beside the doughty Germans and their proudly caparisoned steeds. But, continues the writer, who is himself inspired by the dawning consciousness of Sweden's new-won glory, their past victories in the Baltic had given them strength to attack and enabled them to stand unmoved, like a wall, against the assaults of the enemy.

After the victory at Breitenfeld Gustavus Adolphus's plans, both military and political, became even more ambitious in scope. They were now directed towards central and southern Germany. There the cause of the Protestant princes seemed secure; and, what was more, the German people had met in the Swedish King a new type of war-lord. Gustavus Adolphus had acquired a wider vision and fresh tolerance since his attacks on Sigismund and the Jesuits at the Örebro *Riksdag*, and he soon became an almost mythical figure in Germany, where the sufferings of the long war generated in politics apocalyptic moods of fear and hope. He was regarded as the incarnation of the 'Lion of the North' long prophesied by the seers and astrologers, who was to bring salvation from afar; and this view was strengthened by the moral qualities and discipline of his army. Similar conceptions were also spread by means of leaflets and corantos – as, for example, *The Swedish Intelligencer*, published in London in the 1630's. Even the enemy could not fail to appreciate the King's popularity, and Wallenstein had earlier summed up the general opinion when he said that the people had awaited Gustavus Adolphus as 'the Jews their Messiah'.

# THE
# SWEDISH
# INTELLIGENCER.

*The Third Part.*

*VVHEREIN,*

## OVT OF THE TRVEST

and choyſeſt Informations, are the famous
*Actions of that Warlike Prince Histo-*
rically led along; from the *Norimberg Leaguer,*
unto the day of his death, at the *Victory* of
*Lutzen.* With the Election of the young
Queene of *Sweden:* and the Diet of *Heilbrun.*

### The times and places of every Action,
being ſo ſufficiently obſerved and deſcribed;
that the Reader may finde both *Truth*
and *Reaſon* in it.

Vnto which is added

*The Fourth Part.*

*VVHEREIN,*

The chiefeſt of thoſe Military Actions of other *Swediſh
Generalls,* be related: wherein the King himſelfe, was
not perſonally with the Army.

*LONDON,*
Printed by *I. L.* for *Nath: Butter* and *Nicholas Bourne.*
1 6 3 3.

Meanwhile, the King proceeded from Breitenfeld through
Thüringen to the junction of the Main and the Rhine, with
a view to carrying out an ambitious military manœuvre
against Tilly's forces. It also had results of a political nature,
however. In the winter of 1631–2 Gustavus Adolphus was
holding court in Frankfurt and Mainz surrounded by con-

tinental princes and diplomats. In the spring of 1632 he pushed into southern Germany; entered the august Protestant town of Nuremburg in March, forced the crossing of the Lech after a successful bout with Tilly's troops in April, and marched on Munich in May. These almost incredible advances helped to make possible the plan, which had already been conceived, of a Protestant alliance under Swedish leadership. But the King's position, too, had its obvious weaknesses. In 1631–2 he was commanding six different armies, and the waging of war on so many scattered fronts was proving a heavy strain on his resources. Moreover, Richelieu became increasingly uneasy as the Swedish forces approached the frontiers of France and dominated the southern German provinces, which she had regarded as her special sphere of interest. Meanwhile Wallenstein was again given full powers as Imperial commander-in-chief, and had soon raised a strong army; and Gustavus Adolphus's long line of successes was broken in an encounter with the Imperial troops at Nuremburg in 1632, when he failed to drive them from their strongly fortified position.

Despite the many potential dangers involved, however, Gustavus Adolphus was still in a strong position. He had absolute command of the forces in all the allied countries, he controlled the Baltic coast, and could claim compensation for the expenses of the war and terms which would safeguard the future. His ideas were vast in scope, but his lively imagination was kept within bounds by his shrewd sense of reality. Should he march against the hereditary lands of the Empire, the core of the Emperor's power? Should he organize a *Corpus Evangelicorum* – a permanent Protestant alliance under Swedish protection? It was even suggested that his goal was the Imperial Crown. We cannot be certain; we only know that his mind was never at rest, and that he was apparently able to adapt to circumstances, as they arose, the picture which he had formed by intuition of the problems involved.

At all events, he did not follow up his original intention of proceeding from southern Germany against Austria. Word came that Wallenstein had marched into Saxony, and Gustavus turned in the same direction. On 6th November, a misty autumn day, the two generals met at Lützen, not far from Breitenfeld, and Gustavus Adolphus threw his forces against Wallenstein's well-entrenched position. The fight was prolonged, for Wallenstein had learnt much from his adversary, but indecisive. Nevertheless the German general withdrew from Saxony immediately afterwards, thereby granting Sweden her immediate aim.

Though there were heavy losses on both sides, it was the Swedes who suffered by far the worst blow. For Gustavus Adolphus had fallen in a cavalry engagement at an early stage of the battle. His loss was irreparable, and the death of the King plainly reveals how fragile was the basis of the Swedish policy of expansion. After Lützen it was impossible to foresee whether Sweden would attempt to retire from the fray as soon as possible, or whether she would hold out until she had received some tangible 'satisfaction'. In any case, the war plans would have to be adjusted to the new situation, and much would depend on the generals and diplomats on whom responsibility now rested. But the compelling figure who had wielded both political and military authority had gone, and there was no one to replace him. One of the many professional soldiers from abroad who had flocked to his colours, a Scottish officer called Robert Monro, wrote many years afterwards: 'Such a Generall would I gladly serve; but such a Generall I shall hardly see; whose custome was: to bee the first and last in danger himselfe, gayning his officers' love, in being the companion both of their labours and dangers.' And this appreciation of a unique personality might well have been shared not only by the soldiers of the dead King, but also by all those who had come into contact with him in all the functions of the monarchy.

# XVIII

# Axel Oxenstierna and the Council of Regency
## 1632-1648

When Gustavus Adolphus fell at Lützen his only child, Christina, was six years old, and there were no precise directions as to what form the government should take during her minority. The Chancellor, Axel Oxenstierna, was in Germany, where he was able to assume leadership; while in Sweden the Council temporarily took over control and a *Riksdag* was convened for February 1633.

Various plans were put forward for the minority government, but the one finally adopted was that of Oxenstierna and his supporters. The Regency was to comprise the heads of the five main administrative departments – the colleges which had been instituted by Gustavus Adolphus some years earlier and which included the High Court, the Chancery, and the College of War, the Admiralty and the Treasury.[1] The office of Marshal was already held by Jakob de la Gardie, and that of Admiral of the Realm by Karl Karlsson Gyllenhielm; but two of the other main offices still remained to be filled by the Council. The result of the election was very significant. The Chancellor's brother, Gabriel Gustavsson Oxenstierna, became the Lord High Steward, presiding over the High Court and invested with the old title of *Drots*, and his cousin, Gabriel Bengtsson Oxenstierna, became Lord High Treasurer; this supremacy on the part of one family,

---

[1] It may be of interest to note that during the period of organization of the 1620's a sixth college was planned for education and social services (schools, asylums, houses of correction, and orphanages). An important institution appeared in 1637 with the Mining College, whereby mine administration was removed from the Treasury.

unparalleled since the Middle Ages, enabled the Chancellor to carry out his own policy, in which he revealed a combination, characteristic of him, of obstinacy and flexibility.

Shortly after the death of Gustavus Adolphus, Axel Oxenstierna had sent home a proposed constitution which was marked by both bureaucratic and oligarchical features; for although it was based on the late King's administrative practice it also systematized the rule of the higher aristocracy which had been established when the Council took over at the King's death. This proposal was put forward at the 1634 *Riksdag*; however, its reception in some quarters proved that government by the aristocracy would not be universally welcomed. But for lack of leaders the opponents of the nobles in the Council, and particularly of the Oxenstierna family, were unable to organize any effective resistance, and the proposal went through.

The balance of power now favoured the aristocracy. The six-year-old Queen possessed no disinterested champion, and the royalists among her kinsfolk – foremost among whom was her uncle by marriage, the Count Palatine Johan Casimir – were helpless against the all-powerful Axel Oxenstierna. As in 1611, the victory did not involve any violent struggle but was contrived in a rational manner and in extremely propitious circumstances by a most able statesman.

During the last two decades the economic and social standing of the nobles had been greatly enhanced, largely as a result of the extensive privileges which had been granted by Gustavus Adolphus. Land in the village adjoining the manor was exempt from taxes and services to the crown, and that within a Swedish mile of the manor was immune from the special taxation and conscription which had been imposed more recently. The remaining tenants paid half the crown taxes and a similar proportion of the other obligations of the 'free' tax peasant. It should be mentioned here that most of the estates, even then, consisted of homesteads farmed by peasant tenants in different parts of the country. It was not until later in the seventeenth century that the large estates began to take on a more concentrated form; then, however, they reached considerable proportions. The nobles, moreover, in addition monopolized the most important government offices, and possessed the right to be tried only by their peers. This Estate had also increased numerically during the years of Sweden's expansion abroad and had rapidly absorbed all the most prominent soldiers, diplomats, and civil servants; while the crown was increasingly compelled, by its dwindling resources of ready money, to sell or donate its lands and incomes. A significant illustration of the enormous power and prosperity of the nobles during this period is provided by the monuments they have left behind. Whereas the outstanding buildings of the sixteenth century were the royal castles and strongholds of the Vasas, those of the seventeenth century were the palatial mansions erected by the aristocracy. And the House of the Nobility (*Riddarhuset*), with its motto *Arte et Marte*, which was built in the middle of the century, is a collective memorial to the Estate's golden age.

These lords frequently asserted, with quite genuine intent, that their privileges should not be allowed to stand in the way of the common good. Nevertheless they were little inclined to relinquish them when in fact they began to prove burdensome both to the country as a whole and to other social groups. For the aristocracy felt that they richly deserved their privileges; and certainly the seventeenth-century nobility was an unusually distinguished body of men – able, loyal, and energetic – thanks partly to the ancient traditions of the old-established families and partly to the lack of prejudice with which they received able 'new' men into their ranks. During this period the House of Nobility acquired much fresh and vigorous blood from the Baltic provinces (Wrangel), Germany (Königsmarck), Scotland (Hamilton, Douglas), Holland (De Geer), and – most of all, perhaps – from less well-born families in Sweden (Skytte, Adler Salvius).

Oxenstierna's primary aim was to bring the German war to an end in such a manner as to compensate Sweden for her losses and exertions. It was a very delicate situation which would require all his remarkable diplomatic skill. Following up in part one of Gustavus Adolphus's plans, he managed in 1633 to form an alliance between Sweden and the German Protestant States at Heilbronn. Shortly afterwards, however, Sweden suffered a disastrous setback, when during the later summer of 1634 her troops were decisively defeated at the Battle of Nördlingen. The truce with Poland expired in the following year, and in order to prevent renewed hostilities on this front Sweden was forced to renounce her Prussian customs duties, which since 1629 had been such a valuable asset to the finances of the State. Her allies, too, were becoming restive, and relations with France were particularly strained; while at home many people were clamouring for a speedy peace at any price. But the Chancellor did not, as he put it, intend to 'worm his country out of the war at the cost of reputation, respect, interest, friendship, and everything else'. In the summer of 1636 he returned to Sweden, and set about vigorously putting into effect his political programme. In the autumn of the same year the Swedish general Johan Banér won an unexpected victory at Wittstock, in Brandenburg, over the Emperor and the Elector of Saxony, who had deserted the Swedish alliance in 1635. Banér's bold tactics revealed him as a military genius, and it was now clear that Gustavus Adolphus had had time to train pupils who in some respects outclassed even their master. Pomerania was now safe in Swedish hands and Swedish forces were still active in other parts of Germany; and although Banér himself died shortly after Wittstock, a highly gifted successor was found in Lennart Torstenson, who had commanded the artillery at Breitenfeld.

The Swedish troops who were fighting in Germany at this time differed in many respects from those of Gustavus Adolphus. There is a story dating from the early 1630's which

27. Queen Christina. Painting by S. Bourdon, 1653.

28. Queen Christina's abdication.
Detail of engraving by W. Swidde.

describes how the Swedish soldiers billeted in enemy country used to take the host and hostess by the hand and thank them cordially for their hospitality. Since then, the behaviour of the Swedish veterans and foreign mercenaries, of which the army was now composed, had become less genteel. The rigid discipline imposed by Gustavus Adolphus had collapsed and there was now little difference in this respect between the various armies. Lennart Torstenson's command was the only one which in any way resembled that of Gustavus Adolphus, and his brilliant victories at Breitenfeld in 1642 and Jankow in 1645 resounded throughout Europe. He was also a force in domestic politics, where he seems to have counterbalanced to some extent the dominating influence of the Oxenstierna party.

One of Torstenson's more important tasks, however, was to implement a government decision which was highly typical of Oxenstierna's policy: the war against Denmark in 1643–5. The episode plainly indicated the nature of the relations which then existed between the two countries. Mutual distrust had been fostered by their various quarrels since the Middle Ages and the sixteenth century, and apart from a short-lived defensive union, almost entirely formal in character, their common interests during the 1620's had done nothing to bring them together. Moreover, their hostility had been intensified during the latter years of the Thirty Years War. Sweden's Baltic possessions, together with the territories she occupied in Germany, constituted a latent challenge to Denmark's control of the Sound tolls, as did the close diplomatic and economic relations between Sweden and Holland. The fact that Holland was increasing her Baltic trade and Sweden expanding her rule over the Baltic coastlands made both countries more sensitive to the imposition of the Sound tolls. Moreover, since the time of Gustav Vasa Sweden had always resented Denmark's possession of what are now the southern provinces of Sweden, since this, including as it did the control of the roads from southern

14

Sweden, gave the Danes the opportunity of 'taking the fat from the land' – to use Oxenstierna's expression. In principle, the situation was the same as it had been in the middle of the sixteenth century – with the one important difference, however, that Sweden's expansion to the south-east and the south now encroached on the Danish sphere of influence which extended from Copenhagen through Skåne and the islands of Gotland and Ösel.

The Swedish Council suspected Denmark of harbouring the most evil intentions, and in the summer of 1643 the decision was taken to attack her. Sweden's position in Germany gave admirable opportunity for an assault from the south, the only direction from which Christian IV's cherished fleet could not protect his country. This project, which was a natural consequence of Sweden's Baltic policy and had actually been mooted during the reign of Gustavus Adolphus, would at last, by rendering valueless the girdle of frontier fortifications in Skåne, break Denmark's encirclement of Sweden.

At the direction of the Council, Lennart Torstenson led his army northwards from his position in Moravia in the autumn of 1643 and entered Jutland in the New Year. Soon afterwards Skåne and Halland were attacked and ravaged by Gustav Horn, Oxenstierna's son-in-law, with the effective co-operation of a fleet which had been privately raised in Holland by Louis de Geer for Sweden's benefit. Sweden's victory on this occasion marks a turning-point in an eighty-year struggle for supremacy in the Baltic. After prolonged haggling, peace was signed at Brömsebo in 1645; by the cession of Gotland and Ösel Denmark was deprived of her naval bases in the eastern Baltic, and in addition she was forced to withdraw from Halland for a period of thirty years, thereby exposing a significant breach in her control of Swedish trade routes. Conversely, Sweden became even more powerful in the Baltic; her access to western Europe through Halland was once more assured and she also acquired the Norwegian frontier provinces of Jämtland and Härjedalen.

Meanwhile, Queen Christina had come of age and assumed control of the government. Her position was not an easy one. Could she, an eighteen-year-old girl, assert the power of the monarchy against the higher aristocracy – fresh from ten years' successful rule – at the very time when kings were threatened in France by the Fronde and in England by the Civil War? The situation bears a striking and significant similarity with the state of affairs at her father's accession.

One thing was certain: Christina was a woman of exceptional ability. When she was only fourteen Axel Oxenstierna had expressed to the assembled Council his gratification that 'Her Majesty was not like a female, but courageous and with a good understanding, so that if she escape corruption she will answer every hope.' These words were not intended as a slight on womankind as such – the Chancellor was merely remarking, in the spirit of his time, on the young Princess's unusual character. Her upbringing, too, had followed unusual lines, for in accordance with her father's wish she had received the same education as a male heir would have done. From a very early age she proved a most receptive pupil and imbibed an enormous extent and variety of knowledge under the guidance of the theologian Johannes Matthiae. She was one of the first Swedish women to receive a wholly academic education; in her own words, she had 'an immoderate desire to know all', and she devoured theology, classical languages and literature, politics and modern languages with the same ease and boundless enthusiasm. But not only was she receptive; she also possessed without question a highly independent, scholarly mind of her own.

Her court soon became a centre for scholars and artists, and at the age of twenty she entered into correspondence with the French philosopher Descartes. At the same time she continued her studies of the writings of the Church Fathers and classical philosophers, invariably finding enormous

pleasure in the stiffest and most intricate problems. It has
been said of Christina that she 'was in her way like a finely
attuned instrument, that senses and registers even the slightest
disturbances in the atmosphere. None of the ideological currents of the seventeenth century passed her by. She not only
took an interest in the religious problems, but also made herself mistress of the philosophical, ethical, and – not least –
artistic trends of the time.' But intellectual pursuits did not
absorb all her time. It had never been her intention to neglect
her true vocation, that of a ruling sovereign, and she early
began to prepare herself for it. Among other things she
zealously attended the deliberations of the Council, and she
herself has described her reaction to the political teaching of
the Chancellor: 'There was no book, no sport, no entertain-
ment, that I have not gladly left to listen to him.' Observers
were struck by her interest in and grasp of Council business,
and the French envoy Chanut, who later became one of the
Queen's closest friends, declared that she completely gave
herself up to 'the trade of an old statesman or philosopher'.

The young Queen was fully determined not to allow the
nobles to play fast and loose with the monarchy. But she was
an inexperienced girl, and moreover the monarchy lacked a
direct heir – for under no circumstances would the Council
admit that Gustavus Adolphus's nephews (sons of the Count
Palatine Johan Casimir) had a claim to the Swedish throne.
It therefore looked as though Christina's most obvious
course, in the interests of the monarchy and dynasty, was to
marry, and a most eligible candidate was forthcoming in the
person of her cousin Charles, Johan Casimir's oldest son. But
although they had been fond of one another as children, any
thought of her cousin was soon overshadowed in the Queen's
mind by politics, the state of the country, and intellectual
pursuits; marriage on purely political grounds was unthink-
able to a woman of her proud and sensitive temperament.
She herself had other plans for ensuring the succession and
the hereditary monarchy, and these she would put into effect

when she felt more sure of her own position. However, in 1648, the fourth year of her majority and the last year of the Thirty Years War, she managed to achieve the appointment of Charles as Commander-in-Chief of the Swedish Army. For some years the Oxenstierna party had been opposed to the young man, even if only in secret, and Christina's successful championship of her cousin proved that now, after four years, she was de facto the reigning Queen.

Christina's desire to reach a speedy peace was in line with her personal aims. Nor was she alone in this wish, for the war told heavily on her subjects. Despite the large proportion of mercenary troops in the army and the fact that the latter subsisted largely on German resources, conscription was a heavy burden. And in addition there were the taxes. These could just be tolerated when the harvest was good; but in view of the primitive methods of cultivation and the lack of drainage nothing could stave off crop failures, and the lean years brought great distress. Now and again the peasants would openly voice their complaints in the *Riksdag* and there was no longer a Gustavus Adolphus to cajole them into suffering in a good cause. Negotiations had long been in progress in the Westphalian towns of Osnabruck and Münster, however, and peace was at last in sight. Sweden's position had been improved by Torstenson's victories in the first half of the 1640's, and his successor Karl Gustav Wrangel, together with the famous French general Turenne, had waged a number of successful campaigns in southern Germany. Furthermore, during the last year of the war the Swedish general Königsmarck attacked and looted the part of Prague on the left bank of the river Moldau, which contained, among other great palaces, the famous castle, Hradschin. The rich booty included a priceless manuscript of an old Gothic translation of the Bible – the so-called Silver Bible now in Uppsala University Library – and the statues which now stand in the park of Drottningholm Palace outside Stockholm. The episode is typical, in more ways than one, of the kind of warfare which was carried on during the final phase of the great conflict; indeed, the war booty, both literary and artistic, of the Age of Greatness gradually assumed considerable proportions. But genuine cultural progress had also been made during the war years. In 1640 Finland acquired her own university in Åbo, 'to inspire book learning and other honest living', and a university had been founded at Dorpat in 1632. These disturbed times were also noted for the songs of Lars Wivallius and for the early writings of Georg Stiernhielm, 'the Father of Swedish literature'.

In October 1648 the peace which had so long been desired became a reality; and among the various combatants who claimed compensation from the territories of the German Empire, Sweden came off extremely well. She obtained a large area of Pomerania along the lower course of the Oder, giving her control of valuable river routes to the Baltic. She also received the town of Wismar not far from Lübeck, and was successful in direct competition with Denmark in gaining the sees of Bremen and Verden, both of which had been held by Denmark's future King Frederick III. Thus, although the final results of the Thirty Years War were not those envisaged by Gustavus Adolphus, Sweden benefited both economically and politically. Her Baltic Empire was extended, and an additional and important river mouth had come under her control and others had been brought within her sphere of interest; and from her new positions south-west of Holstein she would be able to exert a marked influence on the power which still held all the inlets to the Baltic, namely Denmark. When, three years later, Axel Oxenstierna proposed to establish a new government department for commerce and related subjects, it was from these great waterways that he illustrated Sweden's achievements during the seventeenth century:

The rivers of the Baltic, then the noblest of the other rivers running through Sweden and her subordinate provinces – these being, besides the rivers of the old kingdom the Neva, the Narva, the Dvina and the Oder, together with the Elbe and the Weser in Germany. Likewise the exceeding rare and precious harbours mainly in the Baltic, and in the North Sea and the Kattegat, asking only wise exploitation to benefit and avail the inhabitants of Sweden.

Only two of the less favourable aspects of the peace will be mentioned at this point. Hitherto Holland had supported Sweden in the struggle for mastery of the Baltic – *dominium maris Baltici*; now that Sweden was so powerful this commercial nation deemed it more prudent to maintain the balance in the Baltic by transferring her support to Denmark, and an alliance between those two countries was made in 1649. Secondly, Sweden's new German possessions had rendered her part of the Holy Roman Empire, and since she was in addition one of the guarantors of the peace she inevitably became involved in complicated political problems outside her natural sphere. And incidentally her control of the Oder estuary was regarded by Brandenburg with anything but a friendly eye.

# XIX

# Problems of Peace and War
## 1648-1657

Thus the war had added to Sweden's territories and brought wealth, honour, and political influence to at least one social class, the nobility. The Chancellor, Axel Oxenstierna, had wholeheartedly espoused the war aims and had bent all his great diplomatic gifts to achieving them. There was, however, another side to the picture.

The burden of taxation was heavy; the increased privileges of the nobility prejudiced the interests of other classes, while its landed wealth was enriched by generous gifts from the crown and the alienation of crown land both by sale and as security for loans. This was not so much the work of the Council of Regency, whose hands had been tied in the matter, as of the Queen, whose inability to deal with the general situation was intensified by her lack of any real grasp of financial problems. The new landed estates tended to take on a more integral form as a result of the assimilation of adjacent peasant holdings, since those near the manor inhabited by the noble enjoyed special immunity from taxation.

Since the noble landowner had considerable power over the peasant tenants (*frälse* or 'free' peasants) on the land he had inherited, they were naturally dependent on him for their welfare; Axel Oxenstierna, for example, seems to have been a humane and considerate master. But not all lords were so mild; and if the crown donated, pawned, or sold the taxes of any one district to a noble, it was generally assumed that the recipient acquired, in addition to the right to collect these taxes in the same way as he collected those of his own peasants, full sovereignty over the hitherto free peasants who resided there. This assumption was inherent in the famous words of Per Brahe, who succeeded Axel Oxenstierna's brother as *Drots*: 'We are all subjects of the crown, the peasants indirectly, and we directly.' This purely feudal conception also affected the attitude adopted towards the old peasant class, which had formerly been wholly free from bondage, paying its taxes to the crown and owning its own lands, and its numbers were steadily diminished by the crown's policy of sale and donation. By the middle of the seventeenth century the crown and the tax peasants together owned only 28 per cent. of the country's land; most of the rest belonged to the nobles. It must be stressed that no form of serfdom resulted from this development; nevertheless the germ was there, strengthened both by the information which Swedish nobles had acquired abroad about the condition of the European peasant, and by the ideas which naturalized foreign noblemen had brought into the country.

The Swedish peasantry, however, had more chances for asserting their independence than their European fellows. One of their main sources of strength lay in their right to self-government, which, though admittedly limited, was a time-honoured and accepted custom according to the legal tradition of the countryside. The village community had many interests in common with the parish as a whole and these were dealt with at meetings conducted by the village alderman. Such parochial business had been greatly reduced by the extensive sequestration of Church property, but during the seventeenth century the parishes regained some of their importance under the aegis of the established Lutheran Church. The vestry meeting (*sockenstämma*) was empowered to deal with disorderly elements in the parish. The rights of the Swedish peasant were also upheld by the old-established legal custom which enabled him to take his grievance to court, on the firm principle that both rich and poor are equally entitled to their rights – as Queen Christina expressed it. It was, perhaps, a different matter when it came to holding his own against nobles who held the judicial office as well as controlling the land, or when a jury had to oppose the hundred judge appointed by the King; but at all events the principle was there. Finally, the mainstay of both self-government and law was the *Riksdag*, in which the peasants were represented by their own Estate, a situation unique in contemporary Europe. Moreover the *Riksdag* had retained much of the influence it had acquired at the beginning of the century, despite the shifting balance of power between nobility and crown. Gustavus Adolphus had been careful to accord the Estates their due standing, and the Council of Regency had sometimes found them distinctly unamenable. All important matters were placed either before them or before a Secret Committee of nobles, clergy, and burgesses. Through the *Riksdag* the people retained their traditional right to tax themselves, despite all the demands of the crown, and the peasants had a frequent voice in the matter – though it should be noted that only the tax peasants who were wholly free were represented in this fourth Estate. Thus the *Riksdag* could preserve its influence by granting taxes for a certain fixed period only – usually two years; and it also had a certain initiative in the traditional and recognized right to lodge with the government those petitions which incorporated the grievances of the people. But, with all these guarantees, there was developing a serious threat to the independence and freedom of the peasant's Estate.

The peasants had already protested against the abuses resulting from the alienation of crown land long before the end of the war, and particularly at the *Riksdag* of 1644, when they demanded that the crown should resume the estates which had been sold to the nobles. Now that peace had relieved the tension in the country, all these grievances began to be expressed with redoubled force, and the young Queen saw that the split between the different social classes might well be exploited for her own political ends.

In 1649 Christina proposed to the *Riksdag* that her cousin Charles should be appointed as the heir to the throne. This would on the one hand ensure hereditary succession and safeguard the monarchy and, on the other, impair the conditions which favoured the present political supremacy of the nobles. The proposal was violently opposed by the members of the Council, who were beginning to realize the Queen's intentions, and even by some of the representatives of the four Estates. Nevertheless Christina managed to win over not only the clergy and burgesses, who were traditionally royalist in attitude and behaviour, but also several of the nobles. Charles was thus provisionally acknowledged heir to the throne in the event of Christina's dying without issue. This brought the Queen considerably nearer her goal, and now that her cousin's position was assured she could lay aside for the moment the open suspicion – accentuated during the peace negotiations with Germany – with which she had come to regard the Oxenstierna faction. Soon afterwards she again raised the question of the succession, however, and managed for the second time to win the support of the *Riksdag* by the device earlier employed by both Charles IX and Eric XIV – the exploitation of the antipathy between the various Estates.

This culminated in a violent encounter at the 1650 *Riksdag*, one of the most remarkable assemblies in Swedish history. A series of bad harvests had fomented unrest in the country and the *Riksdag* itself was faced with a tricky situation: the miserable state of the government's finances, the effects of the extravagant gifts to the nobles, and the hostility between the unprivileged commons and the nobles on one side and the Queen and the higher aristocracy on the other. Moreover the general confusion had been intensified during the two years of peace, for it was no easy matter to disband an army of many years' standing. Sweden's forces could no longer live off former enemy territory; her numerous officers had therefore either to be paid off or appointed to suitable posts, while the troops themselves had somehow to be fitted into civilian life. Furthermore, where was Sweden to find the wherewithal with which to maintain the visible attributes of a great power? The Queen was fully aware of all these problems and their implications.

The *Riksdag* met in Stockholm at the beginning of July and it was soon clear that the unprivileged Estates were out to make trouble. The priests too met together, in the absence of the bishops, to discuss whether it was reasonable that the fruits of peace should be enjoyed only by a few individuals. The Queen intended to use these and similar complaints as a means of breaking the resistance of the nobles to her own projects, and she added fuel to the flames by informing the lower Estates that the aristocracy approved of conscription because it enabled them 'to keep the peasants under submission'. Her methods achieved quick results. Demands were put forward for the restoration of the lands and revenues which had been alienated by the crown, the attitude of the opposition hardened, while the Queen's alliance with the clergy and burgesses in particular appeared to grow stronger.

The Queen probably had no intention of taking seriously the demand for a reduction. But thanks to the split among the Estates, her position was now so strong that she had every chance of carrying her own proposal: the *unconditional* recognition of Charles as hereditary Prince of Sweden. The Council and the nobility, under pressure from the commons, had no choice but to comply; and the Queen persuaded the lower Estates to agree in return to shelve for the moment the issue of privilege, though she guaranteed in general terms her ultimate support.

Thanks to Christina's forceful – and unscrupulous – diplomacy, Charles was now the heir to the Swedish throne. He was a capable, vigorous man in his thirties, and the dynasty's prospects had not looked so promising for half a century. Nevertheless the Queen's tactics in the *Riksdag* had increased rather than assuaged the national unrest. There was still discontent among the peasants, and a Västergötland member of the Estate was heard to declare that they would like to slay every noble in the kingdom. A pretty serious rising broke out in the province of Närke which was only quelled when the leaders had been captured and broken on the wheel in Stockholm. Christina had solved the problem of the monarchy by her devices, but not that of the government's financial position; nor had she done anything to remove the threat to the freedom of the peasant Estate.

In the years immediately following the 1650 *Riksdag*, life at court was conducted, ostensibly, in the most splendid fashion. The Council had refused to allow foreign visitors to attend the funeral of Gustavus Adolphus 'lest they witness our poverty'. But the time had come when the young great power must at all costs make a good impression; and with that in view the Queen modernized the ceremonial side of the court and was constantly organizing fresh festivities and entertainments of the most brilliant kind, in which literature and music, chivalric pageants and ballets in the Continental style, were all represented, as were actors and musicians from various parts of Europe. In verse the heroic ideals of the Age of Greatness were immortalized by Georg Stiernhielm, poet and scholar, in his epic *Hercules*. The Swedish court, which had been the centre of musical life in the country ever since the time of Gustav Vasa, began to employ the services of outstanding German and Italian musicians; as well as those of well-known portrait-painters from abroad. For the first time since the reign of Eric XIV, in the middle of the sixteenth century, a genuine court life had come into being.[1]

But these conventional, fascinating diversions no more represented the Queen's real tastes than did the numerous favourites – Magnus Gabriel de la Gardie, Klas Tott, and others – who were the objects of so much gossip. Her mind was on totally different matters, and it soon became obvious to the merest spectator that something unusual was afoot.

[1] The English legate Bulstrode Whitelocke, sent by Oliver Cromwell to negotiate the Anglo-Swedish peace and trade treaty of 1654, has given in his diary a vivid description of the Queen and her circle during the last year of her reign.

In the summer of 1651 Christina hinted to the Council of her plans to abdicate, though it was not until July 1654 that she finally managed to put her intention into effect. As we have seen she was by no means the first Swedish sovereign to threaten such a move, though she was the first to carry it out.

The reasons behind this sensational decision are among the most baffling and fascinating problems in Swedish history. They will probably never be satisfactorily fathomed; the mind of the chief character was too intricate, she herself was too reserved, and the exact nature of her environment is too difficult to assess. There is little doubt, however, that Christina's decision to abdicate was closely associated with a great spiritual crisis through which she passed during her twenties.

Much later Christina herself stated that, while still a child, 'I reached conclusions which I never forgot, and which were assuredly beyond my years and my understanding.' The words have been interpreted to mean that even at that tender age she felt little drawn to Swedish orthodoxy, harsh, rigid, and combative in character. Her childhood tutor Johannes Matthiae had represented a milder and more feasible conception of religion; while the men on whom she later bestowed her friendship and admiration – the diplomat Pierre Chanut and the philosopher Descartes, both Frenchmen – exemplified Catholicism in a singularly elevated form. Whatever the other psychological factors which induced her decision, there is no doubt that Christina had become a Catholic some time before she announced her proposed abdication, but had chosen to conceal the fact.

Like a heroine of French classical tragedy, she was now torn by conflicting loyalties. According to Swedish law she could not, as a Catholic, continue to occupy the throne of Sweden, since the Örebro Statute of 1617 was still in force. She must therefore choose between her faith and her country. Her ultimate decision has often been twisted to correspond with some garbled version of her character. Many rumours were spread as to the wickedness of her life and to this day she has been presented as an abnormal character, either mentally or physically – anything to explain the outwardly inexplicable.

Be that as it may, Christina did not fail to accept the consequences of her new faith. She resigned her crown at the Uppsala *Riksdag* of 1654; and so moving was the ceremony that it was only with great difficulty that she retained her composure. None of her subjects yet knew she was a Catholic; she had so far settled it only with her own conscience and her Catholic associates. She now left Sweden for the south, taking with her a large number of valuable art treasures – possibly to make the parting easier. In due course, having been officially and with all ceremony received into the Catholic Church, she arrived in Rome – as St Birgitta had done before her. Though for many years she continued to take an interest in politics, she herself was of little concern to Sweden. There she had settled Charles on the throne. In many respects his hands were less tied than hers had been as regards all the significant issues, both domestic and foreign, and it remained to be seen whether he was qualified to solve the problems of peace.

The first year of his reign as Charles X was promising enough. Unlike Christina, he had had practical experience of administration; and his early days on sufferance under the Oxenstiernas had given him an insight into the problems of poverty. Furthermore, he came to the throne in such a fashion as would in no way handicap him by any sense of obligation to the nobles. At his first *Riksdag* in 1655, having intervened with some skill in the protracted negotiations, he succeeded in putting through a preliminary statute which secured the reduction (i.e. restoration to the crown) of 'indispensable' estates (i.e. lands of which the income was essential to the normal course of the administration). Allodial donation (property held in absolute ownership) was abolished, together with the practice by which the crown guaranteed the donation of estates at some future date. The statute also stipulated that, pending their reduction, one quarter of all noble estates should be taxed by the crown.

These proposals not only fanned into flame the old social antagonisms, but actually kindled a new one: namely, rivalry between the higher aristocracy, with its titles and large estates, and the lower nobility. Nevertheless the entire 'quarter inquest' of the 1655 statute was clearly only a temporary measure. Once more the real point at issue had been shelved, largely as a result of the intervention of more urgent questions. For Sweden's attention had been drawn to her eastern frontier by the recent acquisition by Russia of Polish territory. Eric XIV in his time had anticipated the Russians by launching an attack on Esthonia, a device which was now again to be adopted by the Swedish politicians. The King's plans revolved round the project of a new war, this time to be waged against Russia and Poland on Polish soil. It is difficult to say whether the taciturn Charles X in fact regarded a new war as the only solution for the insoluble problems of peace and whether he was committing Sweden, now a great power, to a belligerent foreign policy. It should be borne in mind, however, that he was a professional soldier and, moreover, that the struggles of the 1655 *Riksdag* presaged a state of unrest at home unless attention could be diverted from domestic problems.

Whatever his motive, Charles marched on Poland with an army which had been rapidly recruited and equipped. Like Gustavus Adolphus in Germany, he was unable to make any rigid plans of campaign; he probably altered them even more often than did Gustavus, whose imagination had been more effectively restrained by a sense of reality. For the next two years the attention of the European powers was centred on Charles's army in Poland, even though it won little sympathy. Holland, Brandenburg, Russia, the German Emperor, all plunged into the fray in Poland; the Elector of Brandenburg in particular presented himself now as a power-

29. The House of the
Nobility.

30a. Charles x.
Painting by S. Bourdon.

30b. Charles xi.
Painting by D. K. Ehrenstrahl.

ful ally, now as an opponent of Charles X. It is worthy of note that the Swedish King at this point took over the aggressive plans which Gustavus Adolphus had abandoned when he intervened in the German war. Sweden's leanings towards the east had again been plainly revealed. But it was hardly possible this time to conquer the Prussian ports: such an attempt would certainly have been opposed by both Brandenburg and Holland, of whom the latter was concerned as to the fate of her export trade in grain. These various circumstances greatly complicated Charles's Polish plans.

The fortunes of the Swedish armies were equally chequered. Bold advances and hard-pressed retreats were interspersed with manœuvres of strategic brilliance and skirmishes with levies of Polish nobles and Tartar hordes. In 1656 King Charles and the Elector together fought a magnificent battle at Warsaw, where for three days they engaged vastly superior forces; but, though they emerged victorious, they achieved nothing by their success. As time went on Charles's position grew worse in spite of his victories. The Dutch gradually transferred their sympathies to the opposite side; the Elector of Brandenburg was only waiting for the right moment to improve his position by joining Charles's enemies; the Emperor openly declared war against him; and Russia attacked Sweden's eastern frontier. Moreover, in the summer of 1657 yet another enemy presented herself: Denmark. At the moment it looked as if the war had done nothing but plunge Sweden into the worst possible plight. Yet Charles managed with unerring intuition to circumvent his difficulties in a manner which must have surprised everyone: he marched directly on Denmark. Just as his Polish plans had harked back to those of Gustavus Adolphus, so now his policy towards Denmark revealed the influence of his master Lennart Torstenson. His real strength as a soldier, however, lay in his preference for the unexpected course of action, a characteristic which was to be fully illustrated in the ensuing months.

15

# XX

# The Scandinavian Problem
## 1657-1679

In declaring war on Sweden in 1657 Denmark was influenced primarily by the recollection of her own losses in 1645, together with the opportunity afforded by Sweden's own difficulties and the prospect of help from Holland. But neither her army nor her political leaders were equal to the enterprise. Charles acted quickly and it was barely two months before he was in Holstein, subsequently capturing the stronghold of Fredriksodde and the entire province of Jutland. The Danes were gaining ground in Halland, however, and the Norwegians in Jämtland and Härjedalen; while the Swedish fleet was unable to approach the Danish islands. Moreover by this time Brandenburg had joined Sweden's enemies.

The war ended unexpectedly during the winter campaign at the beginning of 1658. To the initial delight of the Danes and the equal discomfiture of Charles, the sea froze over, thus cutting off the Swedish army from the homeland. But soon the land routes too began to be affected by the exceptional wintry conditions. It was not the first time that winter campaigns had played an important part in Scandinavian history: when the Danes had invaded Sweden in 1520 and 1567–8, for example, the cold had made a pathway over lakes and marshes which were otherwise impassable. Now it was the Swedes who benefited from the heavy frost. During the Russian war, seventy-seven years earlier, Pontus de la Gardie had risked taking several thousands of his men over the frozen Gulf of Finland from Viborg to Ingermanland. Charles and his general, Karl Gustav Wrangel, now undertook the enormous responsibility entailed by a similar decision, once the ice had been tested by Erik Dahlbergh, then a young engineer officer.

After careful preparations the Swedish army proceeded across the Little Belt to the island of Fünen, and then by way of the small islands to Zealand. The possibility of any aid

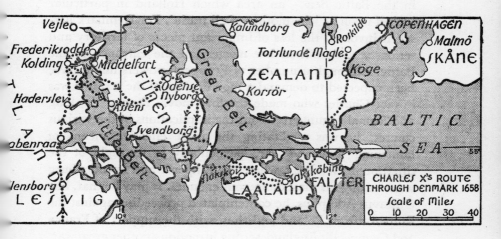

reaching Denmark had been ruled out by the heavy frost, and in the subsequent peace negotiations her representatives were forced to submit to Sweden's demands. These events gave rise to a number of classic observations, from Charles's words when he heard that the ice would bear: 'Now, brother Frederick, we will talk in plain Swedish!' to the sigh of the Danish councillor at the signing of the peace in Roskilde: 'Alas, that I ever learnt to write!'

As a result of the negotiations Sweden gained the Scanian provinces and, in addition, the island of Bornholm, Bohuslän, and the province of Trondhjem in Norway. These acquisitions rounded off her Baltic empire and facilitated access to her possessions in Germany. They also gave her a share in the control of the entrance to the Baltic, extended her Atlantic coast-line, and provided strategic bases in the middle of the Baltic Sea (Bornholm) and in the northern portion of the

Danish realm (Trondhjem). Moreover, since free independence was granted to Charles's father-in-law, Duke Frederick of Holstein-Gottorp, Sweden secured yet another base in Denmark's rear; thus it was now Denmark's turn to fear encirclement. The peace also affected English and Dutch trade in the Baltic Sea – an area which Holland in particular looked upon as 'the mother of all trade'. For Denmark herself it involved the loss of important pieces of territory and seriously undermined her mastery of the entrance to the Baltic. Although a number of European powers might have been expected to demand a modification of the terms it was in fact Charles who made the first move. During the long and formal arguments about the implications of the various clauses, he was meditating the most effective means of launching a second war, particularly in the light of the situation in Germany, where the Emperor and Brandenburg were among his most dangerous enemies. It may be that, like Gustavus Adolphus, he contemplated proceeding against the Emperor from Poland and thus, with the support of France and Cromwell's England, setting in motion another great war.

One of the advantages which Sweden had gained from the recent war lay in the potentialities of her share in the control of the entrance to the Baltic. But to exercise it effectively she needed the co-operation of Denmark and Charles had tried to ensure this by suggesting that the two Scandinavian powers should refuse access to the Baltic to all enemy warships. The chief 'enemy' he had in mind was, of course, Holland; the question was whether Denmark could be induced to sacrifice her friendship with the Dutch. Despite his recent victory, Charles's position was far from easy. With Denmark and Holland as potential enemies in his rear, he could hardly march against his enemies on the Continent. Neither France nor England gave him any effective help; his alliance with Holstein-Gottorp was insubstantial; and in addition to all this there was the difficulty of maintaining the Swedish army.

In the summer of 1658 Charles was with his troops in Kiel,

whence he suddenly embarked them with the fleet. Only those in his immediate circle and a few of the Swedish councillors knew whither he was bound, and great was the astonishment when the fleet was ordered to Zealand. During the voyage the King explained to the French envoy Terlon, who was also on board, that he 'did not intend committing a lunacy by halves', and declared his intention of uniting the Danish lands with his own. The Frenchman protested that the King's reputation would suffer if he violated a treaty which had been signed and ratified. But Charles X, with his usual active imagination, was now beginning to visualize that united Scandinavian kingdom of which Christian II of Denmark had dreamed nearly a century and a half earlier. Norway should have a Swedish Governor, Denmark should be divided into four provincial governments, Copenhagen should be razed to the ground, and Malmö become the main Swedish naval base. Scandinavia in fact was to be transformed into a powerful kingdom under Swedish rule. In view of Charles X's character it was only to be expected that he would thus respond to the deep-rooted tradition of Swedish national aggrandisement.

The course of the second Danish war can be briefly summarized. Copenhagen was besieged and, at the end of October, the Dutch fleet hastened to the assistance of Denmark, and penetrated the defence of the Swedish navy in the north of the Sound, despite Charles's control of the castle of Kronborg. Sweden now suffered a series of rapid setbacks, what with risings on Bornholm and in Skåne, the seizure of Jutland by Polish, Imperial, and Brandenburg troops, and the failure to storm Copenhagen, whose successful resistance was immortalized in Frederick III's moving adaptation of Job's words: 'I shall die in my nest.' Finally, the Swedish troops were decisively beaten on Fünen, and the Dutch fleet and the allied forces thus held Charles in a pincer grip.

Unpredictable to the end, the King, for all his phenomenal energy, was taken ill during the *Riksdag* which had had to be summoned in Gothenburg in 1660 to discuss the forthcoming peace; and within a few weeks he was dead. Though the Roskilde terms were revised in the treaty which followed, Sweden was not too harshly treated; she was only required to cede Bornholm and Trondhjem to Denmark and obtained equally moderate terms from her other enemies. Meanwhile for the third time in this century a minor was next in succession to the throne, and again the rival advocates of monarchical and constitutional principles had to cope with the vexed problems of a minority. In his will Charles X had tried to establish the dynasty's power by appointing as members of the Regency his wife, Hedvig Eleonora of the house of Holstein-Gottorp, and, in the capacity of commander of the army, his brother Adolf Johan. This did not suit either the nobles or the Council; they overruled the lower Estates, who were in favour of the will, and excluded Adolf Johan from the Regency government. Nevertheless the nobles in the Council of Regency did not achieve the supremacy which they had wielded in the time of Axel Oxenstierna; more control over the government was secured by the *Riksdag*, which was to meet regularly every third year and in whose history the next fifteen years were to be an important period.

This Regency, which consisted of the Council led by the five chief functionaries, included some prominent men – Magnus Gabriel de la Gardie, for example, the brilliant Chancellor. But there was no real leader to give it any coherence. Virulent party schisms were a frequent occurrence and all efforts to enquire into the working of the civil service with a view to reform were defeated by the slackness of the administration. But the difficulties confronting the government must not be underestimated. Peace was now essential for many reasons; yet Sweden's status as a great power had to be maintained. Charles X had found the solution in an aggressive foreign policy, but this was no longer possible. The finances were in a precarious state; no military leader with the necessary rank and capacity had emerged, and geographically, too, the country had its weaknesses. Moreover there were plenty of potential enemies, but few allies. The King of Denmark was in constant fear of Swedish attacks from the Scanian coast; Brandenburg was far from friendly; Holland, as a result of her shrewd diplomacy during the critical years 1656–60, had confirmed her domination of Baltic trade. (Though this had been partly counter-balanced by a great increase in Swedish shipping during the European wars in the sixties and beginning of the seventies, the relief was only temporary.) True, Sweden had ranged herself with Holland and England in 1668, but the alliance did not last. In the light of her present situation she must choose between these two nations and her old ally, France; and France, where Louis XIV was beginning to launch his policy of expansion, was considered to hold out the best prospects. In 1672, therefore, a close alliance was made between the two countries. From Sweden's point of view this was sub-sequently to turn out to have been a disastrous step; but for the moment it seemed the only possible means to end Sweden's isolation and also to obtain subsidies for the troops and garrisons which were still required to defend the out-posts of the empire. For in view of their economic interests the aristocratic members of the Council refused to contem-plate bolstering up the national finances by transferring land from the nobles to the crown.

Louis XIV's attack on Holland in 1672 proved to be the prelude to a great European war, in which Sweden became involved as a result partly of her alliance with France and partly of untoward circumstances. In 1675 Swedish troops went to the assistance of France in Brandenburg but were defeated at Fehrbellin the same year. Shortly afterwards Denmark, where the King had maintained absolute power since 1660, adopted the policy of reprisal, which was advo-cated by certain factions in the country, and declared war.

There followed what became known as the 'Scanian War' which, though marked by the violent and bloody Battle of

Lund, the siege of Malmö by the Danes and recapture of Kristianstad by the Swedes, and the various Danish victories at sea, need not be described in detail. One significant feature might be mentioned, however : a rising in Skåne against the Swedish government, prompted by the war, plainly illustrated the extent of Swedish infiltration in these southern provinces. Before crossing to Skåne with his army in the early summer of 1676, Christian V had issued a manifesto to his father's former subjects, urging them to join him. There were no experts in international law available to expound to the Scanian countryfolk the rights and wrongs of the war. But they could recognize hard facts, and few could admit that the early years of Swedish rule had been happy. It is true that they were no more heavily taxed, but certain aspects of Swedish policy had aroused alarm and disapproval. The main grievance arose from the inevitable adjustment of the customs frontiers of the province to correspond with those of Sweden proper, thereby forcing the Scanians to re-orientate their economy. Time and again the potential risks of such a situation have been revealed : the transformation of age-old patterns of culture and economic life cannot be effected at a moment's notice. There were additional grounds for discontent in the oppressive system of army billeting and in certain of the appointments which the Regency, not always wisely, had made in the local administration. In 1669–70 a far-reaching commission had been set up to enquire into these problems, but it had so far got no further than the preliminary investigations.

There was thus plenty of material for revolt at the beginning of the war, and though the rising did not turn into a general insurrection it soon assumed considerable proportions. Men of diverse character joined the rebels, whom the Swedes designated *snapphanar* – which can be approximately rendered as 'marauders'; they themselves chose the name *friskyttar* (literally free shooters). In fact they were vagabonds who put their trust in organized plundering, peasant householders from the hills and forests near the northern frontiers of the province who were tired of seeing their crops trampled underfoot by the Swedish and Danish armies; unemployed youths and deserters – a motley array with no less motley habits. Nevertheless the bands included in addition to mere robbers and looters organized battalions led by peasants or professional soldiers, some of whom are shown by the company rolls to have held the full rank of officers of the Danish King, even if they had originally been no more than sons of the soil. The men of Göinge hundred in Northern Skåne had long been renowned as gunsmiths and marksmen and they now proved of inestimable value to the Danish troops in spying out the land, laying ambushes, and generally obstructing the Swedes. Numerous episodes in their adventurous lives have been preserved in the reports of the trials undergone by the marauders after they had been captured by the Swedes, and their border feuds were also to provide themes for historical romances in the style of Sir Walter Scott.

This guerilla warfare caused the Swedish authorities considerable concern. The marauders were frequently aided by friends and relations who had remained at home in the faint hope that there would still be something left for them after the war; they also received assistance from the Danish troops – often in close collaboration, as in the case of Admiral Juel's attempt in the summer of 1678 to cut off Swedish supplies through West Blekinge. It was plain to the Swedish generals that these freebooters could only be suppressed by brute force. Various methods of coercion were tried, but the one which ultimately succeeded was evolved by the King's friend, General Johan Gyllenstierna: any parishes which housed or in any way assisted the rebels were threatened with such dire punishment that none of them was willing or courageous enough to take the risk. The rebels could therefore expect no assistance from the population; moreover the Danish troops had been repulsed and could no longer reinforce them, and they were therefore completely isolated. In order to live they

had to resort to plundering, without scruple, thereby aliena-
ting their Scanian compatriots; the situation in which they
found themselves during the last part of the war must indeed
have been desperate, and with the restoration of peace the
rising was decisively suppressed. Many of the participants
fled to Denmark; a large number profited from the Swedish
King's amnesty and returned to a regular life; while others
continued to roam the forests until they were captured.
Nevertheless, however, it should be noted that many of the
Scanians had from the outset remained loyal to Sweden.

The problems arising from the conquest of the province
were not new to the Swedish government, for at that time the
country was responsible for extensive non-Swedish areas –
Ingermanland, for example, Esthonia and Livonia, Pomerania and the other German provinces. They were mostly
administered by a governor-general, an office which was
held by prominent Swedish noblemen. This position carried
enormous authority, and there is no denying that on the
whole its functions were discharged in a manner which compared pretty favourably with the state of affairs which prevailed under similar circumstances elsewhere in Europe. For
Sweden already possessed a well-organized system of local
government which had developed on parallel lines with the
central government; and under the constitution of 1634 it
had been rounded off by the division of the country into
provinces (*län*), each administered by a governor (*lands-
hövding*), who provided a useful intermediary between the
government and the royal bailiffs. The functions of a
governor-general were largely similar to those of a governor
of a Swedish province, though the former had military duties
as well. Each, too, was expected to account for his actions in
writing, a practice which had developed during the Regency
of Christina. Important enterprises were frequently carried
out by the men who held these responsible and onerous posts.
Johan Skytte undertook a vast work of reorganization as
governor-general of Livonia from 1629, while Per Brahe

spent two fruitful periods in Finland in the same capacity – not the least of his achievements was the Åbo academy, founded in 1640.

As has been shown in the southern provinces before 1670, a bad administrator could do as much harm as a good one could do good. At this point, however, a significant change took place. Although Johan Gyllenstierna died soon after he was appointed as first governor-general, a worthy successor was found in the warrior Rutger von Ascheberg; and henceforward the provinces began to make remarkably rapid strides. The next Danish attack on Skåne in 1709 provoked no such rising as had that of the 1670's. The new generation of Scanians had become Swedish, a conversion greatly to the credit of the admirable Swedish administration during the seventeenth century, facilitated though it was by similarities of race and language. Appointments were made with particular foresight; Swedish equivalents of Danish hymns were sung in the churches and the children were taught the Swedish catechism. The disturbances which had embarrassed the government during the Regency were effectively checked, and order and obedience were widely enforced. The University of Lund – *Academia Carolina Conciliatrix* – founded in 1668, again came into its own as a stimulus to the increasing naturalization of this hitherto Danish province. Though Skåne would need another century to become wholly regenerated, her absorption into Sweden was already virtually complete by the beginning of the eighteenth century – a process of assimilation almost without parallel in European history.

Certain features of foreign policy between 1650 and 1670 also indicate that the ostensible difference between Denmark and Sweden concealed a common interest, arising primarily from the way in which their territories overlapped round the Baltic Sea. Both countries had dreamt of economic and commercial mastery of these waters, the *dominium maris Baltici*, and this ideal, based on contemporary economic doctrines, had to a large extent determined Sweden's policy of expansion. Since the days of Eric XIV, however, these hopes had never in fact been fulfilled. Holland now controlled Baltic trade; and though Dutch enterprise and Dutch capital had done much to make Sweden what she was, her rulers were beginning to distrust this commercial supremacy and the political influence it entailed.

As time went on, the situation became reminiscent of that which had existed during the Middle Ages when the economic influence of Germany led to political domination. And it produced in the minds of some Scandinavian statesmen a similar reaction in favour of a Danish-Swedish alliance. Nothing had come of it under Gustavus Adolphus or Christian IV. There seems to have been some thought of such an alliance in the interests of Scandinavian trade during the commercial war between England and Holland in 1652–64, but the proposal was no more than tentative, and was in any case curiously confused by issues of traditional rivalry. The war in 1657 had also been preceded by conciliatory overtures; but Charles X's plans for a compulsory union between Sweden, Denmark, and Norway, which echo those of Christian II, were shattered during his second Danish war. Fresh impetus was given to the idea by the prominent Danish statesman Hannibal Sehested, son-in-law of Christian IV, who wrote a political testament in the middle of the 1660's underlining the mutual advantages of a Scandinavian union. At about the same time new negotiations between Sweden and Denmark were begun, and were resumed from time to time in the following years. Thus the idea persisted, though buffeted to and fro by the vagaries of foreign policy, until its last and most remarkable version was presented immediately after the Scanian war by the Swedish statesman Johan Gyllenstierna, who had recently become Charles XI's confidential adviser.

Gyllenstierna made a large number of suggestions, of which one of the most important was the creation of a strong navy and a new Swedish naval base at Karlskrona on the Blekinge coast. He also conducted the peace negotiations in Lund in 1679 and was successful in promoting the marriage between the King and the Danish Princess Ulrica Eleonora. His aim was an ambitious one : to complete the plans cherished by Gustavus Adolphus and Charles X for expansion in Germany; as he expressed it : to make Sweden 'considerable' in Germany through the acquisition of new territories. An important precondition of this policy, of which no details are known and which can only be conjectured, was to stabilize relations with Denmark by the expedient of a Scandinavian alliance, in order to remove all danger to Sweden from this quarter. A treaty was made, but shortly afterwards, in 1680, Gyllenstierna died and the alliance perished in the new danger which was sweeping over Europe. As a result, Swedish foreign policy took a different course. The sources of disagreement with Denmark outweighed the common interests; moreover, after the treaty of 1679 Sweden had a number of more immediate problems to solve. Insistent demands were being made for a further reduction of the estates of the nobles, and the finances were in a pitiful state. The young King's powers of initiative, which had already been revealed during the Scanian war of the seventies, were henceforward to be directed towards a radical reform of the national finances by the reclamation of former crown property. This policy, which in more ways than one recalls the seizure of Church property by Gustav Vasa, was to dominate Swedish history until the end of the seventeenth century.

# XXI

# Reduction and Reorganization
## 1680-1700

During the Battle of Lund, in December 1676, the young
Swedish King Charles XI had shown great courage in the
way in which he commanded his right flank; and having put
to flight the opposite flank of the Danes he had pursued the
enemy far from the field of battle, only returning at the last
minute to save the rest of the Swedish army from a rout and
to win a decisive victory. This is, as it were, our first personal
introduction to Charles XI – a great change from the self-
conscious youth who at meetings of the Regency Council
used shyly to whisper his views into the ear of the presiding
Queen Mother. The characteristics he showed at the Battle
of Lund were boldness and impulsiveness, together with an
unflinching personal courage. Yet his later career gave these
qualities little scope : for unlike either his father or his son he
did not become a soldier, but devoted himself to administration and finance, completely ignoring all Johan Gyllenstierna's projects for expansion.

When the Estates assembled at the Stockholm *Riksdag* in
1680, the common topic of conversation among the King's
friends and the commons alike was reorganization. The
hostility between upper and lower Estates was no less bitter
than during the two previous reigns; it had again revealed
itself during the latter years of the Regency, recalling in some
of its features the atmosphere of 1650. Nor were the higher
and lower aristocracy any more reconciled to one another,
though they had temporarily sunk their differences in their
joint rejection of Charles X's will at the 1660 *Riksdag*. Even
before the Scanian war there had been evidence in the country of royalist tendencies and these had been intensified by

Charles XI's martial prowess. During the war, indeed, he
had become in the real sense a military dictator, and now his
commands took on new force from his position as supreme
head of the army. The administration of the Regency had
already been closely investigated during the war and the
findings could now be used as a weapon against the higher
aristocracy. All these factors enhanced the tension in the
atmosphere when the King met the Estates and the Council
in 1680.

As Gustav Vasa had done at the Västerås *Riksdag* in 1527
Charles described to them the low state of the government's
finances and demanded means for repairing them. He compared the country to a ship which had come safely to harbour
from adversity and peril on the high seas, but was in need of
repairs and refurbishing. The King's description provoked a
demand for an inquiry into the administration of the Regency
and he saw to it that this matter was given priority. The previous investigations were taken over by a Great Commission
of the Estates, which was also directed to pronounce judgment after the inquest had been completed.

An even more long-standing grievance was associated with
the problem of financial reform: the demand for reduction.
The peasants were the prime movers behind this, but the
clergy and the burgesses also supported it and reduction
found other champions in a group of royalist nobles among
the civil servants and army officers who themselves held only
small areas of land. These small landowners had the happy
idea of applying the demand for reduction only to the large
holdings, and in a somewhat questionable manner a group
in support of reduction was formed in the noble Estate. The
members of the higher aristocracy were shouted down, the
political power of the Council having already been destroyed
by the threatened enquiry into the minority government.
Theoretically, the *Riksdag* might well have followed up some
of the constitutional ideas conceived during the Regency
period and assumed full responsibility in the matter. In fact,

however, it was the King who took control with an authority
that was quite astonishing; acting as a sort of powerful one-
man court of appeal to settle the disputes both between the
commons and the nobles and within the ranks of the nobility
itself. In his favour were both the desire for political stability
and the general animosity towards the higher aristocracy;
and it should be remembered also that absolutism was at that
time in the ascendant in Europe, just as Christina's reign had
been marked by an upper-class reaction against strong and
centralized government.

As the *Riksdag* proceeded, therefore, sympathy veered
round increasingly towards the King. How far this was a pre-
meditated plan on the part of Charles and his advisers is a
debatable question. The modern view is that he had no
schemes for reorganizing the actual constitution and that the
urge towards a stronger monarchy was due partly to chance
and, more fundamentally, partly to the post-war royalist
persuasions of the burgesses and lower aristocracy. At all
events when, at the end of the *Riksdag*, the King asked the
Estates to define his powers, he received the astonishing reply
that he was bound neither by the written constitution embodied in the Form of Government nor by the Council, and
was answerable to no law – this last assurance constituting a
break with a century-old political tradition in Sweden. Thus
the political ascendancy of the Council was destroyed, to the
advantage of the King and the *Riksdag*. At the next *Riksdag*
(1682–3), the Estates showed themselves even more accom-
modating in the face of the King's determination to extend
his power in fresh spheres. His tactics were unusual and
apparently unrehearsed. He would seize on a chance
utterance dropped during the discussions and twist it, with a
curious mixture of insouciance and logic, into a further
affirmation in his favour on the part of the Estates. At this
*Riksdag* the reduction was extended and the royal power increased by the granting to the King of the power of legislation.
According to a later statement of the Estates in 1693 he was

Koning Carl den XII.
Sålunda Klädder
enär Han Giorde Sitt
Salttåg A: 1700.

31. Charles XII. Painting by D. von Krafft.

32. Caroline battle scene: the crossing of the Dvina in 1701. Painting by F. Lemke.

an 'absolute sovereign King, responsible to no one on earth, but with power and might at his command to rule and govern the realm as a Christian monarch'. The only power retained by the Estates was that of voting taxes in normal times, though the King was granted special powers in this respect in the event of war.

Quite certainly the King would never have been able to achieve and develop an absolute monarchy if he had failed to achieve, preserve, and consolidate the peace. Thanks to the assistance of France, Sweden had been spared any serious losses; the heaviest was the cession to Brandenburg, by the treaty of St Germain in 1679, of most of her territories on the east bank of the Oder. But France's aid had taken a form which Charles considered humiliating; and it was in accordance with his own wishes that Sweden now abandoned both the French alliance and Gyllenstierna's ambitious schemes in favour of a friendly overture to Holland. While by no means ignoring the latent possibility of war, Charles, like one of the factions in the Regency before him, became increasingly absorbed in the establishment of peace and stability at home. But, unlike his predecessors, he succeeded in solving the problem. The story of how he did so may smack of mere bureaucratic and treasury routine; nevertheless it possesses all the excitement which marks any great and far-flung financial operation.

First came the inquisition into the Council of Regency. The members were charged with dereliction of duty and were made financially responsible, and those who were found guilty received crippling sentences. Parallel with this inquiry – but not to be confused with it – ran the reduction policy already adopted in principle in 1680 and subsequently applied to fresh categories of landed property. The first to suffer were the counts, barons, and other large landowners, after which the smaller holdings were reclaimed. Finally, the crown demanded the return of properties that had been given as security for loans or sold for ready money, arguing that the favourable terms of the original transaction had already allowed for full returns from the revenue which had accrued.

A few figures will help to illustrate the situation. At the end of Gustav Vasa's reign the crown had held 28·5 per cent. of Sweden's land, the nobility 21·4 per cent., and the free-tax peasant-proprietors 50·1 per cent. (the figures refer to Sweden proper). During the latter half of Christina's reign the nobility owned all but 28 per cent.; and they owned little less than this in 1680, as Charles X's few reduction measures had been counterbalanced by the many donations during the Regency. A significant proportion of this land was owned by a few powerful families, for example the Oxenstiernas, the de la Gardies, the Brahes, and enormous properties and rents had also been allotted in the Swedish possessions on the other side of the Baltic. After the virtual completion of the reduction policy in about 1700, the distribution was completely changed. The previously almost non-existent crown property now amounted to about 35·6 per cent. of the whole, that is, more than in the sixteenth century. The peasant-proprietors had 31·5 per cent., and the nobility 32·9 per cent. The reduction appears to have been even more drastic for the nobility in Finland and worst of all in the Baltic territories. The three immediate results of Charles XI's action were that the crown finances were again stabilized; that the threat to the future independence of the peasants was indirectly averted; and, lastly, that the economic supremacy of the nobility was considerably diminished.

The higher nobility, both by the inquiry and by the reduction, were indeed to be pitied, although some of the more heart-rending tales of their subsequent destitution have been refuted by recent research. At the same time, political supremacy was transferred from the aristocracy to an absolute monarchy: the time-honoured high offices of State were no longer refilled on the death of the holder; the departments of the central administration now contained only a handful of the members of the Council, which after 1682 was called not the Council of the Realm but the King's Council; new departments and new commissions were set up under the stringent control of the King; secretaries and special officials replaced the old Council dignitaries.

But this great political and economic revolution by no means saw the end of the nobility as a whole. Military and civil functionaries continued to be recruited from its ranks, though the ancient families no longer had priority, at all events for the time being. Furthermore, the reduction could not touch the core of the hereditary lands of the nobles, who were able to exchange such property for lands threatened by the reduction and thus, by sacrificing the outlying holdings worked by the peasants, maintain possession of their manors and more important estates. In this way the manors and stately mansions of the seventeenth century retained much of their original appearance and status; indeed it was at the end of this century that the large estate, as a result of these exchanges sanctioned by the crown, actually took on its final aspect. Considerable estates were also amassed by new men, not least by the King's co-adjutants, his favoured secretaries drawn from members of both old and new aristocracy. The labour necessary for the cultivation of large compact estates was procured through the *tjänstehjonsstadga*, a new statute which forced the landless poor to take employment offered by landowners – and thus deprived this dependent class, which was a very large one, of any benefits from the reduction.

The first use to which the crown put these new and enormous assets was the building up of an extremely well-planned, sensible budgetary system, in which every expenditure was set rigidly against a specified income. The best example is perhaps the famous *indelningsverk*, with which the King reorganized his army. He fully realized that the problems of peace could not be solved without a regular army, the more so in view of the pressure from abroad in the early

1680's. He therefore permanently assigned to the troops portions of the crown revenues and land (*indela* = to assign). This practice had long been a familiar principle in Sweden, but it had never before been so consistently and effectively applied. It came, however, to form an integral feature of the Swedish countryside and Swedish communal life up to the end of the nineteenth century. The army officers were given farms to live on and cultivate as part of their pay. Cavalry troopers received the taxes due from certain farms, whose holders thus maintained the troopers instead of paying taxes to the crown. The officers lived in the same district and province as the ordinary soldiers; and this link with the soil and common background encouraged a unity and solidarity in these mounted regiments, a little reminiscent of, but infinitely superior to, Gustavus Adolphus's military organization. The infantry were housed and maintained on similar principles, and the reorganization was based on liability not to taxation but to conscription. At the proposal of the crown the peasants were released from the unpopular burden of conscription on condition that they paid the wages of a professional soldier, who was also allotted his own cottage and a small plot of land. In this way the foot soldiers too had a link with the land during peacetime, and their maintenance did not differ appreciably from that of the other troops.

When the *Riksdag* met in 1693 the King was able to inform the Estates that he could release them from all extraordinary taxation except the old land taxes. The State was therefore paying its way, largely thanks to the surplus revenues from the trans-Baltic provinces. The absolute monarch had thus abolished at the same time both conscription and the necessity to impose fresh taxation; and he was able to draw up a model budget on which the finances were to be based.

Apart from some calamitous years during the nineties, when bad harvests resulted in widespread famine, the relative prosperity enjoyed by the State between 1680 and 1700 seems to have been shared by the people – though it is interesting to note that it was during this time of material well-being and normal existence that Sweden was swept by the cult of witchcraft then rife in Europe. Regional statistics for small areas show a rise in population. An increase from 23,000 persons around 1630 to about 37,000 in 1700 has been recorded for the province of Närke, for example: and the same tendency was probably at work in the country as a whole. The area of cultivated land shows a similar increase: for Närke the corresponding figures are 4 per cent. and about 5.3 per cent. That such calculations are possible at all is due to the efficiency of the Swedish administration in so carefully preserving its records. A great deal had been accomplished as a result of the peace and financial reform alone; and, in addition, Sweden received considerable benefit during this time from her Baltic empire, since the corn shipped through Riga from these grain-producing areas helped to satisfy her growing demand for grain. Simultaneously, the earlier improvements in mining and industry were being developed at an increasing rate, and it was during this century that Sweden established a reputation in European markets for her bar-iron, of which certain types in particular were justifiably regarded as excellent raw material for steel. There had been a considerable rise in iron exports even at the beginning of the century; and between 1640 and the middle of the sixteen-eighties they had more than doubled and were still rising. Copper continued to be exported though in smaller quantities, and tar also maintained its position. Iron and tar were especially in demand in England, where there was a shortage of timber and where the possibility of using coal in the manufacture of iron was not yet known. Since the 1630's the pig-iron produced in Swedish mines and furnaces had been further refined at works in and around the Bergslagen district; those outside the mining districts were favoured by the State with a view to reserving the wood supply in the district as far as possible for its own kilns – thus, in particular Western Värmland got its numerous pig-iron works. In time these developments were to produce two very important groups in Swedish society: the ironmasters and the iron-workers.

Ever since the Regency period during Christina's minority the government had been making deliberate efforts to speed up trade and industry, and now Gustav Vasa's policy of en-suring a supply of goods to the country was extended to include a positive trade balance and the protection of home products. This incipient mercantilism had already been apparent in 1667, and subsequently attained a firm footing in Sweden when protective tariffs were introduced after the 1686 *Riksdag*.

Interest in industry and trade brought with it an interest in the towns: these had grown appreciably during the seven-teenth century, both in number, through royal foundations, and in population, as a result of privileges and the growth of trade. The big coastal towns had acquired considerable advantages in foreign trade and had prospered accordingly. The population of Stockholm in the 1670's has been cal-culated at something over 50,000, Gothenburg's at about 5,000, and Norrköping's roughly the same. But the urban population was still only a diminutive fraction of the total, the bulk of which consisted of peasant-farmers and their em-ployees, and workers on the noble estates.

The Church too felt the effects of the urge for efficiency, and in 1686 it was brought under royal control by a new law issued by the King himself. A catechism to be used through-out the country was formulated by Archbishop Olof Sve-belius, and a prayer-book, a national hymn-book, and, later, a version of the Bible – known as Charles XII's Bible – were similarly prescribed. The hymn-book was a devotional work which made a particularly significant contribution to the spiritual life of Sweden. On the other hand the local self-government, which had recovered some of its strength under the auspices of the Church, again began to decline. The King's absolute power was omnipresent. Foreign artists, such

as the portrait painter Ehrenstrahl and the architects Nicodemus Tessin, father and son, were called in to extol it, and
Tessin the younger designed the extensive improvements to
the royal palace in Stockholm.

Very different were the sentiments of many of the nobles.
Johan Gabriel Oxenstierna, when painting the picture of
'the royal bailiff' two generations later, wrote:

'Blessed be the memory of the great royal economist Charles
XI, who took five manors from my grandfather. May God not
admit him among the ranks of the blessed on the Last Day, for we
would be given homespun tow instead of the snow-white garments
that are our due, and sprays of juniper for the promised palm
branches. He will make the Almighty Himself cast about for
means of retrenching.'

These, then, were the characteristics of the Swedish kingdom and the Swedish people at the end of Charles XI's
reign. By the time of the King's death from cancer of the
stomach in 1697, the absolute monarchy was so firmly rooted
as to be virtually immune from all opposition, whether from
the higher nobility or anyone else. The nobles nourished a
vague hope that the reduction policy might be alleviated by
the young Charles XII, who, though only fifteen, had at
once been declared of age; but there were no indications that
this might happen. The royal bureaucracy and its civil
servants continued to rule and foreign policy remained
unchanged.

During the 1680's Denmark had been well on the way to
settling the Holstein-Gottorp problem to her own satisfaction, but Sweden and her allies had managed to intervene.
The alliance with Holstein-Gottorp, which had gradually
become part and parcel of Sweden's foreign policy – even
Johan Gyllenstierna had favoured it – inevitably strained her
relations with Denmark; and although the Scandinavian
countries had united to defend their shipping during the
European war, at the beginning of the 1690's this marked only
a temporary change in their mutual attitude. Since the war

Sweden had gradually improved her somewhat weak position in Germany, largely by the creation of a strong navy. In the middle of the 1690's the Holstein-Gottorp question became more than usually critical. Military help from Sweden had enabled Duke Frederick of Holstein-Gottorp to strengthen his duchy; and there developed around his 'trenches' a state of war, both diplomatic and physical, which continued for several years, with now Sweden, now Denmark, holding the upper hand.

While Sweden was pursuing her fifty-year-old policy of encirclement against Denmark, she herself was threatened with a similar fate, contrived primarily by Denmark in her own defence. The newly elected King of Poland, Augustus the Strong, Elector of Saxony, was also contemplating the extension of his Polish empire by the conquest of Livonia, aided by a Livonian nobleman, Patkul, who had fled from Sweden. Finally, Russia too entered the picture. The Swedish government had long cherished the idea of controlling the whole of Russia's trade; an idea which, as has often been pointed out, had never been fully realized. On the other hand, Russia in her turn was gradually awakening to the necessity for a new commercial policy. Sweden had held part of the route to the Baltic since the time of Eric XIV and the whole of it since the Peace of Stolbova, and this route now appeared as an attractive alternative to (or replacement for) the Archangel route. Russia now manifested an increasing desire to get this Baltic route, hitherto controlled by Sweden, into her own hands. There were strong economic incentives, therefore, for an attack on Sweden's Baltic provinces, though how far the new Czar Peter understood this aspect of the Baltic situation is uncertain.

A series of negotiations between Denmark, Augustus of Saxony-Poland, and Russia, with Patkul playing an active part in the preliminary stages, gradually led to a tripartite alliance directed against Sweden; and Peter terminated a war with Turkey, with a view to releasing Russian forces.

Swedish troops marched into Holstein-Gottorp in 1699, after Denmark had demolished a number of the Duke's defensive outposts. International tension was intensified, and Sweden prepared herself, both militarily and diplomatically, for a trial of strength; complete and highly effective plans for mobilization had long been in existence. Nevertheless, for the moment the Swedish government was unaware of the full extent of the danger, as Augustus and Russia masked their preparations with friendly gestures.

# XXII

# Charles XII : Narva to Poltava
## 1700-1709

In February 1700 Saxon troops without having declared war marched into Livonia and made an unsuccessful attempt to surprise Riga, where Eric Dahlbergh, now an old man, was in command. Denmark then attacked Holstein-Gottorp in March, but Sweden was able, with the assistance of the maritime powers, England and Holland, to invade the east coast of Zealand and thus force Denmark to come to terms. Peace was soon concluded: Holstein-Gottorp's position was established with Swedish help and the tripartite alliance against Sweden was thereby broken up. While the King and the government were considering the next step against Augustus, however, Peter the Great led a large army into Ingermanland in the autumn of 1700 and started to besiege Narva, the main Swedish stronghold there. Sweden at once responded by transferring troops to the Baltic provinces under the King's personal leadership. They landed at Pernau, and during November marched by way of Reval towards Narva, while the war against Augustus in Livonia was reduced to a defensive campaign.

This army, led by the eighteen-year-old King and his second-in-command Lieutenant-General Carl Gustav Rehnsköld, numbered about 10,000 men. Charles XI's new military organization had as yet had little chance of proving itself in war; and none but his immediate circle knew anything about the young King, who with his men was traversing the rough boggy roads which led towards the east, roads which bore the marks of Russian plundering. The King had zealously studied the life of Alexander the Great, as depicted by Quintus Curtius Rufus, and was also very familiar with the

Bible; and it may be that he now saw himself as a new Alexander on his way to encounter the hordes of the East, or as one of the heroes of the Old Testament, called by God to do battle against the foes of himself and his people.

It cannot be denied that many of the turning-points in Swedish history have been determined by war, and it was one of these decisive encounters which awaited Charles XII as he advanced on the Russian army in the late autumn of 1700. His prospects might well appear uncertain. Narva was besieged by an army of 40,000 men commanded by foreign generals of repute, and the Russian camp had been fortified against the approaching forces by a line of strongholds, trenches, and *chevaux de frise*. Contrary to all the rules of prudent warfare, the Swedish commanders led the infantry straight to the centre of this line, their onrush coinciding with a violent snowstorm which spread suddenly from the west. The Russian front was broken in two, and the two halves separated and scattered in the course of bitter hand-to-hand encounters. The last of the Russian troops, fighting gallantly to the end, surrendered after a few hours; many had been drowned or cut down while attempting to escape over the River Narva, while others had fled beyond the line of fortifications, where they were cut off by the Swedish cavalry. Some sections of the Russian army had completely disintegrated and Peter himself had already left the camp two days earlier. The prisoners far outnumbered the Swedish army, and as it would have been impossible to guard and maintain them, they were all set free except for the officers. It is difficult to assess precisely the share taken by the King in the proceedings; certainly his was the order to attack, and he had retained control throughout the battle. This day was undoubtedly the turning-point in his life, for it had revealed to him what he could do and liked doing best – leading troops into battle.

This brilliant victory had an immediate effect on the political situation in northern Europe, and centred the attention of all western Europe on Charles XII and Sweden. The War of the Spanish Succession was about to break out, and both Louis XIV and his opponents, the maritime powers England and Holland, were anxious to gain Sweden as an ally. There were now three alternatives open to Charles: further hostilities against Russia, a speedy peace, or war with Augustus of Poland; and there has always been a difference of opinion among historians – and by no means the only one provoked by Charles XII – as to which would have been the 'correct' choice. Charles XII chose the last. Having reinforced his army he led it to Riga in the summer of 1701 and crossed the Dvina, despite the fact that the south bank was held by Augustus's troops. The enemy was scattered and the duchy of Courland secured.

The situation now appeared similar to that of the spring. Sweden found it difficult to bring either of her enemies to the point of a decisive engagement. Peter the Great was seemingly inaccessible in the vast tracts of the Russian empire; Augustus presented a nice problem in international law since he was theoretically waging war against Sweden solely in his capacity of Saxon Elector and not as King of Poland. Sweden and Poland had been at peace since 1660, and a certain measure of amity had replaced their former hostility. A curious political situation had arisen which suggested to Charles a solution to his problem. He would be satisfied, he said, if Poland would depose Augustus. The idea was a logical one, in keeping with the traditions of Swedish foreign policy. It expressed an attempt to achieve that rapprochement between Sweden and Poland which had once been envisaged by John III, although both the means and the conditions were quite different; and there had been similar projects during Charles X's Polish war. The plan also had something in common with Louis XIV's dream at about the same time of a pro-French régime in Spain. Whether it was practicable, of course, was another matter.

In the summer of 1710, when Charles took this decision,

the Great Northern War entered a new phase which has frequently baffled the historians. Henceforward the problems which arise are particularly tortuous in that they involve two puzzling factors which are so closely intertwined and so complex that it is impossible to disentangle them. The first problem is the personality and temperament of Charles himself; his religious belief in his crown and his calling, his moral principles, his mathematical and logical mind, his inscrutable silences which left even his diplomatists and his generals ignorant of his ultimate intentions, and his devotion to war for its own sake, just as his father had been devoted to the minutiae of the Treasury. In spite of his soldierly uprightness, he was quite ready to turn his reputation for trustworthiness to diplomatic ends. The second problem is the real extent of the power and stability of the Swedish Baltic Empire. Basically, neither of these problems have yet been solved, and much research remains to be done on them.

Poland, ruled by a republican oligarchy under a nominal king, was not easy to tackle, as Charles X had already discovered in his attempt to create a Swedish party in the country or when he had broached the idea of her partition. The loose constitution made it difficult to come to grips with Polish politics. After the Poles had refused to depose Augustus, Charles XII transferred his field of operations to Poland and marched first on Warsaw, and then on Cracow. Now openly at war with Poland, he engaged in battle with Augustus's Saxon troops and the army of the Polish crown, which had meantime been mustered against him, and won a brilliant victory at Kliszow in 1702; and within a short space of time the Poles had been scattered and a large part of the Saxon infantry destroyed. A tremendous impetus was given to the cavalry's attack by the use of the Caroline tactics, at that time unknown in Europe, which involved charging at the gallop, with drawn swords, in tight formation; and corresponding tactics were adopted by the infantry. In the following year the Swedes conquered the solidly built fortress of Thorn on the Vistula, where they captured the bulk of the Saxon infantry, and thenceforth they controlled the most important river basin in the country.

These victories, however, were not decisive. Once inside his Electorate Augustus was safe, as it could only be reached through Imperial Silesia; and though in 1704 Charles marshalled his army close to the Silesian frontier he hesitated for some reason to go any farther. He persisted with his original plan of bringing about the deposition of Augustus and the election of a pro-Swedish King, and gradually built up a Swedish party in Poland. It is not necessary to follow his marches up and down Poland, his sieges, pursuits, and strategic manœuvres, though all were of high military quality. The outcome may suffice. As a result partly of the persistent manipulation by Swedish agents of the noble factions in Poland, and partly of the heavy contributions levied for the maintenance of the Swedish army, a Polish 'Confederation' of a section of the nobility was finally prevailed upon, in 1704, to forswear faith and allegiance to King Augustus. An assembly of Estates, of which the validity was somewhat dubious, then elected as their King a noble from Poznan called Stanislas Leszczynski. This concluded the strange series of events. The next step was to form a regular treaty with the Polish kingdom, and this was accomplished in the following year. The result of the prolonged campaign were now revealed: Poland and Sweden had made an alliance which was plainly directed against Russia, who, though Augustus's ally, was regarded by many people in Poland as the hereditary enemy. In addition a series of trade agreements were made, in conformity with the policy which had been inherited from Eric XIV through Gustavus Adolphus and Axel Oxenstierna, and which had been elaborated by Swedish civil servants during the seventeenth century. Riga was established as the port of export for the Polish hinterland, the Swedes were granted the right to trade in important Polish towns and to buy salt – still a considerable Swedish import – on favourable terms in the Galician mines, and, finally, Poland undertook to prevent any transit trade between Russia and western Europe except that which passed through Riga.

But so long as Augustus retained any power in Poland these would remain paper agreements; and already he was mustering new armies in Saxony and calling on the aid of Russian troops. Constant Swedish victories were of no avail as long as Saxony remained inviolate. There has been considerable debate as to why Charles XII stayed so long in Poland and an explanation has been sought in various external circumstances. He may have been counting on an alliance with Prussia, which would enable him to advance against Russia and settle the issue there; and in fact the two countries entered into prolonged negotiations on these lines, subsequently discussing the possibility of Prussian mediation between Sweden and Russia. In any case Charles plainly wanted to keep an eye on Prussia and check any designs she might have on the Polish territory of western Prussia. Again, by staying in Poland, he may have hoped to lure the Czar's main forces on to Polish soil and meet them there; or it may have been that he found it easy to maintain his army in Poland. Charles's native reticence defies investigation into his motives. The words he wrote to the man whom he most trusted, Rehnsköld, concerning a military plan known only to the two of them are characteristic: 'I have never let fall a word on it to anyone in the world, nor betrayed the slightest sign in my den eanour.' At all events, the protracted negotiations with Prussia came to nothing, for Prussia, one of the Louis XIV's opponents in the Spanish Succession War, obviously did not want to risk severing her friendly relations with Russia. At the beginning of 1706, however, Rehnsköld won a brilliant victory over the Saxon army at Fraustadt, near the Silesian frontier; and in the spring Charles himself arrived triumphantly at the frontiers of Russia. The paths both to the east and to the west seemed to lie open to him. Choosing the latter, he led his troops through Silesia into Saxony, and forced Augustus to make peace in Altranstaedt in 1706. The Swedish army remained there for some months, resting and living comfortably at the expense of the prosperous countryside, while it was being equipped for another great campaign by reinforcements from home.

At this stage the Caroline army was a model one; it was unquestionably one of the most effective military instruments that has ever existed, and imbued through and through with the personality of the King. Charles's strict adherence to the martial pattern made an enormous impression in contemporary Europe by sheer force of contrast, establishing once and for all his rôle as a mysterious, fascinating, and legendary hero. Attired in a simple blue uniform with high cavalry boots and an enormous sabre, and rejecting the wig and other trappings which were then the fashion, he led his troops in person, straight-backed and laconic in his utterances; according to a Swedish observer, he gave the impression of having something indefinable about him, 'awe-inspiring and almost sinister'. He never spared himself, but shared the simple and hazardous life of his meanest soldier. The following anecdote, told by the army chaplain Jöran Nordberg in his famous chronicle of Charles XII, is especially typical of the King's conception of the spirit which should prevail in his nomadic, Spartan military state. The influential counsellor Count Piper had praised a young corporal, the great-grandson of Axel Oxenstierna, and recommended him for rapid promotion. The King refused his consent, saying firstly that a young aristocratic officer can never treat his men properly unless he has learnt what it is to serve in the ranks himself, and secondly that he would favour no one. For, he added, a soldier's qualifications have nothing whatsoever to do with his birth.

While Charles was in Saxony he was being courted by both the antagonists in the War of the Spanish Succession. Neither was successful, however, notwithstanding Marl-

33. A Caroline warrior: General C. G. Armfelt.
Painting by D. von Krafft, 1719.

34. An aristocrat of the Age of Freedom: Count C. G.
Tessin. Painting by G. Lundberg, 1760.

borough's famous visit to the Swedish camp. That the traditions of Gustavus Adolphus were still alive was shown by a
quarrel with the German Emperor over the religious liberty
of the Silesian Protestants; but although it gave rise, as the
case might be, to forebodings or hopes, it brought about no
change in the King's policy. The dispute was settled in
Sweden's favour, a result which not only underlined her
power but also gave her the opportunity to seek recruits
among the German Protestants. But the King was occupied
with other plans than participation in the war in western
Europe, though he did not reveal their identity.

During the deliberations over Charles's next move in the
spring of 1706 the contention was made that 'Sweden's
primary interest is to conserve the army in order to liberate
the provinces of the Swedish Empire'. The fact was that
during Charles's Polish campaigns significant events had
been taking place along the Swedish-Russian frontier. The
Russians had won several victories in Livonia, and as a result
of a determined and persistent campaign the entire course of
the Neva from Lake Ladoga to the Gulf of Finland had fallen
into the hands of Peter the Great, who had caused both St
Petersburg and Cronstadt to be built at the mouth of this
river. The gains which had been made by Gustavus Adolphus
at the treaty of Stolbova were thus threatened, once the Russians had crossed the stream. The Czar had retaken Narva
in 1704, the same year in which Stanislas was elected King of
Poland, and he was then able with his superior forces to consolidate his new Baltic position in face of the fumblings of the
Swedish Council and the uncoordinated command of the
Swedish generals in the east. As long as Charles XII was in
Saxony the position along the frontier remained unaltered;
it was summed up in 1703 by the commandant of Narva:
'Thus are these forsaken territories delivered over to
the foe, for devastation if not for possession.' Yet the King
showed no concern for either the Baltic provinces or
Finland.

17

In the late summer of 1707 Charles XII led his magnificent army of more than 40,000 men – most of them Swedes – from Saxony to the east. By the beginning of 1708 he had succeeded in manœuvring out of Poland and Lithuania most of the Russian troops who had been lording it there during his absence, and it gradually began to dawn on an astonished world what Charles had in mind. He was proceeding against the Baltic provinces, not to relieve the Russian pressure there and recover what had been lost, but to settle the Russian question with a single blow. He left a division of his army in Poland to support King Stanislas, while he himself made straight for the centre of Russian power in Moscow – the same strategy which was to be followed by Napoleon some hundred years later. According to the traditional barbaric custom of impeding the enemy's advance by destroying his bases of operation, the Russians laid waste the route by which he advanced, since Peter did not trouble to reflect that his own country would also suffer as a result of this practice. But Charles had taken precautions to ensure supplies. General Lewenhaupt, previously in command in the southern Baltic provinces, was ordered to proceed with his army south-east from Riga with a large supply train, and join up with the main army later. Russian resistance was beaten back at Holovzin by Charles's troops, who proceeded to march the comparatively short distance to the Russian frontier. The grandiose plan aimed at the heart of the enormous Russian empire, which was already shaken by serious internal crisis. The calamitous turning-point in this great conflict, however, was now not far distant.

So thorough had been the Russian devastations that the Swedish King had little chance of maintaining his army along the northern road to Moscow, even with Lewenhaupt's supplies; and the Russians eluded any direct encounter. He therefore decided to turn south towards Severia, with the aim of discovering a less ravaged route to Moscow. The army was manœuvred in order to clear the way for Lewenhaupt,

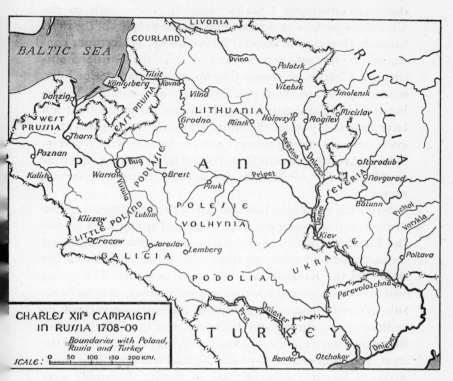

CHARLES XII's CAMPAIGNS
IN RUSSIA 1708-09
*Boundaries with Poland,
Russia and Turkey*
SCALE: 0  50  100  150  200 Kms.

doubtless in the belief that he was quite close, and a strong
corps was sent ahead to safeguard the new base and its approaches. But this vanguard got lost in the unmapped
forests, with the result that the Russians got to Severia first,
ravaged it, and occupied important positions on the route
along which the Swedes had planned to advance.

Simultaneously Charles learnt that he had been mis-
informed as to the position of Lewenhaupt, who had been
overtaken by superior Russian forces; and although he had
sustained a hard battle at Ljesna he had lost both his supplies
and his artillery. It was not until they reached Severia itself
that the remains of his troops joined the main force. Under

these circumstances Charles struck farther south to the Ukraine, where he could calculate on the support of the rebel Cossack Hetman, Mazeppa. Nevertheless, misfortunes continued to pile up. For the second time the Russians outstripped Charles by conducting operations on interior lines, seized and burnt Mazeppa's capital, and completely dislocated the Ukrainian rising. However, since they did not have time to lay waste the entire Ukraine, Charles was at all events assured of good winter quarters, and the King relied on receiving reinforcements from Poland by the spring, when he could press on to Moscow by a third route still farther south.

So far the great plan had failed. For the first time an enemy army had discovered the implications of trying to penetrate the Russian expanses, and the Russian command had shown an alertness and determination very different from earlier days. Yet the King did not lose his equanimity. The spring would soon come and a winter in good quarters was no hardship to sturdy troops. The winter of 1708–9, however, was no ordinary one; throughout Europe it was the coldest within living memory. The French vineyards were devastated by the frost, and in the Russian plains the cold was appalling; hundreds of Swedish soldiers froze to death; thousands were severely frost-bitten. The temperature reached its lowest level at the New Year; and one of Charles's soldiers wrote in his diary that never had they spent 'so lamentable a Christmastide'. Hopes of relief from Poland were also dashed, showing the error of trusting in this country's forced co-operation. On the other hand, Charles received support from insurgent Zaporogian Cossacks farther south and in the spring he also made contact with Russia's old enemies, the Turks and the Tartars, who had already several times, though all unconsciously, eased the Russian pressure on Sweden's expansion in the Baltic. Indeed negotiations between Sweden and Turkey, which had included questions of commercial policy, had been started as early as 1707. It was extremely doubtful, of course, to what extent these theoretical speculations could be realized, but in any case there was no question of a retreat northwards.

The King now pinned his hopes on bringing about a decisive engagement with the Russian forces massed by the Dnieper; and in order to tempt his adversary to fight he laid siege in the summer of 1709 to the fortress of Poltava on the Vorskla, a tributary of the Dnieper. Having assembled on the other side of the river, the Russians proceeded to cross it and established a fortified and entrenched camp. They now numbered about 45,000 men as against Charles's 22,000 (excluding the allied Cossacks), not all of whom were available for battle. This was the same ratio as had existed in most of the campaigns of the last few years; but the military reforms carried out by the Czar during the past ten years were now bearing fruit in troops of a quite different quality from those at Narva. Even so the King decided on battle.

Most unfortunately, however, Charles was in a high fever from a bullet-wound in the foot, and could only be moved on a litter. He was thus unable to lead the Swedish army himself, and his generals – particularly Rehnsköld and Lewenhaupt – did not see eye to eye. Still the campaign was planned with admirable skill: the Russian army was to be taken by surprise and forced to fight with its back to the river. So bold a plan, however, required very skilful handling and this was not forthcoming. The initial moves were ruined by muddled orders and an inadequate grasp of the situation; the surprise attack failed and a third of the Swedish infantry was destroyed before it reached the battlefield; the remainder, already heavily handicapped, were destroyed by the Russian infantry, which was vastly superior in numbers, while the Swedish cavalry failed to come to the infantry's aid. Thus ended the Battle of Poltava, on 27th June 1709. After the defeat the remnants of the Swedish army were rallied under the King's personal leadership, and retired in good order; but towards 7000 men had been killed and 2500 captured; 300 officers had fallen, Field-Marshal Rehnsköld was a prisoner and the King himself had only just managed to escape. Charles XII's army, including those who had suffered from the effects of winter, now consisted of about 15,000 men, mainly cavalry, and these retreated south-west into the angle between the Dnieper and the Vorskla.

SWEDEN
EARLY 18th CENTURY

SCALE OF MILES

# XXIII

# Charles XII: Perevolotjna to Fredrikshald
## 1709-1718

The days immediately after the Battle of Poltava were difficult ones for the Swedish supreme command, which was temporarily camped at Perevolotjna. The roads were bad, the Russians were hard behind, and a rapid decision was essential. Many historians have inevitably held the King or his acting commander-in-chief, General Lewenhaupt, responsible for what followed. But it is easier to be wise after the event than to imagine oneself in the predicament that preceded it. When the soldiers of a dragoon regiment, in common with all the regiments, were asked if they were prepared to fight on they replied: 'Why do you ask us? There were no questions hitherto: the word has been "Forward!" We cannot say that we shall beat them, but we will do all that is humanly possible.' Lewenhaupt, however, simply appears to have given way under the strain.

In order to make contact with the army in Poland the King had crossed the Dnieper with about 1300 men, while the remainder received orders to cross the Vorskla. The next objective may have been the Crimea. But morale gave way and the army of 15,000 men, notwithstanding its superiority, capitulated with all its equipment to the Russian cavalry which had pursued it from Poltava. The Caroline army had ceased to exist. When the King heard of this surrender he directed his march towards the Turkish frontier.

The news of this unbelievable catastrophe spread rapidly throughout Europe and led to a renewal of the original northern league against Sweden. Augustus recovered Poland by force from the adherents of Stanislas, and the Swedish-

Polish forces which had been stationed in Poland retreated into Swedish Pomerania. Meanwhile the Czar was storming Viborg, and for the first time this frontier stronghold was forced to surrender to the Russians in the early summer of 1710, while Keksholm, Riga, Pernau, and Reval fell later in the same year. Denmark had already attacked Skåne in 1709. And meanwhile the King was in Turkey, where he had established his camp at Bender in Bessarabia. In the following years he stubbornly adhered to his original design against Russia, with the only difference that it was now adapted to correspond with his novel situation as 'guest' of Turkey.

At home in Sweden the Defence Commission – composed of royal councillors entrusted with national defence – were working feverishly to replace the shattered military units; considerable forces had also been kept in the country as a safeguard. It was decided that an immediate counter-attack should be made on the Danes in Skåne, where the population was no longer giving them any support. This step was heartily endorsed by the governor-general of the province, Magnus Stenbock, with the words: 'In God's name, let us fall on the enemy, the sooner the better.' And in February 1710, eight months after Poltava, a battle was fought at Hälsingborg and the Danes were driven back over the Sound.

Charles XII now gave a new direction to his great Russian plan. He contemplated obtaining help from Turkey, which would then co-operate with the Swedish army operating from Pomerania and Poland. Any action from the north, however, was prevented by pressure from the maritime powers and the Emperor, though even without such intervention its chances of success were very slim. On the other hand the southern front got off to a promising start. Charles's trusted friend, the Polish nobleman Stanislaus Poniatowsky, successfully collaborated with the pro-Swedish party at the court of Constantinople, while Charles himself had for some time been negotiating with Russia's nearest neighbour and enemy, the Tartar Khan, who owed allegiance to the Porte. The outcome of all these efforts was that Turkey declared war on Russia at the end of 1710. By the summer of 1711 the Turks had surrounded the Russian army – including the Czar – by the Pruth, and Swedish hopes began to run high. However, the peace brought no essential change, for Turkey proved content with concessions from Russia that hardly relieved Sweden's position at all. The complicated intrigues at the Oriental court were not conducive to the stable anti-Russian policy for which Charles had hoped. Nevertheless in December 1711 he once more prevailed on Turkey to declare war on Russia, though with equally little benefit to Sweden.

In the meantime, Charles had continued to ply the Council with instructions to send Swedish troops to Germany without delay, with a view to co-operating with the Turks; but in April 1712, before the troops transports were ready, a fresh peace between Russia and the Porte had already been concluded. The governor-general of Skåne, Magnus Stenbock, making use of his exceptional talent for stirring up public opinion, had extorted both money and ships from the reluctant Swedish townspeople; and in the autumn of 1712 he led a Swedish army to Pomerania preparatory to an attack on Poland. But this third phase of the plan was, like others, doomed to failure, for the Danish fleet managed to destroy all the Swedish transports and supply ships at Rügen – a decisive blow, as without supplies Stenbock could not attack Poland. He had to be satisfied with bringing relief to the hard-pressed province of Pomerania and defeating the Danes at Gadebusch in December. It was true that in November Charles XII had managed to extract from Turkey a third declaration of war against Russia, but this proved ineffective, since any possible co-operation between Swedes and Turks had now been ruled out. Instead, Stenbock entered southern Jutland, where in January 1713 he found sanctuary in the Holstein-Gottorp fortress of Tönning but was forced to give himself up with his exhausted army in May of the same year.

Charles's Oriental diplomacy, Stenbock's action, the negotiations simultaneously going on with regard to Sweden's Baltic territories (in which both Prussia and Hanover were now interested), the Holstein intrigues – all these features created during this period a labyrinth which it is almost impossible to penetrate. Moreover, in the spring of 1713 the war of the Spanish Succession had at last been brought to an end by the Treaty of Utrecht, enabling the powers of western Europe to turn their attention to the Northern War. In February Charles's friendly relations with the Turks had been destroyed as a result of a remarkable *Kalabalik* (Turkish: 'tumult'); in a final attempt to rid themselves of a guest who had become an embarrassment to them, and whom they called 'the Iron Head', they attacked and subsequently set fire to his quarters in Bender, and took him prisoner as he was leaving the burning building. Meanwhile the Czar, no longer worried about his Turkish front, attacked Finland and ruthlessly laid waste the country. With the defeat at Storkyro in February 1714 of Finland's valiant defender, General C. G. Armfeldt, the Russians gained control of the Swedish Empire's most valuable defensive outpost and, at the same time, of her recruiting ground for soldiers of the highest quality. Sweden's most effective counter-move during these years was the blockade, with the aid of privateers, of Russia's new Baltic provinces. Denmark had already recovered Bremen. In addition, Stettin and the area of Pomerania south of the Peene had become Prussian possessions, as a result of a series of diplomatic intrigues in 1713, in which the Holstein diplomat, Baron G. H. von Görtz, had played a prominent part. At that time Prussia could not yet officially be counted among Sweden's enemies; in 1714, however, an alliance was made between Czar Peter and the Prussian King, Frederick William I. In 1712 the Elector of Hanover had already occupied Verden, ostensibly to 'pro-

tect' this region for the Swedes. Such were the main outlines
of the situation when Charles XII escaped from Turkey and,
having travelled most of the way on horseback, rode disguised and bearded through the gates of Stralsund in
November 1714.

The numerous fronts which resulted from the geographical
structure of Sweden's Baltic empire were an obvious disadvantage in view of Charles's curiously one-track ideas of
warfare and diplomacy; doggedly he had staked all for the
one great end and had failed to attain it. Nevertheless the
hopelessness of the situation must not be exaggerated; France
had been in an almost equally disastrous situation on several
occasions during the War of the Spanish Succession, and yet
Louis XIV had managed to weather the storm. But Sweden's
situation was desperate enough. Charles's peace-time army
had proved inadequate even in the initial stages of the war,
and reinforcements had been hastily mustered, without
regard to privileges, by methods suspiciously like the old
policy of conscription which had been superseded by the
military reforms of Charles XI. Heavy taxes had been imposed right from the first year of the war; distress in the
country had been increased by bad harvests, together with
an epidemic of bubonic plague which had spread from the
east in 1710; and the capitulations at Perevolotjna and Tönning had resulted in the best of Sweden's manhood being sent
to captivity in Siberian prisons, Venetian galleys, and elsewhere. Finland and the Baltic provinces had been laid waste
and the grain imports from Riga had been cut off. Various
means were employed in an attempt to restore the Treasury,
which was sadly impoverished, and in 1713 the King had
despatched from Turkey a new government ordinance which
aimed at bringing such efforts under more effective central
control; and meanwhile extensive loans were being negotiated in the country. Still, the economic situation had its
brighter side. During the first ten years of war the ravages of
the enemy had not extended to Sweden proper, and the

Swedish armies had been able to live largely on foreign resources. Good harvests had helped matters; until 1710, trade with western Europe had continued to be good, and the subsequent decline was temporarily checked by the Treaty of Utrecht. Exports of copper and iron could therefore continue much as usual, though the Swedish tar industry was beginning to feel the effects of competition from America and Russia. In the most critical period the economic conception of mercantilism had been confirmed by the new Swedish customs tariff of 1715.

Charles XII's intention now was to continue the war to the bitter end. Despite his defeat at Poltava, his reputation as a general was still untarnished. By far his greatest asset, however, was Caroline Sweden herself. The divine right of the monarchy had taken on distinctive Swedish features which were enhanced by the various religious ideas expressed in contemporary literature. Even during the reign of Charles XI the learned and versatile professor at Uppsala, Olof Rudbeck – naturalist, historian, architect, musician – had tried to show in his four mighty tomes on *Atland* that Sweden was identical with Plato's Atlantis and the legendary Isles of the Blest, from which all culture had sprung. The 250-year-old edifice of 'Gothic romanticism' here received its ultimate crown, and none doubted that Rudbeck was right in attempting to show Sweden in this light.

Meanwhile in Stockholm, Nicodemus Tessin the Younger was commissioned by the King to build a new palace to replace the one that had been destroyed by fire in 1697. The new building was to express in stone the absolutism which underlay contemporary Swedish politics and to incorporate those characteristics of instinct, imagination, and severity which marked the King himself. To the Sweden of Charles XII the monarch was an all-pervading national symbol, and the signs of discontent are no evidence to the contrary. The solidarity and endurance of the country are reflected in miniature in the behaviour of the prisoners who were scattered throughout Russia and Siberia. Supported wherever possible by the resources of a Swedish chancery and a Swedish treasury in Moscow, directed by Piper and Rehnsköld, these prisoners continued to teach and work, bowed but unbroken.

They were further sustained by a spiritual revival in their ranks; and one of them has left the following significant words written in a prayer book: 'A simple that cureth all things . . . the apothecary hath it not, yet is it prescribed by the physician. The soil beareth it not but Heaven yieldeth it: *Patience!*' A similar outlook can also be discerned in Sweden, where the spiritual currents of the period found their favourite expression in the practical aspects of life, allowing less scope for research, literature, and art.

It was against this background, then, that Charles spent the next few years feverishly recruiting all that was left of Sweden's resources. In 1715 he obtained a certain amount of diplomatic support from France, and refused to regard as fatal the fall of Stralsund, Sweden's only remaining possession on the other side of the Baltic. The King had escaped over the sea to Skåne on the eve of the siege in December 1715, and he now took up his headquarters in the university town of Lund.

Here the absolute King put forth all his energies, firmly suppressing both opposition and obstruction on the part of the Council and officials and the growing discontent among the population generally, reflected in the committee *Riksdags* of 1710 and 1713. Agents untrammelled by Swedish political traditions, chief among whom was the Holstein baron, Görtz, were commissioned to maintain the consistency of Charles's foreign policy, while at home a new department, the 'Purchasing Deputation' (*upphandlingsdeputation*), was created with unrestricted authority; its first measure was to put into circulation a new type of government bonds, which were made out in the name of the Estates on the security of public and private property, and came in time to be used extensively by the state as a means of payment. The Deputation's most noteworthy step was the creation of the so-called emergency coinage of 1716; a token copper currency of high nominal value, this coinage was to be regarded as legal tender throughout the country, and the government made every effort to put it over at its face value. Meanwhile the army was replenished by means of scarcely concealed conscription and compulsory enrolment, heavy taxes were imposed, forced loans extorted, Dutch credit was exploited, and foreign exchanges manipulated. The Deputation took over control of the export of metal and from 1718 the towns were granted export licences only on condition that they imported specific goods. The administration became even more centralized, and members of the old Council were completely superseded by officials of quite different type. The King made a personal contribution to the new ordinances and enforced them vigorously; consistent in theory, he generally preferred to follow a logical plan rather than attempt to adapt his ideas to the shifting requirements of reality.

The King's right-hand man in planning and carrying out this economic policy was the very able Baron Görtz, the chief member of the Purchasing Deputation. Many of his projects were already familiar to the country or had been in force elsewhere, but it was he who put them into practice in Sweden. In addition, he took over control of Swedish diplomacy and the country thus obtained a skilled representative, according to the practice of the time. At one period Charles XII had brought his own peculiar technique to bear on Swedish diplomacy, but after his stay in Turkey he conformed to contemporary methods and finally he allowed Görtz to act as he thought best. The one-eyed Holsteiner was an extremely able diplomatist. Like the King, though in a different way, he kept his distance; he was wholly lacking in moral scruples and, whether from personal or from ideological motives, was a strong adherent of authoritarian principles. Few details are known about the nature of the collaboration between this inscrutable couple, but it is plain that Charles gave Görtz a fairly free hand. Consequently the final years of Sweden's period of greatness were no less tense than any of the previous phases, though the focal point had now shifted from the military to the diplomatic sphere.

Charles's reputation in Europe for inflexibility and stubbornness now stood him in good stead. The period from 1716 to 1718 might almost be described as that of a cold war, since each protagonist determined to hold out the longest. And although Sweden's domestic difficulties and burdens increased each year, so too did those of her adversaries, among them Russia and Denmark. Moreover, Swedish diplomacy could count on an ever-widening breach between the allied Powers, especially between Russia and Hanover-England.

Though the Elector of Hanover was also King George I of England, he turned against Sweden primarily in his former capacity, intending to link up his two kingdoms by the conquest of Bremen and Verden. At the same time he watched with trepidation the continual inroads which Russia was making into northern Germany, where the Czar maintained large bodies of troops and had occupied important territories. George's English subjects provided him with indirect support in the form of naval expeditions to the Baltic, and, in 1717, provoked by the injury which was being done to English shipping by Charles XII's blockade of the Baltic provinces, England imposed a ban on trade with Sweden. Nevertheless, England needed Swedish exports – Sweden normally supplied 90 per cent. of her iron – and the English were no less dismayed at the sight of Russia's increasing power in northern Europe; and in 1716 the hostility between George I and the Czar was intensified by the Russo-Danish plans to land in Skåne. Meanwhile Görtz paid a visit to Holland in order to raise a loan, and at the same time both he and the Swedish envoy in England, Karl Gyllenborg, began to intrigue with the exiled English Jacobites, who were bitter enemies of the House of Hanover. But their machinations were discovered, and in 1717 both Görtz and Gyllenborg were imprisoned; though the former, who was a captive of the Dutch, was released after six months and resumed his activities where he had left off. He now set himself to widen the breach between the allies by every diplomatic means, primarily that of conducting separate negotiations with Russia and Hanover-England, and playing them off against each other. The wildest rumours were circulated as to the scope and success of his diplomacy and even in their most fantastic form they seem to have gained credence. It is impossible here to follow Görtz's devious tactics, but some of them at least appear to have had a certain success. Among other things he was generally believed to have emerged victorious from his separate negotiations with Russia on Åland in the summer of 1718, which had been undertaken in an attempt to attract the Czar into the Swedish alliance and regain Sweden's lost Baltic provinces by giving compensation to Russia elsewhere.

It cannot be denied that much credit is due to the Swedish people for managing to put up such a show of resistance during the critical years of 1716–18, considering that each year losses were felt more keenly; a large part of Finland was already in ruins, and men, women, and children had been dragged from their homes away to slavery. The first reliable estimate of the Swedish population can be dated about 1720, and reveals a figure of 1,440,000 persons in Sweden proper (corresponding to a figure of 1,120,000 for the 1630 frontiers). This is a considerable increase since the first years of the Age of Greatness, and indicates that the Thirty Years War probably cost more lives than the campaigns of Charles XII. But there had been widespread plague, homesteads all over the country were deserted, and the continued recruitment into the armed forces took heavy toll of the male population, even supposing that Charles XII's last army still consisted of soldiers of normal age, and not of children and old men. The people were now heartily weary of war and the new prepara-

35a. The factory of the Swedish
East India Company in the
international quarter of Canton. Contemporary painting on
glass.

35b. Dannemora Iron Mine.
Engraving by J. F. Martin,
*c.* 1790.

36a. Emanuel Swedenborg.
Painting by K. von Breda.

36b. Carl Linnaeus.
Painting by A. Roslin.

tions aimed, in Görtz's words, 'Not to continue the war but to end it.'

Swedish warfare in this period had tended to spare the soldier, as it had been confined to home defence and to attacks on Norway; this last, incidentally, gave rise to the fear that Sweden would support the Jacobites in Scotland from across the North Sea. In the autumn of 1718 Charles XII had for the second time marched, with a well-equipped army, on south-western Norway, while General Armfeldt advanced towards Trondhjem. In November the King laid siege to the fortress of Fredrikssten at Fredrikshald (Halden); but as he was watching the progress of the operations from the trenches on 30th November, a bullet struck him in the temple. Death was instantaneous. It was rumoured that the shot was fired at close range by an intimate of his brother-in-law, Prince Frederick of Hesse; and, though different theories have also been advanced, this view is still held by a number of modern historians. The considerable force with which the bullet entered the King's head lends weight to the theory of murder, which is also supported by certain features of the general political situation. For Prince Frederick was fervently hoping to succeed to the Swedish throne through his wife, Charles XII's youngest sister, Ulrica Eleonora. His rival was Duke Charles Frederick of Holstein-Gottorp, the son of Charles's oldest sister, Hedwig Sophia, who was believed to have the support of his compatriot, Baron von Görtz. At the very moment when the King fell, Görtz was on his way to Fredrikshald; it was believed in Hessian circles that he had brought with him favourable terms from Russia which would finally decide the tug-o'-war in favour of the Holsteiners. The only certainty is that Charles XII fell at Fredrikshald – but whether by the hand of an assassin or from a stray enemy bullet is likely to remain a matter of controversy.

The century and a half of war in Sweden's history was drawing to a close.

18

# XXIV

# The Age of Freedom. The Peace Crisis and Arvid Horn
## 1718-1739

As there was no direct heir to the throne after Charles XII's death, the hereditary Prince Frederick of Hesse and his wife Ulrica Eleonora immediately took appropriate steps to win supporters and out-manœuvre Charles Frederick of Holstein-Gottorp. The money in the field treasury was distributed among the officers of the main army in Norway, and Görtz was arrested before reaching Fredrikshald, to be subsequently sentenced to death and executed for having aided and abetted the absolute monarchy and having proved a danger to the Hessian party. Nevertheless, Ulrica Eleonora soon realized that she would have to renounce all thoughts of absolute power if she wished to be acknowledged Queen. The Council, in its original bureaucratic form, automatically resumed its seventeenth-century status, and the new government departments created by Charles XII in his later years, together with their officials, were disregarded. 'The King's Council', as it had been called during the period of absolutism, again became 'The Council of the Realm'. Duke Charles Frederick's claims to the throne were frustrated and he soon left the country. A *Riksdag* was convened and Ulrica Eleonora was acclaimed as the *elected* Queen. In 1719 a new constitution was established, and in the following year Ulrica Eleonora managed to bring about the election of her husband as Frederick I, King of Sweden.

Caroline absolutism now became a thing of the past. There had always been in the country an opposite current which had kept alive the noble tradition of constitutionalism in Swedish political life. This was expressed in an aristocratic form by the mediaeval Council, by Erik Sparre, and by the great nobles of the seventeenth century. The Council had asserted its power during Charles XII's absence in Turkey, and there had even been rumours of a projected *coup d'état*. There had been signs of open opposition in the *Riksdag* of 1713–14, and a similar attitude later found silent expression in the unwillingness shown by many civil servants to serve under the more extreme forms of absolute government, and in their critical observations on the state of the country and its resources. A change had long been desired, for, during Charles XII's final years, the bureaucracy established by Charles XI, which had been recruited mainly from lesser nobles, had been disregarded as coolly as had the upper aristocracy, and its place had been taken by the new government departments controlled by Görtz. Members of the Council and other officials had therefore provided the nucleus of a concealed opposition, and they now came forward with demands based on new constitutional principles. Royal authority was side-stepped, and as a result of the Forms of Government accepted in 1719 and 1720 and of the *Riksdag* Ordinance of 1723 the Estates, i.e. the *Riksdag*, became the most powerful element in the government. The Estates were dominated by the office-holders, and at once annulled Charles XII's administrative innovations and re-established the old order. This involved the reinstatement of the former collegial departments, although from 1720 onwards they included only a few members of the Council. The five great offices of the crown were allowed to lapse, and these honourable titles dating from the early Middle Ages thus disappear from Swedish history. The Council of the Realm came to contain sixteen members, and the Council itself was divided into two sections, its chief official being the President of the Chancery. The Chancery secretaries, on the other hand, were not members of the Council, an omission which still showed traces of the old dividing-line between secretaries and high-born councillors.

It was not immediately clear how the new constitutionalism was going to develop. Both Ulrica Eleonora's own
temperament, which was not unlike that of her brother, and
the fact that she was the daughter of a Swedish King guaranteed her considerable authority during her first year, when
she was reigning alone. The situation was changed, however,
by the accession of Frederick I in 1720, when the authority
of the sovereign further declined. Nevertheless Frederick, too,
assembled all his available resources with a view to retaining
the power that still remained to him; and he regarded it as
one of his first tasks to secure his position by obtaining the
recognition of a Hessian relative as successor to the Swedish
throne – for he and Ulrica Eleonora had no children – and
thus thwarting the plans of Charles Frederick. Meanwhile
he sought his main allies inside the country from among the
royalist peasant Estate.

The future development of the constitution would, obviously, depend to a large extent on the nature of King
Frederick's rule during the first critical years of peace. The
first step, however, was to bring the war to an end. Inevitably
Sweden had suffered heavily both in vigour and in prestige
from the death of Charles XII; and, once his inflexible will
had disappeared, there could be no more thought of continuing the war to the bitter end. So enormous a strain,
concentrated in a comparatively short period of time, had
engendered a war-weariness which proved impervious to any
further challenge. Nevertheless, the former opportunities still
existed and they were increased at the beginning of 1719,
when open controversy broke out between England-Hanover
and Russia. This gave the Swedish government a fresh
chance for diplomatic manœuvre, despite the fact that there
was nobody left to lead an army, that the Russians were
making raids on Sweden's east coast, and that the Danes were
moving into Norway. This time, however, Sweden made
no attempt to play off Russia and England-Hanover against
each other; she declared unconditionally in favour of the

latter, and in November 1719 procured peace at the cost of
Bremen and Verden. Through the mediation of England and
France peace was then made with Prussia, to whom Sweden
ceded the southern portion of Pomerania, including Stettin
and the islands of Usedom and Wollin. Signed in January
1720, this treaty at last gave Prussia access to the coveted
Oder estuary, even though Sweden still retained her control
of it. In June 1720 the mediation of England brought about
a treaty between Denmark and Sweden, by which Sweden
renounced her exemption from the Sound tolls and withdrew her traditional backing of Holstein-Gottorp – a concession which was the less painful to her in that Frederick I
was not particularly desirous of assisting the country of his
rival. Thus denuded, Sweden sought the powerful backing of
England in an attempt to regain some of her former Baltic
possessions now in Russian hands.

England's support, however, proved somewhat shadowy,
and when the Czar reinforced his demands by fresh raids in
1721, Sweden found that at the crucial moment she was
alone; England's one desire was to extricate herself at all
possible speed from the Scandinavian crisis. By the Treaty of
Nystad in 1721 Sweden was compelled to yield Livonia,
Esthonia, Ingermanland, and East Karelia (including
Viborg) to Russia. Her position suffered considerably as a
result of these terms – both strategically in that she could no
longer rely on Finland as a bulwark, and economically by the
loss of the rich province Livonia. At the same time, however,
she was granted the right to import large quantities of duty-
free grain from Riga.

During these critical negotiations there is no indication
that Frederick I subordinated his own interests to those of
his country. At that moment Russia was supporting Duke
Charles Frederick of Holstein, who had taken refuge with
the Czar when he left Sweden, and it was known that Peter
was planning a marriage between the Duke and his daughter.
Situated midway between his rival and his chief ally,

England, Frederick I had shown few scruples in his political manœuvres; even so, he failed to attain either of his objectives – the enhancement of his authority and the recognition of a Hessian dynasty. Equally unsuccessful were the methods by which he attempted to pilot his country through the storms of these difficult years. Nevertheless he was still sanguine and he hoped to consolidate his position at the *Riksdag* of 1723 with the help of the peasant Estate and other royalists. In this he also failed; a Holstein party emerged whose members criticized Frederick's part in the peace negotiations, and favoured the claims of Charles Frederick, in the hope that he, together with the Czar, might help to restore to Sweden some part of what she had lost; reference was also made to Peter's intention to hand over Livonia to the Duke as a marriage settlement. Thus King Frederick's schemes were all completely frustrated, the more so as during the 1723 *Riksdag* an ordinance was passed which increased the power of the Estates. The Swedish monarchy was beginning to lose its traditional place in the political life of the country, and signs of the new order became immediately apparent. The King had become nothing more than the chief member of the Council, and his influence was limited to the exercise of two votes on important issues; nor was Frederick's personal authority, already seriously diminished, such as to make up for so drastic a curtailment of royal power.

The first years of this so-called Age of Freedom were also marked by grave social problems similar to those which had so frequently occurred before. The barriers between the Estates were still as strong as ever, despite the isolated protests from the unprivileged classes – not to mention the levelling-out process which had been indirectly stimulated by Charles XII. On the other hand, in the Age of Freedom the social problems were consciously brought out into the open and debated with more vigour than in the previous century. And now that a strong monarchy had ceased to function as mediator and leveller, and could no longer exploit the differences between nobility and non-privileged, these differences loomed even larger than before, and came up regularly for discussion. Although these social conflicts were sometimes overshadowed by party quarrels on foreign policy, they remained important throughout this period.

The abolition of 'feudal' privileges and the levelling-out of the old class differences took roughly ninety years, from 1719 to 1809. From shortly after Charles XII's death to the 1723 *Riksdag*, the question of privileges provided material for a series of important disputes. These were resumed about 1771, until peace was finally made less than a century after the beginning of the Age of Freedom.

The noble Estate in Sweden had been to a certain extent remodelled after Charles XI's reduction; although the landed nobility had not disappeared, the newly ennobled officials had been proportionately strengthened. During Sweden's Age of Greatness the division between upper and lower nobility had been emphasized by a three-fold division in the House of Nobility: Counts and barons formed the first class; members of the Council and their descendants the second, and other nobles the third; and the power of the higher aristocracy was secured by the allocation of one vote to each class. The lower aristocracy had asserted itself under Charles XI, and now, in the general reorganization, the House of Nobility was made into an integral unit and individual voting was instituted. At the same time, as a result of the rapid development in industry and commerce, the unprivileged Estates, who were fully conscious of their importance in the new constitution, had acquired determined and experienced leaders. Attention was also drawn to inequalities in privilege by the fact that during the great economic upheavals a few of the privileged estates of the nobles had passed into the hands of unprivileged landowners; and it should be remembered, too, that both Charles XI and Charles XII had regarded merit and not birth as ground for promotion. All in all, the question of privileges was bound to be raised once the absolute monarchy had gone and the crisis had been weathered.

It came up at the 1719 *Riksdag*, immediately after the King's death. It was not raised by the lower Estates, however, but by the nobility. With the collapse of absolute government the nobles had taken over control and had already been granted far-reaching privileges by Ulrica Eleonora, who had agreed that henceforward all reduction should cease. As was to be expected, the other Estates strongly protested, and in 1720 the *Riksdag* rejected the more extreme demands of the nobles. Moreover, the privileges granted in 1719 were not confirmed, and the matter was temporarily shelved. At the *Riksdag* of 1723 a compromise was reached, following the King's attempts to extend his power, and the commoners forced the nobles to climb down. The outcome was, to all intents and purposes, a codification of the Caroline practice. Positions in the Council and other high offices were reserved for the nobles, whose exemption from taxation was confirmed in accordance with earlier custom; at the same time they were refused the right to enlarge those estates which were particularly profitable and which carried the most far-reaching privileges. Though the nobles also retained other financial advantages, the right of the clergy and burgesses to hold certain types of 'free' land was now uncontested. The peasants also gained. It was an old custom that a crown peasant – that is to say, one who cultivated a crown farm – might acquire ownership of his homestead by purchase. In 1723 this practice was regularized, and it remained in force, with only a few interruptions and modifications, until 1773. In consequence large areas of crown territory passed into the hands of the peasants, and between 1700 and 1772 the proportion of land owned by 'free' tax peasants rose from 31·5 per cent. to 46·9 per cent. of the total number of homesteads.

Once peace, external and internal, had been restored the next step was to restore prosperity. As a result of the war both territories and population had diminished; revenues and custom duties were no longer coming in from important commercial towns, and the century-old dreams of economic control of the Baltic seem to have been shattered. Finland had been badly ravaged; thousands of its inhabitants had been deported, and the war had left traces of misery everywhere. War losses were estimated at about 30,000 dead and captured, though about 7,000 prisoners returned to Sweden from Russia in 1722-3.

The work of rehabilitation was started at once. All the emergency measures, administrative and economic, were cancelled, and the token copper currency was devalued, though the heavy taxes were retained for another ten years. Sweden proved surprisingly resilient, and it was not long before the national economy began to recover; largely thanks to the mere fact of peace. The leading figure of these years was Arvid Horn. He had been a captain in Charles XII's bodyguard and shortly after Charles's death he had become President of the Chancery. He had retired for a short period as a result of disagreement with the Queen, but had resumed office shortly afterwards. He was an elusive personality but an astute and level-headed politician. Slowly but surely the nature of his policy and leadership was revealed. In 1724 the Holstein party, still very active, made an alliance with Russia and maintained its support of Duke Charles Frederick; and in the same year representatives of the same party, adhering rigidly to their mercantilist outlook, achieved their so-called 'Products Edict' (*Produktplakat*), directed against England. This edict, which recalls Cromwell's Navigation Act of 1651, laid down that foreign ships should only be allowed to carry to Sweden the products of their own countries, a restriction which had long been among the aims of Swedish commercial policy.

Horn was successful in defeating the ambitious schemes for restitution conceived by the Holstein party, which had to a certain extent inherited Görtz's outlook in foreign policy.

He directed his policy first towards the western powers, who had united with Prussia in the Hanoverian alliance of 1725, and finally towards England alone after she had drifted apart from France. The deaths of Czar Peter and the Empress Catherine I deprived Duke Charles Frederick of his influence in Russia and the Holsteiners, therefore, of their most powerful ally. In due course the Estates were persuaded to approve Horn's foreign policy, and he was soon able to displace the Holsteiners on the Council and obtain a majority for his own party; and subsequently the opposition was disbanded. The Products Edict, however, remained in force, for, although slightly detrimental to trade, it naturally stimulated Swedish shipping and ship-building. England's demand for high-quality iron from Sweden was still so great that no conflict ensued from the new navigation act, notwithstanding the threat of Russian and American competition. Sweden's commerce now flourished apace, thanks to the maintenance of peace and Horn's moderate mercantile policy. Although the trade in copper had declined, a new industry was beginning to arise alongside the export of iron to England. This country had for some time been importing tar from America instead of from Sweden; but the great Swedish forests could also yield another commodity, timber. At that time the annual export was no more than could nowadays be produced by a single sawmill and comprised only 5 per cent. of the total exports; nevertheless it constituted the beginning of a tremendous enterprise. Meanwhile, trade with France and the Mediterranean countries increased, the share of foreign vessels in Swedish commerce diminished, and in more remote continents trade was in the hands of the Swedish East India Company. About 8·5 per cent. of the population of Sweden was now occupied in crafts and industry (including mining).

On the other hand agriculture, the most important means of livelihood, was still unaffected by the new prosperity. Sweden's need for grain imports was intensified by the ever-increasing rise in population during the period of peace, yet for centuries agriculture had made virtually no progress. It had been retarded by the antiquated codes of the village community, inefficient cultivation, and stringent State regulations which were more concerned with ensuring the taxes of the crown than with improving agriculture and rural conditions. In spite of this, about 75 per cent. of the population were still employed in husbandry and cattle-breeding.

As we have seen, the monarchy was also non-existent as a political force during the first part of the Age of Freedom, and power was centred in the Council. It has also been noted that Horn's rule recalled that of the old aristocratic Council during the Regencies of the seventeenth century. He found his main support among the bureaucrats and the clergy, though many burgesses and peasants also sided with him. Indeed, it was not only in the Council that the seventeenth-century tradition was carried on during this period. The essence of Charles XI's reorganization was preserved in the revival of the *indelning* system for the army and the re-imposition of the old taxes in kind. His model budget, too, was still the ideal, and served as a framework for the unified budget of all State income and expenditure which was ultimately achieved in 1723. Meanwhile the pietist revival which had taken place among the imprisoned Caroline soldiers spread rapidly, and a young priest called Erik Tolstadius began vigorously to attack the activities of the Church. A violent controversy ensued, and the outcome was the Conventicle Edict of 1726, which enforced orthodoxy and banned other religious sects. The spiritual legacy of the Caroline Age was also expressed in more positive ways. The mediaeval national code and town laws were superseded at the 1734 *Riksdag* by a new law which restated the former codes in admirably concise and appropriate terms. Since 1710, Gustav Cronhielm, the Council member who was largely responsible for this new law, had been chairman of the legal commission which had started its work under Charles XI.

The views of the leading scientists also had their roots in the Caroline period, though new tendencies can be discerned in Olof Dalin's *Then svenska Argus* (The Swedish Argus), a didactic periodical based on English models and published at the beginning of the 1730's; or in the contemporary French taste in architecture represented by Carl Gustav Tessin, who completed the interior of the Stockholm Palace. The ideas of the period of enlightenment and rococo were already beginning to influence Swedish taste, though they did not become fashionable until the middle of the century.

The potentialities of the new constitution had not yet been fully realized, however, nor had the new ideological currents then sweeping Europe yet penetrated Sweden. Nevertheless a new outlook was gradually gaining ground: it could already be perceived at the 1734 *Riksdag*, and by the time the next *Riksdag* met in 1738–9 it was shared by the majority. Its strength was revealed in the emergence of the first real political party of the Age of Freedom. The members of this group called themselves 'Hats', in contradistinction to those of Horn's party, whose policy was deemed worthy of 'night-caps' and who were therefore known as the 'Caps'. The Hats, who included among their number several former Hol-steiners, had formulated a systematic programme for both home and foreign affairs. Horn's foreign policy, which had been based on an alliance with England and France, had been thrown out of gear when these two Powers drifted apart, and it was not easy for Sweden to maintain her equilibrium. The Hats now demanded a foreign policy designed to exploit the various diplomatic alignments in Europe with the aim of recovering Sweden's territorial losses, particularly her losses to Russia. Charles XII became for them a political symbol; indeed, this was among the first of many illustrations of the way in which any accurate judgment of him on the part of posterity has been distorted by his appeal to the emotions. On this occasion he was made to personify a policy of retribution against Russia which, it was hoped, would restore to Sweden her share in the control of the Baltic and promote Swedish trade. The Hats also demanded that mercantilist doctrines should be more consistently applied, insisting that Horn was too moderate in this respect. The demands of the Hats found support in various quarters, among young military and civil officials, for example, and among wholesale merchants and rich nobles who were engaged in all the new economic projects. At the 1734 *Riksdag* the Hats, having vigorously launched that part of their programme which advocated a union with France, obtained the upper hand in the Secret Committee: they then approached the French envoy in Stockholm, who provided them with money. The new trend was also beginning to find favour in the Council, and at the *Riksdag* of 1738 the Hats proceeded to attack Horn in an atmosphere of lively agitation. A new era was dawning in the Age of Freedom.

# XXV

# The Rule of the Hats: Politics, Scholarship and Letters
## 1739-1764

In the 1738–9 *Riksdag* the Hats succeeded in bringing about a fundamental change in parliamentary procedure. Under the prevailing constitutional practice members of the Council could be convicted, on the evidence of incriminating Council protocols, of failing in their duty to the Estates, and accordingly expelled. Their successors were then proposed by a committee of the three upper Estates, and appointed by the King and his councillors. This somewhat complicated system opened the door to a form of parliamentary action which the Hats now put into effect for the first time. They had already, in the autumn of 1738, forced through an alliance with France, and they now accused the Council of failing to follow up the foreign policy sanctioned at the previous *Riksdag*. In December Horn resigned, at his own request, from the Presidency of the Chancery, while most of his adherents in the Council were indicted on more or less genuine charges and were dismissed. The Hats then took over the control of the government. They confirmed the alliance with France and, as soon as the situation in Europe allowed, they intended to carry out a vigorous foreign policy. Their mercantilist outlook was expressed in more active support of industry (especially the new 'factories') and trade through export bounties and loans.

All this led to a remarkable change in constitutional practice. Just as the power of the monarchy had been broken before, so now that of the Council, based on seventeenth-century traditions represented by Arvid Horn, was similarly destroyed and the ascendancy of the Estates was virtually complete. Under the new constitution the Council had already been deprived of its former position as pivot of the bureaucracy and the colleges. Now it became purely political in character, and its members were chosen for their political rather than their administrative qualities. The system of parliamentary government which resulted from this change was a significant phenomenon of the Age of Freedom, and it is interesting to compare it with the older English form, with which it had certain features in common.

The Hats now ruled the country from 1739 to 1765. Their first Chancery President was Karl Gyllenborg, Charles XII's envoy in London and later a prominent member of the Holstein party, and he was succeeded as party leader of the Hats by Carl Gustav Tessin. These twenty-six years were not lacking in crises, some of which were provoked by features inherent in the Hat rule. The first arose as a result of their foreign policy. Having incapacitated their opponents at the 1740–1 *Riksdag* by a charge of treason, the Hats decided on war with Russia; in so doing they were prompted partly by the prospect of support from France, partly by the European situation in general (Russia was at war with Turkey), and partly by hopes of co-operation with the Russian Princess Elizabeth, who was planning a *coup d'état* in St Petersburg. Yet, for various reasons, this war of revenge was a complete fiasco. Such preparations as were made proved wholly inadequate, the army was in a wretched condition, and Finland's military problems still awaited solution. Moreover, Elizabeth made herself Empress by her own unaided efforts and was therefore little inclined to help Sweden. The Russians proceeded to occupy a large part of Finland, and the situation became threatening in the extreme.

Sweden was forced to make peace, and the negotiations became involved with the question of the succession. After various proposals the choice stood between Empress Elizabeth's candidate, Adolf Frederick of Holstein-Gottorp, a kinsman of Charles XII's brother-in-law, and the Danish

Crown Prince Frederick. When the *Riksdag* reassembled, the Hats had to face a storm of well-organized opposition among the commons against the bureaucracy, and, indeed, against the entire constitution. The Swedish peasants, traditionally royalist in outlook, were attracted towards Danish absolutism, and Prince Frederick's cause gained considerable support. Rarely, since the old days of military conquest, had a union between Sweden, Denmark and Norway seemed within such easy reach; the peasant Estate even formally elected the Crown Prince as successor to the throne. The people of Dalarna, exasperated both by the policy of the government and by their own acute distress, marched on Stockholm, and there were also signs of unrest in a number of other districts. But it was in vain. Elizabeth remained adamant; the Dalarna rising was defeated, and those who took part were severely punished. Nevertheless, in return for the election of her candidate, Elizabeth had already agreed in principle to terms of peace, and these were ratified in Åbo in 1743 after her candidate, Adolf Frederick, had been elected. The peace was relatively mild, but the strategic value of the Finnish frontier was diminished by the cession of part of south-east Finland to Russia, and the whole episode had raised serious doubts as to the general effectiveness of Finland's defence.

Although the Hats had gained a temporary, if ignominious, reprieve, their position was still precarious. The greatest danger arose from Russia's increased influence in Sweden, which threatened to become almost a protectorate, and which resulted from Russia's having secured her own candidate as heir to the throne; and it was with Russian support that the opposition – the Caps – now took the offensive. On the other hand, Adolf Frederick and his gifted and very ambitious wife Louisa Ulrica, sister of Frederick II of Prussia, were now on the side of the Hats. At the next *Riksdag* in 1746–7 the Caps, with their Russian supporters, were overwhelmed by a wave of intense national feeling, and the

Russian partisans received summary treatment. The second crisis had been weathered.

Nevertheless, Sweden's military reputation, which had been such a powerful asset to her foreign policy since Caroline times, had suffered badly as a result of the war and its outcome. Plans for strengthening her defences were vague, though there was a general feeling that extensive reforms were necessary. These were eventually accomplished on lines projected at the beginning of the Age of Freedom by Major-General Axel Löwen, and they throw an interesting light on the changes which had taken place in Sweden's geographical and strategic position. An oared fleet of the Mediterranean type, which became known as the Army's fleet or the Skerries fleet, was created for purposes of warfare in the Gulf of Finland; work was begun, under the direction of Augustin Ehrensvärd, on the construction of a great fortress, Sveaborg, outside Helsingfors, and a careful study was made of schemes to improve the defence of Finland by collaboration between the various arms. By these means a foundation was laid for future development. The situation was well summed up by J. Serenius, a famous Cap politician and one-time chaplain of the Swedish church in London, in the words: 'Finland had borne the brunt of all Sweden's tussles with her worst enemy, and yet she outdid all the other Swedish dominions in undaunted faith and loyalty to the Swedish Crown.'

At the time when the Hats had won over the Holstein-Gottorp couple to their independent anti-Russian policy (thanks largely to the skill of their new leader, C. G. Tessin), they had promised the future King that once he was on the throne his power would be increased. When Frederick I died in 1751, however, this promise was not kept, and a further cause of tension was introduced into Swedish domestic politics. A struggle developed in which the goal was not so much power within the framework of the existing constitution as an extension of the royal power and a revision

19

of the constitution. A court party was formed, centred round the King and Queen, and it remained in existence throughout this period. The parliamentary practice which had developed in Sweden was now confronted with new constitional doctrines imported from the Continent, above all by the conception of a strong central government advocated by the Physiocrats. The resultant clash gave rise to the Hat party's third crisis, which culminated in an abortive royalist coup at the 1756 *Riksdag*. The humiliation which the King and Queen incurred by this failure led to an inevitable break with the Hats. Nor were matters improved when in 1757 the Hats tried to push forward their foreign policy by joining the enemies of Prussia and Frederick II during the Seven Years' War. Louisa Ulrica took this as a personal insult, though the real motive was to safeguard the mouth of the Oder against the designs of Prussia. But this move, too, was unsuccessful, and it was only with the greatest difficulty that the Hats managed to extricate themselves from their fourth serious crisis. As a result of the Queen's intervention, however, a tolerable peace with Prussia was effected in 1762 on a *status quo* basis.

The policy of the Hats also included an economic and financial programme. The prevailing topics were not all controversial; the parties were more or less agreed, for example, on their attitude to the iron industry. The Hats formed it into a monopoly under State control, and subsequently aimed to stabilize both production and prices, and save charcoal and wood. The result was that Sweden's iron exports remained fairly steady at about 50,000 tons per year throughout the Age of Freedom. Other questions were less easily solved. As has already been mentioned, the Hats were fervent mercantilists, anxious to promote home production, and in 1740 one of their most prominent members, A. J. von Höpken, formulated this economic doctrine in a famous speech on the 'virtue of abundance'. As a result, industries acquired a spurious prosperity while the goods remained poor and costly, and the policy owed its long but misguided acceptance solely to energetic propaganda. Moreover, the mass of paper money which was issued, especially in war time, produced considerable confusion in the monetary system, and uneasiness was intensified by a total disregard of the relation between the mass production of notes and the rapid fall in the value of minted coins.

Although the ruling party was predominantly interested in the manufacturing industries, progress was also made in agriculture from about 1740 onwards. It is true that this more liberal agricultural policy was determined by mercantilist doctrine rather than by any desire to benefit agriculture as such, since its main aim was to encourage larger families and so increase the population. This involved the abolition of former restrictions, for example the prohibition against the division of holdings which, after 1747, could be divided down to an eighth of a *mantal* (the original cameral entity supposed to represent a 'normal' family). This was followed in 1757 by the *storskifte*, which enabled a farmer to consolidate his scattered strips into a more convenient working unit independent of his neighbours in the common fields. This process of consolidation was not yet very extensive, but it paved the way for a consistent policy of enclosure and consolidation some decades later. Meanwhile, the area under cultivation increased; between about 1700 and the latter half of the century Närke, for example, showed an increase of from 5·3 per cent. to 7·5 per cent. of the total area. Potatoes, which were now being harvested for the first time in modest quantities, were later to become one of the staple crops of the country. The interest in population had yet another significant consequence during the Age of Freedom: population statistics – the oldest of their kind in the world – were introduced, and it is thanks to these that it is now possible to give exact figures for Sweden's population during the eighteenth century.

All these decisions on agricultural policy, though ultimately

of the greatest significance, were calmly taken in the
middle of party wrangles without stirring up anything like
the same acrimony as did the discussions on many less
important questions. All in all, a good deal of useful work
was accomplished during the Age of Freedom, which has
sometimes been unduly overshadowed by the feuds and party
quarrels in the *Riksdag*. It may be that the peaceful spirit of
progress was to a certain extent a reaction against what
had gone before. Yet the tendency was towards modification
rather than renunciation. And indeed, the commercial enterprises in remote lands, the zeal for scholarship and discovery,
and the courageous way in which the legislators responded
to the demands of progress – all these are imbued with that
audacity and fearlessness which characterized the Age of
Greatness. It is the contrasts which are more sharply
revealed, especially perhaps in the field of foreign policy.
The plea that bribery and corruption were common to
Europe at this time does not excuse the behaviour of the
different parties of the Age of Freedom in exposing their
country to danger by their subservience to foreign Powers.
Those who attempted to carry out an independent foreign
policy too often failed to foresee the consequences of their
actions, and, as far as military planning was concerned, it
sometimes seems as though party leaders had no notion of
how to cut their coat according to their cloth.

The rule of the Estates had, besides, certain rather un-
pleasant aspects which were plainly revealed during the
years of party strife. Individual liberty and security were
frequently endangered as a result of the bitter struggles, and
victories were ruthlessly exploited for party ends. Much was
determined by party reward and party justice. Here again,
however, historians should not overlook the positive features
of political life, of which one of the most important – as
modern historians tend to emphasize – was the development
of a constitution which was peculiarly Swedish.

The *Riksdag* acquired its shape first, in theory, from the

ordinance of 1723, and subsequently from practical experience. To a certain extent the old framework of the sixteenth and seventeenth centuries was retained; the nobility remained the leading Estate; and as a result of the abolition of the class division in the first Estate in 1719, the lower aristocracy, numerically the strongest, gained the upper hand and the House of Nobility was democratized, most noticeably from the 1730's onwards. Each family could be represented by its head or his deputy, and the number of representatives varied considerably according to the importance of the issue under discussion; three hundred was about the normal figure, though this might swell to over a thousand when vital questions were to be raised. Both Hats and Caps were represented in the House of Nobility, whose President, the *Lantmarskalk*, was elected by the members.

The Estate of the clergy comprised about fifty members. The bishops were members *ex officio*, while the other clerical members were elected. The archbishop or, in his absence, the Bishop of Linköping, presided. The Caps, incidentally, had always had a firm footing in this group. The representatives of the burgesses were elected from among the leading citizens by direct or indirect vote, and their number was about ninety; their chairman was often the chief magistrate of Stockholm. This Estate was a traditional stronghold of the Hats on account of the benefits which accrued from their economic programme to the section of society it represented. The peasant Estate contained about one hundred and fifty members who were generally elected by indirect vote. Though royalist by tradition, many of them later transferred their allegiance to the Hats. The inevitable lack of political maturity and experience in the fourth Estate was frequently revealed in the earlier years, and it was not unknown for violent scuffles to break out during debates. Peace might sometimes be restored for a short time by a resourceful member striking up a hymn in which the entire assembly would join, only to be at loggerheads again as soon as it was over. The most influential person in the peasant Estate was the Secretary, who was elected by the speakers of all four Estates.

The basic constitutional law had invested this *Riksdag* of the Estates with almost supreme power. Theoretically, the King was supposed to approve its legislation; in practice he had little say in the matter. The *Riksdag* had sole authority to impose taxes, duties, and tributes. It controlled the work of the Council and the government departments by inspecting their protocols for the years between its meetings; it determined both general objectives and specific matters of foreign policy; it appointed courts of justice to deal with special cases, especially those of a political nature, and it could also intervene in the ordinary course of justice. Through the Council and by means of the instructions it gave for the periods between its meetings, the *Riksdag* virtually controlled the entire policy of the country – the Council might almost be called the executive committee of the four Estates. The King's stubborn refusal to put his name to certain decisions was rendered nugatory by the adoption in 1756 of the familiar expedient of a royal stamp, which had the same validity as the King's own signature. And it was not long before the Estates had evolved a distinct constitutional theory based on their own infallibility as 'the sovereign Estates of the realm'.

Nevertheless it was plain that the rather clumsy process whereby each Estate met and deliberated separately called for joint committees similar to those of the seventeenth century. Of these the most important was the Secret Committee (*sekreta utskottet*), from which the peasants were excluded and which was concerned with foreign policy and other questions of a confidential nature. In addition there were a number of other permanent or temporary committees, usually known as 'deputations', which in all essentials provided the basis of the committee system which characterizes the Swedish *Riksdag* to-day.

In the House of Nobility the art of politics and rhetoric, not to mention that of intrigue, flourished with exceptional vigour and found magnificent exponents in such distinguished Hat leaders as C. G. Tessin, A. J. von Höpken, and Axel von Fersen the Elder. The recorded debates were not without brilliance, and were marked by both wit and authority, while the House of Nobility, with its clubs and its whips, possessed also a highly perfected party organization. Political theories were propounded in numerous reports, chronicles, and treatises on political economy; not to mention the pamphlets and lampoons which were provoked by political agitation.

The public mind, in fact, was gradually becoming politically conscious, though the process was slow and, so far, limited to small sections of society. Evidence of this growth of political consciousness was provided by the development of the party system and its recognition as a legitimate piece of political machinery. Formerly, party quarrels had often merely caused the bewildered peasants to mistrust both sides. Now a different attitude prevailed towards the party as such, for the old political Estate of nobles was matched with new and able men from other classes, well-read clergy and rich and experienced merchants, who were not slow to make their mark in the party politics of the *Riksdag*. Despite their incongruities and distortions, the new political conceptions were a tremendous advance on those of previous centuries.

Swedish letters and Swedish scholarship also played a significant part in the Age of Freedom. Just as Arvid Horn was dismissed by a new political generation, so the old school of literature was being superseded by more recent trends. A departure from the old culture had already been effected in Dalin's *Then svenska Argus*, published in 1730. Influenced by English models, this marked a departure from the old culture with its strong classical flavour, its pronounced element of theology, and its chauvinistic antiquarianism. Moreover, the Hats idealized France, the Caps England – the two countries which had done most to produce the Age of Enlightenment, and each now had an influence on Swedish culture. From France came the classical poetic form, which had been evolved during *le Grand Siècle* but had hitherto found no great echo among Swedish poets; and a treatment of history and philosophy which was at once elegant and popular; while philosophical, economic, and political theories, together with new scientific and antiquarian ideas, spread from England.

The early 1740's saw the first appearance of the Swedish poetess Hedvig Charlotta Nordenflycht, a typical figure of the Swedish Enlightenment. Her circle included G. P. Creutz, from Finland, and F. Gyllenborg – two aristocratic poets who represented respectively the Epicureans and the Stoics of the period. Creutz's beautiful versification was something quite new in the Swedish language. In art, too, Sweden moved with the times, and by the middle of the century rococo had replaced the Caroline baroque as the prevailing fashion. The Palace of Stockholm was decorated in the new style, a China Pavilion was built for Queen Louisa Ulrica in the gardens of Drottningholm Palace; the seventeenth-century strongholds of the nobles were modernized and new more elegant ones were built. A further characteristic of the age was to be found in its patrons; foremost among them was C. G. Tessin, who, besides being a politician, was an art-collector and a gifted amateur author and was responsible for some of the finest collections in the National Art Gallery of Stockholm to-day. And finally, societies of a new kind, either scientific or learned, began to be founded in which nobles mingled with scholars and authors with men of business. The Academy of Science was founded in 1739 and the Academy of Letters, History, and Antiquities in 1753.

The culture of the Age of Freedom was thus rich and varied, and full of contrasts. Traces of the Caroline period and contemporary utilitarianism flourished side by side with rococo elegance, ambitious dreams of political expansion, and practical research. In fact the Age of Enlightenment was not so exclusively rational as the romantic would have us believe. Religious movements which appealed to the emotions – Herrnhutism, for example – won many converts, while in the 1740's Emanuel Swedenborg was evolving his mystical doctrine of the world of spirits. Such developments reinforced the new freedom of thought in its attack on the rigid orthodoxy of the past.

The outstanding figure in Swedish culture was Carl Linnaeus, ennobled as von Linné, a typical product of the age. Although he had visited foreign countries, his finest literary achievements are to be found in the books which resulted from his tours of investigation at home during the 1740's; in these he recorded the features peculiar to the Swedish provinces and anticipated the development of modern Sweden in his view that 'one province can be helped by the agricultural practices of the other'. In the 1730's he had visited Lappland, thus following up the ethnographical interest which had been taken in this area since the sixteenth century; and he gave a new stimulus to botany with his world-famous sexual system (*Species plantarum*, 1753). No other contemporary source recreates the epoch so vividly as the descriptions of Linnaeus's botanical excursions round Uppsala with his pupils: 'They were undertaken in a certain order . . . and were made to eight places near the town. At this time he had not less than two to three hundred who accompanied him, all clad in light linen garments, and bearing all necessary devices for the collecting of herbs and insects. . . . During each excursion, certain resting-places were ordained, where the scattered students would assemble, and where lessons would be given on their most important findings. When the young men had thus disported themselves in the country from morning to night, they were marshalled for the return march and, with their teacher at their head, the young men trooped to the house in the Botanical

Gardens, where a repeated shout of *Vivat Linnaeus* wound up the pleasures of the day. The mirth, delight, and eagerness with which the youths listened to the words of their teacher inspired foreigners, no less than Swedish scholars, to share in these pleasures.'

This is the bright, idyllic side of a period which was at the same time rent with ideological strife, party divisions, and an unfortunate and over-ambitious foreign policy. The Hats had now been in power for more than twenty-five years; by the middle of the 1760's, however, the final crisis was at hand. During the long and stormy *Riksdag* of 1760–2 the position of the Hats, already precarious, was further shaken by the efforts of the Caps and the Court party, not to mention the behaviour of the malcontents in their own ranks. There were various attempts to reach a compromise and the Estates gratefully accepted the Queen's help in the peace negotiations with her brother Frederick II of Prussia. The King and Queen, with the support of the Court party, were anxious that the constitution should be altered to give the monarchy more power. Though this scheme came to nothing, the proceedings did at least result in the adoption of the so-called 'composition policy' (*kompositionspolitiken*), which aimed to secure a mutual understanding between the different parties; and it seems that a temporary rapprochement between the Court and some of the party leaders had actually been achieved before the next *Riksdag*.

Shortly after the 1760–2 *Riksdag*, however, circumstances played into the hands of the Caps. In 1763 the financial confusion in the country was intensified by a general European crisis. The rule of the Hats offered abundant openings for attack which the oft-defeated Caps were not slow to exploit, and they began to prepare for a general onslaught. Even more important than the traditional party quarrels, however, were the serious rifts in society itself, which were to reveal themselves during the immediately following years.

# XXVI

# Social Problems and Conflicts. The *Coup d' État* 1765-1772

At the 1765 *Riksdag* the Caps, as had been anticipated, came into power with the support of the Court party, to whom they had given a promise that the constitution would be revised. The Hats were removed from the Council and their rule was made the object of a comprehensive judicial inquiry. The finances were put on a sounder basis and a reduction was made in the extravagances of the mercantilist policy. The former close relations with France gave way to a rapprochement with Russia and England, who had now been on friendly terms with each other for some time. Augustin Ehrensvärd was recalled from his military activities in Finland, though this involved no abandonment of the plans for the defence of Finland. The culprits among the Hats were tried. At the same time an important innovation was made in quite a different sphere. Hitherto only the polemics of the dominant party had appeared in print, those of the opposition being distributed in handwritten copies. An Ordinance passed in 1766 established for the first time the principle of freedom of the press – a notable step towards liberty of political opinion.

The revised constitution, however, failed to materialize and the Court party therefore again approached the Hats, who, in their turn, were holding out promises of a stronger monarchy. The Caps had made many enemies by their deflationary policy; and with the help of France on one side and the Hats on the other the King forced a *Riksdag* to be held in 1768. He refused to carry out his constitutional functions and the government departments, which were dominated by the Hats, followed his lead; and the Hats were restored to power, if only for a short time. By this time the nature of the differences between Hats and Caps had altered in a manner which became fully apparent at the 1771-2 *Riksdag*. During the last years of the Age of Freedom the Hats represented the interests of the bureaucracy and the nobles, while the Caps championed the lower Estates against the nobles, and the 'people' against the bureaucrats.

It will be remembered that the right of members of the lower, unprivileged Estates to hold government office had been a burning question during the debates on privilege during the 1720's. Since then, except for an occasional reference, the matter had receded into the background, and the close co-operation between the Hat nobles and the burgesses prevented any serious conflict. Towards the end of the period, however, as the party struggles became more complex, the subject was revived and the hostility between the nobles and the lower Estates flared up over a specific case. In 1770 the Council had proposed three nobles for the Vice-presidency of the Åbo court of Appeal, passing over two lawyers from the lower Estates. This gave rise to a flood of furious protests – resembling in form the pamphleteering literature which preceded the French Revolution – against the Council in particular and the nobility in general, and when the Estates met in 1771 they were all set for a battle.

The opposition party of the lower Estates was led by the Caps, who supported its demand for equal rights of promotion. At the 1771-2 *Riksdag* the Caps regained power in the face of formidable competition from the Hats and appointed some of their own leaders to the Council. The privilege question was then bandied to and fro with a lack of dignity which makes the *Riksdag* debates of that period somewhat unedifying. Nevertheless they had significant political and social implications. A typical representative of this closing phase of the Age of Freedom was the chaplain Anders Chydenius, a member for the clergy, who attended his first

*Riksdag* in 1765-6. He was a clever and original economist and provided in his work *The Nation's Profit* (1765) a classic exposition of liberal economic doctrines. He was unusually humane in his attitude to his fellow-men, and had been an enthusiastic champion of the new freedom of the press in 1766. Meanwhile, the burgomaster Alexander Kepplerus of Lovisia in Finland, with the assistance of a social philosopher issued a publication in which he was going a step farther than a mere stubborn defence of the rights of the lower Estates, and was seeking to improve the lot of those who were too lowly even to be represented at all – the agricultural labourers. Since Charles XI's time this unpropertied class had been subjected to regulations which had been imposed in order to procure labour for the large estates and recruits for the army and which had treated the landless labourer as a vagrant with no rights whatsoever. Kepplerus protested vehemently against such bondage, asserting that there should be equal liberty for all men except those of evil character. This embryonic democratic ideology, which was based on the desire so to establish the rights of the commons as to remove all possibility of an aristocratic revival, has been compared to some of the declarations of the French Revolution and was subsequently to be given even more radical expression by Chydenius.

Needless to say, the majority of the spokesmen of the unprivileged Estates harboured no such far-reaching or consistent democratic ideas, and were content to champion the interests of their own particular group. The nobles found even this more than they could stomach, however, and terrible threats issued from the House of Nobility: 'In the last resort we shall go forth sword in hand to defend the rights of our absent fellows.' All the same, the nobles were forced to give way over the question of right to office, and no one could now foretell at what point the Caps and the lower Estates would cease in their demands. In this way the specifically political issues became linked during the 1771-2

*Riksdag* with social differences, and the perpetual disputes produced an atmosphere of tension. Moreover the country-side, too, was showing signs of unrest as a result of poor harvests and the threat of famine, and the general discontent was intensified by the apparent inability of the government to alleviate the distress.

It has been suggested that at this point the constitution might have been repaired sufficiently to withstand attacks at home and to make Sweden powerful abroad. But this was not to be. Many were the forces by which constitutional life was being undermined: widespread disgust with the constant party squabbles, often purely selfish in motive, and with the dependence on foreign Powers; dissatisfaction with bureaucratic government; the anxiety of the nobles (particularly the officers) to preserve their privileged position; the unrest in the country due to famine; the attractive personality of the young King Gustav III; the desire on the part of France for a constitutional revolution in Sweden which would destroy the influence of Russia, Prussia, and even Denmark, and would restore the former alliance with France. The longing for a change in this respect was reinforced both among Swedish Russophobes and in France by the action of the Caps in following up their victory at home with an approach to Catherine II of Russia. Such was the setting, then, for the *coup d'état* of 1772.

The kings who reigned in Sweden during the Age of Freedom were not attractive personalities. Each had conducted himself honourably and energetically in early life, Frederick I as a general and Adolf Frederick as a military expert who did valuable work in reforming the Swedish army. But each in his later years lost all capacity to inspire or stimulate. Frederick is said to have had in his dotage only three names for the animate objects he came across: General, Doctor, and Pug; while Adolf Frederick is reputed, rather unfairly, to have given all his attention to his turning-lathe. Moreover, both were foreigners by origin and were therefore lacking in adequate knowledge of conditions in Sweden. Adolf Frederick's son Gustav, on the other hand, was a Swedish-born Prince, the first since Charles XII; in addition, he was talented and early showed signs of promise. The Court party had naturally gathered round him when he had witnessed his father's refusal to carry out his functions in 1768, and much was expected of him in the future. The death of Adolf Frederick occurred in the middle of the stormy 1771-2 *Riksdag*; he was succeeded by Gustav, who, though travelling in France at the time, was immediately recalled.

Gustav III was then twenty-five years old. He had had a curious boyhood, as the ruling Estates had ordained that, politically, he should be educated according to their views, and on one occasion their spies protested that the tutor of the ten-year-old Prince had allowed Pompey the Great to be eclipsed by Caesar, who 'unlawfully usurped the government'. The mind of the young Prince must have been influenced during these impressionable years by direct contact with political intrigue and violent party strife – and with detrimental results, as even his contemporaries acknowledged. Moreover the Estates had compelled him to make an unfortunate marriage with the Danish Princess Sophia Magdalena, daughter of Frederick V, and there is no doubt that this union of two entirely different personalities, prompted as it was by political motives, changed the highly strung Prince for the worse and tended to dehumanize him. Gustav was a precocious young man, with artistic leanings and a vivid imagination; and in his youth he revealed certain characteristics which recall those of his famous uncle, Frederick the Great of Prussia.

The Crown Prince had early become acquainted with the new political doctrines and particularly those held by the Physiocrats, who advocated a strong monarchy in the hands of an enlightened despot, and he was fired with a boyish enthusiasm for the great Swedish Kings, above all Gustav

Vasa and Gustavus Adolphus. He had already come into contact with the leaders of the Court party; and since then, during his extensive travels abroad in 1770–1, his outlook had become coloured to a large extent by French influences, and he yearned to shine as one of the heroes of French classical tragedy. This was the man who was to consolidate the opposition to the regime of the Age of Freedom.

When he returned from his French tour on the death of his father, Gustav tried various expedients to reconcile the different parties, but none met with any success. Towards the end of 1771 the Hats were thrown into complete confusion by the withdrawal of French support. France urged instead that Gustav should carry out a *coup d'état*, a project in which he could also count on the support of the nobles who had rallied to him after they had been expelled from office when the Hats were defeated in the Council in 1772. The Court party was thus rapidly increasing its numbers. And not only was revolution in the air: a leader too was available in the person of Baron J. M. Sprengtporten, assisted by the crown forester J. C. Toll and others who had been deprived of office by the Caps.

The services of a large group of noble officers and State officials, all of whom were threatened by the policy of the Caps and the lower Estates, were secured and in May 1772 Sprengtporten submitted a comprehensive plan of campaign; this was approved by the French ambassador and preparations were set on foot. The King's adherents were to attack in Finland, while Gustav III's brother, Duke Charles, with the aid of the ex-Hat Toll, was detailed to raise the banner of revolt in Skåne. Meanwhile the King himself would prepare a coup in Stockholm, which was to be carried through by the Finnish troops when they arrived in Sweden after the successful completion of their enterprise in Finland. The King and his party also drew up a new constitution which was to presage a return to the good government of Gustavus Adolphus. The *coup d'état* was thus very carefully planned.

On 12th August a rising, contrived by Toll, broke out in Kristianstad. Duke Charles hastened to the spot, ostensibly to subdue the rebels but actually to join the Kristianstad garrison. The Council was informed of the revolt on 16th August, and on the same day Sprengtporten attacked in Finland. So far, all had gone according to plan. But now the tide began to change, owing partly to the fact that the troops from Finland were held up by a head-wind. The Council, who mistrusted both Duke Charles and the King himself, took counter-action in Skåne and concentrated troops in Stockholm as a precaution against a possible royalist plot. Gustav III lacked the immediate assistance of his intimate friends and counsellors, and in this awkward predicament was forced to think for himself – and quickly. He found his main support among the Guards regiments, whose officers were ardent royalists, and it was with their help that he made his real debut on the political stage. On the evening of 18th August he attended an opera rehearsal and afterwards presided, with the utmost equanimity, at a State supper in the Palace. At 10 o'clock on the following morning, under dramatic circumstances, he accomplished the first public coup of his career. It was brilliantly successful. By the evening everything was over; the members of the Council had been arrested, together with the dangerous political conspirators, and the King's emblem – a white band round the left arm – was freely displayed. Not a drop of blood had been spilt. Gustav III had been observed by everyone riding confidently through the capital in the midst of his people, and even conversing with them. Not one of his powerful opponents seemed capable of action. Two days later the King delivered an inspiring speech to the Estates assembled in the *Riksdag*. In eloquent terms he described the *coup d'état* against the background of hate and party strife which had hitherto prevailed; and he disclaimed both any desire for power and any intention to restrict the people's liberty: 'I have promised to rule a free people, and the promise is the more sacrosanct in that

20

it was self-imposed. Far from desiring to encroach on your liberty, it is only the despotism of party rule I would abolish, replacing arbitrary rule by firm and established government, such as is ordained by Sweden's ancient law, and was the custom in the days of the greatest of my forebears.'

Many of his listeners were uplifted by the high-flown sentiments of the speech, and opposition either melted away or was relegated to the background. Even the Cap leaders swallowed their resentment. Thus the constitution of the Age of Freedom was discarded, shortly to be replaced by that formulated by the King during the summer. Urgent questions of finance and other matters were dealt with according to his wishes, while he was in turn authorized to allay the threatened famine by prohibiting the distillation of spirits from grain. The Estates then adjourned; according to the King's promise they would meet again in six years' time.

A particularly fortunate concatenation of events had precluded any interference from the Powers which had previously pledged themselves to defend the old constitution. Russia was occupied with the partition of Poland and war with Turkey, Prussia with the Polish question. Denmark was in no condition to protest, and was further intimidated by military demonstrations ordered by Gustav. England, in accordance with her policy of maintaining the balance of power in Europe, remained neutral, though France, having helped to instigate the *coup d'état*, now aided the King with fresh subsidies and diplomatic support. There were thus no signs of any hostile reaction. The King's name was on all lips, and the people expected him to take strong measures against famine and economic disorder, and put an end to party strife and general insecurity. Having formed an all-party Council, the King skilfully pleaded the cause of appeasement and tolerance: no 'slanderous diatribes' were to be printed, and the abhorrent party names were forbidden. 'Gustav revealed himself, armed with truth and heroic courage', wrote the poet Gyllenborg. 'In a trice the spell was broken.' In France Voltaire sang his praise: 'Jeune et digne héritier du grand nom de Gustave – Sauveur d'un peuple libre et roi d'un peuple brave.'

These restless and creative years also left their mark on intellectual life, and they were a remarkable period in the history of Swedish culture. In 1769 Sven Lagerbring began to publish a critical history of Sweden which was in many respects a pioneer achievement. Meanwhile Torbern Bergman was breaking fresh ground in chemical research, and disciples of Linnaeus were enthusiastically and indefatigably carrying on their master's work in almost all the four quarters of the earth. During the 1740's Pehr Kalm had already undertaken a voyage to North America; his fellow Finn, Peter Forsskål, had visited Arabia in the 1760's, and Carl Petter Thunberg was at that moment travelling to Africa and Asia. Music, which had hitherto been confined solely to the Court and the Church, now began to flourish among the bourgeoisie of Stockholm and Gothenburg, assisted by the followers of the distinguished composer Johan Helmich Roman (d. 1758).

Poetry, too, reflected the life of the period, and commercial enterprise provided the occasion for Jacob Wallenberg's lively and amusing description of his East Indian voyages, *Min son på galejan*, a literary counterpart to the more learned approach favoured by Linnaeus's pupils. It was also during this period that the composer-poet Carl Michael Bellman wrote a great number of the songs which were published in 1790 under the title of *Fredman's Epistles*. His poems give a realistic picture of Stockholm, though it is somewhat stylized and even playfully satirical in places. The watchmaker Fredman is made the central figure of an assembly of various characters drawn from Bohemian life and the bourgeoisie of the age of rococo. The mood varies from gaiety to melancholy and the whole is a curious mixture of elegance and crudity. Bellman has caught something of the Sweden of his day; and incidentally this was the first time that contemporary conditions had been reproduced in outstanding literary form since, four hundred years earlier, St Birgitta and the author of the *Chronicle of Eric* had reflected in their writings the chivalric and religious culture of their age.

# XXVII

# Gustav III

## 1773-1792

During the years 1768–9 a number of schemes were put forward for re-organizing the Swedish constitution according to the division of powers advocated by Montesquieu. Nevertheless, so strong was Sweden's own political tradition that when Gustav III sought a formula for his new government he went not to the fashionable doctrines of the Enlightenment but to the practice of Gustavus Adolphus. The violent reaction during the Age of Freedom against Caroline absolutism had taught him to curb his own undeniable leanings in that direction.

At the same time the constitution of 1772 was full of contradictions and obscurities. It laid down that the King should rule the kingdom, that a Council appointed by the King should 'advise but not govern', and that a group within the Council should act as final court of appeal. But the functions of the Council were left rather vague and the influence of that ancient institution was much diminished. The Estates were convened at the King's pleasure; and although they retained their right to grant taxes they had little chance of controlling or influencing actual financial policy. The King himself appointed the chairmen of each Estate. The *Riksdag*, as well as the King, could initiate legislation, and two special prerogatives also remained to it under the new constitution: its sanction was required for a war of aggression, and it could grant new taxes for a limited period, at the end of which a new *Riksdag* would become necessary. And the *Riksdag* retained also its rights over the State Bank.

It remained to be seen how the constitution would work out, for a good deal depended on the manner in which its terms were applied. Several of its features savoured strongly of its author's personality – his historical romanticism, his lust for power, his reluctance to go to the root of problems, and his general, rather vague optimism which stemmed, as is often the case, from an unstable, highly imaginative, and sanguine temperament. The actual form of government, too, became imbued to a large extent with the personality of the King; the affairs of the State, more often than not, were dealt with in cabinet councils, where they would be laid before the King by departmental secretaries in the presence of one or more members of the Council.

The situation in the country was serious; another bad harvest had succeeded that of 1771 and the mortality rate had reached a record figure: the country was infested with bands of starving beggars who provided a tragic illustration of the difficulties brought about by the rapid increase in population, which, at the end of the Age of Freedom, numbered 2,000,000, compared with 1,400,000 at the beginning. Additional imports of grain became necessary, and meanwhile a lower-class population was growing up in the country districts with few opportunities of earning a living, a phenomenon which became particularly apparent in times of distress when fewer servants were employed. The potato was still not one of the regular crops, though the culinary possibilities of the new 'earth pear' were not lost on those who tried it.

It would be a mistake to suggest that the Gustavian period marked a completely new era. Domestic problems had been inherited from the Age of Freedom, and the solutions which were devised differed only in their political aspect. Numerous schemes had already been aired during the violent debates in the last *Riksdag* of the Age of Freedom. Attention continued to be focused on the question of privileges and on the struggle between the nobility and the lower Estates; demands were still made for an official inquiry into the bureaucratic rule which had flourished at the end of the Age of Freedom, and there was a fervent desire that the administration should be reformed and the laws humanized. The King and his counsellors at once began to investigate several of these problems. A ban had already been imposed on the distilling of spirits from grain in order to save this commodity for food, although it was sometimes contended that moderate tippling was the peasants' 'best cure and apothecary'; and at the same time the crown arranged for an increase in the imports of grain. Though it was not until 1774 that the situation really began to improve, no one could have accused the government of idleness.

The problem next in order of urgency was that of the budget and the currency, which were in a considerable state of confusion. Before they had dispersed, the Estates had virtually given the King a free hand, and the problem was ultimately tackled on the basis of the devaluation proposals which had already been made before the revolution. Gustav himself had little knowledge of such matters, but he found a competent adviser in Johan Liljencrantz, a cautious and trustworthy financial expert; and it was he who, in 1776–7, prepared and put into effect a careful scheme of currency stabilization, whereby depreciated money was called in and redeemed at a reduced rate. Furthermore, some of the old restrictions were raised from the trade in grain, thereby reducing the danger of famine.

The same general principles underlay the long-awaited reform of the abuses in the bureaucracy. Here, too, Gustav III modelled his policy on former ideas. Negligent officials were tried, and improvements were made in the schedule of work. Greater efficiency was introduced into the administration in Finland, where the number of provinces was increased from four to six; and a new Court of Appeal was established at Vasa to serve the northern part of the country. All these measures, which had been inherited from the Age of Freedom, were widely acclaimed; and the new humanitarian outlook received positive expression in the abolition of torture, a step worthy of an enlightened

monarch and all the more desirable in that this barbaric
method of extorting information, commonly used in the
treason and witchcraft trials of the seventeenth century, had
even been employed as recently as the Age of Freedom.
Diplomatically, too, Sweden's position was not unfavourable.
Neither Russia nor Denmark made any real effort to intervene, but were content merely to form in 1773 a new secret
anti-Swedish alliance by which each promised to help the
other in the event of a Swedish attack, and agreed to promote the restoration of the old Swedish constitution. Swedish
diplomacy was conducted at the time by the new President
of the Chancery, Ulrik Scheffer, who succeeded in re-
enlisting the support of France and subsequently adopted a
policy of appeasement towards Russia. A further notable
achievement, one of the greatest of the Gustavian era, lay in
the reorganization of the Swedish defences, which involved
strengthening the Navy proper and speeding up the work on
the infantry galley, or Skerries fleet. By such means did the
new regime successfully espouse several of the ideas initiated
by the Hats and the Caps.

A more difficult problem remained, however, and one
which Gustav III was at present unable to solve on account
of his own paradoxical position. The desire for a levelling of
social distinctions was as strong as ever. But it was the nobles
who, jealous of their threatened privileges, had been largely
instrumental in putting Gustav where he was, and they now
looked for their reward. The King was anxious to fulfil their
expectations, but what would be the reaction of the unprivileged sections of society? The new constitution decreed
that appointments, in which the King had the last word,
should be made according to merit and experience and without regard to birth and favour 'when they are not found
together with ability'. The paragraph was ambiguously
phrased and liable to be misconstrued, whether intentionally
or otherwise. The King had already made it clear that he
favoured the nobles, both on personal grounds and on prin-

ciple, quite apart from the fact that they had become allies as a result of the *coup d'état*; and now, by way of a temporary sop, he gave rewards to those who had been directly concerned in the 1772 venture. At the same time he was compelled to take account of the demand of the unprivileged Estates, who had by no means relinquished their hopes; and he therefore found himself in a dilemma which was later to bring about his downfall.

For the rest, Gustav III and his associates made considerable headway for some years – with one exception. The increasing addiction to drink, with its detrimental effects on health and behaviour, was a serious blot on eighteenth-century life; and in 1775, prompted by his constant need for money, the King took advantage of a proposal to centralize all manufacture of spirits in crown distilleries. The saving of grain was more than outweighed, however, by the indignation caused both by the 'crown toping' and the ban on private distilling, not to mention the contraband production which flourished as the result of prohibition. Gustav nevertheless succeeded in many respects where the leaders of the Age of Freedom had failed, even if most of his reforms had actually been initiated by them. The question remained whether loyalty to the crown could permanently triumph over the tradition of opposition that had grown up in the preceding period. Count F. A. von Fersen, the most brilliant exponent of the political tradition of the House of Nobility, had already resigned from the Council, to be followed later by Höpken.

Gustav III convened his first *Riksdag* in 1778, so timed to coincide with the general rejoicing at the birth of an heir to the throne. In its meetings, however, many differences of opinion and many defects in the constitution became apparent, and disappointment was general. To a certain extent this was a natural reaction from the exultant atmosphere of 1772. But there was not yet a tangible opposition, and the King helped to strengthen his own position by his skilful account of the first years of his rule, for which he could in fact claim considerable progress. Furthermore, the deputies of the Estates stood godfathers to the Prince Gustav Adolf, who was born during the proceedings. One of the more important decisions of this *Riksdag*, for which some credit must go to Anders Chydenius, concerned the extension of religious freedom, then largely a matter of economic policy; and in the following year the Jews, too, were granted the right to settle and hold services in certain towns.

Few Swedish Kings have been the subject of so much controversy as Gustav III. His enemies among the aristocratic writers of memoirs usually cannot vilify him enough; the courtiers and artists who admired him saw in him 'a ray of eternal life'. The glowing picture drawn of him by Tegnér is classic but not true to life; 'In purple sat the enchanter on the throne, and his sceptre was a magic wand.' Yet it contained one important grain of truth. The age was one of great cultural activity, particularly in the sphere of *belles-lettres*, and the King did what he could to foster it. He himself had a passion for the theatre and the opera, and even wrote plays which throw considerable light on his outlook and his romantic view of the past glory of Sweden. Distinguished professional writers assisted the King with these dramas, in which Gustav Vasa and Gustavus Adolphus appeared on the stage and were made to play an almost up-to-date rôle in the art of national propaganda. The rising bourgeoisie possessed its intellectuals whose training, though academic, was devoid of pedantry. By contrast with the seventeenth century, when it had been choked with words and constructions from Latin and German, the Swedish language now adopted French models, though it was not long before even these were abandoned. The literary renaissance inaugurated by the poets of the Age of Freedom, and above all by Linnaeus, was firmly established.

Four of the Gustavian authors deserve special mention. The writings of Carl Gustaf af Leopold – poet, journalist, philosopher and courtier – were largely classical in tone, while Bengt Lidner was a typical pre-romantic poet of the emotions. The other two, Johan Henric Kellgren and his antagonist Thomas Thorild had, as it were, a foot in each camp, for they achieved in their works that remarkable blending of what, in retrospect, appear as irreconcilable opposites – a characteristic of transitions in literary fashion. At the same time Bellman was writing some of his best poems and other scholars and lesser poets were also flourishing; and in 1786, poetry, scholarship, and rhetoric received royal sanction in the foundation of the Swedish Academy. Meanwhile a learned coterie had been formed at the University of Åbo in Finland, led by the widely-read historian Henric Gabriel Porthan. Painting flourished under A. Roslin, C. G. Pilo, and N. Lafrensen (who was known in France as Lavreince), each of whom had acquired an international reputation during the Age of Freedom, while the Swedish sculptor Johan Tobias Sergel introduced fresh blood into the Neo-classic school. Although it was essentially similar to the rococo which had preceded it, the elegant Neo-classic style of decoration and furnishing came to be called 'Gustavian', after this justly famous age. In short, culture, which had previously been restricted to scientific research and pure scholarship, was liberalized. Music was the one exception; at court a high standard continued to be maintained by Italian and German composers, but interest in the community at large gradually dwindled into an amateurish dilettantism.

There is no doubt that the age of Gustav III at least partially deserved the aura of romance shed around it by its poets. But so great were its contrasts that it is not easy to give a coherent picture. The apparent political harmony belied the numerous and persistent discords beneath, which, though muffled at the 1778 *Riksdag*, were soon to be heard again, penetrating the ear of the King himself. Meanwhile his rule became increasingly despotic, while his private unofficial council, attended by members whom he himself selected, enlarged its power; the old counsellors either retired or were deprived of their influence, and the King was able to suppress the rising opposition with the help of those directly dependent on himself – statesmen such as Toll, Erik Ruuth, and Gustav Mauritz Armfelt. By the time the *Riksdag* met in 1786, however, all factions were bitterly resentful at the mismanagement of the finances, which were again in a precarious state, and at the King's frequent intervention in the government; and ill-feeling was aggravated by another series of bad harvests. In the face of this atmosphere of unrest and resistance the King and his new counsellors found it necessary to resort to various expedients. One of these which had been under consideration since 1783 was to focus the attention of the nation on an active foreign policy to meet the threat of Russo-Danish encirclement. At the same time there were deeper motives behind this policy. As a result both of the loss of her Baltic Empire and of the Russo-Danish alliance, Sweden had been reduced to a position similar to that which she had occupied before the expansion of the seventeenth century. For a time Gustav had adopted a conciliatory attitude towards Russia, and during the great European conflicts around 1780 Sweden had made a trade agreement with Russia, Denmark, and Prussia. But Denmark's policy was now openly anti-Swedish, while Gustav, for all his occasional overtures, was stirred by his Holstein blood to similar hostility. Among the fantastic schemes which he cherished, particularly towards the end of his reign, was an attack on Denmark and the dreams of a conquest of Norway. Gradually he developed the further notion of attacking Russia, whose rapid expansion under Catherine II, especially in view of the Empress's known attitude to the Scandinavian problem, had caused some alarm in Sweden. Meanwhile, however, the domestic unrest demanded more immediate palliatives and the King now adopted a line of action which was to bring the abolition of privilege within easier reach. The opposition was centred mainly in the nobility and Gustav had given up hope of winning them over. Instead, immediately after the 1786 *Riksdag*, he planned to split the opposing forces and court the favour of the commoners by granting a number of their specific demands. The freedom of the press was already being curtailed.

It was not long, however, before the King, together with certain of his counsellors (since 1785 he had been his own Foreign Minister), was completely engrossed with his Russian policy. A bold plan of attack had been drawn up, based on the improvements made in the Navy during the previous years. After defeating the Russian fleet the Swedes were to direct their attack straight at St Petersburg, while the Russians were busy with their Turkish war. Having, as they believed, completed their preparations the King and his entourage light-heartedly declared war in the summer of 1788, regardless of the fact that in so doing they were contravening the constitution.

But the plan foundered. The naval attack was unsuccessful and the advance of the army was retarded by bad generalship and poor equipment. Meanwhile it became evident that the King would have to fight simultaneously on two fronts at home. The officers, who were naturally drawn from the nobility, were now concentrated in the army, and the opposition had moved into camp. Furthermore, a movement for independence had for some years existed in Finland, where it was led by Göran Magnus Sprengtporten (half-brother of Gustav III's ally during the *coup d'état*), an able soldier who had played a large part in the defence of the province. His goal was an independent Finland under Russian protection, a proposal which agreed with Russia's plans for buffer states on the frontiers.

Sprengtporten's schemes were favoured by the prevailing discontent in Finland, which derived both from the policy of the *storskifte*, the first enclosures, and from a conviction that the defences of the province were inadequate. Some members

of the Finnish party managed to enlist the sympathy of
friends among the others, who were ignorant of their ultimate
aims, and they also appealed to the Empress Catherine,
writing her a letter in which they criticized the King's policy
and declared that they were willing to make peace. The
ringleaders persuaded about a hundred of their fellows to
make a formal declaration of their allegiance to the Anjala
League, so called after the locality north-west of Fredrikshamn where this meeting of the officers was planned. Soon
afterwards Denmark was compelled reluctantly to enter
the war under the terms of her treaty with Russia.

The King's position seemed hopeless; the enemy, however,
had failed to take into account his amazing resilience. He
refused to treat with the Anjala men and, returning to
Sweden, he proceeded to travel round the country stirring
up patriotic fervour for the royalist cause. He took his
historic romanticism so seriously that he addressed the
countryfolk of Mora in the open air, as if he were staging a
scene from his own opera *Gustav Vasa*. It was not long before
the league of Finnish separatists and the aristocratic opposition disintegrated. The Anjala army went into winter
quarters, its leaders were arrested in November, and at the
same time England and Prussia offered to mediate.

Resistance had by no means ceased, but it was now
counterbalanced by a surge of royalist feeling, ably fed by
the King. The Anjala men who had been arrested were
transferred to Stockholm in the New Year of 1789, a month
after the summoning of a *Riksdag*. This *Riksdag* had originally
been demanded by the nobles; but the King, with his innate
political adroitness, succeeded in turning the public mood in
his favour.

When the Estates met at the beginning of February 1789,
the King, with logical, almost cynical insight, repeated his
former tactics. Once again he exploited the split in the
Estates which had made possible the coup of 1772, merely
reversing his choice of allies. Before, they had been the

nobility; now he wooed the three lower Estates with concessions on the all-important question of privilege. In this
way the nobles were subdued and a new constitution, 'the
Act of Union and Security', was drawn up with the help of
clergy, burgesses, and peasants. Following a disagreement in
the House of Nobility, the King summoned all four Estates to
a joint meeting in the Palace on 17th February, when he
publicly reprimanded the nobles and ordered them to leave;
he then requested each of the three lower Estates to select
three of their members for direct discussions with the King,
and he prevailed upon these nine men to agree to the newly
proposed constitution. The leaders of the noble opposition
were arrested, a further joint meeting was held, and the
constitution was pushed through in a manner which was
plainly illegal. The designs of the Anjala League could hardly
have been more effectively parried.

From the King's Act of Union and Security there
developed a new form of royal absolutism. The King's power
extended to all spheres; he could settle the affairs of the
State as he thought best, he could dispense in practice with
the Council, since he had been granted the right to determine
its numbers and appoint and dismiss most of those who held
office – a blow at the old bureaucracy – and he could declare
war. Powers of taxation alone were withheld from him. In
return, extensive privileges were granted to the lower
Estates. They were allowed to sit in the new High Court,
which had taken over the appellate jurisdiction of the
Council, they had equal rights with the nobility to most of the
offices, and they were equally entitled to all types of land
except that carrying special privileges,[1] to which the nobles
retained exclusive right. The peasants were again allowed to
acquire crown homesteads, and they were granted, in principle, the absolute right to dispose of their own land and
farms as they pleased; this has been called the first decisive

[1] This specially privileged land was situated near the lord's manor and
enjoyed greater taxational exemptions than the noble's 'ordinary' land.

victory of the peasant Estate. These concessions were made
by the King himself, only three months before the meeting
of the States General in France, where similar demands for
equality contributed to the outbreak of the great Revolution.

As there was now virtually no one to question his actions,
the King could concentrate his whole attention on the war,
which had to be kept going until peace could be made under
favourable circumstances. The heavy defeat suffered by the
Skerries fleet at Svensksund in the summer of 1789 was followed by a second, but less humiliating, reverse at the beginning of July 1790, when the Swedish navy, blockaded at
Viborg, broke out with serious losses. Six days later, however,
when it was again fighting at Svensksund, against the Russians, the navy won perhaps its greatest victory. Thus the
King's inveterate optimism had prevailed over faintearted-
ness and now, although at considerable cost, the two
antagonists were even; and as conditions in Europe were
not in Russia's favour, peace was concluded at Värälä a
little over a month later. The status quo was restored, but at the
same time Russia formally surrendered all right to interfere
in Sweden's home affairs, and the two countries signed a
treaty shortly afterwards which was to Sweden's advantage.

One immediate outcome of the war was tremendous
internal inflation. When paper money began to fail, the King
is reported to have said: 'Are there no paper-mills in
Sweden?' At the 1789 *Riksdag* the Estates had attempted to
deal with the national debt by the expedient of a new
*Riksdag* department (*riksgäldskontor*), but the situation was
still extremely grave. Discontent, though silenced, had been
kept alive by the autocratic behaviour of the King and
also by the thorough reorganization which followed the
establishment of the new constitution. Serious plans for a
counter-revolution were being discussed, and antipathy
towards the King drew inspiration from the works of classical
history in the fashion of the time. Gustav himself realized the
necessity of convening a new *Riksdag* in order to reduce the

37. Gustav III. Painting by A. Roslin, 1777.

38a. Gustav III opening the *Riksdag* of 1789.
Painting by J. L. Desprez.

38b. View of Stockholm Palace.
Painting by E. Martin, *c.* 1783.

financial situation to some kind of order, and it met in Gävle in 1792; but although on the surface proceedings followed the usual routine, the ill-will and hostility of the nobles towards the King could not be concealed.

In March 1792, shortly after the *Riksdag* ended, several of Gustav III's bitterest enemies made contact with each other. They included civil servants from among the nobility who had seen the downfall of their Estate, army officers who cherished a grudge from the time of the Russian war, and personal enemies of the King. Proposals for a new constitution were discussed, under the leadership of Jakob von Engeström, the theoretician of the group. Many of the disgruntled nobles were in favour of using violence; among them was the former Captain of the Lifeguards, J. J. Anckarström, a fanatic who regarded the King as his personal enemy and himself as a classical tyrannicide. A conspiracy was launched; and on 16th March, 1792, when Gustav III was attending a masquerade at the Opera, he was shot down by Anckarström and died from his wounds two weeks later.

'The enchanter on the throne' was a fascinating and diverse personality, a strange mixture of infant prodigy, cold-blooded intriguer, high-principled hero, and unworldly aesthete. His entire reign was marked by a curious, paradoxical logic; the path towards equal privileges for all was a tortuous one, but it was followed to the end. The most important event in his reign occurred during the 1789 *Riksdag* when, on the spur of the moment but with swift, unerring instinct, he pointed the way to that equality, the lack of which was so soon to convulse the rest of Europe. In other words, the historical romanticist, who regarded the traditional Swedish aristocracy as excellence incarnate, was at the same time the man who started undermining the time-honoured privileges of the nobility and threw open the gates to the burgesses and peasants – the social classes of the nineteenth century; and it was this personal and tragic paradox which cost the King his life.

21

# XXVIII

# Sweden during the Revolutionary and Napoleonic Wars

## 1792-1809

In the last years of his life, Gustav III had dreamed of leading a crusade against the French Revolution. This characteristic plan was thwarted by the assassination at the Opera; nevertheless, the European storms of the next seventeen years had considerable influence on the history of Sweden, although until 1804 there was little direct contact between Sweden and the rest of Europe.

When Gustav III died, his son and successor Gustav IV Adolf was only fourteen years old. This meant that a Regency had to be set up for the first time since Charles XI's death ninety-five years earlier. The opposition factions, and particularly the nobility, had doubtless hoped to utilize the King's murder as a means of bringing about a violent revolution; for various obscure reasons, however, no revolution materialized, though new constitutional projects had already been discussed. The hateful nature of the murder in itself acted as a deterrent; and in addition there was the personal charm of the King, which he exerted from his sick-bed as never before – the noble and generous side of his character seems to have become fully apparent during the last two weeks of his life. The transition to a Regency was therefore uneventful, and Duke Charles, Gustav III's younger brother, took control of the government; he co-operated at the outset with the late King's counsellors – the Gustavians – but before long his trusted friend Gustav Adolf Reuterholm had become the real leader of the government. Although Reuterholm was not an outstanding man, he is of interest in that he reflects to a large extent the contemporary outlook; he was a mystic

and a spiritualist, and he had originally been an ardent supporter of the French Revolution, whose slogans were frequently on his lips. His main characteristic, however, was an
intense lust for power, which before very long absorbed his
whole attention – the enthusiast for liberty became himself a
despot. His exceptionally bad reputation derives from his
pedantry and narrow-mindedness, his dislike of new ideas,
his suppression of free speech (although he had originally
been an advocate of the freedom of the press), and his vindic-
tive treatment of the Gustavians, whom he accused of various
conspiracies and sentenced to heavy punishments. But his
four years of power left no special mark on Swedish history;
nor did he achieve any significant results by his experi-
mental and vacillating foreign policy, in which he was
mainly concerned to secure the assistance of France against
Russia.

Once the eighteen-year-old Gustav IV became King in
1796, Reuterholm was forced to leave the country; while the
young sovereign, on whom his father had pinned high hopes,
was universally welcomed. Despite a narrowness of vision,
which was revealed in his actions against real or assumed
Jacobinism, he made a personal positive contribution to
practical reform, and many far-reaching improvements were
accomplished during the eight years of Gustavian absolutism
from 1796–1804. The ground had been well prepared both
under Gustav III and under the Regency, for the pettiness
and court intrigues of the latter period must not be allowed
to overshadow its positive achievements – the attempt to
clean up the State finances, the co-operation with Denmark
in 1794 to protect trade during the Revolutionary wars, and
the investigations into agrarian problems.

In addition to these egalitarian and humanitarian measures,
important reforms were now undertaken in a sphere of
economic life that had hitherto been only rarely favoured –
agriculture. Since agriculture was infinitely more important
as a source of livelihood for most of the country than either

mining or manufactures, which, though generously treated, were of little quantitative significance, such reforms were urgently needed. According to calculations, about three-quarters of Sweden's population was directly employed in agriculture at the beginning of the nineteenth century. Yet farming was still based largely on mediaeval methods. The only major change seems to have been the introduction of a two- and three-field system in the more important agricultural districts; though modern implements had also been improved as a result of edging them with iron. In the first thousand years A.D., the rigid peasant communism of the village had resulted in greater security and a more efficient organization of available labour; but now its disadvantages began to outweigh its advantages. It was essential that agricultural productivity should be increased; this need had become clear when Sweden lost the grain-producing Baltic provinces at the Peace of Nystad; it had been preached by the eighteenth-century Physiocrats and had been further driven home by the disastrous effects of the bad harvests of the 1770's and 1780's on the increasing population. The consolidation in 1757 of strips belonging to one farmer, the freeing of the grain trade in the 1770's, and the annulment of certain old privileges in 1789 had all helped to improve working conditions on the land, both for the peasant-farmer and, even more, for the larger *entrepreneurs*. The latter corresponded in agriculture to the ironmasters and big merchants and, like them, they were demanding more freedom of movement in the community. Nevertheless much yet remained to be done.

The demand for grain in all the more important markets had been intensified both by the industrialization of western Europe, and especially England, during the latter half of the eighteenth century, and by the great increase of population throughout the Continent; and the question was how production could be stimulated in Sweden. A few Scanian agriculturalists (notably Rutger Maclean of Svaneholm), doubtless inspired by Danish methods, had been active in this cause since the 1780's, and interest increased during the reign of Gustav IV, who took a personal interest in finding a solution to the problem. The outcome was the adoption of the *enskifte* system – that is, the right to consolidate and enclose the scattered holdings of the peasants into a few larger fields. *Enskifte* was enacted for Skåne in 1803 and for the rest of Sweden in 1807; Skåne's priority was doubtless due to a desire to check the active emigration from that province.

By the turn of the century, agricultural societies in the various provinces were beginning to work for a more progressive system of agriculture, and the last period of Gustavian absolutism therefore ended constructively. This was underlined in 1807, when Gustav IV abolished serfdom in Pomerania during a complete reorganization of its government.

The progress of modern Sweden owes much to the *enskifte* system, which facilitated more intensive and efficient production and broke up the thousand-year-old village community, thereby transfiguring both the appearance of the Swedish country side and the life and civilization of the Swedish farmer. At the same time there is no denying that many of the peasant-farmers found it irksome; the dissolution of the old villages was not an unmixed blessing, nor was it accomplished in an instant.

Meanwhile other domestic questions were demanding attention. The most urgent was the coinage, as the Russian war had again upset the monetary system. The country was also suffering from more bad harvests, the herring fisheries on the west coast had failed, and trade was adversely affected by the great European conflicts. The economic situation, indeed, was critical; and the main task of the *Riksdag* summoned at Norrköping in 1800 was to arrange for a revaluation of the currency, a proposal which was approved by the Estates. At the same time it was clear that there was strong opposition to absolutism, particularly in the House of

Nobility, several of whose younger members had renounced their titles purely as a gesture – among them was Hans Hierta (afterwards Järta), who was later to play an important part in Swedish affairs. But this resistance was not so intense as that which had been aroused during the latter part of Gustav III's reign; the young King was by no means personally unpopular and everyone paid tribute to his good will and honesty. The stormy events in Europe had also induced some of the nobles to attach themselves more closely to the monarchy, thereby swelling the ranks of the Gustavians. No very serious clashes, therefore, took place. The *Riksdag's* most important achievement was the revaluation of the currency, though it was based not on the proposals of the Estates but on a more radical plan drawn up by the King himself, whereby the Swedish State pawned Wismar in order to procure the necessary silver.

These beneficial and important domestic reforms were accomplished without undue difficulty. Much more complicated were Sweden's foreign problems, as these were bound up with the tremendous political upheavals which were transforming the entire face of Europe. Sweden had already revised her foreign policy to conform with the altered situation in northern Europe. During the Age of Freedom Swedish politicians had appealed both to Russia and France for support against possible attempts to encircle the country, while Gustav III had oscillated between the two, again making friendly overtures to Russia after the Peace of Värälä. But there were two other important factors to take into account besides Russia and France. One was Denmark, whose policy towards Sweden during the eighteenth century had alternated between a close alliance with Russia against her and attempts at co-operation with her, and especially to protect their commerce by a joint policy of neutrality. The second important factor was England, whose influence in the affairs of northern Europe during the same period was determined partly by her demand for Swedish iron at the time of the Industrial Revolution and partly by her desire to prevent Russia from becoming too powerful in the north. This latter consideration had frequently worked to Sweden's advantage during this century, first about 1718, when Russia and England had fallen out with each other, then at the time of the *coup d'état* of 1772, which had been indirectly supported by England, and finally during the Russo-Swedish war in 1788–90, when England by her efforts at mediation had helped to ensure Sweden's success. But although some of these basic influences were still apparent at the end of the century, great developments were at hand as a result of the Revolutionary wars. It was clear that the old order was changing and it was necessary for Sweden to seek some security and support.

The obvious difficulties of Sweden's position had already been revealed in the irresolute overtures made by Reuterholm and Gustav IV, first towards France and, in the last resort, to Russia. But it appeared that Revolutionary France had outgrown that country's traditional attitude towards Sweden; and in 1799, therefore, Sweden formed an alliance with the Emperor Paul of Russia, a step which for the moment determined her foreign policy. By this time Paul was definitely hostile to England; nor was the latter popular with the Swedes, as during her great war with France she showed no regard for the legitimate commerce of neutral countries and had even confiscated important Swedish convoys. In 1800, therefore, Denmark, Sweden, Prussia, and Russia formed another of their leagues of neutrality. England retaliated by seizing any of their ships that lay in English ports, and by attacking Copenhagen in 1801 and threatening the Swedish fleet in Karlskrona – the expedition in which Nelson played an important part. Sweden had thus placed herself, as a result of her policy, in a very awkward position between England and Russia; however, when Russia adopted a more pro-English policy after Paul's death the Swedish government were able to co-operate with her in reaching a friendly settlement with England. Thenceforth, Sweden abandoned her previous policy, with its attempts at strict neutrality, and drew closer to England – a course which was justified by the King with weighty and convincing arguments.

The motive for this approach to England was primarily commercial. In the eighteenth century the policy towards the iron industry had aimed, with some success, at ensuring a constant level of production and export, and Swedish iron had maintained its place in the European market without any very great variations. At the beginning of the new century (1801–3), an average of 40–50 per cent. of Sweden's iron and steel, by far her most important export, went to England. The maintenance of good relations with this country was therefore essential to Swedish economic life; and it had been shown in the preceding years that England controlled the seas. Moreover, in the great commercial war that she was then waging with Napoleon, England could repay such friendship by supplying Sweden with essential goods. Thus Gustav IV was able to defend his foreign policy on realistic grounds; nor, for the moment, did it jeopardize his good relations with Russia. He was also doubtless influenced by the general pressure of Napoleonic imperialism, which might directly affect him in his capacity as a ruler of territories in Germany. As yet, however, he did not abandon a neutrality which was, at all events theoretically, unambiguous.

In 1804, however, a curiously irrational and personal element was introduced into this otherwise sane and realistic foreign policy. In the summer of 1803 Gustav IV had gone to visit his parents-in-law in Baden, where he had remained for a year – a journey which was sharply, and indeed at times justifiably, criticized at home. During this visit the King visualized himself more and more clearly as the embodiment of opposition to Napoleon. He was imbued with an historical romanticism which, though less aesthetic than that of Gustav III, moved him to uphold the historic German Empire and rise up against Napoleon's impious disregard of tradition. He also possessed a fervent, if rather rigid, sense of justice which made him react strongly to the capture within the territory of Baden of the *émigré* Duke of Enghien.

'Abhorrence' and 'contempt' were the words he used to describe his feelings when told of this event. It was this uncompromising hatred of Napoleon, combined with his own commercial policy, which influenced the King in 1805 to join with England and Russia in forming the third coalition against the French aggressor, though at the same time his highly developed business sense caused him to stipulate for considerable subsidies. Gustav IV has been condemned for thus abandoning the position of neutrality and involving Sweden in the great European war, though his action can be vindicated by comparison with the policy of neutrality pursued by Denmark, which did not prevent the latter from joining in the war. There is also strong justification for Gustav's action in the fact that Charles John (Charles XIV) subsequently carried out a very successful foreign policy largely on the lines laid down by his predecessor. Nevertheless Gustav IV's implementation of his policy entailed grave risks for Sweden, and it became even more remote from his original sane and rational designs.

During the third and fourth coalition wars against Napoleon, Swedish assistance was confined to Pomerania, where some of the time the King himself took command. The Pomeranian war was a lamentable fiasco. This was undoubtedly due partly to Gustav's defects as a military leader and partly to the poor quality of the Swedish troops and officers. The King's reputation in military circles also suffered at this time from his foolish and unreasonable behaviour, and it was obvious that he had no clear idea of the extent of Sweden's war resources. The agreement between Napoleon and Alexander of Russia at Tilsit in July 1807 had disastrous results for Sweden; a month later her army was surrounded by French troops at Rügen, and it was only by a combination

of ingenuity and good luck that the level-headed Toll
(Gustav III's old councillor, and now the most trusted
adviser of Gustav IV) was able to manœuvre their embarka-
tion to Sweden.

The effect of the Treaty of Tilsit on Sweden did not
immediately become apparent. It soon became clear, however, that in two quarters, at any rate, her position had
deteriorated. Firstly Denmark, who had hitherto managed to
remain neutral, was attacked and deprived of her navy by
England. This led to an alliance between the Danes and
Napoleon in October 1807, as a result of which Denmark
now became Sweden's enemy; and the subsequent presence
of French troops in Denmark, under Marshal Bernadotte,
Prince of Ponte Corvo, constituted a tangible threat. The
second danger lay in the east, for the implications of the
Tilsit alliance were becoming clearer. Czar Alexander had
originally urged Gustav IV to come to terms with Napoleon,
but with no success. He also proposed that Sweden should
combine with Russia in an attempt to protect the Baltic by
closing it to belligerents. Gustav categorically refused,
however, since such a move would have been directed against
England, with whom he was anxious to maintain his old
alliance. Alexander then finally broke with England and
continued his diplomatic pressure on Sweden; and at the
same time, with Napoleon's approval, he concentrated his
troops on the Finnish frontier. Russian troops attacked Finland at the end of February 1808, and on the same day
Russia issued an ultimatum to Sweden requesting her to
join forces with Russia, France, and Denmark. Denmark
declared war in March, in obedience to Napoleon; while the
latter's troops, led by Marshal Bernadotte, prepared to
invade Skåne – though he did not in fact intend to advance
farther.

Finland was badly fortified and deficient in good military
commanders; and in addition the strength of the Russian
troops had been much exaggerated. By April the Swedes had

retired to the extreme north, while Admiral C. O. Cronstedt, commander of the huge stronghold Sveaborg, outside Helsingfors, had simultaneously promised the Russians that, failing reinforcements from Sweden, Sveaborg would capitulate at the beginning of May. Cronstedt's action is hard to understand; he had no lack of troops and stores and there had hardly been time for a prolonged siege. But he had been infected by the political atmosphere which had become evident, for example, during the Russian war of Gustav III, and the spirit of resistance was in any case generally weak. The position had become desperate.

There has been frequent controversy as to whether this desperate situation could have been avoided by a complete reversal of Swedish policy immediately after Tilsit in 1807; Napoleon might not have been altogether disinclined for a friendly settlement with Sweden. Still, we shall never know as Gustav IV made no such move. During all his reverses and Napoleon's successes, the Swedish King's antipathy to the French Emperor had, if anything, intensified. It was plain that a strain of fanatical mysticism had by this time been added to his stern legitimism and sense of justice, which caused him to identify Napoleon with the beast of the Apocalypse. Friction was intensified by aggressive diplomacy, both in word and deed, and it seemed as though Gustav IV was implacable. He went into the crisis with his eyes open, and there were various indications that his grip on reality was weakening; fits of exaltation alternated with violent outbursts of rage and suspicion. But the course he had chosen could still be justified on material grounds, for Sweden continued to be dependent on her trade relations with England. Furthermore, Sweden was now almost the only outlet through which England could be reached by the rest of the Continent, since all the other countries were affected by the Continental System by which Napoleon hoped to subjugate England. Great profits therefore accrued from the transit trade, which had its chief centres at Gothenburg in the west, and Karlshamn in the south. Even so there were many people in educated Swedish circles who were friendly to Napoleon at this time. The King, on the other hand, unhesitatingly pursued his pro-English policy, depending for his sole support on English subsidies and the English navy.

At the end of April 1808 the retreating Swedish troops in northern Finland counter-attacked bravely at Siikajoki, and a considerable area of central Finland was recovered during the summer, when generals such as Adlercreutz, Döbeln, and Sandels distinguished themselves. At the same time plans were made for a Swedish attack on Norway, which had been cut off from Denmark by English sea-power. In the long run, however, the Swedish troops were unable to keep the enemy at bay. Their victories in Finland were indecisive, their position was particularly difficult after the surrender of Sveaborg, and help from Sweden was inefficiently organized. In the autumn the retreat began anew, and in November 1808 the Swedes evacuated Finland. At the beginning of 1809 the Russians began to attack Sweden proper on several fronts. An English auxiliary expedition under General Sir John Moore had already reached the western coast in May 1808, but so different were the aims and outlooks of the allies that this projected Anglo-Swedish co-operation was rendered ineffective and Moore's troops never disembarked. Nor was anything accomplished by the battles on the Norwegian front; and a further misfortune occurred in the middle of the crisis, when it was found that the territorial army which had been mustered not only lacked adequate equipment but was ravaged by camp fever.

A generation later the poet Johan Ludvig Runeberg used some of these dire events as the theme for his *Fänrik Ståls Sägner* (Tales of Ensign Stål). There is something almost uncanny in the way that he managed in these poems to convey to posterity a picture of the Finnish war which is so completely divorced from reality; it is a picture of heroes and great deeds, of determination, endurance, and selflessness; it was an inspiration to subsequent generations and is still alive to-day. Runeberg turned defeat into victory, for his time and for posterity.

The hapless warfare and diplomacy had revealed many weaknesses in civil and military administration. There was general chaos in the spring of 1809, and the King's rule was capricious and muddled. Money was scarce, despite issues of bank-notes, and crippling taxes had to be imposed. There are various indications that by this time the King was mentally unbalanced; he passed military sentences which were both ferocious and unjustified, and he even came close to a break with England.

At this point plans to depose the King were being discussed in certain unofficial and, to begin with, unconnected groups. Public opinion, as so often before, had been persuaded to blame the King for all the country's misfortunes; historians, on the other hand, differ as to how far he was personally responsible, the more so as the issue is confused by the increasingly tortuous workings of the King's own mind. All that can be said is that Gustav IV lacked the gifts and the self-control necessary to deal with the extremely complicated European situation with which he was faced, though at the same time we cannot accept the distorted caricature which was drawn of him by his enemies.

At all events, in many circles – chiefly among civil servants and officers, less often among townsfolk and peasants – Gustav IV was made the scapegoat even for events beyond his control, for the complicated international situation, for the widespread inefficiency at home and for the obstruction in the civil service and the army. The plans to remove the King and summon the Estates were largely initiated by two factions; one comprised a fairly heterogeneous group of officers and officials in Stockholm, which was centred round Jacob Cederström, while the other was the officers' corps of the Western Army on the Norwegian frontier, led by Lieutenant-Colonel Georg Adlersparre. It was not long before the two joined forces. The first plan for a coup, which had emanated from Stockholm, came to nothing. On 9th March, however, Adlersparre marched from Karlstad towards the capital and issued a proclamation which, though expressed somewhat vaguely, was concerned with the necessity for peace, a *Riksdag*, and an alliance with Napoleon. Meanwhile the Stockholm group had a new plan ready; after their previous failure, they had induced General Adlercreutz, who had distinguished himself in the Finnish war, to be their leader. Having been informed on 12th March of the approach of the Western Army, the King began to take immediate military countermeasures. Adlercreutz therefore proceeded to act. Barely allowing time to discuss what was to be done after the *coup d'état*, a new plan was improvised, and on the morning of 13th March the King was caught unawares and taken prisoner. He escaped through a secret door, but was again seized and was carried screaming and vomiting up to the Palace. He was subsequently exiled and spent the rest of his life in poverty and obscurity on the Continent.

At the time of one of Gustav IV's encounters with Napoleon early in the century, Wordsworth had written: 'Call not the royal Swede unfortunate.' But it would seem, after all, that the appellation cannot be avoided.

# XXIX

# The 1809 Constitution and the Policy of 1812

## 1809-1818

In 1808 the Emperor Alexander had proclaimed Finland to be united with Russia, and his campaign against Sweden proper continued throughout 1809. The war with Denmark proceeded uneventfully on the southern front, while on the Norwegian front there had been an armistice since the end of 1808. There were many important problems and tasks which awaited the attention of the men who now took over responsibility, including the question of a sovereign, a new constitution, the convening of the *Riksdag*, and an urgently needed overhaul of the State finances.

On the day that the King was captured, his uncle, Duke Charles, was persuaded by Adlercreutz and his followers to form a Regency; his 'government' consisted mainly of those who had held high office under Gustav IV, together with some of the instigators of the *coup d'état*. On the following day they issued a summons to the *Riksdag*, a reversion to the practice in force before the period of Gustavian absolutism. The situation was still obscure and opinion was by no means unanimous. A section of the new leaders, the Gustavians, wished to see the nine-year-old Crown Prince Gustav on the throne; Adlersparre, who arrived at the capital with his troops some days after the *coup d'état* and immediately became a member of the government, was determined that Duke Charles should be proclaimed King, while a third group favoured Adlersparre's earlier suggestion that the matter should be shelved until the *Riksdag* assembled. In the event, it was this last course that was followed.

The provisional government now drafted a constitution,

in which a fairly strong monarchy was retained despite the more liberal ideas which had been put forward during its preparation. The government also approached Napoleon and planned a reorientation of Swedish foreign policy with a view to obtaining his approval and support. Another urgent problem, and one which became the centre of interest and intrigue, was that of the succession if the childless Duke Charles became King. The Gustavians naturally worked on behalf of Prince Gustav, while Adlersparre put forward as candidate the Danish Prince Christian August of Augustenborg, Commander-in-Chief of the Norwegian army, who was known to have Scandinavian sympathies. Adlersparre had been in contact with him at an early stage, when the Prince had been responsible for concluding and maintaining the armistice with the Swedes which had assured the success of their *coup d'état*; and there were those among Adlersparre's followers who, together with certain Norwegians, believed that Christian August might help them to unite Norway with Sweden, though in fact the Prince had remained loyal to the Danish government. Finally, Frederick VI of Denmark presented himself as a candidate for the throne, though without success, while the Regency government, for its part, appealed to Napoleon to suggest some one suitable.

However, when the *Riksdag* met on 1st May these various schemes and speculations were temporarily overshadowed by a question which was regarded by the radicals of the Estates as of supreme importance; the substitution of a more liberal constitution for the one proposed by the provisional government. 'First the constitution, then the King', was their slogan, and their programme combined the constitutional doctrines inherited from the Age of Freedom with the progressive political ideas which had gained ground more recently. Chief among its advocates were the nobility and the burgesses. The hopes cherished by Duke Charles and his counsellors, as well as Adlersparre, that the Duke should succeed in his own hereditary right, came to nothing.

39. Charles XIV as Crown Prince.
Painting by F. Gérard, 1810.

Gustav IV and his heirs were declared to have forfeited the Crown, a step which at the same time invalidated the programme of the Gustavians. A constitution committee, composed largely of those whose viewpoint was mid-way between that of Adlersparre and that of the radical 'Jacobin' wing, began to drew up the new constitution; and so quickly did the work proceed that the task was completed within fourteen days. Their proposals were discussed and accepted with equal rapidity on 6th June, when the constitution was expounded and defended by the committee's secretary, Hans Järta, in a classic memorandum which revealed in its weighty content and elegant language the hand of a brilliant jurist. The constitution incorporated a division of powers on the lines laid down by Montesquieu: an executive with full powers within its prescribed limits; the legislature, the *Riksdag*, which was slow to act but powerful in obstruction; and an independent judiciary. This was presented by Järta as a continuation of the basic conceptions of Swedish constitutional life, on the ground that such traditional forms should not be lightly jettisoned. English history had shown, Järta concluded, that these constituted the strongest guarantee of the nation's rights and the citizen's freedom.

The Swedish constitution of 1809 is the oldest written constitution in force in Europe, and though frequently altered and modified, it has provided the basis of Swedish government for nearly a hundred and fifty years. It is truly a remarkable document, rapidly put together and yet embodying the experience of centuries of discussion and experiment. It has been said of it that 'both the constitution as a whole and each of its paragraphs records a piece of history and an event in the life of the people'. In accordance with the experiences of the preceding century, care had been taken to achieve a balance of power between the various component parts of the government. The main features of the constitution can be summarized as follows: (1) 'The King shall alone rule the kingdom.' (2) 'The Swedish people's ancient right

22

to tax themselves' shall be exercised by the Estates of the realm at the general *Riksdag*. (3) The *Riksdag* and the King shall jointly make and amend the civil, criminal, and ecclesiastical law. (4) Before taking his decisions, the King shall consult with a Council of State, whose nine members he shall himself appoint. (5) The members of the Council of State shall be answerable to the *Riksdag* for the advice they give, according to different rules in different cases. (6) The *Riksdag* shall meet at least every fifth year; according to fixed rules, it shall control the activities of the Council and ensure that the State finances are correctly administered. The constitution was completed by an ordinance concerning freedom of the Press.

A great deal had been achieved; but among the problems that still remained to be dealt with were two of the utmost importance: the question of privileges and the basis of representation in the *Riksdag* (i.e. whom the deputies were to represent). A small advance was made in the process, begun during the eighteenth century, of levelling down the privileges of the noble Estates. All the Estates received equal rights of appointment to the higher offices. Further, the nobility renounced their exclusive right to own privileged land, and in conjunction with the clergy and burgesses they made certain concessions in taxation in order to reduce the discrepancy between themselves and the peasants. Still the peasants were not satisfied. Notwithstanding that everyone was equally entitled to any type of land, the old order still imposed a graduated scale of taxes on the various categories, which included 'special' nobles' land, 'ordinary' nobles' land, tax and crown land. The 'free' land owned by the nobles was still exempt from some of the old land taxes imposed on other types of landownership, whereas the peasants wanted all land to be taxed equally. They refused to authorize their chairman to sign the new constitution, and it was only after strong pressure of a rather questionable nature that the peasant Estate was finally induced to give way. As regards the right to be represented in the *Riksdag*, the existing constitution made no allowance for those important social groups that had emerged since the growth of the *Riksdag* of the four Estates, chiefly the ironmasters and those farmers who did not belong either to the peasant or the noble Estates. Furthermore, the *Riksdag* of the four Estates was still strongly bureaucratic in character; most of the nobles and all the clergy were civil servants, and many of the representatives of the burgesses were mayors and aldermen, which made them crown servants. This disparity had long been under discussion, and it was given fresh prominence by the restoration of bureaucratic rule in 1809. Finally, the working classes in town and country lacked any direct representation. Various schemes were suggested with a view to bringing up to date the right of representation, even the device of a *Riksdag* with two Chambers on the lines proposed by the theorists of the French Revolution; but these came to nothing, and the *Riksdag* Ordinance of 1810 was, in all essentials, no different from the old one.

In each of these important questions, therefore, the sponsors of the constitution had stopped short at half-measures. The constitution was functioning in practice long before the topics had even been fully discussed – indeed, even before the peasants had withdrawn their demands with regard to taxation. The new form of government had already been approved by Duke Charles, who was at once proclaimed King as Charles XIII; and a new Council was appointed, dominated by the same influences as those which had stamped the constitution. Two more questions now awaited attention: foreign policy and the succession.

The new government's foreign policy was determined by the general desire for an alliance with Napoleon, which would involve making peace with Russia and breaking away from England. But neither the tentative approaches made to the French Emperor nor the counter-attacks on the Russian troops in Västerbotten yielded any result. All the hopes of the government were destroyed, and Sweden, now completely isolated, was forced in September 1809 to make peace with Russia at Fredrikshamn, whereby she ceded the whole of Finland, the Åland islands, and the north-easternmost strip of Sweden itself. Century-old ties were broken; both the territory and population of Sweden were reduced by more than a third, and the geographical aspect of the country was completely transformed. The loss caused great grief and indignation, which continued to be felt for generations afterwards. 'As Heaven is my witness,' declared the Swedish diplomatist Stedingk, 'I would have signed my own death warrant sooner than this peace.' In addition to making these territorial cessions, Sweden was compelled, though with certain qualifications, to join the Continental System. Peace with Denmark followed in December without further loss of territory; and the following January (1810) Sweden came to terms with Napoleon. She thus regained Pomerania, but had to break off all trade with England, retaining only her imports of salt.

The question of the succession had been closely associated with the peace negotiations. The chief candidates were now Gustav IV's son, Gustav, and Duke Christian August. The former, however, was soon forced to withdraw. During the heated debates in the *Riksdag* on the subject, the Duke found a zealous advocate in Adlersparre, who declared that this choice would assist the country to attain a more favourable peace with Denmark and prophesied, as before, that a union between Sweden and Norway would 'attend' the Duke. During the negotiations, Christian August remained with the Norwegian army and disregarded Frederick VI's orders to attack; when he was elected in July, however, he announced that he could not accept the throne until peace had been concluded between his present and his future fatherland. Nevertheless, though Adlersparre's predictions were not fulfilled, the election still held good; and after peace had been concluded Christian August proceeded to Sweden,

where he was adopted by the King and took the name of
Charles August.

Thus by the beginning of 1810 a number of problems had
been solved, if not in the manner anticipated by the opti-
mists. But the position was still far from stable. In the field
of foreign policy none of the extensive and confident hopes
had been realized; Napoleon had given no help, Norway
had not united with Sweden, and the negotiations throughout had been badly handled. Meanwhile the *Riksdag* was a
hot-bed of intrigue. The Gustavians and their followers were
conspiring to overthrow the new constitution on the ground
that it gave too much power to the *Riksdag*, and they had
succeeded in gaining the support of the King; while at the
same time, the more radical elements wanted to reorganize
the constitution in the opposite direction – though there
were occasional approaches between the two factions. Various efforts were also made to change the form of representation. The atmosphere was stormy, the general mood one of
disillusion and weariness; and there was acute hostility
between the Gustavians and the 'men of 1809'. Many
people, however, concentrated their hopes on the new Crown
Prince, who endeavoured impartially, and with some success, to reconcile the different parties. But while he was in
Skåne at the end of May 1810 he had a stroke and died
instantly. His death seemed to open up new prospects for
the Gustavians and provoked intrigue and agitation in the
opposing party. Wild rumours were put about that Charles
August had been murdered by the Gustavians; and when
his dead body was brought to the Palace in Stockholm there
was a rising among the populace. One of the foremost
Gustavians, the Marshal of the Realm, Count Axel von
Fersen – well known during the French Revolution as Marie
Antoinette's friend and helper – was attacked and killed by
the mob, without any effort on the part of either the troops
or the officials to rescue him. This was the appalling climax
of the incessant intrigues which had followed the *coup d'état*.

And a further sequel seemed probable as a new heir to the throne had to be chosen.

The Danish King tried hard to assert his claim, and a united Scandinavian kingdom again seemed within reach. A brother of Charles August was also mentioned. But the final choice was completely unforeseen. During a visit to Paris a Swedish lieutenant, Carl Otto Mörner, got into touch, on his own initiative, with one of Napoleon's most celebrated marshals, the forty-seven-year-old Jean Baptiste Bernadotte, Prince of Ponte Corvo, and suggested that he should launch him as heir to the Swedish throne. Bernadotte consented, and Mörner hastened home to win support for his impromptu idea. Napoleon did not oppose the project, and when the elective *Riksdag* met in Örebro in August 1810 Bernadotte was proclaimed heir-apparent – though in fact Sweden had exaggerated both the significance of the French Emperor's approval of the candidature and the extent of the help which she could consequently expect from him. In such manner did the lawyer's son from Pau, former General of the Revolution, Napoleon's foremost rival at the *coup d'état* of Brumaire and now one of his ablest but most independent servants, become the Crown Prince of Sweden. In October 1810 he came to Sweden, where he was adopted by Charles XIII, now quite senile, and given the name of Charles John. He soon achieved widespread popularity; he was admired for his quick intelligence, and his lively charm was almost irresistible: 'every inch a Prince' was the Queen's impression. Among his less attractive qualities were a hasty and violent temper and a very suspicious disposition; he gave Sweden both a secret police and a spy system, an indication of the nature of his origins and earlier environment.

It was not long before Swedish politics felt the impact of his strong will and wealth of ideas, and under his leadership Sweden struck out in new and sometimes unforeseen directions. The desire to propitiate Napoleon and to take revenge on Russia still dominated Swedish opinion; and it was at

first hoped that the new King would take the offensive against
Russia and win back Finland. That Charles John was
interested in these schemes was shown in the early stages of
the new régime when Sweden allied herself closely with
Napoleon; and in response to ruthless pressure from the
Emperor she formally declared war on England in accordance with the Continental System, though in fact her action
was more apparent than real and she continued to carry on
an extensive clandestine trade with her supposed enemy.
It gradually became clear that Charles John was relying for
his purpose on forming unexpected combinations. Even
before the Swedish episode he had taken a positive attitude
to Russia, and he shared none of Sweden's strong and understandable sentiments towards her. He was also speculating
on the weaknesses in Napoleon's position. Influenced by the
Revolutionary doctrine of natural frontiers he conceived the
idea of seeking compensation in Norway for Sweden's loss of
Finland, although it is a little difficult to ascertain how far
he had abandoned the possibility of regaining Finland herself. For a time he carried on negotiations simultaneously
with Napoleon and Russia, without coming to an agreement
with either; gradually, however, the project of an alliance
with Russia gained precedence. Charles John's Norwegian
policy began to take shape in 1811. It followed a long-
familiar pattern, last adopted by Adlersparre, and previously
by Gustav III, Charles XIII, and Eric XIV; Charles John
introduced a completely new element in that he intended to
achieve his purpose with the help not of Napoleon, as envisaged by the Swedes, but of Russia. Napoleon himsel
helped to turn Swedish opinion against him when, in the
New Year of 1812, he again sent French troops to occupy
Pomerania; his object being to crush the flourishing clandestine trade which was being carried on there with England
from Sweden proper. By 1812 the long-anticipated break
between Napoleon and Russia had become imminent;
Charles John was therefore able to make definite proposals

to Czar Alexander, and in April Sweden and Russia effected their first treaty of alliance.

The main outlines of the new policy soon took shape. In the spring of 1812 a *Riksdag* introduced conscription into Sweden and granted supplies for armaments; while the miserable budgets of the last four years were to some extent repaired by the simple expediency of writing off those Swedish foreign loans which were held by French subjects in, for example, Holland, Italy, and Germany. Meanwhile the royal adherents were planning a reform of the constitution, as the King was having difficulty in coping with the unruly Estates. Once the King had in practice gained complete control of policy, however, these projects became unnecessary, and in fact they never materialized. The Press ordinance, on the other hand, was altered so as to enable the government to suppress the newspapers of the opposition.

In the summer of 1812 Sweden joined with Russia in making peace with England, thus far reverting to the much-decried policy of Gustav IV; and in August Alexander and Charles John came to a final agreement in Åbo, on territory of which Sweden had been deprived three years earlier. On this occasion, also, the question of Finland was discussed between the two parties; nothing was accomplished, however, since Norway was the price demanded by Charles John. The long-desired war between Napoleon and Russia had by then been in progress for two months, and the King was therefore in a position to improve on his original terms: Sweden was to be assisted by a Russian army of 35,000 men in her projected attack on Denmark, with the object of forcing the latter to give up Norway; Charles John would then lead the united Swedish and Russian troops against Napoleon in Germany. The Russian auxiliary troops, however, were not forthcoming, as Alexander felt that they could not be spared from the great conflict in Russia. The original plan therefore had to be both postponed and modified. Despite the fact that Charles John's designs in Norway were approved by

England and Prussia in the spring of 1813, circumstances
were such that he was compelled to lead his army not into
Denmark but into Pomerania, in the hope that Russia would
then help him to attack Denmark through Holstein. But
again his hopes were frustrated. In view of Napoleon's successes in Germany at the beginning of the year's campaign,
Alexander was unwilling to allocate troops for such an enterprise; the Czar and the other allies demanded instead that
Charles John and his troops should immediately assist them
against the French. Charles John was thus in a difficult
situation, since he was playing for high stakes with allies
more powerful than himself. It was only after long and
exasperating negotiations that he agreed to this arrangement,
and his compliance provoked discontent among the Swedish
officers. In the summer Russia and Prussia were forced to
make a truce with Napoleon; and only then, threatened with
a French victory, did Charles John yield to their demands for
direct action against the French Emperor. The allied Princes
met at Trachenberg in July, when they drew up a plan for
the subsequent campaign. The Swedish Crown Prince, who
had played a significant part in these discussions, was given
command of the so-called Northern Army.

Charles John's relations with his allies were still not particularly good, however, and they did not improve perceptibly
as time went on. He was still in a difficult position; on the
one hand he had to hold his own against allies who were
infinitely stronger than he was, and carry out the Norwegian
policy on which he had staked so much; on the other he had
to endeavour to impose as little as possible on Swedish troops,
and so he contented himself with sending only his artillery
into action in the battles of Dennewitz and Grossbeeren which
preceded the decisive encounter at Leipzig. His allies,
moreover, questioned his willingness to fight against his
former compatriots, and on this account deeply mistrusted
him. Even at this stage he seems to have considered the
possibility of re-entering French politics in some capacity

after Napoleon's fall, after having acted as mediator between his present allies and his former compatriots in an attempt to save the Rhine frontier for France. Consequently, during the march to the Rhine after the Battle of Leipzig, he broke away with some of his troops and proceeded northwards. His position was indeed complex, for both political and psychological reasons.

Having manœuvred his men past a Napoleonic army commanded by Marshal Davout on the lower course of the Elbe, he launched an attack on the Danish troops in Holstein, who were by this time Napoleon's only real allies. This was the fourth time that Swedish troops had attacked Denmark from this direction, for Charles John was following in the steps of Lennart Torstenson, Charles X, and Magnus Stenbock. The Danes retreated and fighting took place at Bornhöved and Sehested; a truce was made shortly afterwards and, in January 1814, peace was finally concluded at Kiel, a little more than a month after the invasion of Denmark. Charles John had thus achieved his end unaided, in circumstances quite different from those originally envisaged. Metternich, anxious to maintain the balance of power, now brought Austria to the assistance of Denmark. Charles John, however, supported by Russia, successfully secured the desired peace terms; the King of Denmark joined the coalition against Napoleon and surrendered all claims and rights in Norway, and the latter was thenceforward to be united with Sweden, though retaining her old laws and privileges. Frederick VI was compensated with a large sum of money and Swedish Pomerania with Rügen, which in due course was exchanged with Prussia for Lauenburg. Charles John then returned with his army to the main theatre of war.

The period of France's final collapse was for him a time of frustration and mental strife. His position was all the more difficult in that the French plans to enlist the services of the Swedish Crown Prince – possibly even as Napoleon's successor, or as a kind of *major domo* under the Bourbons – had not been abandoned, and were revived after the Hundred Days and Waterloo. By that time, however, Charles John had long been back in Sweden, and was compelled not only to disregard the appeals of the French but even retire altogether from the European scene.

The great successes and the skill with which the 1812 policy had been implemented had brought about a swing in Swedish opinion and, with a few exceptions, warm gratitude was extended to Charles John. The newly-won territory was now to be taken over, and Norway's attitude remained to be seen. The Swedish government had invited her to submit proposals for a free Norwegian constitution, thereby giving her the opportunity to replace her absolutist régime by a constitutional one. At the time of the Treaty of Kiel the Danish Governor was Frederick VI's cousin, Christian Frederick; and when he was informed of the peace terms he aroused public opinion and contended that the Danish King had no right to cede Norway. A liberal constitution was adopted at the Assembly of Eidsvold, and on 17th May 1814 Christian Frederick was elected King of Norway. In the optimistic hope that this course would win support in other countries, the Swedish proposals for a settlement were rejected. But the hope was not fulfilled, and Charles John himself led a Swedish attack which procured a speedy, if not decisive, result. In the event, Charles John behaved with extreme generosity, both because he wanted to conciliate European liberal opinion and because he had not completely abandoned his French hopes. The freedom accorded to Norway was, he said, 'homage to the principles and love of liberty which I have been fortunate enough to find inherent in every Swede. This union between two peoples under the aegis of freedom will confute all envious detractors and prove a monument to human dignity, invoking the admiration of every enlightened person, and giving comfort to those who have the cause of humanity at heart.'

No later than August, a convention was signed by the two
countries in the town of Moss. In accordance with its terms,
the new Norwegian King renounced the throne; while
Sweden recognized the new constitution and the new parliament, the *Storting*. The latter then assembled at Christiania
and on 4th November King Charles XIII was elected and
acknowledged as King. The problems common to both
countries were regulated by an Act of Union adopted both by
the Swedish *Riksdag* and the Norwegian *Storting* in August
1815. The Union was drawn up rather hurriedly, as Charles
John wanted to present the Congress of Vienna with a *fait
accompli*, and consequently some of its articles might have
been more clearly expressed. But the Union was a fact.
Sweden and Norway were one kingdom, each with its own
constitution, and the goal of 1812 had been achieved. At the
same time, any idea of regaining Finland was put on one side.
Charles John had done much to shape the events of this year,
since it was he who had turned Sweden's attention from east
to west; and the results were confirmed at the Congress of
Vienna, in which the exchange of Pomeranian territory played
a significant part. Another attempt to unify the Scandinavian
kingdoms had been made, the word *brödrafolk* (lit. 'brother
nations') entered the vocabulary, and the poet Tegnér sang
of one power and one united will in the north – 'What God
hath joined let no man put asunder.'

But there were still large adjustments to be made, for the
constitution contained many features which proved difficult
to apply and interpret. In 1809–10 the *Riksdag* had dominated,
and from 1811 the King – or rather the Crown Prince
Regent. The actual provisions of the constitution offered scope
both for the sovereign and the *Riksdag*. Meanwhile the country
had experienced serious inflation since 1808–9, the question
of right of representation in the *Riksdag* was still unsolved, and
social problems, specially those connected with the rapid
rise in population, called for attention. The primary concern
of the next two meetings of the *Riksdag*, in 1815 and 1817–18,

was the state of the currency; a general economic crisis had begun in 1812–13, which had intensified the general unrest. The government, however, failed to find a solution to the problems. There was only slight opposition, which consciously endeavoured to follow English parliamentary custom; nevertheless it provoked in Charles John a reaction which is best described in his own words at the time: '*Opposition – c'est conspiration.*' The projects for a reform of the *Riksdag* electoral system led nowhere, and the solution to all these questions was postponed until the 1820's and 1830's.

During the years immediately following 1809 Sweden passed through a period of strain and vicissitude which in certain respects paved the way for modern Sweden. It is estimated that between 1805 and 1818 the land under cultivation in Sweden increased by about 17 per cent., owing to the *enskifte* system, which had been initiated under Gustav IV and which involved, besides increased cultivation, an extension of the settlements of peasants who departed from the old villages. It was about this time that the potato came into its own, and became a favourite crop on the new plots; its popularity was further enhanced by the discovery that it could yield both spirits for human consumption and wash for animals, which was considered a happy combination. The population, too, had been increasing rapidly in the last century, mainly among the farm labourers and other workers on the land; this brought about a change in the structure of society and was constantly creating new social problems, though most people were as yet hardly aware of them. As time went on, however, they were to become increasingly apparent and urgent, and Sweden began to realize the necessity of compensating for her territorial losses by making increased efforts within her now reduced frontiers.

# XXX

# Neo-romanticism and Gothicism; Liberalism and Conservatism; the Rise of the Middle Class

## 1818-1844

The features peculiar to Swedish history clearly emerge if we compare the manner in which Sweden and France respectively applied, at the beginning of the nineteenth the social and political lessons of the preceding centuries. The summary treatment of feudal privileges under the French revolutionary régime is paralleled in Sweden by a process lasting nearly a century from 1719 to 1809; and the confiscation of land from the French nobility and Church corresponds to the reductions of Gustav Vasa and Charles XI. The uneven constitutional development in France, where a liberal constitution was not achieved until 1830, has its Swedish counterpart in a remarkable, almost unique, series of experiments through the centuries, which finally attained their equilibrium in the constitution of 1809. For several hundred years the right to be represented in a national assembly had been more widely extended and more firmly established in Sweden than in most other European countries, and the political tradition and life of Sweden had few parallels.

While Sweden was seeking the visible expression of her political life in constitutional documents and practice, Swedish letters and scholarship, prompted by a fundamental desire both for regeneration and for contemplation of the past, were entering an age of brilliance. The first representatives of modern Swedish intellectual life flourished between 1750 and 1790: Linnaeus, Bellman, Kellgren, and their contemporaries. They were followed in the 1810's and 1820's by the generation born in the heyday of the Gustavian era. The beginning of this golden age of Swedish literature exactly coincides with the political crisis about 1810. Most of the new writers were sons of clergymen, merchants, or ironmasters, who had attended a university and who often ended up as professors or bishops; and in these respects they foreshadow the rise of the middle class in the first half of the nineteenth century.

In 1810 the Neo-romantics published the first number of their journal *Phosphoros*, and thus became known as the Phosphorists. In its pages the foremost representative of the movement, P. D. A. Atterbom, made his début as a lyric poet, and it also launched a violent attack on the traditions of the Enlightenment and French Classicism. In the following year Tegnér wrote *Svea*, his great political and patriotic poem; and the same year saw the foundation of the Gothic Society (*Götiska förbundet*), in whose journal, *Iduna*, E. G. Geijer published his first poems. While the Phosphorists were strongly influenced by German Romanticism, and the Gothicists favoured a return to the early traditions of Nordic history, Tegnér, with his diversity of outlook, combined all the trends of this creative period; Romanticism, Gothicism, Fichte's philosophy, the Neo-classicism of Goethe and Schiller, and the best of Gustavian culture; and he synthesized them into a national whole which was yet personal and individual. It was during the 1810's and 1820's that he wrote his lyrics and his famous *Fritiofs Saga*. Meanwhile Geijer produced many poems, of which the most notable were *Vikingen* (The Viking) and *Odalbonden* (The Free Peasant), and at the same time planned his *History of Sweden*, which was published between 1832 and 1836; and Atterbom composed his romantic lyrics and his philosophical fairy play *Lycksalighetens ö* (The Isle of Bliss). Other writers of the period were E. J. Stagnelius, with his strange, fervent emotion, and C. J. L. Almquist, who made his début as a romantic with works which were both horrific and mystical.

A large number of lesser lights fill out the picture with lively debates on the literary events of the Old and the New School. J. O. Wallin's hymns, the pioneer work of the chemist J. J. Berzelius, and the many and varied activities of the economist and botanist C. A. Agardh, all provide further evidence of the creative enthusiasm of the period. The sphere of music boasted several composers of intimate romantic songs; and it was during this time that Sweden's greatest composer, Franz Berwald, developed to the full his own peculiar style, which struck an unromantic and unsentimental note in a romantic age.

Several of these poets and scholars shared a longing for a new order, a striving towards moral, aesthetic, and educational renaissance. The adherents of the Gothic school, including the poet P. H. Ling, founder of the famous gymnastic system, were particularly keen to popularize this movement. The new literary currents sprang from the same soil as the political currents which provide a direct parallel, and a spiritual bond can be discerned between the men of 1809 and the poets of the same generation – for example, in their respective reactions to the changes in contemporary Europe.

The years between the restoration and the middle of the century were marked by a great ideological war between Conservatism and Liberalism, between the desire to maintain traditions and the urge to move with the times. The sympathies of such Swedish romantics as Atterbom and Stagnelius were with the Conservatives; and so at the outset were those of the leading Gothicist, Geijer. A similar fundamental conflict of ideas also became apparent in many other spheres. The conception of Conservatism as a philosophy of life, in the spirit of Burke, was taking shape; and besides Geijer its chief exponents were Hans Järta, the man who played so large a part in the events of 1809, and the politician and civil servant A. von Hartmansdorff. From 1818 to the mid-1840's politics in Sweden were coloured by the interaction between Liberalism and Conservatism; the latter

represented by the King and the Council, the former by
the opposition in the *Riksdags* and the Press.

These two political schools of thought usually found themselves on opposite sides in current controversies. Nevertheless,
they were agreed in the main on the reforming of the monetary system, which had been under consideration as long ago
as the 1810's. Gradually a plan of action was evolved, though
it was not until 1834 that the new revaluation programme –
the third since 1775 – was ready, whereby paper money was
redeemed at almost half its value and stability was restored.
This question had been discussed at length and attracted
considerable interest, and on the whole the government and
the *Riksdag* had worked tolerably well together in the matter.
But there were also other and more important economic
questions on which the old and the new elements were able
to co-operate. They were agreed on the expansion of the
policy of enclosure and the consolidation of strips (with the
consequent break-up of the old village community – a process completed in 1827), and on the further extension of
the area of cultivation. Experiments were made with new
methods and implements, outworn habits were abandoned,
and great opportunities were offered to the energetic and
enterprising agriculturalist. But country life in this transitional phase also had its sombre aspect. The debts and other
unfortunate consequences of enclosure were of minor importance compared with the vital question of the position of the
agricultural labourers. The population continued to grow
rapidly; as a result of 'the peace, vaccination and potatoes',
to use Tegnér's slightly cynical, but extremely apt words, it
increased from about 2,400,000 in 1810 to nearly 3,500,000
in 1850. The traditional class of peasant-farmers could ill
afford to support this increase, despite new methods of cultivation and increased productivity, and the division of existing
holdings could not go on indefinitely. Nor was there any big
industry to absorb the growing population, and surplus
labourers had to remain on the land either as farm hands or

23

as casual workers. There were the crofters (*torpare*), who tilled a small piece of ground under the peasant-proprietors; there were the men who owned a cottage but no ground (the *backstuga*), and supported themselves with any work they could find; and there were the *statare*, an agricultural employee who was housed by his employer and received a part of his wages in kind – a system which was introduced into the larger farms at the beginning of the nineteenth century. The rapid growth of these groups during this period, added to their precarious economic position, presented a serious social problem, and the provision of poor relief became one of the most urgent necessities. Bad harvests could cause real hardship, and there is no question that at times the distress was very great. It was certainly no worse than in previous centuries, but we are more fully informed of it through the copious records contained in contemporary poor relief reports. The Liberals believed that these problems could be solved by a new order of *laisser-faire* and free trade, whereas many of the Conservatives considered the trouble to be more fundamental in character.

The absence of any big industry to absorb the surplus population can be attributed to the almost complete lack of development in the iron industry during the last hundred and fifty years. Though Swedish iron production had remained constant and was assured of a steady market, it was still strictly regulated both as to output and in its geographical distribution. In his memoirs, Geijer has given a justifiably famous description of a Swedish mining-village of about the turn of the century:

These flames rising from deep snow, the water gushing forth beneath vaults and pillars of ice; the heavy reverberating blows of the hammer that in a landscape frozen into repose show that man is awake; straining sinews and sweat amid cold and snow-drifts; carters of charcoal and pig-iron in long rows, with rime-frost in their beards; the whinnying of horses sending warm steam from their nostrils; the eddy of human life and business: it is a picture to behold, it is a picture to live! How many evenings have I not watched the flames rising from the forge, and followed the wandering sparks till they faded in the dark expanse!

This is a vivid and attractive picture. At the same time it reveals how remote was this community from the Europe of the Industrial Revolution. Geijer is describing an idyll which was doomed; for some decades earlier England had invented the puddling method of using coke in the smelting of iron, a discovery which reduced and ultimately dispensed with the use of wood in this sphere of industry. Sweden's position was thus completely altered: she was now compelled to modernize her ironworks and abolish the antiquated methods which dated from the seventeenth century. This reorganization was largely carried out by the new class of industrialists and ironmasters, although many civil servants and ministers, too, actively supported a moderate and liberal economic policy. From the 1820's, therefore, fresh fields were opened up for the iron industry; within a short time the old techniques were replaced by the Lancashire smelting process, introduced from England by energetic and wealthy ironmasters, and the modern ironworks soon began to flourish. Although the new developments occasionally aroused bitter resentment, the principles of economic liberalism generally prevailed.

At the same time, a lively discussion took place in the *Riksdag*, in pamphlets and in the Press in favour of a similar relaxation of the old guild system and of other restrictions on crafts and trade. This movement was initiated at the 1823 *Riksdag*, though it was not completed until 1846, when controls were removed both from crafts and trade in the towns and from the production of iron; in country districts, too, crafts were wholly freed, and all trade except that which was carried on in the immediate vicinity of the towns.

The main struggle between Liberalism and Conservatism, however, was waged over the purely political and constitutional issue. Here there were sharp, even violent clashes, and the history of the *Riksdags* during this period was chiefly

distinguished by the conflict between the government and
the opposition. The opposition gradually began to advocate
constitutional and parliamentary government, for the middle
classes, which included large-scale agriculturalists, businessmen, industrialists and journalists, hoped by this means to
obtain the political power which they considered to be the
rightful consequence of their social advancement. The conflict was not at first serious, as Charles John still wielded
great authority. Gradually, however, the former revolutionary became intensely conservative in outlook; his
pertinacity, his suspicious nature and his desire for power
turned him increasingly into an absolute monarch, intolerant
of opposition; and his decisions on important issues, whether
taken alone or in consultation with trusted advisers, tended
to exceed his constitutional powers. He strongly opposed the
constitutional demands of the Liberals. The members of the
Council were appointed by him alone and were usually
chosen from among the higher officials; moreover they held
the appointments for years at a time and many of them only
retired, it was said, when they were too decrepit to hold
office any longer. It was difficult for such a Council to stand
up to the King; the more so as it was increasingly lacking in
able men, since those of stronger personality and greater
talent than Charles John did not always find it easy to work
with him. In addition, it was often hard for the less practised
members to hold their own in a foreign language in deliberations with a sovereign of brilliant rhetorical gifts; for Charles
John always used his mother tongue and never learnt to
speak Swedish. In these circumstances, the administration
was imbued with the King's personality, and 'one-man rule'
soon became a slogan of the opposition. There was also talk
of 'bedroom audiences', prompted by the King's habit of
getting up late, and to the 'Brahe régime', so-called after his
personal friend Magnus Brahe, who was believed to exercise
an unconstitutional influence, specially over appointments,
and who even acted as the King's mouthpiece in the Council.

A conflict was thus inevitable. Violent clashes took place in the *Riksdag* of 1828–30, and reached their climax during that of 1840–41. New opposition leaders emerged at the end of the 1820's who were more aggressively and consistently Liberal-minded, and the middle classes rose up against the 'Bureaucratic Sweden' which had been established as a result of the 1809 constitution. The leaders of the opposition included such prominent men as L. J. Hierta, who, besides being an important industrialist and merchant, was editor of the main Liberal paper *Aftonbladet*, and the lawyer J. G. Richert, one of the ablest of the Liberal spokesmen. In 1838 they were joined, after a notable *volte-face*, by E. G. Geijer, formerly one of the leading Conservatives. Briefly, the Liberal programme demanded more power for the *Riksdag* and greater control over King and Council, and a reform of the suffrage so as to bring it more into line with the new social order (primarily, therefore, to benefit the middle class) and make it less unwieldy in form. The tactics of the opposition were determined by the existing constitution; a majority in the *Riksdag* did not entitle the Liberals to attack the King personally, but they could impeach those councillors who were thought to have pandered unduly to him, to have disregarded the welfare of the State, or to have overstepped their authority. The opposition duly employed this expedient to attack measures or persons that it disliked, and the legal grounds were argued both in the *Riksdag* and its Examining Committees with considerable skill and eloquence. The Press, too, joined vigorously in the battle; the most notable contribution was made by *Aftonbladet*, which since 1830 had been the main organ of the opposition and whose editor Hierta had a rare talent for appealing to his middle-class readers and criticizing the King and the Council. The government for its part responded to the Press attacks by means of its official newspapers, and it also made use of the powers of confiscation enacted in 1812; by successively changing the title of his journal, however – from the Second right up to the Twenty-third *Aftonbladet* – Hierta was able to wage his newspaper war uninterrupted, and even managed to ridicule the frequent confiscations.

The persistent pin-pricks of the Liberals may seem petty and ignoble, and indeed they provoked Tegnér to write of 'the calumny' which 'is loose six days of the week and scarcely rests on the seventh'. Nevertheless, the constitution was to some extent modified as a result of these perpetual battles. By such means an unremitting check was kept on the government's proceedings, above all in its use of the revenues granted by the *Riksdag*. The government successfully routed the opposition attacks during the 1828–30 *Riksdag*, but thenceforward its task became increasingly difficult. At the end of the 1830's the feud between Liberals and Conservatives culminated in actual riots. The opposition journalist C. M. Crusenstolpe, who was a personal enemy of the King, was charged with libel and was sentenced in the summer of 1838 to three years' imprisonment. This decision was followed by prolonged mass demonstrations in the capital, which stemmed partly from the proletarian character of the surplus population. The party conflict became noticeably sharper in the period before the 1840 *Riksdag*, when certain Liberal factions formed a 'coalition', with the avowed aim of forcing the King to abdicate in favour of Crown Prince Oscar, who had Liberal sympathies and was popular with the opposition. The Conservative view of the state of the country was thus defined by a contemporary witness:

I passed six months at home in Sweden, after an absence of seven years. I did not recognize the country: it lay there glorious, blooming, cultivated, advancing in all things. I did not recognize the people . . . snatching after illusory betterment, with no reverence for what was previously held sacred; out of humour, ill-mannered, impudent in censure both with and without cause, politicizing even in the army, demoralized, preaching freedom. Journalism insolent, cynical, shameless beyond bounds. The members of the government dispirited, indolent, fearful, stifled by the opposition.

By the time the *Riksdag* met at the beginning of 1840, all the opposition groups in the four Estates were in active co-operation; having gained important successes in the committee elections, they determined to strike a death blow at the King, the Council, and the Conservatives. In the High Court, actions were brought against ministers on thirty-eight counts, and in seventy-two cases indictments were made according to the two methods decreed by the constitution; and only the heterogeneous nature of the opposition and the skilful resistance of the Conservatives saved the government from decisive defeat.

The previous *Riksdag* had determined on an important constitutional change by which the old Council was to be remodelled on departmental lines; seven of its members would each become the head of a department dealing with a specific subject, while three members, who had no department, were given consultative status. This had many advantages. In the old Council the secretaries had been specialist advisers, but their status did not correspond to their actual qualifications, and they had only limited influence. The new heads of departments were intended to be both councillor and secretary; the councillor would himself become an expert, and his position *vis-à-vis* the King would thereby be strengthened. The scheme was to be approved at the 1840 *Riksdag*, and the opposition made use of the occasion to get rid of a number of the old councillors. This led in practice to a change of government, the first under the new constitution, and among the new men there were several who, despite their Conservatism in politics, professed to support a moderate Liberal policy in economic questions.

The opposition had not won a decisive victory; nevertheless the 1840–1 *Riksdag* was epoch-making in that it constituted the most successful attempt yet made by the middle classes to exert their influence. Moreover, one effect of the recent conflicts had been to change the balance of power as conceived by the men of 1809 in favour of the *Riksdag*, primarily through its having gained practical control of State expenditure. Charles John died in the spring of 1844, and in his last years there was a noticeable relaxation of tension.

The violent *Riksdag* controversies tend to overshadow several important reforms which were accomplished outside the sphere of economics; important projects were initiated during the 1830's and early '40's, generally with somewhat grudging co-operation between Liberals and Conservatives; such co-operation introduced a novel and significant feature into Swedish politics which still persists to-day. At the 1840–1 *Riksdag* the government put forward a proposal for organized primary education; the *Riksdag* adopted it in a revised form, and in the following year an elementary-school act was passed which laid the foundations of Sweden's existing educational system. Following the *enskifte*, local government councils had been remodelled by a statute in 1817; and this offshoot of Sweden's tradition of self-government was now further strengthened by an ordinance of 1843. Careful reports on the question of poor relief were presented at the same *Riksdag*, and these were later to have a practical outcome.

But no solution had yet been found to a question of paramount importance, at all events in the eyes of the Liberals. This was suffrage reform; in other words, the extension of the right to send representatives to the *Riksdag*. It had been to the fore ever since the end of the 1820's. A scheme worked out by two Liberals, Anckarsvärd and Richert, had been published in 1830, and others soon followed. In most of these projects representation in the *Riksdag* was based not on the corporate Estates but on the individual citizen. No agreement was reached, however, even after the opposition's strong attack in 1840. Fresh proposals were made at subsequent *Riksdags*, but the demands were too numerous and diverse even for the opposition to agree among themselves. Still, some modifications were made from the 1820's onwards, with the aim of incorporating in the *Riksdag*, within the framework of the four Estates, those sections of society which were formerly unrepresented. By this means the universities and the learned societies obtained representatives in the Estate of the clergy in 1823, the ironmasters in that of the burgesses in 1828–30 – thereby considerably swelling the ranks of the Liberals – and the nobles' peasants (the so-called 'free' peasants) in the peasant Estate in 1834–5.

It was not until the middle of the 1860's, however, that this vexed question was finally settled. Nor was any fundamental solution found for the social problems arising from the increasing proletarian character of the rural population, for which no remedy had yet been provided in the poor relief reports. Such a remedy must depend in the last resort on a general improvement in the national economy, and a thorough exploitation of the natural resources of Sweden would obviously take some time.

It was true that the Liberal middle class had failed to achieve some of its basic aims, that it had not accomplished any great reorganization of the constitution, and that parliamentary government was still remote. Nevertheless it had managed to abolish many features of the old society symbolized in the four Estates, and it was about to make great advances in its liberal economic policy. There was also emerging a middle-class literature which was realistic in approach and expressed the new contemporary outlook. The lyrical and romantic outpourings of former times were followed by straightforward prose, best exemplified in the novel. C. J. L. Almquist, originally a romantic, wrote a series of prose works during the 1830's in which he discussed modern problems, portrayed the life of the nation, and made some penetrating observations on 'the meaning of Swedish poverty', the most burning question of the time. Fredrika Bremer and Emilie Flygare-Carlén wrote of the daily routine; the former, a true representative of her period, espoused the question of women's rights, while the latter depicted the life of the people on the west coast.

The debates in the *Riksdag* and the affairs of the constitution should not be allowed wholly to dominate the picture of Swedish history during this period, for in fact they merely reflect movements that can more easily be traced in literature, in economic activity, and in social life. During this period one is able to observe afresh and at close quarters the significant developments and intellectual activities that were taking place among hitherto obscure classes of society; and it becomes possible to follow in detail the thoughts and aspirations of the people. For the first time the great popular movements are beginning to affect the lower-middle-class town dwellers and the rural population.

This is the real starting-point, for example, of the Free Church revivalist movement. Hitherto confined to certain areas and social classes, the new trend now became widespread. L. L. Laestadius, the unconventional Norrland priest, worked with indefatigable zeal and self-denial among the Lapps, the message preached by the Lund churchman H. Schartau yielded in Western Sweden a strict form of piety which became known as Schartauism. In Stockholm, the English preacher George Scott, followed by the Swede C. O. Rosenius, instigated a popular revival which was soon to have important consequences and, indirectly, give rise to the Free-Church pietistic movements in the late nineteenth century. The dissolution of the old village community and the social and economic crises of the time had prepared the ground for such influences.

The Temperance movement, which originated in the 1830's, might also be described as a kind of revivalism. Heavy drinking, which had increased since the Gustavian period, was rife in all classes of society. Home distilling on a small scale had been legalized in 1798, and the peasants made their own spirits from grain or potatoes. Familiarity had blinded people's eyes to the sordid aspects of intemperance. Nevertheless they were at last beginning to realize the connection between drunkenness on the one hand, and poverty and criminality on the other; and in the middle of the 1830's the priest P. Wieselgren initiated an intensive nation-wide campaign in favour of abstinence, or rather moderation. And although he met with stubborn resistance at first, his efforts were to bear fruit in the end.

The Revivalist movement, the Temperance movement, and the new elementary schools were to have important consequences for the Swedish people and for the development of modern Sweden. They are among the brighter aspects of the confused developments which characterized the first half of the nineteenth century.

# XXXI

# Scandinavianism
## 1815-1875

---

After the successful termination of her 1812 policy, Sweden continued to maintain her pro-Russian attitude. The situation in the west had changed and the danger which had for so long influenced political calculations had been removed by the Union with Norway. It was some time before relations with Denmark became really friendly; but difficulties were not very likely to arise, the less so since the difference of opinion over Norway's share in Denmark's national debt had been settled by an agreement in 1819. There thus began a period of peace, during which Charles XIV wavered cautiously between the two main powers in Northern Europe, Russia and England, though his sympathies inclined towards the former. On the other hand, official pro-Russian policy had never been popular in Sweden, and the opposition urged the King to make an approach to England, which was regarded as the antithesis of 'despotic Russia'. The government itself had often chafed under Russian influence, and while Alexander I was alive relations were far from satisfactory.

Meanwhile new conceptions of foreign policy were beginning to be mooted among certain groups, and the contemporary liberal and nationalist outlook gave birth to 'Scandinavianism', the idea that the three Scandinavian countries would form one unit. This movement developed rapidly between the end of the 1830's and the middle of the '60's, and has played an important part in Scandinavian cultural life.

The idea of a unified Scandinavia has a long and remarkable history. In its mediaeval aspect it was evolved partly from feudal and dynastic conceptions, and partly from a joint aversion to the strong influence of the Hansa League and Mecklenburg in the fourteenth century. Once achieved, however, the union met with opposition in various parts of the powerful state created by Queen Margaret, and not even the many common political and economic interests were sufficient to preserve it intact. Christian II was unsuccessful in his assiduous attempts to restore the union by war, and the sporadic efforts subsequently made by Gustav Vasa and Christian III were engulfed by the Northern Seven Years War and the numerous wars in the later 16th century. The idea was next revived by Charles X, who, like Christian II, envisaged a union through conquest, only this time it was the Swedes who would be the conquerors; and he all but succeeded in his project of following up his second Danish war by creating a Scandinavian state centred in Sweden. Notwithstanding the persistent conflicts between the two countries, it was not long before enterprising Swedish and Danish politicians were again promoting the idea of a union, though it is difficult to say how far they really believed they would achieve anything.

In the middle of the eighteenth century, during the Age of Freedom, the idea cropped up in a new form, and for a little while it looked as though Crown Prince Frederick of Denmark might succeed to the Swedish throne; while towards the end of the century, Sweden and Denmark-Norway co-operated, to their mutual advantage, in defence of their commercial neutrality during the wars of the great powers. From 1809 onwards Frederick VI of Denmark was again projecting plans for a dynastic union, both before the election of Charles August to the Swedish throne and after his death. Then came the Union of Sweden and Norway which, by its subsequent amalgamation of two states with separate constitutions under a common sovereign and foreign ministry, incorporated in practice one of the main features of the earlier proposals. This Union worked fairly smoothly at first, owing chiefly to the feeling of security induced by co-operation in foreign affairs; and although clashes sometimes took place, they did not become really serious until the second half of the century.

During the eighteenth and the early part of the nineteenth centuries, therefore, Scandinavian solidarity had been taking on a new form. True, its appeal was limited to certain groups, such as scientists, writers and artists; but among these it aroused considerable interest, and it was at the outset an expression of the intellectual internationalism of the Age of Enlightenment. Swedish and Danish historians, who had hitherto only exchanged political diatribes, now began to collaborate. The Swedish sculptor Sergel formed a personal friendship with the Danish painter Abildgaard under the aegis of Neo-classicism. At the beginning of the nineteenth century, Swedish and Danish scholars of prehistory promoted the new science of archaeology, which was to throw light on the ancient history of Scandinavia, while study of early Scandinavian culture infused into the Gothicists in Sweden and Grundtvig in Denmark a sense of its contemporary oneness. And at the degree-giving ceremonies in Lund in 1829, Tegnér, who was officiating, bestowed the formal laurel wreath on the Danish poet Oehlenschläger, with the words:

Now is divorcement no more – it should never had been in
                                                     the boundless
liberal world of the mind . . .

All this was something new, and it involved a degree of intellectual contact between Sweden and Denmark which, if not yet very extensive, at all events had potentialities. The university students were the first to be affected. The winter of 1838 was an exceptionally severe one, and students from Lund and Copenhagen walked over the frozen Sound to visit each other. A more permanent means of access had already been created as a result of technological progress in the form of a regular steamboat service between Malmö and Copenhagen, and in the summer of 1839 a conference of Swedish and Danish students was held in Copenhagen.

Signs of a political Scandinavianism were also beginning to appear. This conception was first mooted in the 1830's, when war seemed likely between the two rival great powers in northern Europe, England and Russia. At that time Charles XIV had momentarily considered embarking on a joint policy of neutrality with Denmark in order to keep the Scandinavian countries out of the threatened conflict, a heritage of Sweden's attitude during the eighteenth century. However, he soon gave up the plan in deference to the feelings of Russia, who would hardly have benefited from the step and who in any case disapproved of the Scandinavianist tendencies. But although the great powers in fact refrained from fighting, Swedish uneasiness at Russia's influence became increasingly marked, not only in the Liberal opposition but also among members of the government. Shortly afterwards, nationalism became a burning issue in the south of Denmark; and with Russian pressure on Sweden and German pressure on Denmark, the time for political Scandinavianism had come.

Oscar I of Sweden was clearly determined to move out of the Russian orbit into that of England; in this, as in much else at the beginning of his reign, he was at one with the Liberals. This departure in foreign policy was dictated partly by Sweden's economic relations with England, which had been growing closer since the middle of the century, and which will be described elsewhere; partly by Oscar's desire to enhance the international standing of both Sweden and himself; and partly by his enthusiasm and rare talent for the game of diplomacy.

In 1843, the year before Charles XIV died, a large meeting of Scandinavian students, excluding those from Norway, had been held at Uppsala; it was followed two years later by a similar one in Lund, and the two together inaugurated a series of lively interchanges in the following years, during which considerable rhetoric was expended on the subject of Scandinavian ties.

Meanwhile, however, serious trouble was brewing in Denmark. Holstein and Southern Schleswig, where German was the dominant tongue, wished to be allied wholly with Germany. In the spring of 1848, there was a rising in the duchies assisted by Prussia and the German *Bund*, and by Easter the Danish troops had been routed. This event fired the adherents of Scandinavianism in Sweden with the desire to follow up their numerous orations with action. Oscar I, too, considered that the time was ripe for intervention, and at the beginning of May he outlined his scheme to a Secret Committee in the newly assembled *Riksdag*. He did not propose to intervene directly in the question of the duchies, but rather to dispatch 15,000 men to assist Denmark in the event of Jutland and the islands being threatened by German troops. The *Riksdag* approved his plan, and shortly afterwards the King informed Prussia of his intention. Russia followed suit and brought pressure to bear on Prussia in Denmark's support, with the result that the Prussian troops evacuated the occupied areas of Jutland even before the Swedish forces had arrived; still, the combined diplomatic and military demonstration had in itself done something to further Denmark's cause. At the beginning of June the Swedish troops, now 4,000 strong, started to disembark on Fünen, while a larger force was kept in readiness in Skåne; and it was largely due to Oscar I's mediation, backed by pressure from the neutral powers, that an armistice was concluded between Denmark and Prussia at Malmö in 1848. War again broke out in 1849, but this time Oscar disapproved of the Danish government's action and refused any further assistance, though he endeavoured to bring about a settlement by diplomatic means. Nor was this the extent of Sweden's contribution, for it was her 4,000 soldiers who, after the preliminary armistice in 1849, occupied northern Schleswig until the definitive treaty was signed in 1850. In addition, Sweden joined with the great powers in signing both the 'London protocol' in 1850, which established the integrity of the Danish State, and the agreement as to the succession in 1852 which made the future Christian IX heir to the throne. As to the latter move, Oscar I may have hoped for a different outcome: to become himself heir to the Danish throne and thus pave the way for a united Scandinavia. But there is no reliable evidence for this. Whether or not he was disappointed, however, he had had to face another discovery during the Danish crisis: that Russia's influence in northern Europe was still very great and that it was her policy that had largely determined the outcome of the Danish question. All these various events between 1848 and 1850 no doubt influenced the outlook of the Swedish King, who was now more than ever resolved to develop his foreign policy on his own lines.

He was soon to be offered an ideal opportunity to do so. In 1853 there occurred a crisis in the Eastern Question in Europe which led to the outbreak of the Crimean War, and the tension between Russia on the one side and England and France on the other increased every day. In view of this, Oscar I revived the project of a league of Scandinavian neutrals, directed principally against Russia, and it was carried through in December on the basis of a joint declaration by Sweden-Norway and Denmark, which was approved by all the powers, though only grudgingly by Russia. The Crimean War broke out in March 1854, and Oscar I now made a cautious but determined approach to the Western Powers, adroitly utilizing for his purpose the Press and other means of propaganda, both in Sweden and abroad. In the same year the navies of the allied powers destroyed the Russian fortress of Bomarsund on the Åland islands; and in the following year Oscar I helped to procure the November Treaty with England and France, by which the Western Powers guaranteed Swedish-Norwegian territories against Russia. There is no doubt that Oscar had intended to enter the war; peace, however, was made in 1856, and was accelerated, indeed, by Russia's fear of the implied threat in the November Treaty. Sweden's new policy had gained for her a

24

guarantee on the part of Russia, given when the peace was signed, not to fortify the Åland islands.

These events gave a fillip to the idea of Scandinavianism, which now emerged in a new form. It was clear that one of the King's main aims was to strengthen Sweden's position as a Baltic power. His plans in the east having been frustrated by the termination of the war, he employed other means to counteract Russia's now unfriendly attitude and obtain an influential position for Scandinavia in the Concert of Europe. All at once Scandinavianism became the dominant political issue, and plans to create a new great power in northern Europe were enthusiastically ventilated. Oscar I negotiated with Scandinavianist circles in Copenhagen with a view to implementing the Ejder programme (Schleswig's incorporation with Denmark) and forming an offensive and defensive alliance, or even a dynastic union, between the three Nordic countries which would supersede the succession decree of 1852. In 1857 a proposal for such an alliance was laid before the Danish King, Frederick VII, who rejected it. Prompted by increasing fear of Germany, the new Danish President of the Council, C. C. Hall, resumed negotiations in the autumn of the same year; but by that time severe illness had forced Oscar I to withdraw from active participation in the government, and all that remained to him, politically, was thus a sense of disappointment at the failure of his ambitious Scandinavianist policy. And since the Crown Prince-Regent Charles, supported by the Foreign Minister, L. Manderström, felt unable to respond to Hall's overtures, the preliminary Danish proposal of alliance was declined. The *Riksdag* evidently shared this view, and for the time being political Scandinavianism was abandoned. Thus ended Oscar I's dreams of a Scandinavian great power.

The change of sovereign in 1859 had a marked effect on Swedish foreign policy. Oscar I had himself acted as Foreign Minister, just as he had done his utmost to maintain personal rule, occasionally tinged though it was with Liberalism. His son and successor Charles XV lacked Oscar I's personal qualifications for sustaining the power of the monarchy; and in addition he appointed at the outset of his reign a Council which, under the leadership of the able Minister of Justice Louis de Geer, acquired a new independence in political affairs. The changed situation was underlined by an episode which occurred inside the Swedo-Norwegian Union about this time. Under the terms of the Union of 1815, the King had the right to appoint a Governor in Norway. This had always been an unpopular office, and during the 1850's its abolition was demanded by the growing Liberal-Democrat opposition in the *Storting*. While on a visit to Norway Charles XV had rashly agreed, and the *Storting* accordingly did away with the Governorship in December 1859. This action was strongly resented by the *Riksdag*, the Council and Swedish opinion generally, and it was only with difficulty that de Geer was able to find a solution that more or less satisfied the various parties. This in fact constituted a severe defeat for the King, while at the same time the authority of the Council was enormously increased. At all events those who were cognizant of affairs could now see that it was no longer the Swedish King who determined foreign policy, as in Oscar I's time, but the Council, and this development throws considerable light on the course of Scandinavianism in the years that followed.

Interest in Sweden was now concentrated on a proposal for electoral reform which de Geer had persuaded the 1862–3 *Riksdag* to accept, and whose fate was ultimately to be decided at that of 1865. But meanwhile a serious crisis was blowing up in Denmark over Schleswig-Holstein and Germany. We shall confine ourselves here to the effect of these complicated problems on the ideas of Scandinavianism and the plans for alliance. Hall's policy of March 1863 had been to link Schleswig closer to Denmark and leave Holstein alone. It was based to some extent on the hope of Swedish support, and not without good reason, for at the beginning of the

1860's Charles XV had guaranteed to assist the Danish government in the threatening crisis. His lively imagination was captured by the prospect of playing a great political rôle, and he did not always stop to think of the possible consequences of his words. In practice, the change in the control of Swedish foreign affairs, which had been implicit in the matter of the Norwegian Governorship, detracted increasingly from the value of the personal promises which the King made so lavishly; it was the Council that now had the last word. These circumstances helped to bring about the defeat of Charles XV's Scandinavianist policy in 1860–5.

Charles XV and Frederick VII of Denmark were close friends; each was characterized by a certain affability and a love of good living. In the summer of 1860 they had met in Skåne to discuss the more urgent questions, and mention was made of an alliance. With the exception of the Foreign Minister Manderström, the Council was not as a rule very fully informed of the King's actions or intentions, and the negotiations were therefore marked from the outset by a deplorable confusion, which grew worse. After the proclamation of the March policy of 1863, Charles XV, who was spending part of the summer in Skåne, crossed to Skodsborg and there met Frederick VII and Hall. The Swedish King had previously discussed with Manderström the basic essentials of the attitude Sweden should adopt, and the Swedish envoys in London and Paris had expressed their support of Danish policy. At the Skodsborg meeting, however, Charles went much further; he promised, on certain conditions, to send 20,000 Swedish soldiers to defend Schleswig if Germany attacked Holstein. Though he tried to curb Charles's exuberance, the Swedish envoy in Copenhagen, H. Hamilton, was himself in favour of a defensive alliance, and Manderström also considered it advisable. Negotiations to this end were started in August, and a preliminary draft, embodying Charles's terms, was ready at the end of the month.

At that time Manderström was the only Council member who had detailed information of the progress of events; and when the others were told at the beginning of September, one of the leading councillors, the Minister of Finance, J. A. Gripenstedt, declared himself strongly opposed to the project. At a meeting with the King at Ulriksdal on 8th September, which was attended by de Geer, Manderström, Hamilton, and the Norwegian Prime Minister G. Sibbern, he won over de Geer and Sibbern to his views; the other two felt that they ought to take the consequences of the previous negotiations. Gripenstedt and de Geer insisted that before any alliance was effected England and France, preferably both, should promise to co-operate in any assistance that Denmark was given; and this view was subsequently favoured by other members of the Council. The King tried to carry his point and even threatened to appoint a new Council, but he was not successful; his well-known oddities of character probably helped to discourage councillors from giving him their unconditional support. Manderström and Hamilton were thus in an awkward intermediate position, since they felt themselves personally bound to Denmark by their share in the previous negotiations; and they chose the unfortunate course of trying to postpone any decision about an alliance, in the hope that the Western Powers would intervene in Denmark's favour. The Danish government therefore received no definite answer, and were consequently over-optimistic as to the support that might be expected from Sweden; and this in fact was wholly contingent on the attitude of the Western Powers in the approaching conflict. But the Western Powers also failed to give a definite answer; and the confusion was increased by the evasive manner in which Manderström and Hamilton felt obliged to explain the altered situation to the Danish government. A new and less far-reaching form of alliance was discussed at the end of October; but in this, too, no decision was reached. After the death of Frederick VII and the publication of the Danish

November Constitution, linking Schleswig with Denmark and excluding Holstein, Sweden gave up all thought of an alliance; and it was not until then that Manderström gave any precise information about Sweden's attitude. It is true that, in December, Charles XV munificently agreed to assist Denmark with 22,000 soldiers, but it soon became clear that this was merely one of his customary unfounded promises and it was immediately revoked by the Council; for the King had not yet succeeded in replacing the Council with a new ministry that would implement his programme. Any hope of achieving a union of the three Scandinavian States under Charles XV was now over.

There is no need here to go into the reason why, in spite of this lack of support, Hall adhered to the earlier Danish policy; nor to describe the tragic events of the subsequent war, when Prussia and Austria jointly attacked Denmark and conquered Schleswig and Holstein. No help was forthcoming from the Western Powers, and Denmark remained isolated. In Sweden, Scandinavianism was vigorously promoted both in the Press and among the Swedish volunteers who went to Denmark. The confusion which marked Swedish policy during the disastrous months of 1863 was (as we have seen) due primarily to the lack of co-operation between King and Council, together with the King's ill-considered and unfounded promises and his lack of realism; moreover the Swedish diplomats, convinced that things would right themselves in the end, refused to admit categorically that the situation had changed – an understandable but dangerous attitude, while responsible statesmen were restrained by the obvious imperfections which existed in the organization of the Swedish army.

Since the beginning of the nineteenth century the Swedish army had been composed of two basic elements. Firstly the *indelning* system, by which officers and cavalry troopers lived on crown lands and received taxes in kind from the peasants. The infantry soldiers cultivated small holdings which were provided by the peasants in order to escape conscription. The system brought stability and linked the army with the soil; its main defects arose from its rigid adherence to an outmoded economic system of payment in kind and the antiquated methods of training. The second basis of the army was the *beväring*, or conscription. Training was brief and spasmodic, however; and the government inquiries and attempts at reform which had been made during the nineteenth century had led nowhere. Moreover, anyone who was liable for military service could hire a substitute to do the training, though in 1860 this practice was superseded by that of buying oneself out of the army. A Defence Committee was considering these problems during the first half of the 1860's, but it had as yet only reached the preliminary stages. This being so, it would have been most rash to involve Sweden in an extensive war – a consideration which might also be applied to Oscar I's plans to join in the Crimean War – and conscientious politicians could hardly have agreed to it. And it was in fact many years before the Swedish defence system was finally reorganized.

By 1864, the day of political Scandinavianism seemed over, for its lamentable miscalculations had made a deep impression and aroused widespread indignation and bitterness. At the same time the electoral reform of 1865 struck a much-needed note of enterprise and regeneration. Charles XV's efforts to emulate his father's independent and active foreign policy had been frustrated, and his consequent hostility towards Prussia was manifested in the Franco-Prussian war, when Swedish opinion was almost unanimously on the side of France. But foreign policy took a fresh turn under the new King Oscar II (1872–1907), who, in the course of a significant visit to Germany in 1875, declared his sympathies with the new German realm; in this view he was supported by the Foreign Minister O. M. Björnstjerna, who considered that Sweden should regard Germany as 'her best friend'. A brisk cultural and economic exchange sprang up between the two countries, and persisted in many spheres right up to about 1910; Swedish scholarship, as well as her fiscal and social policy, tended to be based on German models, and there was a marked increase in trade between the two countries.

What, then, did Scandinavianism amount to in the end? The generation which lived through the disappointments of 1864 were inclined to put it down as a failure. But this is a complete delusion, if an understandable one. In the middle of the century the Scandinavian peoples acquired knowledge of one another's culture, a process that was made easier by their similarity of language; and the foundations were laid of a fruitful collaboration in scholarship, legislation, economic life, and art and letters that has since been expanded and is now of the greatest significance. Politics in Norway reacted on those of Sweden; the Danish Folk High School was taken as a model for similar educational institutions in Sweden, and writers such as Strindberg, Ibsen, and Georg Brandes had a great influence in all three countries. These were permanent gains, and were far from being endangered by the destruction of political Scandinavianism. Indeed, the essential strength of the movement was such that even the Union crisis of 1905 failed to weaken for more than a few years the co-operation between the three peoples, as is evidenced by the policy of the governments of the Scandinavian States during the First World War.

# XXXII

# The Beginnings of Industrialism. Railways and the Reform of Representation
## 1844-1865

The vast wooded tracts in Sweden had changed little in the course of the ages. In the middle of the nineteenth century there were still largely virgin forests, haunted – to simple minds – by the trolls of pagan times. And although the cultivated area had gradually spread and summer pastures for the cattle and land worked by Finnish colonists had been added to the area of peasant settlement, most of the more remote parts of Sweden was still under forest. Those responsible for economic policy, exaggerating the risk of depletion, had endeavoured for centuries to limit tree-felling in order to ensure an ample supply of charcoal for the ironworks. Forest products – timber and tar – had been exported for many years and from the eighteenth century onwards in increasing quantities, but the timber trade was not yet a dominant factor in Swedish economic life. The second half of the nineteenth century, however, brought with it the overwhelming impact of industrialization, and it was this economic development that was chiefly responsible for Sweden's vicissitudes during the last hundred years.

There are divers reasons why Sweden's industrialization took place at this moment. The Industrial Revolution and the huge increase in population in western Europe had created an enormous demand for timber. For a long time most of it was provided by Norway; but by the middle of the century she was no longer able to meet the demand, and it was natural, therefore, that the more remote areas of Sweden should enter the field. Large-scale exports had become possible as a result of the great development in maritime transport. Moreover, during the 1840's a crucial change had taken place in the policy of Sweden's foremost importer, England. Since the beginning of the century the latter had favoured timber imports from her colonies in preference to those from other countries; now, however, her acceptance of free trade doctrines opened up new and profitable prospects for Swedish exporters.

Important advances were also being made in technology. The water-driven Swedish sawmills, introduced in the eighteenth century, were already in common use by the beginning of the nineteenth, and the old coarse-bladed saws, which turned much of the log into sawdust, were gradually replaced by more economical saws with fine blades. But at the critical moment an even more important innovation was made. The water-driven sawmills had to be placed near rapids and waterfalls; and as these did not exist along the coast the sawn timber could not be floated and therefore had to be taken to the ports by more costly overland means of transport. With the advent of the steam engine, however, sawmills could be erected beside a suitable harbour at the mouth of a river, and logs could be floated down to the mills along the numerous waterways. The clearing of these waterways was the only expense involved, and the first steam-driven sawmill was set up on the Norrland coast in 1849. A further reason for the rise of the timber industry lay in the fact that since 1823 the crown had relinquished to the peasants large areas of forest in Norrland, which could thus be freely exploited. In 1846, after long dispute, virtually all restrictions were lifted from trade and industry; two years later fresh possibilities of economic expansion were opened up by a new company law; and with these developments forestry in Sweden entered a new era.

Energetic large-scale *entrepreneurs* now began to turn their attention to lumbering and the export of timber; and among

the leading businessmen who helped to discover the latent
resources of northern Sweden were J. C. Kempe, originally
from Swedish Pomerania, and members of the Scottish
immigrant family of Dickson. The forests of western Sweden
were exploited first, as they were nearer the ports of export.
But Norrland's turn soon followed, and modern sawmills
were established all along the coastline of the Gulf of Bothnia.
Much energy and money were expended on clearing the
river courses, proceeding higher and higher up as the
demand for timber increased. Huge areas of forest were
bought up and ruthlessly stripped, and at times the very
existence of the Norrland peasant class seemed threatened by
the speculations of timber firms. Coastal towns from Gävle
to Luleå hummed with life, and the general rate of progress
can be illustrated by some significant figures. The average
annual export of sawn and planed timber at the beginning
of the 1830's was 190,000 cubic metres – and by the 1860's it
was six times this figure, the greatest increase coming after
1850.

It was not only in forestry, however, that great advances
were made. The freeing of the iron industry, too, resulted in
a steady, if less rapid, rise in the exports of iron. In the 1820's
the average annual production of pig-iron was 80,000 tons;
by the middle of the century it was about 145,000 tons, while
between 1861 and 1865 it rose to 205,000 tons, an increase
for which the new type of ironmaster who appeared during
the first period of Liberalism was largely responsible. As the
restrictions on trade were eased and the iron market completely freed, the antiquated co-operative associations of
peasant miners were superseded by larger and more modern
forms of organization. And at the end of the 1850's, Swedish
iron production was further revolutionized. Widespread
experiments were then being made in the mass-production of
steel, and the English engineer Henry Bessemer had worked
out a theoretical, but as yet impracticable, process. In 1858,
however, the method was perfected, after many setbacks, by

a Swedish iron industrialist, G. F. Göransson. The process consists in passing a current of air through the molten pig-iron in order to purify its carbon content to the desired degree. This discovery made possible the establishment of the modern Steel Age, and the first successful Bessemer furnace thus marked an epoch in the history of modern technology. It was some time, however, before the method was generally adopted; in 1870 the amount of Bessemer steel manufactured was still less than 5 per cent. of the total production of malleable iron and steel. A new method on similar lines, the Martin process, owes its development partly to the Swede J. F. Lundin, who helped to confirm the results of the French inventor.

Meanwhile, the countryside was becoming dotted with factories. English inventions were ousting the old domestic system in the textile industry; English machines were imported, and cotton mills and looms sprang up round Borås in Västergötland, which had long been the centre of the cotton industry. The leading man in this sphere was Sven Erikson, another of the pioneers of modern industry. His mother had for many years woven cotton fabrics for sale in the poor district where she lived, and this was her legacy to her son. As far back as the 1830's he had set up a weaving-mill in Rydboholm in Västergötland, and his example was followed in many parts of the country. The woollen industry was mainly, though not exclusively, centred in Norrköping, and the mechanized loom was introduced into Sweden about 1850. Motala provided the centre for a new engineering industry, which produced such goods as large steam engines. It was not until much later, however, that these industries developed into large-scale enterprises. At the same time the industrialization of Europe had an indirect influence on Sweden's oldest economic activity, agriculture, which procured a good market for its surplus grain, particularly oats. The community was changing in character, if not yet very perceptibly.

Thus between 1845 and 1865 Sweden began to merge into the greater unit of the modern industrialized world. Her immediate need was for improved communications to enable her diverse products to reach the world market, and during this period great advances were made in her transport facilities, largely owing to the introduction of the steam engine. From 1850 onwards the tonnage of Swedish merchant shipping and sailing vessels showed a considerable increase, though it was not until the 1880's that steam ships became a significant factor. But still more urgent was the need for communications inside Sweden, in view of her long distances and widely scattered communities. Ever since the sixteenth century many Swedes had favoured the introduction of a canal system, and in 1809, when the country was at its lowest ebb, the *Riksdag* had decided that the Göta Canal should be built to form a central artery through the country from the Baltic Sea to the Kattegat. This enterprise, which was directed by Baltzar von Platen with the assistance, in the preparatory stages, of the famous Scottish canal-builder Thomas Telford, was completed in 1832. But although it still exists as a means of communication and a tourist attraction, the canal was soon out of date. Other demands had arisen, and technology offered new solutions. The railway age was at hand.

A competition famous in railway history had been held in England in 1829, to which the Swedish inventor John Ericson sent a locomotive of his own construction. During the 1830's, railways were being built extensively throughout the world; and in the 1840's the question was mooted in Sweden by Count Adolf von Rosen, who had studied the system in Europe and was anxious to promote it at home. The topic provoked some lively debates in the *Riksdag*, and it even aroused the personal interest of Oscar I. The new ideas prevailed despite some opposition from the anti-Liberals, and at the next *Riksdag* it was decided that the main lines should be built by the State with the help of foreign capital, while local lines should be left to private enterprise. The great undertaking was directed by Colonel Nils Ericson, who was a brother of the inventor, and who had been trained by von Platen. Building started during the 1860's and gathered speed during the '70's, and the opening of new railways became gala occasions. A *Riksdag* member has described the inauguration of the main line between Stockholm and Gothenburg in 1862 : 'The King, the popular Charles XV, drove in an open carriage in the first train, stopping for a shorter or longer time at each station to talk to the people, who had everywhere assembled in countless numbers to gaze on the splendour. Here and there triumphal arches were erected, and at one station in Södermanland there was a salute of cannon. The jubilation was universal and the cheering almost deafening, not only at the stations but also at other suitable spots where a crowd was collected. In the evening you could see here and there the reflection of burning tar barrels or piles of twigs, and at Hallsberg the rockets flashed and burning squibs crackled in the bushes, so that nowhere was one safe from sparks and flames.'

This triumphal procession of the product of mechanical skill through the old peasant settlements was like a modern fairy-tale; and the birth of the railways has perhaps contributed more than anything else to the growth of modern Sweden. Sweden's links with other countries were further developed by the introduction of the electric telegraph in the 1850's and the modernization of the postal system. At the same time, and in close co-operation with industry, a modern banking system was created: *Stockholms enskilda bank* (the Private Bank of Stockholm) in 1856, *Skandinaviska Kreditaktie-bolaget* (the Scandinavian Credit Company) in 1864, and *Svenska Handelsbanken* (the Swedish Trade Bank) in 1871. It was indeed a dramatic and exciting era in Sweden's history. Nor was the political development without interest; closely interrelated as it was with these industrial and economic events, it embodied the final victory of Liberalism.

Oscar I had succeeded his father in 1844, and the change of sovereign was accompanied by a fundamental change in the government. As Crown Prince, Oscar had sympathized with the Liberals, who regarded his accession as a favourable augury. He had taken a great interest in the proposals for humanitarian reform, and he possessed knowledge of current problems. He was a widely cultured person of considerable gifts and strength of purpose, though he lacked the will-power and arresting personality of his father. Reference has already been made to his diplomatic propensities, his desire to hold the centre of the stage and his attempts, regardless of means, to sway opinion. Notwithstanding it all, he was very sensitive to what people thought of him and anxious to stand well with his subjects. During the first year of his reign he conceded certain of the Liberal demands. He admitted moderate Liberals to the Council, thus ensuing steady progress in the work of reform. The restrictions on the freedom of the Press were abolished in 1844, equal rights of inheritance for men and women were established in 1845, and an extensive reform of the law on humanitarian lines was undertaken; it was promoted by, among others, J. G. Richert, and was strongly opposed by the Conservatives. A new poor relief ordinance was enacted in 1847, and revised in 1853; and while it could not solve the most urgent problems of the rural population, it did at least provide for the first time an organized system of relief. The February Revolution of 1848 in France gave a stimulus to the opposition in the *Riksdag*, with the result that the Council was again reshuffled; it was now composed almost entirely of new men, who included moderate Liberals from various groups. These ministerial appointments were influenced, to a greater extent than before, by political motives; at the same time, the overall political colour remained what was then called 'grey'. The King continued to impose his personality on the Council; but instead of the old conflict of government versus opposition, the grouping in the *Riksdag* became more variable. Oscar I's 'modern' outlook did much to smooth out the worst disputes; and although he established what was to all intents and purposes a 'Liberal one-man rule', it can be said that the Liberals won their decisive political victory in the second half of the 1840's. It should, however, be emphasized that the most important reforms were accomplished through the co-operation of Liberals and Conservatives.

At the end of the 1840's, however, Oscar I began to espouse the Conservative cause, and by 1852 the composition of his government was exclusively Conservative; though a few years later it was leavened by the appointment of K. E. Günther as Minister of Justice. One of the most important measures of reform was enacted at the *Riksdag* of 1853-4; this was the prohibition of the domestic distillation of spirits, which, despite the protests of the peasant Estate against such an attack on their freedom, ultimately benefited both the peasants and public behaviour.

Towards the end of his life, Oscar I was compelled, as a result of illness, to give up the practical work of administration, and in September 1857 it was taken over by the Crown Prince Charles, who became Charles XV two years later. Of equal importance with the change of rulers was the change in the position of the Council. Its influence had been increasing ever since it was divided into departments under departmental ministers, and by this time the Council had acquired, through its members, a fund of expert knowledge and a political standing in the *Riksdag*. It was not yet regarded as a unified whole, however, nor had a leading spokesman emerged from any of the various groups. All this was now altered, and in 1858 Oscar I's personal government, with its tinge of Liberalism, was replaced by a new system.

Charles XV had decided Conservative sympathies and disapproved of his father's Liberal tendencies; moreover he was determined, mostly on personal grounds, not to retain Günther as Minister of Justice. In his own words, his aim was to pursue a policy 'according to his own mind', and with this in view he made radical changes in the Council, to which he appointed capable experts with whom he hoped to maintain good relations. They included the diplomat, L. Manderström, Foreign Minister, the brilliant Conservative nobleman, H. Hamilton, who was expected to become the dominating figure, and the Minister of Finance, J. A. Gripenstedt, a member of the previous ministry. The new Minister of Justice was the skilful lawyer Louis de Geer (who belonged to the same family as the great seventeenth-century industrialist), of whom little was known, but whose appointment was attributed mainly to his professional qualifications. In fact, although he lacked brilliance, he was exceptionally competent and clearsighted, intelligent, restrained, and fearless; politics he conceived as the art of the possible, and at the same time he was a talented author and essayist, and his memoirs are among the most notable of their kind in Sweden. As Minister, he did not fulfil the King's hopes. Charles XV was gifted and artistic; but whereas his father had merely been sensitive to public opinion, Charles deliberately courted popularity, and Oscar's pliancy became in him an over-confident insouciance. Some of his characteristics have already been illustrated with regard to his foreign policy. When faced with Louis de Geer's firmness, he always came off the worse; and the result was that Sweden obtained for the first time, and to the surprise of all, a united ministry under a recognized first Minister, similar to the English Cabinet system. As leader of a capable Council de Geer could wield a greater influence in the government than any of his predecessors had done: the effect of his attitude during the conflict with Norway has already been mentioned. A fundamental change took place in the working of the constitution, and greater co-operation was achieved between the government and the *Riksdag*. De Geer's term of office saw the final triumph of the Liberal policy of reform, which now entered its third phase, and it was not long before the King's Conservative hopes were shattered.

25

A bold and comprehensive programme of reform was now initiated. The corporal punishment of servants by their masters was forbidden, and it was decreed that an unmarried woman should reach her majority at twenty-five years of age. Religious freedom was introduced as a concession both to the Free Church revivalist movements and to the views of the Liberals. In 1862 local self-government was given a more efficient and popular basis by the introduction of the *Landsting*, with functions similar to those of an English County Council; and in 1864 a new and more humane penal code was adopted which abolished the old medley of obsolete and cruel punishments and made imprisonment the main penalty of crime.

Internal free trade was established in 1864, and freedom was also introduced by degrees into trade with other countries. The chief advocate of, this was the Minister of Finance, Gripenstedt, the most enterprising and vigorous exponent of economic liberalism of his age. Free Trade had become for him an article of faith, and he was deeply convinced that economic liberalism could solve all social problems. He had an almost unlimited belief in progress, and he propounded his ideas with wit and eloquence in the *Riksdag* and the Press. The principles of free trade were finally confirmed by a commercial treaty with France in 1865. This treaty was indirectly connected with the beginnings of economic expansion, and showed that Sweden was about to take her rightful place in international trade.

Since the middle class believed that it was mainly responsible for the upsurge of industry and reform, it was all the more surprising that the ultimate reform was still lacking. This was the right to be represented in the *Riksdag*, and it would give to the middle class uncontested political leadership. Though many proposals had been put forward and the subject had been discussed at length in the *Riksdag*, nothing had been achieved. The burgess and peasant Estates were now making definite demands for reform, and there were also strong forces at work among the nobles. And then, at the

Riksdag of 1862-3, de Geer himself put forward a proposal for a reform of the *Riksdag*. He suggested that it should consist of two Chambers. The First Chamber was to be based on indirect election with voting on a graded scale based on income, while the Second would be elected on a direct basis, with individual voting, and there was to be a property qualification for the franchise. By this means the First Chamber would represent the upper classes, whereas the elections to the Second Chamber would favour landed property, since the electoral qualification was an income of 800 crowns a year, or real estate to the value of 1,000 crowns. De Geer said that his aim was to give the majority of the electors the deciding vote and at the same time, by the two-chamber system, to prevent hasty decisions and protect existing interests and rights. The proposal was accepted, and was to be confirmed at the next *Riksdag*. There was great excitement when the Estates met in October 1865. Was the *Riksdag* of the four Estates really to crown its work of reform by abolishing itself?

Lengthy and brilliant debates took place in the House of Nobility in December 1865. Everything depended on the nobles; for the peasants and burgesses were all in favour of the reform, and the clergy had decided to follow the nobles. Public opinion brought strong pressure to bear on the issue, deputations from all parts of the country urged the demands of the middle classes, and at last the King reluctantly assented to the proposal. It was then carried in the House of Nobility by 361 votes to 294. Thus the *Riksdag* of the four Estates was abolished, and the Leader of the House of Nobility, Count Lagerbielke, addressed to the first Estate the following classic words, which embodied a proud memorial to the nobles who were now of their own accord renouncing their last privilege: 'Laws may undergo change, rights cease to exist, but duty to the mother country endures; and while this duty is well performed, the true noble little cares what his position and place in society may be.'

The new suffrage was naturally expected to bring about the political predominance of the middle classes. With some reservations, Liberalism had proclaimed individualism as the lodestar of reform; education, capacity, and social influence were regarded as pre-requisites of the right to vote. From the contemporary and Liberal viewpoint, the citizen's capacity and education were largely indicated by his economic position, and this was the idea behind the property qualification. Failing any adequate statistics of income, it was not easy to foresee the practical consequences of the new system. One thing, however, was certain: neither the labourers in the country nor the workers in the towns would ordinarily be entitled to vote in the reformed *Riksdag*. The towns obtained many more seats, proportionately, than the country, and this advantage was considered to cater satisfactorily for the urban middle classes. The exact distribution was unknown, but expectations ran high, and there was great satisfaction throughout the country. No protest was heard from those large classes which were still without any representation, and in any case the reform had brought within the constitution a large number of hitherto unrepresented voters. The former distress in the countryside had now been temporarily eased, part of the surplus population was being absorbed into the new industries, and for a time agriculture had been enjoying comparatively favourable conditions.

Among the groups of society which had now been granted a hearing, the mood at the beginning of 1865 was definitely optimistic. Nevertheless, omens of storm were not lacking. Among them was *Bibelns lära om Kristus* (The Bible's Doctrine of Christ), a courageous book by the young Viktor Rydberg which was published in the early 1860's and which reflected one aspect of the Liberal culture that was now reaching maturity in Sweden.

# XXXIII

# Industrial Development and the Great Agricultural Crisis. Protection and Free Trade

## 1865-1887

The results of the first *Riksdag* elections to be held after the reform disappointed many of those who had supported the measure; for it was the peasant-farmers, not the urban middle class, who triumphed. The assessment of 1861 had greatly increased the value of the farms, and it turned out that a large number of farmers qualified for the suffrage. The opponents of the reform referred to the imminence of a 'peasant rule', and to a certain extent they were right. This development was due to the progress which had been made in Swedish agriculture as a result of the *enskifte* system, and which had been reflected since about the middle of the century in increased exports of grain.

The *enskifte* was a turning-point in Swedish agriculture. Enterprising farmers were able to experiment with a more effective rotation of crops, and the hay from meadowland was supplemented by specially grown fodder, a practice hitherto almost non-existent. Drainage was improved by the use of covered drains; lighter and more efficient ploughs were introduced and other farming implements were brought up to date – wooden pitchforks, for example, which had at best been reinforced with iron, were replaced by those made of steel. Better equipment, and perhaps somewhat better strains, reduced the need for draught animals, while, thanks largely to the fodder crops, the number of cows could be increased. Under such circumstances it was not surprising that agriculture should have made some progress, for which it was praised by Oscar I in his accession speech in 1856.

In the light of this development, the peasant domination in the first reformed *Riksdag*, though regarded with apprehension, was only to be expected. It should be remembered, however, that although the peasant-farmer electorate proved a large one, it only formed one section of the rural population; it is estimated that in 1870 2,690,000 persons were occupied in agriculture, of whom 1,400,000 were independent farmers, against 1,290,000 labourers and casual workers; and many of the homesteads were too small to ensure their owners a vote, or even an adequate livelihood.

The whole system of parties had been expected automatically to disappear in the new *Riksdag* of 1867, an outcome for which de Geer had fervently hoped. But instead, the farmers combined at the outset with certain estate-owners in the Second Chamber to form a new group called the Agrarian Party (*Lantmannapartiet*). Its leaders included the landowner, Count Arvid Posse, who was to play an important part in its history. It was antagonistic to the government and actively supported the interests of the agriculturalists; and it formed a front against the higher civil servants, big landowners, and industrialists who held the majority in the First Chamber, and against the urban and intellectual middle class in the Second Chamber. The Agrarians quickly drew up a detailed programme, in which they demanded firstly the abolition of what they called 'century-old injustices'. These included the old taxes and the military system of the *indelning*, both of which were related exclusively to the land worked by peasant-farmers and had been excluded from the privileges already abolished. The party also advocated strict economy in State expenditure and stringent control of civil servants. The age-old opposition between peasants and civil servants now again flared up into open hostility. 'Bureaucratic Sweden' had seen her best days, and she was tottering on her foundations. Equally marked was the clash between the Agrarians and the rising industrialists. Both the civil servants and the urban middle classes regarded themselves as the creators of modern Sweden; and they did not welcome, therefore, the growing political influence of the farmers, who had by this time acquired a considerable knowledge of political affairs.

The Liberal policy of reform which was being carried out by de Geer's ministry was now temporarily checked, and from 1867 until the mid 'eighties political activity was diverted into less fruitful channels by two complex questions. First, the Agrarians' demand for the abolition of land taxes and other burdens on peasant land; and secondly, the reorganization of the defence system, which was brought forward by the government, and won support both among certain groups in the first Chamber and among the 'intelligentsia' in the Lower. The problems of foreign policy in the middle of the century proved the necessity of such a step, and it was made even more urgent by the Austro-Prussian and the Franco-Prussian wars. The Agrarians, on the whole, were against army reform, arguing that there was no longer any danger now that Sweden was not involved in the European conflicts. It must be admitted that the programme and policy of the Agrarians often struck a petty note; perhaps psychologically they had not yet assimilated the effects of the break-up of the old village community.

De Geer, who remained at the head of the government until 1870, failed to solve the issue. There followed 'a reconstructed de Geer ministry – without de Geer', as contemporary commentators put it. In 1872 the political situation was changed by the death of Charles XV and the accession of his brother Oscar II. The new King was anxious to restore the dwindling influence of the monarchy, and he was well equipped for the task. He was superior to his brother both in ability and character; he was eager for power, but desired also to act as a mediator in political conflicts – an attitude not unlike that of de Geer. With the King's co-operation, a 'compromise' was effected in 1873 with a proposal to buy the reform of the army by satisfying the Agrarians' demands.

This compromise was never put into practice, however. In 1874 the civil servant Edvard Carleson took over with a ministry that was no stronger than the preceding one, and was shaken by a succession of minor crises. Bureaucratic ministries, lacking any strong personality at their head, proved unable to solve the two vexed questions; and things were no better even when a Premiership was created in 1876[1] and de Geer returned as leader of a ministry which included several new men. Though he wished to carry out the compromise, he lacked the power to do so, and his army proposals were rejected by the Agrarian Party. This Party now held the majority in the Second Chamber, and in 1880 its leader, Count Arvid Posse – a party politician and an estate owner and not a civil servant – became Prime Minister. There followed what was almost an experiment in government by a parliamentary majority; but it failed to solve the questions at issue. On Posse's resignation in 1883 a kind of transitional ministry was formed; and it was only when O. Themptander, formerly Minister of Finance, became Prime Minister in 1884 that there seemed any prospect of positive action in the related questions of taxation and army reform. Themptander was a capable civil servant and familiar with the procedure both of *Riksdag* and government; he was also a level-headed and skilful politician who combined determination with flexibility, and in 1885 he achieved a preliminary settlement in the spirit of the 1873 compromise. Military service was to last for forty-two days, as against the former period of thirty, the land taxes were reduced by 30 per cent., and the State took over a similar proportion of the costs of the *indelning* system. Nevertheless, other problems

---

[1] Since 1809 the Council had contained two ministers of higher rank than the others; the Ministers of State for Justice and for Foreign Affairs. Neither was the actual leader of the ministry: there was constitutionally no such functionary until the Premiership was created.

dominated Swedish politics during the next three years. There was impending a great battle over protection, owing to Sweden's involvement in the fundamental changes in the world economy. But before describing the transformation in the Swedish party system, we must refer to other domestic events, more important even than the *Riksdag* issues, which took place between 1865 and 1885.

Briefly, the essential features of Swedish history in these two decades were the progress of industrialization, emigration, the labour problem, the popular religious movements, and the social criticism in contemporary writing. It is even more difficult than in earlier periods, however, to piece together these events from the reported debates of the *Riksdag*.

Although these twenty years were distinguished by fewer outstanding developments than in the years either before or after, they are nevertheless significant. There was, to begin with, the increase in the production of timber, iron, textiles, and machines. Railway construction had been expanding since the 1870's, and in the 1880's steamships acquired greater importance in the Swedish merchant navy. By 1885 the average exports of sawn and planed timber had risen to 3,750,000 cubic metres; it had thus been more than trebled during the last twenty years and now constituted almost half the total export trade. The long-neglected expanses of Norrland had by this time surpassed other districts as producers of timber, and had begun to experience both the advantages and the difficulties of industrialization: in the 1870's the poet Elias Sehlstedt could sum up his impression of the coast round Sundsvall in the oft-quoted line: 'Saw by saw I saw, nor else I saw.' The first serious labour conflict was connected with the Norrland timber industry; this was the Sundsvall strike in 1879, which the State countered by calling out the troops.

The production of pig-iron rose from 145,000 tons in about 1850 to an average of almost 440,000 tons during the eighties, though even in 1890 the old bar-iron methods were still predominant. The Bessemer and the Martin processes were further developed, and this period saw the real beginnings of the mass production of malleable iron. Rolling mills, factories for nails, sawblades, files, etc., were set up, and between 1870 and 1875 the engineering workshops were remodelled and brought up to date; machines, agricultural equipment, and locomotives were manufactured, and shipbuilding proceeded more rapidly. Swedish matches began to be much in demand. Joineries grew up in various parts of the country, and important experiments were carried out in the chemical production of pulp. Many new companies were also formed. Indeed, the 1870's were a boom period, which produced wide repercussions.

Since the middle of the century the problem of the indigent rural population had been eased by the expansion of industry. The population continued to increase, however; at the beginning of the 1870's it was about 4 million, and in 1890 it was 4,785,000. But whereas in 1870 it was estimated that 72·4 per cent. subsisted on agriculture and 14·6 per cent. on industry and crafts, the corresponding figures twenty years later were 62·1 per cent. and 21·7 per cent. Since the middle of the century the absorption by industry had been supplemented by emigration to the United States; and although this left more work available in the Swedish countryside, it involved heavy losses of young and active people, and deprived the country of their strength and energy.

Industry was attracting more and more workers at this time. It is estimated that between 1865 and 1885 the number increased from 54,000 to 102,000, and the demand for labour continued to grow. Social policy could not keep pace with the phenomenal rate of industrial development, and although the workers had started to combine in trade unions, they had not yet found any way of pressing their claims. The time was not far off, however. In 1874, while taking the waters in Karlsbad, de Geer had seen the famous socialist Karl Marx.

He tells how 'they glared at one another between glasses, without getting acquainted', and adds that a congress of one section of the International was gathered at Karlsbad under Marx's leadership. Seven years after this odd meeting, the socialist agitator August Palm, who had encountered Marxism in Denmark, began to preach the doctrine with considerable success. Socialist ideas were also gaining ground elsewhere. In 1886 the Stockholm trade union movement, which until now had not taken up any clear position in political matters, was won over to Socialism, and in the same year Hjalmar Branting and Axel Danielsson were appointed editors of the paper *The Social Democrat*. A great and popular political movement was thus emerging into prominence. Attention had already begun to centre on the new social problems arising from Sweden's rapid industrialization, and investigations were being made into such matters as working hours, child and female labour, and occupational risks and safeguards. But all these were mere beginnings, and it was only in the subsequent twenty years that Sweden began to lay the foundations of a modern social policy.

The Labour movement within the trade unions, which had accepted Socialism as its political creed, was not the only popular movement during these years. There was also the Temperance movement, which was to have both political and general effects on Swedish society and which assumed definite shape after the introduction of the Order of Good Templars in 1879. More important still were the Free Church societies. These were of an even earlier date, and they obtained fresh scope when freedom of religion was granted during de Geer's reform period. The Baptist Free Church movement provides an interesting example of the reaction of the American Swedes on their homeland; for during the 1850's the ground was prepared for the formation in the mid-sixties of a Baptist Church, which owed its encouragement to personal links with those on the other side of the Atlantic; and the same was true of Swedish Methodism, which developed some ten years later. A similar and notable 'free church' of Swedish extraction started during the 1870's with the Swedish Mission Society, whose members had broken away from the State Church. Just as the first revivalist movements had owed their origin to the dissolution of the old village community, so now their growth was accelerated by the changes brought about in the community as a result of industrialism and railways. When the church was no longer the geographical centre of the village, the chapel or the tabernacle often became the place of worship in the new type of industrial settlement. During this period the distribution of the Churches in Sweden became localized; e.g. the Free Churches were centred in Northern Småland, as also in Närke and other provinces where smaller industries flourished, and most of the adherents of these religious movements sprang from among the hard-working members of the lower-middle classes.

Literature, too, was influenced by the new developments. Young radical authors, intent on criticizing and even improving society by their writings, formed a group called 'Young Sweden'. Less single-minded according to their viewpoint, but incomparably the greatest writer of them all, was August Strindberg. In 1879 Strindberg published his novel *The Red Room* (*Röda rummet*), in which, with his characteristic mixture of acerbity and good humour, he criticized civil servants, speculators, and the petty bourgeoisie. Although he was only sporadically in touch with the Labour Movement, its influence is apparent at one stage of the novel, when a carpenter from the poorer quarters of Stockholm speaks his mind to two charitable ladies from the upper bourgeoisie:

'I assure you, ladies, things are already unbearable. And a day will come when they will be even worse; but then – then we will descend from our slums with a roar like a waterfall, and we shall demand back our beds. Demand? nay, take! and you shall be made to lie on carpenter's benches, as I have been, and you shall

eat potatoes till your bellies are tight as drums, just as if you had
gone through the ordeal by water, as we have.'

In his great autobiography *Son of a Servant* (*Tjänstekvinnans
son*), written during the eighties, Strindberg described the
period as a time of ferment not only for himself but for the
country as a whole. Making effective use of paradox, he contrasts the traditional concept of Beauty with the idea of un-
varnished Truth, declaring that the old must be pulled down
to let in air and light. This new style of writing has become
known in Swedish literature as 'the eighties school', and it
reflected in a peculiar fashion both the unrest and the hopes
of the time.

All this seething activity, both intellectual and economic,
had virtually no impact on Swedish parliamentary life
during the first twenty years after the reform of the *Riksdag*.
In the mid-1880's, however, Sweden's close links with the
world economy led to political as well as economic repercussions. Booms and slumps outside Sweden had already been
to some extent reflected at home. But the crisis in the 1880's
was particularly significant in that its chief victims were the
agriculturalists, who still comprised nearly three-quarters
of the population. It is true that this basic industry had continued to develop and that Scanian farming was entering a
golden age under the influence of immigrant landowners and
farmers from Denmark. Elsewhere, too, methods had been
brought up to date. But this progress was not enough to
counteract the effects of the great crisis. These first made
themselves felt at the end of the seventies, and by the middle
of the eighties the situation was serious, an illustration of
the way in which improved communications had drawn the
once remote Sweden into a world economy.

As a result of the development of navigation, which had
already assisted Swedish emigration to America, grain could
now, for the first time, be brought from other continents to the
European market at prices far below the normal. It came
chiefly from America, though Sweden also imported cheap

Russian grain. About the middle of the nineteenth century, Sweden was producing enough wheat and rye for her own needs, and she had also been exporting large quantities of oats. After 1865, however, though oats continued to be exported for some years, the wheat and rye harvests proved inadequate, and there was a consequent rise in imports. But as soon as cheap American and Russian grain appeared in the Swedish market, there was a steep fall in prices – as, indeed, was generally the case at this time. The Swedish wheat and rye growers were hard hit by the changes in the world market. At the same time, the butter exports were rising, and the increase in animal husbandry provided a possible solution to the crisis, as Denmark, also, was beginning to realize. Further remedies, however, were needed.

The second generation of Liberals, the contemporaries of Gripenstedt, had accepted Free Trade as an article of faith; the crisis of the eighties, however, caused many of them to change their minds. Large numbers of farmers, specially those in the grain districts, demanded Protection, a demand which was also made by many industrialists from the point of view of their own economic interests. On the other hand, townspeople and those farmers who were not dependent on grain crops were in favour of retaining the former system of Free Trade. Thus in the middle of the eighties Protection suddenly became the dominant issue in Swedish politics. Everyone was deeply affected by it, with the result that the old party system was completely destroyed. The change started in 1885 and was completed at the *Riksdag* of 1888. When the *Riksdag* met in 1886, the agricultural and industrial Protectionists had joined forces, and thenceforward the supporters of Protection in both Chambers formed a united party, with 'Sweden for the Swedes!' as their slogan; the demand of the Free-traders was 'No starvation tariffs!' – the Swedish equivalent of the English Free Trade cry of 'Cheap bread!' The Prime Minister, Themptander, who had successfully handled the great questions of the army and the land taxes in 1885, favoured Free Trade, as did the rest of the ministry, though he did not consider it his task to solve this new problem. At that time he had a small majority in the *Riksdag*. In the autumn of 1886, the First Chamber elections went against him; but, though he was prepared to resign, he remained in office at the King's request; in this great struggle, as in previous ones, Oscar II was anxious to act as mediator and reconcile the conflicting opinions. Themptander's position at the beginning of the 1887 *Riksdag* was not very strong; and the joint voting in both Chambers was expected to result in a small Protectionist majority. Under these circumstances the King decided, with the agreement of Themptander, to exert for the first time a royal prerogative which he feared would become a dead letter for lack of use: the right to dissolve the *Riksdag* and hold a new general election with a view to obtaining a clearer picture of public opinion. The Second Chamber was dissolved accordingly, and the subsequent elections attracted more interest and a larger number of voters than ever before. Nearly half of those who were entitled to do so recorded their votes. The Free-traders obtained a clear majority, and the government thus found itself in a stronger position.

A further ordinary election to the Second Chamber was held in the autumn of the same year, but the result was roughly the same. But before a *Riksdag* had time to meet, it was discovered that some minor formality had not been observed with regard to a Stockholm voting sheet, and all the names on it were therefore invalid. The places of the elected Stockholm members – who numbered no less than twenty-two – were taken by their Protectionist rivals. The Protectionist party thereby gained the majority, and Themptander asked to be allowed to resign.

The main events of these last twenty years can be summarized very briefly. The rapidly rising middle classes – in the sense of the term current in the 1840's – had hoped that the suffrage would bring them final victory. Instead, the power fell into the hands of the farmers, particularly the more prosperous ones, who used it primarily to abolish any privileges that were left over from the older 'Estates' society, personified in the unreformed *Riksdag*. Meanwhile, the new 'fifth Estate' of industrial workers, like the petty bourgeoisie and the less well-to-do among the rural population, had as yet no place in the political life of Sweden, and they found temporary compensation in the new Labour movement and in Free Church and Temperance organizations. Themptander was far from pleased when, during the Protection crisis, a workers' meeting led by August Palm assured him of their confidence; that he was clearly aware of the problem, however, is shown by his reference in his diary to the position of those excluded from the suffrage: 'The blindness of those in power will teach those below the line (i.e. not entitled to vote) finally to realize their position; but then I fear the reaction will be complicated.'

41. Swedes and Indians in New Sweden.
Contemporary engraving by P. Lindeström.

42. 'America in sight.'
Scene from an emigrant
clipper. Contemporary
woodcut.

# XXXIV

# Swedes Abroad

The first indication that Swedes were leaving – and not, as hitherto, merely entering – the country came in the era of the Teutonic migrations. From about A.D. 500 there is archaeological evidence of a Swedish settlement on the other side of the Baltic Sea, the area which subsequently became the Baltic provinces and States; and the Ansgar legend tells a similar story. In the ninth, tenth, and eleventh centuries Swedish Vikings travelled westwards to the British Isles and Iceland, and even more frequently to Russia and the lands beyond, where they founded states, traded, and plundered. The traces of this eastward emigration gradually disappeared, and it can only be pieced together with the help of prehistoric finds, place-names, and Russian and Arabic sources.

Quite different is the case of those Swedes who settled sometime during the early Middle Ages or possibly even before, along the east and south-east coast of Finland, whence they penetrated inland and mixed with the Finnish tribes who were coming from other parts. The descendants of both these and later Swedish immigrants still form an important tenth of the population of modern Finland; they are concentrated mainly in the provinces of Österbotten, Åboland, and Nyland, and on the wholly Swedish-speaking Åland islands, but small numbers of them are also to be found as far east as Karelia. Up to 1809, they, in common with the rest of Finland, shared Sweden's history. The influence of Swedish culture and civilization was apparent in Finland's legal system, which is based on the same principles as that of Sweden, and in the fact that up to 1906 her parliamentary representation was founded on the old Swedish system of the four Estates. On this subject, the Finnish historian B. Estlander writes:

Who would have thought that, a century and a half after the Swedes had abolished as tyrannical Gustavus III's Swedish constitution of 1772 and the Act of Union and Security of 1789, these laws should still hold in Finland and be invoked as a protection against Russian tyranny?

Finland's Swedish-speaking writers have contributed in full measure to Scandinavian culture. There was, besides Runeberg, Zachris Topelius, whose historical tales and children's books are regarded as popular classics in Swedish literature; and later writers have worked in close collaboration with their Swedish colleagues. The language problem, on the other hand, has caused much bitterness. For a long time the Finnish language was virtually ignored by the educated classes; but by the mid-nineteenth century the national and romantic ideology was beginning to find expression in attempts to make Finnish the dominating tongue. It was a long struggle, and acrimony was intensified at times by its social implications. Gradually, Finnish sentiments prevailed and ultimately took on a definitely anti-Swedish character. Yet Finland's constitution of 1919 states that: 'Finnish and Swedish are the national tongues of the republic. The right of the Finnish citizen to use either his Finnish or his Swedish mother tongue in courts of law or before other authorities, and to have his case dealt with in the same tongue, shall be ensured by law, with equal respect for the rights of both the Finnish- and the Swedish-speaking populations'. In spite of this the matter continued to be discussed in various quarters, until both sides buried their differences in the joint heroism of the Winter War of 1939.

Sites of old Swedish settlements also exist south of the Gulf of Finland, which from 1721 shared Sweden's fate. It is difficult to say when these came into being, but it was probably in the early Middle Ages. In any case, the 6500 or so persons that were recorded in the 1941 census lived on islands and in coastal districts in the north-west part of Estonia, though earlier they had been spread over a larger area. There they preserved the old Swedish methods of farming, fishing and sealing, as well as some interesting dialects; latterly, their education has been ensured by elementary schools, Folk High Schools, and secondary schools. In recent years their numbers have been reduced, largely as a result of deportation to Russia. A small section of this Estonian-Swedish population has had a particularly curious fate. In the eighteenth century the Swedish villages on the island of Dagö, north of Ösel, were owned by a Count Stenbock. He and the Swedes quarrelled over a legal matter, however, the villagers appealed to the Empress Catherine II, and at her command they were transferred in 1781 to Potemkin's new Governor-generalship in southern Russia. Some 1,200 of them therefore set off on foot through Russia, of whom only half reached their destination. They were given land to cultivate beside the Dnieper, and they inhabited their *Gammalsvenskby* (lit. Old Swedish village) until 1929; in that year their request to come to Sweden was granted, and nearly 900 arrived. They still spoke Swedish in a strange dialect. Many of them settled down comfortably in Sweden; since then, however, about one-quarter have returned to Russia, while others have gone to Canada.

Such emigrations as these later became rare in Swedish history, and for some centuries it was immigration that predominated. The immigrants included German burghers and miners during the Middle Ages, Finnish settlers in the sixteenth and seventeenth centuries, Dutch merchants and Walloon smiths also in the seventeenth, and craftsmen and industrialists from Germany, England, and elsewhere at the beginning of the industrial era. But isolated cases of Swedish emigration still occurred, and illustrated various aspects of the country's history. There were, for example, the exiles during the civil strife in the period of Union and the Vasa Age; some of these made contributions to Swedish culture during their exile, including the brothers Johannes and Olaus Magnus, who published their books on Sweden in Italy.

The Swedish emigrants who followed King Sigismund to Poland were also a remarkable group, but they quickly disappeared without trace; whereas most of the Swedes who took service in foreign armies during the seventeeth and eighteenth centuries later returned to Sweden. There was no return, on the other hand, for those who abandoned the faith of their fathers and went over to Roman Catholicism, of whom Queen Christina is the most notable example. A case of collective emigration occurred after the rising in the 1670's, when several of the *snapphanar* from Skåne and Blekinge crossed to Denmark and settled there on lands allotted them by the Danish State.

During the eighteenth century many Swedes fought in French armies, mainly in the Royal Suédois; this regiment was formed at the end of the seventeenth century from French mercenaries, but Swedish soldiers were to be found both in the ranks and to an increasing extent in the officers' corps. Having distinguished itself during the War of the Austrian Succession, it acquired the reputation of being a crack regiment; and only then, half a century after its formation, did it receive its title. Many other Swedes took part in the North American War of Independence on the side of the colonists, including Marie Antoinette's friend Axel von Fersen, who had also experienced long service in France. Those who were sent into exile after the *coup d'état* of 1756 and the murder of Gustav III had an unusual variety of fates: of the banished Gustavians, G. M. Armfelt entered Russian service, and so did G. M. Sprengtporten and several of his Finnish followers. But these aristocrats were isolated cases, emigrés rather than emigrants. At the same time a significant, more anonymous, exodus took place among the lower classes at the end of the eighteenth and beginning of the nineteenth century, when farm hands of both sexes from the southern and western Swedish provinces went over to Denmark; this showed that the rise in population was already having adverse effects on the labouring classes.

It was North America, however, which subsequently received the bulk of Swedish emigration. And here a new type of Swedish emigrant emerged in the colonist who was sent out to other continents by the State, with the object of creating wealth for the home country in accordance with the principles of mercantilism. In the 1650's an attempt of this kind was made in Africa, at Cabo Corso on the Gold Coast, but it came to nothing. Similar enterprises in North America had more positive results. Plans had been made as far back as the 1620's, but they were not put into effect until Christina's Regency. Then, however, Dutch merchants and Swedish aristocrats put their capital into a colonizing enterprise, and in 1638 two ships moored in the Delaware river near the present town of Wilmington. A somewhat vaguely defined piece of ground was bought from the Indians, and here Nova Svecia, or New Sweden, was established with Fort Christina as its centre. The Swedes conducted missions among the Indian tribes, with whom their relations were remarkably friendly; the Indians bought cloth, implements, and trinkets from the settlers, who in return received not only maize and other foodstuffs, but above all valuable furs which it was hoped would form, together with tobacco, their main exports. Occasionally a new expedition arrived from home; and the colony came to comprise, in addition to craftsmen and tillers of the soil, soldiers, deported poachers, army deserters, and Finns expelled from Sweden for despoiling the forested settlements. From 1645 to 1663 this little community was ruled with a fair amount of success by the Governor, Johan Printz – a colourful figure, vigorous, impetuous, and reckless. No gold or spices were found, and even fur and tobacco were only to be had in small quantities. Nevertheless the settlers did much to turn the virgin forest into fertile ploughland. For a long time the colony included only about one hundred male adults, but with the inception of voluntary emigration, several hundred more were added. Among them was an engineer officer, Per Lindeström, whose experiences form one of the most entertaining Swedish books of the seventeenth century. Of the Indians he writes:

These wild men are not called wild because they are believed mad or witless; but for their idolatry and erring faith. They are a kind of people of brownish *couleur*, nimble, deft-fingered, willing, adroit, and quick to learn and apprehend. . . . A well-proportioned people, straight and slender as a rushlight. A courageous race, vengeful, pugnacious, bold in heart, heroic, strong of arm but weak across the back, very supple and light-footed, running like horses, and with a good scent like hounds . . . patient and strong to endure hardship. On the other hand they are vicious, arrogant, prone to boasting, wanton, bestial, distrustful, mendacious and thievish. . . . *In summa*, these Indians are a people of all manner of qualities, more apt to evil than to good. . . .

Lindeström was accompanied on this expedition by the last Swedish Governor of New Sweden, Johan Rising. The latter had but a brief rule. Just as the work seemed to be bearing fruit, the colony was conquered by the Dutch, who were its nearest neighbours. The Swedish King was too busy with the Polish war to spare much thought for his distant subjects, and Fort Christina fell in 1655.

The Swedish settlers remained in the farms and fields where they now felt at home, and at times they were reinforced by newcomers from Sweden, mainly Finns. They were reputed by no less a person than William Penn to be 'a plain, strong, industrious people, proper and strong of body.' They carried on their arduous existence first under Dutch and then under English domination, and continued to speak Swedish up to about 1800. Swedish clergymen were sent out to them, and an interesting literature has grown up around the lives and customs of these Delaware settlers. One of their descendants, John Hanson, was president of the colonial congress at the beginning of the War of Independence in the 1780's; another, John Morton, was a signatory of the Declaration of Independence. By that time they regarded themselves as wholly American, and gradually the little

Swedish colony was absorbed into the great American one, and its native tongue was heard no more.

Thirty or forty years later the Swedish language was being spoken in another part of North America. A rumour had reached Sweden that in a foreign country fertile land was to be had for the asking, with every prospect of future riches for the owner; consequently many of the indigent rural population felt the urge to go out and try their fortunes. Groups of these people followed each other across the Atlantic in small and uncomfortable boats; they pushed inland from the east coast until they reached the frontier, moving ever westwards. A group from Kisa, in Östergötland, founded a colony in south-east Iowa in 1845; and in the following year Erik Jansson, a fanatical sectarian from Hälsingland, reached Illinois with a band of followers who had fled from unsympathetic treatment at home and who established a colony which they called Bishop Hill. Minnesota, Kansas, and Nebraska were peopled by an increasing number of Swedes, who spread by degrees over the entire Middle West; they cleared and cultivated the land, and the earth huts of the early settlers were soon turned into properly built farmhouses. The number of emigrants swelled rapidly after the middle of the nineteenth century when, as a result of the huge steel passenger steamers, mass transport became possible for the first time. The bad harvests of 1867–8 and the agricultural crisis at the end of the 1870's are plainly mirrored in the emigration statistics. Between 1867 and 1886 nearly 450,000 Swedes left Sweden; most of them were country people and the majority aimed for the U.S.A. During the eighties alone, the period of the agricultural crisis, the emigrants numbered 347,000; in 1887, a record year, the figure was 46,900.

Some of the Swedish emigrants remained in New York or in other big centres near the coast; but most of them proceeded westward. And although a few of these stayed in Chicago, the majority went on to the great stretches of forest and prairie in the Middle West which had been thrown open to colonization by the homestead law of 1862. The number of Swedish nationals in America rose from 194,340 in 1880 to 478,040 ten years later, an increase of nearly 283,700, which was balanced by a population growth of 220,000 in Sweden during the same period. Since their first arrival in North America, the Swedes have put under cultivation between 9 and 10 million acres of land – more than the total area of arable land in Sweden. Like the New Sweden colonists, they concentrated on agriculture, though they also went in for engineering and building.

Some of the Swedish settlements which were established during the latter half of the nineteenth century still exist in their original form, and bear a strong resemblance to those in the old country. There is an interesting parallel with contemporary events in Sweden in the revivalist movements which swept over the Swedish portions of North America; the Baptists and Methodists, in particular, won many adherents, and reference has already been made to the inter-action between the religious impulses on both sides of the Atlantic. A Swedish church was set up for the emigrants with the Augustana synod. Thus the Swedes lived and worked in the area which extends west of Lake Michigan to the Rocky Mountains, and from the southern frontier of Kansas in the south to the borders of Canada in the north. The scenery in the north resembled that of Sweden, and the emigrants were often observed to gravitate towards places which offered similar natural conditions to those of their home province. Here we find places with genuine Swedish names – Falun, Stockholm, and others. But although Swedish agricultural settlements are to be found in the New England States, a large number of Swedes settled in the towns: in 1930 there were in Chicago 65,700 born of Swedish parents, and no less than 150,000 of pure Swedish origin. In the same year New York had 37,300 Swedish nationals, Minneapolis 24,900, and Seattle, on the Pacific coast, 10,000. Many

Swedes have also found a permanent home in Canada, largely in Ontario, owing to its proximity to similar settlements in the United States. In 1931 it was estimated that in the whole of Canada there were 34,500 Swedish-born subjects and about 81,000 of Swedish origin. In 1930 the corresponding figures for the United States are 595,000 Swedish-born subjects, and about 1,500,000 if one includes members of the second generation, many of whom have attained to leading positions in the country.

There has been much discussion as to the fundamental causes of this emigration, but here we must confine ourselves to certain pointers. A vital contributory factor was, of course, the overcrowding in the Swedish countryside during the nineteenth century. But there was, as well, a general feeling that at home there were too many restrictions and no prospects. Significant evidence of this is provided in letters from the immigrants. In 1852 a Swede in America writes:

As for me, I have missed Sweden but little. I long realized the oppression of her less fortunate citizens . . . the undue power of the higher classes, the disregard and harshness with which they used it to oppress the poor – A free land where all men have equal right to the benefits bestowed by the Creator – this is what I sought, and found indeed.

Those in Sweden were slow to appreciate the seriousness of the emigration problem; and although a few people realized its implications, the *Riksdag* debates reveal, during the most critical years, an inexcusable unawareness of the situation. By the time the first preventive measures were being taken against the great drain on the population, other factors had entered the picture; industrialization, together with the new democratic trends, had so transformed Swedish economic and intellectual life as to reduce the former strong incentives for emigration. The steady fall in the figures after the 1880's is significant: in the 1860's the average figure per year (for the United States) was about 8,900, in the 1870's over 10,000, in the 1880's about 32,000, in the 1890's about 20,000, in the first decade of the twentieth century nearly 22,000, and in the second 8,150. Moreover, between 1890 and 1910 there was an average annual repatriation of 4,000–5,000.

Necessity and a desire for adventure were among the reasons that had sent Swedes to many quarters of the world during the past hundred years. In Europe, no less than 85,000 Swedish-born subjects were living outside Sweden in 1930. The majority of them had settled in Norway and Denmark (about 31,500 in each), but a large number had gone farther afield. Among the Swedish engineers, business-men, and others who have performed valuable services in Imperial Russia were the Nobel family, who took a vigorous and successful part in the exploitation of the Russian oil-fields, besides making their mark in other industries.

But Swedes have also penetrated lands outside Europe. C. J. Andersson, for example, made a notable contribution to the exploration of Africa in the middle of the nineteenth century. The 'Congo Swedes' worked as colonial civil ser-vants in the Belgian Congo, and for some years Swedes have been active in Abyssinia as military and medical organizers, and political and cultural advisers. Swedish scholars have helped to organize the modern educational system in Egypt, and both here and elsewhere they have engaged in plant breeding. Swedish planters and businessmen are also to be found in various parts of the African continent.

In Asia, too, Swedes have made their mark. Swedish officers have organized the gendarmerie in Persia, while others have directed geological research and other scientific enterprises in China. A Swedish 'Duke Larsson of Mongolia' suddenly emerges as administrator in the Chinese provinces, while Swedish engineers, foresters, lawyers, and businessmen have worked in different parts of the continent, and Swedish explorers led by Sven Hedin have penetrated its undiscovered territory.

Australia has had a steady flow of Swedish settlers, who

were estimated in 1930 to number about 4,000. There is still a small group of some 700 Swedes in the virgin forests of North Argentina; having reached Brazil in the 1890's, they found the climatic and other conditions there too trying, and proceeded farther south. In the Argentine there are Swedish specialists in dairy-farming, and many Swedish engineers and businessmen also hold important positions in South America; while Swedish scientists have contributed to the research into the races and unknown areas of South and Central America. And finally, large numbers are employed in overseas branches or as foreign representatives of modern Swedish industry, of which such a large proportion is concerned with export to remote areas.

# XXXV

# The Triumph of Industrialization:
# The New Issues
## 1888-1905

In February 1888 the Marshal of the Realm, Baron Gillis Bildt, succeeded Themptander as Premier, with a ministry which included both freetraders and moderate protectionists. Protection was now an accomplished fact, and it later became firmly established. Industry was granted protection in 1892, and adjustments were made in the grain duties in the following year. The new system, which ran parallel with the extensive development of dairy farming, came increasingly to form the basis of modern Swedish agriculture; its effects were also felt in industry, specially in those sections that were concerned with supplies to the home market.

Further progress in agriculture resulted from the important technical advances that had been made in recent years, and from the 1880's dairy-farming, too, was stimulated by the manufacture of separators and other modern machines. The completion of earlier developments also brought about an important extension of the cultivation of sugar beet, while sugar refineries sprang up in the areas where this new crop flourished, and sugar became more plentiful in private homes.

The early and mid-eighties had been a period of acute economic crisis; and although the situation became easier towards 1890, another crisis followed. When this had been overcome, however, there ensued what was perhaps the quickest and most remarkable recovery in the history of modern Swedish industry – the third great period of development, if we count those of the 1850's and 1870's as the first two. In addition to the expansion of existing industries, there occurred a succession of remarkable technical innovations. There is room here to mention only a few typical examples of the new features that emerged at the turn of the century.

The export of timber, which had at first been responsible for the industrialization of Sweden, had by this time reached a fairly constant level. This did not mean, however, that there was any stagnation in the timber industry as a whole. New fields of development had been opened up, and the manufacture and export of wood pulp, which had been intensified in the 1880's, now showed a steady increase, owing to the modernization of the newspaper press in the larger countries. Wood pulp had been produced in mechanical mills in Sweden ever since the end of the 1850's; the rise in demand, however, led to the discovery of chemical methods of producing paper pulp, which came into use in Sweden in the 1870's. Swedish technicians helped to perfect these methods; in 1885 the engineer A. Müntzing invented the 'sulphate method' of making brown kraft paper, while C. D. Ekman, who divided his time between Sweden and England, worked out the 'sulphite method' of producing fine white cellulose by other chemical processes. The development was rapid and continuous; moreover, the new methods made no demands on the heavy timber needed by the saw-mills, as they were able to use inferior and even waste wood. Pulp factories were set up in different parts of the country; and although they polluted air and water with evil-smelling fumes and lye, they yielded enormous export returns. The figures speak for themselves; at the end of the 1880's the average yearly production of pulp was 62,100 tons, whereas between 1901 and 1905 it was 430,400 tons, of which more than three-fifths was chemical pulp that had been largely produced by the sulphite process. Norrland gradually increased its contribution to this industrial progress.

A new method of utilizing Sweden's mineral resources was discovered about the same time. The Gilchrist Thomas process, so-called after its English inventor, made it possible for the first time to produce first-class iron from ores containing phosphorus. The method was first tried out in Sweden in the 1880's, and by the 1890's it had acquired far-reaching significance. It so happened that certain of the largest Swedish sources of ore were of precisely this type – as, for example, the ores of Grängesberg in Bergslagen, and the large iron-mines in upper Norrland. A new export trade in ore was immediately launched, since large profits could be gained by sending it in its raw state to the coal-producing industrial countries. Ore was first exported from Grängesberg in 1887, from Gällivare in 1892, and from Kiirunavaara in 1902, by which time good transport facilities were available in the railroad to the ice-free Norwegian harbour of Narvik. The various Norrland orefields north of the Polar Circle soon became important centres of operation, where blasting went on in the mines all the year round. Gradually the Klondyke-like settlements gave place to model communities, which provided the amenities to compensate for the bitter climate. By 1913 Sweden's ore exports had risen to 6,440,000 tons, of which the largest proportion went to Germany.

Another flourishing concern was the metallurgical industry, whose main source of profit lay in the engineering workshops. Although its origins go back a long way, in its existing form it dates only from the 1890's; and since then the industry has never looked back. Its scope was greatly increased as a result of the modern methods of mass-producing steel, and between 1896 and 1900 its annual production rose in value from 43 to 84 million crowns. The predilection of the Swedes for technical work – a bent which the enterprising statistician, G. Sundbärg, in a paradoxical and stimulating study of the national character has related to their lack of interest in people – has established a centuries-old tradition of mining and forging, and produced workers of exceptional quality; and this quality was reflected in the products of Swedish engineering. Many of these continuing achievements were based on Swedish inventions; of these the most important were De Laval's separator and steam turbine, L. M. Ericsson's various contributions to weak-current technique, Jonas Wenström's three-phase engine, F. W. Lindqvist's Primus cooker, G. Dalén's acetylene gas units, C. E. Johansson's instruments for precision measurements, and S. Wingquist's ball-bearings, besides such inventions as Westman's woodcutting instruments, which gave wider scope to earlier enterprises.

Technological developments in electricity have made a particularly significant contribution to the modernization of Sweden. The discovery of how to transform water power into electric energy and transfer it over long distances offered tremendous opportunities to Swedish engineers in the following years. Industry and private homes have benefited equally from electrification, and it is difficult now to imagine the thick winter darkness that was once an integral part of Swedish life. Domestic lighting had originally been provided by means of sticks dipped in resin, candles, or colza- and sperm-oil lamps; and it was not until the second half of the nineteenth century, when oil was tapped in greater quantities, that it was revolutionized by the introduction of the paraffin lamps. Gas, too, was already being used both for street lighting in the big towns, and indoors. But now both paraffin and gas were superseded by electricity, which was generally adopted in Swedish homes in the second decade of the twentieth century.

Life in Sweden was being increasingly influenced by technology and industry. The industries which were producing goods for home markets naturally acquired an increased significance also. Signs are not lacking of the great expansion of economic activity in Sweden at the turn of the century. The development of the joint-stock companies is a striking example; in 1896 they owned 24 per cent. of industry; by 1905 35 per cent. The growth in the size of joint-stock banks was particularly marked; their capital had increased tenfold since the beginning of the 1880's, and

business undertakings as a whole were being brought rapidly
up to date.

As for the people, this progressive industrialization had a
notable effect on their choice of occupation or prospect of
livelihood. Despite emigration the population, which had
numbered about 2,500,000 at the beginning of the nineteenth
century, had increased by 1905 to nearly 5,300,000. In 1880,
about 68 per cent. were still living from agriculture and only
17·5 per cent. from industry, mining, and crafts; the corresponding figures for 1900 were 55 per cent. and 28 per cent.,
and for 1910, 49 per cent. and 32 per cent. The urban
population showed proportionately a similar increase. In
1865 about 12 per cent. of the total population were living
in towns, compared with 22 per cent. at the turn of the
century; furthermore, many small urban communities had
grown up at railway junctions and in the neighbourhood of
the rural industries. The structure of society was undergoing
a radical change.

In 1891 the whole problem of industrialization was ventilated in one of the most important Swedish literary creations
of the century. This was the poem *Den nya Grottesången* (The
new Song of Grotte) by Viktor Rydberg, who, thirty years
before, had contributed to the Liberal discussion of religious
issues with his *The Bible's doctrine of Christ*. His great poem
borrowed its symbols from the Edda myth of the mill Grotte.
The mythical mill became, in Rydberg's hands, the
machinery of industry; and the poem ends in a mood of
dark foreboding which offers but a small ray of hope. The
hustle of modern methods of work, the ruthlessness of
economic competition, child labour, and materialism – all
conduce in the poem towards gloomy prognostications of
imminent disaster. Man, after all, was not yet master of
mechanical development, and the situation in the heavily
industrialized countries of Europe perhaps gave Rydberg
grounds for his fears. For Sweden also was experiencing
similar conditions to those elsewhere in Europe, though in a

43. Bessemer blowing at Sandviken ironworks. Contemporary woodcut.

milder form. Working hours were long: at the beginning of the 1890's factory hours varied between nine and eleven, though usually they were about ten and a half. Child labour was not used to anything like the same extent as in other European countries, and moreover was steadily decreasing; but it was still a serious problem. The justified demands of the women were too often disregarded. The state of the premises was unsatisfactory, hygiene was neglected, and the protection of dangerous machinery inadequate; there had either been no time or no scope for devising improvements. The efforts of the workers to protect their own interests and organize themselves were frowned upon; the 'muzzle law' of 1889 is a typical example of the government's desire to forestall agitation. It is worthy of note, however, that the protection of dangerous machinery had been under consideration since 1884, and in 1889 the safety of workers and factory inspection were regulated by law; such was the modest beginning of social legislation in Sweden. Gradually, almost reluctantly, it was realized that such measures were both desirable and just. Friendly Societies, which had been instituted in the 1870's, were legalized in 1891, and ten years later a Workers' Compensation Act was passed. Viktor Rydberg was to be proved wrong; his vision bore little resemblance to reality.

Having put its trust in the power of Socialism to build a new world, the workers' movement was faced with a momentous task. Nor did the workers lack grounds for confidence. The first signs of progress came at the beginning of the 1880's, and in 1889 the Social Democratic party was formed. Socialist doctrines were enthusiastically expounded on public platforms, and recruits were attracted in ever-increasing numbers. In 1897 the first representative of the Social Democrats, Hjalmar Branting, took his seat in the Second Chamber of the *Riksdag*; and in the following years the Swedish trade unions combined to form a centralized organization, *Landsorganisationen* (the Swedish TUC).

27

The popular movement thus acquired a permanent structure, almost reminiscent of Sweden's strong bureaucratic tradition. In due course the rights of combination and collective bargaining were recognized by the employers, and the workers achieved appreciable results. Frequent use was made of the strike weapon, and conditions of employment were subsequently modified by collective bargaining. This progress is reflected in the rise in wages; those of a skilled industrial worker doubled between the 1860's and 1905, though certain types of manual labourer still had no share in these benefits.

In 1902 the employers, too, joined forces in the Swedish Employers' Union, which was originally intended as a general precautionary measure against strikes; the employers' counter-weapon was the lock-out. The conflicts between the two were sometimes bitter and violent, and extreme language was used on both sides. From 1889 strike-breakers were protected by law, and it was over this question that the most violent clashes of opinion took place, involving two very distinct legal viewpoints. By degrees, virtual agreement was reached on the basis of negotiation, but it was a slow process.

While Social Democracy was making its entrance into Swedish politics – including, ultimately, the *Riksdag* – there had been significant changes both in the party system and in the questions which engaged the *Riksdag* and public opinion. At the 1888 *Riksdag*, during the tariff battle, the Agrarian party had split into a protectionist section, the 'new Agrarian party' and a free-trade section, whose views coincided with those of the centre. The Agrarians joined up again in 1895, but the old party alignments had already begun to crumble; and, after various combinations, they were replaced by a 'Right' and a 'Left', that is, by Conservatives and Liberals in the modern sense, though the dividing-line between them at the outset was so fluid as to be more like a border region. In 1891, after the main points of the protectionist programme had been accepted in a moderate form, the King took an almost unprecedented step in choosing as his new Prime Minister E. G. Boström. For Boström was not a civil servant, but a landowner; he had had a political career in the *Riksdag*, however, and was familiar with its methods and personalities. With the support of majorities of varying composition, he set out to solve, in turn, all the main problems of the day. He generally aimed at achieving a compromise, and to this end he utilized, with frequent success, the joint voting of the First and Second Chambers on questions relating to the budget and taxation. He first tackled the problem of the old land taxes and the organization of the army, and after skilful preparation he finally settled it at an extraordinary *Riksdag* in 1892. A military service of ninety days was prescribed, thus laying the foundations of the modern conscript army; the expense of the *indelning* system, which was retained in a modified form, was to be borne by the State; and the old land taxes were abolished by stages. The nation's budget was now at last wholly based on a money economy instead of on the old natural economy. Boström's reputation increased as a result of this success. He was supported both by the diehard Conservative 'Great Party' in the First Chamber, by the large moderate Conservative group in the Second, and after 1895, by the reunited Agarian party; while his 'national policy', as he himself liked to call it, was opposed by the Radical and Liberal groups, representing the urban districts, in the Second Chamber, by the less Conservative elements in the countryside, and, in due course, by the Free Church members, who, since the 1890's, had been taking an increasing part in politics. One of Boström's most notable achievements was in connection with his defence policy; important additions were made to the navy – not unnaturally, in view of the boom in foreign trade – and extensive fortification was undertaken at Boden, in Norrland. In 1901 the army was further reorganized by Boström's successor, F. von Otter;

thenceforward all males were to undergo a military service of from 8–12 months, and the *indelning* system was completely abolished.

Meanwhile another important problem arose – the question of the franchise; and this was in fact to determine the new party alignments at the turn of the century. The constant rise in wages, specially those of the industrial worker, meant that an increasing number of voters were embraced by the property qualification. Between 1870 and 1905 the electorate rose from 5·6 per cent. of the population to over 8 per cent. The cry was now raised for universal suffrage, and it became particularly insistent at the time of the protection battle and after; it was maintained that this was a natural and just consequence of military service, as a man whose duty it was to protect the country should have a share in deciding questions affecting its welfare. The Conservative Boström was not in favour of the reform and did little to further it; and the fact that his Conservative supporters in the *Riksdag* were strongly against it only strengthened him in his attitude. But the demand was pressed by organized agitation and with the co-operation of the more Radical elements in the *Riksdag*. More and more people came to regard democracy as both necessary and natural. The Radicals in the Lower Chamber, who became known at the turn of the century as the 'People's party', took a particular interest in the franchise question; and in 1900 there was formed the 'Liberal coalition party', which included the solution of this issue among its aims. The need for action was also felt among the Conservatives. Boström had put forward a proposal of reform in 1896, though it was hardly intended to be taken very seriously. After the army was reorganized in 1901, however, it became clear that the franchise must be extended; and von Otter's government made a fresh proposal at the next *Riksdag*. No agreement was reached, for ideas as to the form the franchise might take had not yet germinated. It was obvious, however, that a solution might be achieved on the lines of a compromise proposed by Bishop G. Billing, which offered 'universal franchise with guarantees' against oppression from the majority – that is to say, for those who already had the vote.

Meanwhile another issue had come to the fore – the Union with Norway. Cynical as it may sound to describe this as a source of irritation, it was little else at the time. Indeed, the material advantages which Sweden had gained from the Union during the nineteenth century were surprisingly small – at all events compared with the storms it raised. These cannot here be described in detail, but a few words are necessary to provide the setting for the crisis which came to a head in the early years of the twentieth century.

In an earlier chapter the progress of Scandinavianism was traced as far as the destruction of early hopes, because of political factors, in the 1860's. One positive gain seemed unaffected by this failure : the Union of Sweden and Norway. But it was already showing serious cracks, owing to constitutional and temperamental differences and divergent trends in economic and foreign policy. The Union had been hastily and imperfectly made, and tension was increased by the fact that the two countries had different types of constitution. In the 1880's Norway had established a real parliamentary system, and the Liberals were violently opposed to any features in the Union constitution which might wound the sensitive national feelings of the Norwegians; the attacks were mainly concentrated on the Union's diplomatic representation, which consisted of a joint Foreign Minister (a Swede) and a joint Consular system. The long-drawn-out and monotonous negotiations which took place towards the end of the century need not be described; their main interest lies in their revelation of Norway's growing discontent and her ultimate desire to abolish the Union, and they also indicate the vague and confused character of the Swedish programme. On several occasions the Union question had had a direct impact on Swedish home policy; Boström's

predecessor had owed his resignation to an unguarded
utterance about Norway. Furthermore, Swedish Radicalism
found stimulus in the ideas of its Norwegian counterpart. All
these issues came to a head at the beginning of this century,
and the possible dissolution of the Union had to be faced;
the real point at issue, it might almost be said, was the means
by which this was to be effected.

Meanwhile the negotiations proceeded as usual, and they
centred chiefly on the diplomatic representation of the
Union; this was a question on which the Norwegians, in
view of their recent advances in trade and navigation, were
naturally particularly sensitive. Norway demanded firstly
that she should be granted a Consular Service and then a
Foreign Minister of her own, and finally that arrangements
should be made for dissolving the Union; whereas Sweden
took her stand largely on the view that the various problems
should all be solved together.

This was the state of affairs when, in 1902, von Otter
resigned over his failure to solve the franchise question, and
Boström again became Prime Minister. Boström's second
ministry was less Conservative than the first, and tended to
take an intermediate position with a foot in each camp. He
was now determined to solve the two great questions of the
franchise and the Union, in his usual spirit of compromise.
A government proposal on the franchise was put forward at
the 1904 *Riksdag*; it granted universal and uniform suffrage
for elections to the Second Chamber, but at the same time
suggested certain safeguards; of these, the most important
was proportional representation, which was intended to
protect the interests of the minority. The Liberals rejected
the proposal both at this and the following *Riksdag*, however,
as in their view a majority vote was preferable to proportional representation. This view was shared by certain Conservatives, and indeed there was great diversity of opinion
on the subject.

Meanwhile, the Union crisis was becoming more acute;

differences of opinion arose in the Swedish government, and the Foreign Minister, who had been contemplating certain concessions, resigned in the autumn of 1904. The negotiations which were being conducted by Boström in Christiania broke down at the beginning of 1905. The Norwegians had been increasing their fortifications on the Swedish frontier since 1901, the year that Sweden adopted her new army organization. The situation looked threatening when the *Riksdag* met in January, and 1905 promised to be a stormy year. It was the task of the next decade to solve the questions of Union, franchise, and defence, in that order.

Intellectual achievements were added to material progress in these early years of modern Sweden. There was a new awareness of the Swedish heritage and tradition which was finding its first full expression. A new generation of writers, whose works began to be published in about 1890, reacted against the contemporary world in a very different fashion from that of the contemporaries of Strindberg and the Young Sweden group. The most prominent authors of the nineties – Verner von Heidenstam, Gustaf Fröding, Selma Lagerlöf, Erik Axel Karlfeldt – found their inspiration in the old Swedish civilization of the ironmasters, lords of the manor, and tillers of the soil, a civilization which was being submerged under the great weight of industrialization; and they reacted in their writing against the manifestations of the new age. They harked back to a world of fantasy that bore no relation to modern Sweden. At the same time they based their conception largely on Swedish history and traditions, and therefore created fresh links with the past, not only for themselves but also for their readers. But their patriotism, which did not prevent them from criticizing certain aspects of society, had nothing in common with the sentimental or arrogant forms of patriotism which are sometimes encountered; it had its roots in a real and living tradition. During the eighties and nineties the various Swedish provinces each produced writers who portrayed its peculiar features in literary form; and a similar spirit prompted Artur Hazelius to found the Northern Museum of Ethnology (*Nordiska museet*) and the open-air museum *Skansen*, where monuments of local culture could be assembled. Archaeological research on modern lines was initiated by Oscar Montelius and Hans Hildebrand. The historian Harald Hjärne, discarding the out-worn platitudes, provided a fresh and critical approach to Swedish annals, while a philosophical counterpart to the literary currents is found in the work of Hans Larsson.

Nor were similar achievements lacking in the other arts. Painters who had been trained abroad, such as Ernst Josephson, Anders Zorn, Carl Larsson, Bruno Liljefors, and Karl Nordström turned for their themes to the legends and life of their own country, and the same nationalistic tendency was apparent in the music of Wilhelm Stenhammar, Hugo Alfvén, and Wilhelm Peterson-Berger.

An interesting comparison with this group of writers and artists is to be found in the draughtsman and author Albert Engström, who began working in the 1890's. His humorous sketches, which are of considerable historical value, depict the environment of his childhood and youth in the Sweden of transition. In a pungent caricature of the Free Church preacher and the advocate of temperance he illustrates the reverse side of the popular movements, while the Swedish worker in the period before the labour movement is represented by the famous Stockholm characters of Kolingen and Bobban. The old 'Bureaucratic Sweden' is held up to ridicule in the parson, and the out-dated army system in the ludicrous upper-class lieutenant, the country corporal and the raw recruit; the disappearing traditional peasant type and the country youths and maidens appear in countless variations. The modern upsurge of economic enterprise, on the other hand, can only be glimpsed in the dandified stockbroker and the self-satisfied agricultural expert. With a curious, almost unconscious acuteness, Engstrom has captured and preserved in his comic drawings all the aspects of Swedish life which were ceasing to exist at the turn of the century.

The general philosophy of the writers of the nineties was quite alien to the Swedish working-classes and Social Democrats; the workers, who had as yet made no independent contribution to culture, found Strindberg more to their taste. Nevertheless they, like many others, had begun to study on their own account. Women were demanding emancipation, equal education, and the franchise. Adult education was being vigorously promoted in workers' organizations, temperance societies and elsewhere, and it would not now be long before the Universities' monopoly of culture was broken. Yet this growth of education and self-confidence among the lower classes only intensified their feelings of social injustice and frustration, and increased the bitterness of the class conflict. There was little peace in the society which, at the beginning of 1905, was preparing for the Union crisis and the franchise debate.

# XXXVI

# The Union Crisis; the Franchise Crisis; the Defence Crisis

## 1905-1914

After the failure of his Union negotiations, Boström resigned the Premiership for the second time in the spring of 1905. He was succeeded by J. Ramstedt, a capable civil servant without, however, very wide political experience or authority; and under him the Council was a mere machine for dealing with current business. It was at this moment that the Norwegian government elected to take the offensive. The *Storting* adopted a new consular law; and when this was vetoed by the King on 27th May, the entire Norwegian Cabinet in Christiania tendered their resignations. The King refused to accept them, declaring he could not at the moment form another Norwegian ministry. The *Storting* took this to mean that the Norwegian monarchy, and with it the Union, had ceased to function, and it therefore authorized the Norwegian Council to take over the government of Norway. This 'revolution' in Norway immediately brought the Union crisis to a head. Surprise tactics had been skilfully planned and were carried out at a well-chosen moment: except for those few in the know, everyone, and most of all Sweden, was taken unawares by the decision.

If Swedish sympathies had previously been undefined, and decidedly pro-Norwegian in left wing quarters, they now were no longer so. Norway's action was regarded as a humiliation for the old King, who was not even given the opportunity to abdicate if he wanted to do so. Astonishment soon turned to indignation, and measures were discussed whereby the situation might be saved. Crown Prince Gustav felt that the Union should be declared unconditionally dissolved, since he thought this would greatly advance Sweden's standing with the great powers. But the general opinion was different.

An extraordinary *Riksdag* was summoned, and the question was handled by a special committee which decided on a course of action for the immediate future. The old ministry was dismissed and the *Riksdag's* programme was entrusted to a national coalition government under the chief representative of the right in the Upper Chamber, the ironmaster Christian Lundeberg, who had once before been suggested for the Premiership. This step was in several respects a new departure in Swedish politics. The previous custom on a change of Prime Minister was for some of the other ministers, if not all, to remain in office. This time there was a completely new government. Moreover, the Lundeberg ministry was to implement the *Riksdag's* programme, and in this respect it became, despite earlier attempts, the first ministry to be politically responsible to the *Riksdag.* It was also the first coalition government formed to meet a crisis, and including representatives of the most important groups in the *Riksdag.* In this it foreshadowed the suspension of party strife at the beginning of the First World War, and the coalition government at the beginning of the Second. Furthermore, this was the first Swedish government to include among its members a farmer, Alfred Petersson, and a professional lawyer, the leader of the Liberal coalition party, Karl Staaff; and, curiously enough, it was probably also the first time that the telephone and the telegraph had played a large part in the formation of the government.

The *Riksdag* agreed on a programme, which was successfully carried through by the Lundeberg ministry; after a referendum or a general election, the *Storting* was to present Sweden with Norway's request for secession, and the terms would then be settled. Sweden's conditions were to be the demolition of Norway's recently erected frontier fortifications and the institution of a neutral frontier zone, transit trade agreements between the two countries, and rights for Swedish Lapps to pasture their reindeer in Norway. After careful consideration these terms found general approval among the Swedes, irrespective of political creed and despite the sympathies with Norwegian demands which had earlier been particularly marked among the radicals. Relations between the two countries became increasingly strained during the subsequent negotiations in Karlstad, war seemed imminent, and both countries made military preparations, for which the Swedish *Riksdag* had already granted a credit of 100 million crowns. In the end, the Norwegians accepted the Swedish terms, with certain modifications regarding the frontier fortifications and the neutral zone. A new extra-ordinary *Riksdag* ratified the settlement in October of the same year, and the Union was dissolved towards the end of the month. The wise restraint shown by the King and the Crown Prince, the firmness and unanimity of the Swedish *Riksdag*, and the rational manner in which the government and the negotiators handled the matter – all these factors, together with the relatively good state of Swedish military preparedness, brought Sweden honourably out of the conflict.

The general reaction in Sweden was certainly a great sense of relief, and it was in this mood that the burning domestic questions were attacked. There is little doubt that the separation had, on the whole, a stimulating effect on Swedish life, despite isolated demands for violent action and disappointment when it was not forthcoming. Psychologically the effect was similar to that produced by the loss of Finland a hundred years earlier: the Swedes felt that they must now achieve twice as much as before within their own frontiers. And just as the early nineteenth century was distinguished by great economic and cultural advances, so now there was continued expansion of industry and social legislation. It is significant that the emigration figures, which had already started to fall during the 1890's, now dropped still lower: the mother country was beginning to provide openings as good as those of the New World.

The great progress in engineering and its related industries continued unabated. South American businessmen were using Swedish telephones, Russian farmers installed Swedish separators, there were Swedish engines in Australian power plants, navigation on the seven seas was protected by Swedish lighthouses and buoys, and Swedish matches had a world-wide market. Several of the world-famous Swedish firms, such as Asea (1883), Separator (1883), Atlas-Diesel (1891), Aga (1904), and Skefco (1907) were founded; and meanwhile Sweden's modern merchant fleet was augmented by steamships, the shipbuilding industry was developed, and Swedish trans-Atlantic shipping was launched on quite a large scale. The increase in foreign trade is shown by the fact that between 1911 and 1913 the average yearly export of agricultural products (mainly livestock produce) rose to a value of 126,800,000 crowns, forest products and timber to 196,500,000 crowns, products of the paper industry to 133,900,000 crowns, minerals and their products other than metals (ore and matches came under this heading) to 114,900,000 crowns, and metal products to 151,600,000 crowns – figures that were three times those of a generation previously. The most important imports now included coal and coke, and the artificial manures and the concentrated cattle foods which were demanded by modern methods of agriculture. Nevertheless, economic life in Sweden changed little during the period from the Union crisis to the First World War. The only exception was in the increased industrial standardization and mechanization. Electrification was also carried further and a special State Water Board (*Vattenfallsstyrelsen*) was set up for this purpose. Huge undertakings, both State and privately owned, began to utilize 'white coal' (as water power was picturesquely described) from Lagan in the south to Porjus in the north. Another feature of the time was the advance in home industries; and the steady rise in the standard of living, due to industrialization, was accompanied by a growing market for protected home-produced goods.

Politically, the domestic scene was far from quiet in the decade after the separation from Norway. Foremost among the questions that clamoured for solution was that of the franchise, which many people had come to regard as a political restorative. The autumn elections of 1905 gave fresh scope to the left, and the Liberals possessed both a nation-wide 'Liberal Association' and an able and determined leader, Staaff, whose primary aim was to establish a Swedish 'House of Commons'—that is a 'Lower House' parliamentary system on the English model. When Lundeberg's ministry took a well-earned rest, Staaff was asked to form a Liberal ministry with the specific object of solving the question that had defeated von Otter and Boström – the franchise. Backed by the Liberals, Staaff presented a programme that differed fundamentally from those of his predecessors. His proposals included universal suffrage for the Second Chamber (with certain reservations) and single member constituencies, with simple majority voting; the First Chamber was to remain unchanged, since Staaff believed it would thereby lose its power. This system would lead to parliamentary government on English lines. Against this, the right advocated universal suffrage based, in order to protect the minorities, on proportional representation; this was the system that had been contained in the reform proposal of 1904, now reinforced by proportional voting for both Chambers, the so-called 'double proportional representation'. As his proposal only obtained a majority in the Second Chamber, Staaff resigned in 1906. It was now the turn of the right to devise a solution.

Among the many new phenomena of this year was the birth of modern party organizations. The Liberals were first in the field having achieved theirs, while the right was still in process of organizing itself. The Agrarian party in the

Second Chamber still existed, though since 1902 it had been inferior in numbers to the Liberals. In the 1905 elections the Liberals obtained 106 seats; the right (i.e. the Agrarians and the unattached members who had combined to form the 'Friends of moderate reform') had 99; the Social Democrats 13. The right-wing parties were further regrouped during the 1906 *Riksdag*. In the First Chamber, they were divided between the diehard 'Great party' and a more moderate group. The Conservatives had taken over from the Liberals the idea of a nation-wide organization, and a constituency party association – the *Allmänna valmansförbundet* – had been formed in 1904, which gradually became the right wing counterpart to the Liberal Association. The right wing was thus being steadily consolidated, and on Staaff's resignation it was in a position to take over the government. The task of forming a ministry which, at the King's express desire, was intended to solve the franchise problem fell to one of the most capable of the moderate Conservatives, the naval officer and industrialist Arvid Lindman. Besides being an energetic, conciliatory and popular representative of the industrialists, Lindman was also to prove a fine *Riksdag* tactician, and with great skill he succeeded in uniting the various right-wing industrial and agricultural factions.

In the 1907 *Riksdag* Lindman's ministry proposed an electoral reform on the basis of universal suffrage for all taxpayers for the Second Chamber, proportional voting for both Chambers, and, finally, proportional voting for those local-government bodies which selected the members of the First Chamber. Graded voting in local government elections was to continue, but in a reduced form, and the maximum number of votes was to be limited to forty per person. The right hoped that these provisions would reduce the violence of the 'democratic avalanche', and that the moderately democratized First Chamber would have a sufficiently restraining influence. The moment was a suitable one; many people were weary of the fight, and certain left-wing circles were now willing to accept such proposals. By skilful tactics Lindman secured a majority for his scheme, though with certain modifications, in both Chambers, and the majority in the Second included votes both from the right and the left. According to the provision in the constitution relating to alterations in the fundamental laws of the kingdom, the question had then to be brought up in another *Riksdag*, of which the Second Chamber must be newly elected. The elections were held in 1908; the right gained 83 seats, the Liberal coalition party 98, and the Social Democrats no less than 34; and in addition there were eight non-party members who inclined to the right, and seven inclining to the left. At the 1909 *Riksdag*, the Liberals having withdrawn their opposition, Lindman's proposal was finally approved.

The results of the first elections to the Second Chamber after the reform were eagerly awaited. They took place in 1911, and produced a bigger response than any since the 1887 tariff disputes; 57 per cent. of the electorate (which now formed 19 per cent. of the total population as against 9·5 per cent. just before the franchise reform) went to the polls. Never before had so many Swedes taken part in a political issue. The Liberals obtained 102 seats, the Conservatives 64 – a significant, if not unexpected, reverse – while the Social Democrats rose to 64. The modern party alignment had been established. The right were recruited from farmers, industrialists, and the upper-middle class; the Liberals partly from the old urban Radicals but above all, thanks to the increasingly powerful Free Church and Temperance movements, from the small farmers and tradesmen. The Social Democrats formed a well-organized party of factory workers under the leadership of Trade Unionists and Radical intellectuals, though they were also beginning to turn their attention to other groups among the lower-middle classes.

By this time parliamentary government was so well established that Lindman resigned after these elections. He was succeeded by Staaff, whose new ministry was more Radical

45a. (*above*). 'Bondetåget' (Farmers' demonstration to the King in 1914). Contemporary photograph.

45b. (*below*). Workers' counter-demonstration to the Prime Minister in 1914. Contemporary photograph.

46. Hjalmar Branting. Painting by R. Bergh.

than his previous one. Staaff proceeded to dissolve the First
Chamber, which, like the Second, now received considerable
Liberal reinforcements in the elections as a result of the
1909 reform, though the Conservatives were still in the
majority: the figures were 86 (−42) for the right wing; 52
(+37) for the Liberals; and 12 (+10) for the Social Democrats. The questions that had hitherto been decided by a
joint vote could thereafter be solved on liberal lines. A
further outcome was that the Conservatives now comprised
a consolidated 'National Party' in the First Chamber, and
an Agrarian and urban Conservative Party in the Second,
both corresponding to the constituency party association,
*Allmänna Valmansförbundet.*

During the battle over the franchise, the country as a
whole had taken an increasing interest in politics, and it was
intensified by a great social and political conflict in 1909.
Reference has already been made to the bitter disputes
between workers and employers; wage disputes were frequently accompanied by strikes and lockouts; clashes had
taken place between strikers and blacklegs; and in 1908
there was a bomb outrage by strikers in Malmö on a ship
carrying imported English strike-breakers to Sweden (the
Amalthea incident). Moreover, the international economic
crisis led to reductions in wages − hitherto, real wages had
been rising roughly in proportion to prices − and fresh conflicts, minor lockouts, and strikes ensued. A big lockout was
determined on by the Employers' Union, and the workers
countered with a general strike in August 1909. It was well
organized and proceeded smoothly, and was an impressive
demonstration of the power of the Swedish Labour movement. The movement's progress during the last few years is
illustrated in the membership of the trade unions − 66,000
in 1902 and 231,000 in 1907, though subsequently there was a
slight drop in numbers. Nevertheless, although as many as
300,000 downed tools during the strike, it failed in its object
of proving that society depended on the industrial workers.

28

Gradually, in the late summer and autumn, the various disputes were settled, and the central trade union organ, *Landsorganisationen*, suffered a notable reverse. In the same year, however, the reform of the franchise gave the workers a chance to exert political influence, and they did not fail to make the most of it. The trend of Socialist discussion at the beginning of the century reveals that the original Marxist ideology, had weakened its hold; and at the party congress in 1911 the party programme showed a departure from the strictly Marxist viewpoint in favour of 'humanist' principles, which were advanced chiefly by Carl Lindhagen. The party's representatives in the *Riksdag* adapted themselves without difficulty to its procedure, and there was a certain co-operation between Liberals and Social Democrats.

A factor of vital importance arising from the social conflicts was the general work of reform. This was finally set in motion in the years after the Union crisis, when there was an awakening of the social conscience and a realization of the need to go to the roots of the great social changes that had been so rapidly brought about by the recent industrialization. This work of reform continued steadily and significant results were achieved, often as a result of compromises. One of the most important between 1905 and 1914 was the legislation for industrial safety, which had been shelved since 1889; and the still existing law dates, in a revised form, from 1912, when earlier statutes were consolidated and brought up to date. An extensive inquiry into the temperance problems was begun in 1911, and a law providing for old-age pensions was passed two years later. A new method of settling labour disputes had been introduced as early as 1906, by which government arbitrators were to mediate at the request of the disputants – a step which was to prove of great significance in Swedish society. The so-called Norrland questions were settled as a result of an inquiry in 1904; the farmers were given protection against the timber companies in

1906-9, and in 1907 it was decided that the State should progressively take over the Lapland orefields. By no means least in importance was the comprehensive inquiry into the emigration problem, and the subsequent attempts to improve the chances of livelihood in Sweden by means of 'home loans'. By these means a stable social democracy was being formed, and the basis was laid of the system of social security for which Sweden later became celebrated. In accordance with former practice, the parties co-operated in this work; and although relations were not always harmonious, there was a fair amount of genuine give and take in the committees. The consequent progress was assisted by economic expansion, making possible the installation of water supplies and drainage by the towns and larger communities – a move of equal importance with the legislative steps. Thanks to all these measures, Sweden was soon to be regarded as a pioneer in social legislation. At the same time, curious relics of former times continued to persist: the auctioning of paupers to those who demanded least for their support, for example, was still practised in Sweden during the first years of the twentieth century.

In the task of laying the foundations of modern Sweden and preparing the ground for future reforms, politicians worked together with profit and in a matter-of-fact spirit which survived political conflicts. There was less unity on questions of defence. The Liberals were inclined to be pacifist, while the general outlook of the Social Democrats caused them to oppose defence on principle and regard the army as an institution designed for the protection of the propertied upper classes. Violent anti-militarist agitation was stirred up in various quarters, and this negative attitude was stimulated both by inadequate knowledge of and interest in problems of foreign policy, and by wishful thinking with regard to a future rational world order. Many people in Sweden failed to realize that the competition among the great powers for world trade and world power was already assuming a strong military flavour, and that the regrouping of the alliances during the first years of the century would be followed by a terrible conflict. Nor did many realize that Sweden's new economic power was something that might need to be defended against the covetousness of others. The Liberal's election programme of 1911 included economies in defence expenditure to pay for further social reforms; and at the beginning of his second term as Premier, Staaff cancelled the building of a new type of warship, the F-boat, and set up committees to investigate the defence question – primarily with a view to limiting defence expenditure; and it was this question that provoked the next great political battle.

The cancellation of the F-boat caused a great sensation, and it soon became apparent that there was a considerable desire for a strong defence policy. As a result of a well-organized subscription in 1912, money was raised for building the debated ship. The danger from Russia was emphasized in a sensational pamphlet by the explorer Sven Hedin (*A Word of Warning*, 1912), whose views were heatedly discussed. At the same time, many of the Liberals who took part in the defence inquiry – and above all Staaff himself – believed that the general situation called for development of defence on the lines laid down during the 1890's and in the reorganization of 1901. In December 1913 Staaff published the results: defence must be strengthened. But he did not feel able to achieve this all at once, as such a measure would be incompatible with the previous Liberal programme, and he felt that an increase in the period of military service, for example, could only be obtained after a new election. The subsequent conflict was both violent and unusual. The Conservatives, supported by certain Liberals, demanded immediate and full reform of the army – a view which Gustav V had held since 1911, sometimes in sharp disagreement with the Government. A wave of opinion in favour of strengthening the national defence now swept the country; it was stimulated by skilful agitation, and on 6th February 1914,

30,000 farmers assembled in the courtyard and on the slope in front of the Stockholm Palace – the so-called *bondetåget* (lit. farmers' procession) – and presented the King with demands for a rapid strengthening of the army and navy.

In his famous 'courtyard speech', the King declared his sympathy with the demands of the gathering, and summarized the immediate needs as follows:

'There are undoubtedly those in our land who consider that this is not the moment for regulating the infantry's term of training, but I am by no means one of them; on the contrary, I share the views you have just advanced, namely, that the entire question of defence should be dealt with and decided now, without delay and as a single proceeding. I fully uphold the demands for the efficiency and preparedness of the army, which my military experts declare to be indispensable. Furthermore, to execute its great tasks, my fleet must not only be maintained, but must also be appreciably strengthened.'

Staaff protested against the unparliamentary nature of this procedure, but the King declared that he felt unable to forgo 'the right of communicating freely with the people of Sweden'. The Premier and his government thereupon resigned; and, Liberal attempts to form a ministry having failed, a substantially Conservative government in favour of defence was assembled under the Governor, H. Hammarskjöld, with K. A. Wallenberg, director of the Private Bank of Stockholm and the leading financier of Sweden, as Foreign Minister. The subsequent elections to the Second Chamber were preceded by an election campaign which was marked by several unusual features; Staaff and the Liberals were accused of treasonable tendencies, while the Liberals asserted that the events of the spring embodied attempts to overthrow the constitution. The elections brought gains for the right wing and the Social Democrats (80 and 74 seats respectively), but there were losses and splits among the Liberals (70 Liberal seats, and 6 for the new group of 'Prodefence Liberals'). However, there seemed little prospect of

Hammarskjöld's government being able to carry through its defence programme. Then came the international crisis of the late summer, and on 1st August the First World War broke out. The whole question took on a fresh complexion.

It is almost impossible to describe this complicated and important phase of Swedish history in a few pages, and, since certain essential evidence is not yet available, it is equally impossible to put all the events into the right perspective. But it is one of the key periods for an understanding of modern Sweden. The 'middle way' and the tradition of co-operation were established. The process was accompanied by violent domestic conflict, which was intensified by the unaccustomed novelty of a modern party system, the unnecessarily long delay over important reforms, and the marked distrust of the workers for the traditional elements in Swedish society. Nonetheless, most of these battles had positive results, not least of which was the development of a political awareness in almost all classes.

Meanwhile, popular movements, already foreshadowed during the nineteenth century, were gaining ground. Among them were the Adult Education movement, which now assumed its modern form, and the Co-operative movement, which had made great progress during these years, although it was not finally established until the following decade. Founded in 1899, the Co-operative Association instituted its retail trade in 1904 and its wholesale manufacture in 1908; by 1910 it had 68,000 members. And although the labour movement at first gave it a rather doubtful reception, the subsequent relations between the two were such as to merit the description 'benevolent neutrality'. Interest in athletics and sport also increased during this period, and was greatly stimulated by the Stockholm Olympic games in 1912; and this movement was later to make a significant contribution to the levelling out of class distinctions and the promotion of a new patriotism. The women's movement, too, found a firm footing in these years.

While the great writers of the nineties continued their work, while Strindberg was creating a drama which combined realism and imagination and which was to hold a significant place in European literature, and while these two schools sometimes clashed violently on questions of the day, the romantic dreams and bitter speculation of the *fin-de-siècle* began, in about 1909, to take on a different tone. A new generation made its appearance and embarked on voyages of discovery in the new Sweden. There now emerged the first proletarian writers, above all Martin Koch, and a series of middle-class novelists such as Gustaf Hellström, Sigfrid Siwertz, Ludvig Nordström – the literary apostle of the modern industrialized Norrland – Elin Wägner, and the master of imaginative writing, Hjalmar Bergman. And although some of them endeavoured to be cosmopolitan in this period of intense preoccupation with world affairs, their work retained a typical national flavour.

The Swedish tradition had not been destroyed, either materially or intellectually, by the tremendous changes arising from industrialization. But its stability was to be sorely tested in the world crisis which began in the late summer of 1914.

# XXXVII

# The First World War and the Peace Crisis

## 1914-1922

In the summer of 1914, just as the exchange of notes which followed the Sarajevo murder was about to begin, a political speaker in Sweden announced that 'peace in Europe proper has at present far firmer foundations than the modern pessimists will admit.' This pronouncement must be read in the light of the sanguine belief in future progress which then prevailed, and which had increased after the Union crisis. For many people the downfall of these hopes was a terrible blow; and although the country was not involved in the 1914-18 War, she felt its repercussions until the early 1920's. The main threat was to her chances of self-sufficiency – in politics, in economic life, and in the world of ideas.

When war broke out in August 1914, the defence problem was still unsolved, and party differences were remarkably violent. Swedish policy held to the tradition which had first emerged in its modern form during the Union crisis in 1905, and it was agreed that Sweden should preserve unconditional neutrality. On 2nd August Branting informed the Premier that, as in the present crisis the government was doing its utmost to maintain Sweden's neutrality, it could rely on the full confidence of a united people. And Staaff publicly informed Hammarskjöld that, since there was plainly no hope of concessions from all parties, the Liberals were prepared – in the interests of national unity, and realizing the necessity for an immediate decision – to withdraw their earlier opposition to the proposed extension of the infantry's period of training. The government could therefore depend on Liberal support in the matter.

A party truce was thus declared. Shortly afterwards the new army organization was adopted with the support of the Conservatives and most of the Liberals, although certain Liberals, and also the Social Democrats, had voted against it. The period of training was increased to 340–365 days for ordinary conscripts, and 485 days for student categories who were to be trained for a non-commissioned officers reserve; it was also decided that the navy should be enlarged. Hammarskjöld's government retained office after this reform; as a widely recognized expert in international law, Hammarskjöld was well equipped to carry through the policy of strict neutrality that was declared at the beginning of the war and which had so far been approved by the entire country. And although both Russia and Germany seem to have considered the possibility of Sweden's joining the Central Powers, she maintained a strict neutrality. This policy had a firm basis in the new army reform and the rearmament that this had entailed, and in the mobilized defence forces. And it was soon reinforced by a significant demonstration of co-operation between Sweden, Denmark, and Norway.

The initiative was taken by King Gustav V, whose experience and knowledge of foreign policy proved a valuable asset to Sweden during the long international crisis. In December 1914 he arranged a meeting in Malmö between the three Scandinavian monarchs, who were thereby able to proclaim to the world the joint desire of their kingdoms to remain outside the war. The three Kings continued to maintain contact through their leading statesmen; and three years later they met again, this time – apparently on the suggestion of Gustav V – in Christiania, where the Swedish sovereign's tact did much to efface the painful memory of the Union quarrels:

'I should not be honest, either to myself or to history, if I said that the events of 1905 could yet be forgotten. The rupture of the Union instituted by King Charles XIV . . . inflicted a deep wound on the conception of unity in our Scandinavian peninsula, to whose healing I for my part zealously desire to contribute. It is for this reason, Your Majesty, that I have come here to-day to say to Your Majesty and the one-time partner of the Union: Let us create a new unity, not of the old kind, but an alliance of the understanding and of the heart, whose power will, I trust, be of more enduring nature than the former one."

This new conception was to acquire great importance in the following decades, and has provoked continuing discussion. King Gustav expressed the view that at that stage the basic principle of a Scandinavian policy should be the protection and maintenance of the neutrality determined upon by the three kingdoms. As far as Sweden was concerned, the task made considerable demands both on her statesmen and on the forces responsible for naval and coastal defence. At times, pressure from outside was considerable. One critical situation arose immediately after the outbreak of war, when Russia contemplated making a swift naval attack on Sweden. There was another in 1915, when the Entente were discussing plans to establish a direct link between the Western Powers and Russia through Scandinavia. As Churchill put it: should the English strike a blow through the Belt towards the Baltic Sea or through the Dardanelles towards Constantinople and the Black Sea? As it happened, the latter alternative was chosen. Germany on her side tried both in 1915 and 1916 to induce Sweden to enter into an alliance against Russia, but the Swedish government firmly refused. These crises were not noticed by ordinary Swedes, and they have only since become common knowledge. More noticeable were the problems of foreign trade and supplies; and in its treatment of these questions the government had to take into account both the Entente's blockade policy against the Central Powers and the existence of German mines, not to mention the unrestricted submarine warfare which developed later.

In several important respects, Sweden was not self-supporting at the beginning of the war; she was chiefly lacking in certain foodstuffs. Agricultural progress had continued, and although the farming population had decreased both relatively and absolutely – it constituted about 47 per cent. of the total in 1914 – the constant improvement in methods had led to an increase in production, particularly in that of wheat. But the country was unable to produce enough grain for her needs. In the years immediately before 1914 about 17 per cent. of the country's rye, 48 per cent. of her wheat, and 29 per cent. of all her cereals had to be imported. Besides, agriculture was now more dependent than before on the international situation, as many of the ordinary farmers' needs, such as artificial manures, had to be imported. The position of dairy-farming was for the time being less acute, as improvements had continued steadily since the great crisis in the 1880's, and under normal conditions many dairy products, notably butter, could be exported. But dairy-farming called for maize and concentrated cattle foods, and these came from abroad. Moreover, to maintain its normal production modern Swedish industry required coal, lubricating and fuel oils, machines, and a large number of primary products, including certain metals and raw materials for the textile and rubber industries. Finally, in order to exist Sweden had to keep up her exports, above all timber and wood pulp, machines and other engineering products, and iron ore. The whole economic life of the country was thus far more dependent on a stable foreign trade than it had been in the days of a more primitive economy.

Its policy of strict neutrality brought the country into repeated conflict with the belligerents. The Entente kept a wary eye on all imports to Sweden which might indirectly benefit the Central Powers, while German mines and submarines threatened Swedish ships sailing to England. It was in the interest of the belligerents to keep as tight a control as possible on Sweden's foreign trade. Nevertheless, Sweden adhered consistently to her chosen line, and a large proportion of her foreign trade was brought under State control; for the government was determined to resist all attempts on the part of foreign powers to influence the Swedish economy. Sweden maintained and even considerably increased her trade with Germany during the early years of the war, thereby ensuring herself, among other things, sufficient supplies of coal. In exchange, she sent to Germany not only ore but also goods which depleted her own stocks, such as food and skins. Sweden also continued to export many goods to England, though the imports from that country were greatly diminished. All this resulted in 1916–17 in a large export surplus.

Gradually the scarcity of supplies became noticeable, the more so as harvests were poor. Prices rose rapidly as a result of shortages and inflation. The cost of living, which had doubled between 1914 and the first part of 1918, continued to rise. Attempts were made to control prices, but with unfortunate results; grain was promptly used for other purposes, and crops which were not controlled grown instead; clandestine trade and profiteering in food and other necessities flourished as soon as these became scarce. Supplies were regulated by various commissions: sugar rationing was introduced in the middle of 1916, and flour, bread, fats, and coffee were rationed in 1917. The food and fuel commissions naturally became somewhat unpopular; the latter in particular had to contend with great administrative difficulties, as well as a certain amount of ridicule; wood supplies, however, were sufficiently well organized to ensure that the nation kept warm.

Negotiations were started with England with a view to relaxing the import position, but they came to nothing. The real difficulties began on 1st February 1917, when the Germans launched their unrestricted submarine warfare. The United States then entered the conflict, and the Entente increased its pressure on neutral trade. More and more of Sweden's merchant shipping was mined or torpedoed, and between 1914 and 1918 her shipping losses amounted to 280 ships. Many ships, often carrying valuable cargoes, were also detained in English harbours. The import of concentrated cattle foods during 1917–18 was very low and the output of milk suffered accordingly, although few cattle were slaughtered. The production of substitute goods in industry was small by modern standards. It is true that there was no very serious unemployment, since lumbering provided work for those formerly employed in textiles and other crippled industries. But the rise in prices was very marked and there was widespread discontent.

By 1917 the political unity of 1914 had disintegrated, and at the *Riksdag* of that year the left wing parties made an attack on the government. It was believed in some quarters that the latter was responsible for the shortage of supplies, and members of the left also asserted that on various occasions the government had acted on its own and disregarded the *Riksdag*. At the autumn elections to the Second Chamber a shift had taken place in the position of the parties: the Conservatives, including a number of independent members, had 86 representatives, the Liberals, also taking into account the unattached members, fell to 57, while the Social Democrats had no less than 87. There was thus a considerable left wing majority; and in face of its concerted attacks, Hammarskjöld's government was forced to resign in March 1917. It was succeeded by a moderate Conservative administration, with Carl Swartz as Premier and Arvid Lindman as Foreign Minister.

By the spring and early summer of 1917 the situation had deteriorated so greatly that it was beginning to have marked social consequences, despite the partial success of the government's counter-measures. Food riots broke out, induced largely by the potato shortage. Nor was the opinion on foreign policy so united as it had been in 1914. A section of the right wing sympathized with the Central Powers, while the left inclined towards the Entente; as far as the immediate problems were concerned, this division of sympathies was manifested by a demand from the left that commercial policy should be adjusted in favour of the Western Powers, who might thus help to relieve some of the shortages. The March Revolution in Russia in 1917 and the growth of radical opinion in the Central Powers also had repercussions in Sweden and led to an increasing demand for a democratization of the constitution. The guarantees which the right wing had won for the First Chamber in the electoral reform of 1907–09, above all the graded plural voting in local elections, were now hotly debated. The Social Democrats had long been urging that universal franchise, without a graduated scale, should be extended to local government elections, a view which after 1915 also came to be held by the Liberals; and they had put forward the proposal, though without success, at the 1916 *Riksdag*.

At the 1917 *Riksdag* they tried again, but with no better success. The demands became louder, and in May an extreme left wing group within the Social Democrats formed an independent 'Left Wing Socialist' party containing 15 members. There were heated debates in the *Riksdag*, and on 5th June Branting, who had paid a visit to Petrograd, put a question to Swartz. While the Premier was replying, the police came into collision with the crowd that had assembled for a demonstration in the square outside.

The *Riksdag* debates, however, had failed to clarify the issue, and it was under the slogan of a democratic constitution that the left wing parties approached the trial of strength in the autumn re-elections to the Second Chamber. During the election another, and equally effective, slogan emerged as a result of what was known as the Luxburg affair. It transpired that the German chargé d'affaires in the Argentine, Luxburg, had through Swedish diplomatic channels been sending code telegrams to Germany concerning the torpedoing of Argentine boats. The various Swedish governments had naturally been ignorant of the contents of the communications; nevertheless the affair provoked a considerable scandal. The election produced material changes in the strength of the parties; in the final results the Conservatives obtained 57 seats, the Liberals 62, the Social Democrats 86, and the left wing Socialists 11. In addition, two new parties emerged, each of which represented the farmers as a social group, and had been brought into being by the disputes between the agriculturalists and the rest of the population; disputes which had continued throughout the process of industrialization and were intensified by the war situation. The two parties were the Farmers' Party, which was recruited mainly from smallholders and which gained 9 seats, and the Agriculturalists' Union, representing large farmers, which gained 3; the latter party was later joined by two more members of the *Riksdag*. These rural parties followed earlier attempts at organization on an economic basis in other spheres; and they constituted the beginnings of a popular movement that was to develop after the war and ultimately to comprise a large section of the rural population.

After the elections, Swartz was succeeded in 1917 by the Liberal leader and Professor of History, Nils Edén, who since Staaff's death in 1915 had been the foremost member of the party. As in 1905, however, an attempt to form a coalition of the larger parties failed owing to disagreement over the constitutional question. The reformist tactics which the Social Democrats had gradually adopted were now fully expressed in their willingness to co-operate with the Liberals in forming a government, and Edén's ministry included, in addition to seven Liberals, four Social Democrats. Branting became Minister of Finance, but was soon afterwards relieved by his party colleague, F. V. Thorsson. Parliamentary government, for which the ground had been prepared by the events of 1905 and the ministries of Staaff and Lindman, is considered to have been achieved with the left wing government of 1917; it now obtained a more or less firm footing in Swedish constitutional life, though its

subsequent development had little in common with the programme laid down by the most fervent supporter of responsible parliamentary government, Staaff.

The new ministry was faced with the task of piloting
Sweden through the last hazardous stages of the war, and
one of its first steps was to regulate supplies. In May 1917
Swartz's government had already achieved an agreement
with England, whereby as many as thirty-three ships were
permitted to return home from American and English ports.
Three of these were torpedoed by German submarines,
whose commanders had not been informed that a German
safe-conduct had been granted; the rest brought home
valuable cargoes of grain, concentrated cattle foods, and
maize, which arrived just when the food situation in Sweden
was at its worst: the subsequent harvest failed almost completely as a result of the unusually dry summer. The position
was only partially alleviated by commercial co-operation
between Sweden and the other Scandinavian countries, and
it became a matter of vital importance to procure fresh
imports. Rationing was extended to more and more necessities, including potatoes and lentils, and the number of substitute foods and ersatz goods was increased. Although it had
certain satisfactory features – electrification was speeded up,
for example – the situation was almost out of control. The
food shortage was so serious that it led in some cases to
actual malnutrition, and too little account was taken of
the social effects of the crisis. And since the United States
was beginning to tighten up her commercial policy, the
import problem had now to be approached from a different
angle.

On 1st March, 1918, Edén's government achieved a
*modus-vivendi* agreement with England. Later complemented
by others, this provided for the importation of wheat and
rye, maize, concentrated foods, fertilizers, oil, and coffee,
while restrictions on their distribution guaranteed that the
goods were not passed on to Germany; during 1918 about

47. August Strindberg. Painting by R. Bergh.

48. Gustav v. Painting by E. Österman.

half a million tons' worth of goods were either imported or granted permits. In return, Sweden leased out shipping of 400,000 tons deadweight – about half her merchant tonnage – to the Entente, by whom her ships had for a time, in any case, been forcibly requisitioned. At the same time she agreed to place limits on her exports to Germany, though she carried on parallel negotiations with this country in order to prevent a rupture with the Central Powers.

Although it involved some humiliating concessions, Sweden's neutrality policy was to some extent maintained and for the moment her supplies were more or less safe. But there had been violent differences of opinion on trade policy, as well as an increase in domestic strife which, because of its rancorous nature, helped to weaken the country's collective powers of resistance. It became particularly apparent with regard to two important problems that arose in the last year of the war, one external and one internal.

The Bolshevik Revolution in Russia in November 1917 led to the liberation of Finland but also to the outbreak of violent civil war there. The leaders of the Finnish (so-called White) government requested assistance from Sweden against the Red leaders and their Russian allies. In January 1918 the Swedish government recognized Finland as an independent State; she did not feel able to do more, however, since it was felt that this would constitute a departure from her policy of strict neutrality and involve the risk of her being drawn into the war. A further important factor was the attitude of the Social Democrats, particularly the left wing section, who sympathized with the Red government that was formed in Finland at the end of January, and vigorously opposed the idea of sending help to the other side. Middle-class Conservative opinion in Sweden, on the other hand, demanded that unconditional assistance should be given to the White government. The Edén government considered, and with some reason, that the risk of internal dissension and even

29

civil war over the Finnish question was too great to allow it
to meet Finland's demands for arms, and therefore confined
itself to assisting the return of the Finnish volunteers who
had been trained in Germany. At the same time, a number
of Swedish volunteers joined in the conflict and distinguished
themselves in several encounters. The situation was complicated in February 1918, when a Swedish naval expedition
was sent to the Åland islands in order to protect the inhabitants against the Russians. A deputation from the islands
had already requested, on their behalf, a union with Sweden.
The situation on the islands was a complex one, for, besides
the Russian soldiers, a White Finnish corps had arrived and
was followed later by a Red one. Having negotiated with
these groups, the Swedish expedition arranged that they
should all be removed from Åland under Swedish auspices.
Soon afterwards a German squadron landed on the islands –
part of the military aid which Germany was now beginning
to send – and the Swedish troops were withdrawn. The
significance of the episode stemmed from the anti-Swedish
feeling aroused in Finland, where in certain circles it had
been supposed that the object of the expedition was to
detach the Åland islands from Finland and reunite them with
Sweden. Inside Sweden, the Finnish question had provoked
a dispute, which had a distressing outcome in the prolonged
persecution of the Swedish volunteers. Fortunately, these
differences were expunged by subsequent events.

The disputes over the predominating domestic problem of
democratic constitutional reform were less violent; but this,
too, felt the impact of the critical international situation
which at times increased the bitterness of the conflict.
Demands for reform had become more radical in tone. Not
only had the election strengthened the position of the left
wing and an extreme left wing independent party had been
formed but its whole attitude to the problem stimulated by
the crisis of 1914–18 had become more radical. The conception on which De Geer's system of property qualification

had been based – that money could be used to assess personal, moral, and intellectual capacity – was falsified during this period by revelations of the seamy side of the business world: even during the *Riksdag* debate of 1917 it had been stated as undesirable that 'skill in profiteering should be regarded as a qualification for an influential position in society.'

At the 1918 *Riksdag* Edén's government put forward a proposal to make the local government franchise more democratic, but it was rejected by the First Chamber. In the autumn of the same year an extraordinary *Riksdag* was summoned to deal with certain questions of minor importance. To the assembled members there came the news of the November revolution in Germany, an event which had an immediate and marked effect on Swedish opinion. The possibility of violent revolution was discussed, and the government considered it necessary to intervene in order to calm the atmosphere. Edén had already made contact with the Conservatives in the hope of reaching an agreement by the methods of compromise that were now traditional in Swedish politics, but these negotiations did not have time to mature. Having regard to the great international upheavals, the government gave an assurance to the extraordinary *Riksdag* on 14th November that they would submit proposals for a municipal franchise to correspond with the parliamentary franchise (the proposals were in fact presented eight days later), and announced that they also intended to take up the question of extending the parliamentary franchise itself at the next ordinary *Riksdag*. There were probably several reasons which prompted the Conservatives to agree: pressure was brought to bear on them by the extreme left, the international situation provided an object lesson, various prominent members of the right were doubtless in favour of democratization in principle, and the King was also urging the right to find a solution to the problem. The result was that the Conservatives in both Chambers agreed, with certain provisos, to the introduction of universal suffrage. All the parties thus came to an understanding on the reform question as a whole.

As a result the new regulations for extending the franchise were approved by the following *Riksdag*. These included the lowering of the voting age in Second Chamber elections from twenty-four to twenty-three years, the abolition of certain property qualifications, the introduction of women's suffrage, and the right of women to stand for the *Riksdag*. After fresh elections, these changes in the fundamental law of the constitution were confirmed in 1921. With this franchise reform the final triumph of democracy, foreshadowed by the establishment of parliamentary government in 1917, was achieved. Whereas hitherto just over 19 per cent. of the population had been entitled to vote in the Second Chamber elections, the figure now rose to just over 54 per cent. The result was that the left gained a majority both in the local elections and in the 1919 election to the First Chamber, in which the Conservatives were reduced from 86 to 38, the Social Democrats increased from 19 to 49, the Farmers' parties obtained 19 seats, the Liberals 41 (as against 43 before) and the Left Socialists 3. A further step towards democracy was taken when a Foreign Affairs Commission to control foreign policy was set up, and in 1921–22 the referendum was introduced on similar lines to that in Switzerland and other States.

Taking the war years as a whole, it can be said that Sweden weathered the storm reasonably well. At the end of the war many people fell victim to the influenza epidemic, the more so as malnutrition had lowered resistance to disease. But defence and supplies had been well organized on the whole, and there had been little restriction on freedom of opinion. In about 1916 the 'Activists', who included both Conservatives and Social Democrats, were inspired by the reported threat from Russia to press for 'a bold alliance' with Germany. But this, although hotly debated, did no more than cause unrest, and had no effect on Swedish policy; and most suggestions of this kind were regarded as attempts to surrender Sweden's independent foreign policy. Later, the Bolshevik revolution, the German collapse and the upheavals within the Central Powers led to demands in Sweden for councils of workers, soldiers, and farmers on Soviet lines, but such demands were ephemeral in character and vaguely formulated, and had little direct significance. Sweden's political tradition remained unbroken.

The effects of the revision of the constitution soon became apparent. Greatest of all was the increase in the influence of the Social Democrats; and it was only to be expected that the Edén coalition government should be succeeded in March 1920 by the first purely Social Democrat ministry, headed by Branting. A shift of opinion was revealed in the autumn elections, however, probably due simply to the fact that a number of voters had been scared by talk of socialization. The result was that the Conservatives and the Farmers' parties headed the poll, and Branting's ministry was replaced by a moderately Conservative administration. But this proved no more than a stopgap and, in 1921, after the first Second Chamber elections under the new constitution had taken place, Branting returned to power with the second Social Democrat ministry. In the Second Chamber the Conservatives now held 62 seats, the Farmers (the two parties had now amalgamated) 21, the Liberals 41, the Social Democrats 93, the Left Wing Socialists 6, and the Communists 7; the latter had broken away from the Left Wing Socialists and were wholly imbued with Soviet doctrines and sympathies. Branting's second government remained in office until the spring of 1923.

During these critical years there had been a number of social reforms, some of which were the practical and political outcome of the constitutional revision. Continuation schools were instituted, and a new poor relief law was passed. In 1919 an eight-hour working-day was

provisionally established – it became permanent much
later – thus fulfilling a long-standing demand of the workers, and a new code of marriage laws, which had also long
been desired, was passed by the 1920 *Riksdag*. But the
greatest and most urgent social problem was of quite a
different nature, and was bound up with the economic
difficulties of the peace crisis.

Soon after the Armistice the economic administration
organized by the State during the war was abolished and it
was hoped that conditions would soon return to normal. But
although there was a short period of prosperity, the world
slump of 1920 had repercussions in Sweden and serious unemployment followed. At the beginning of 1922 more than
160,000 men were out of work. Prices fell rapidly and the
inflation of the war years was followed by deflation. The
Unemployment Commission tackled the crisis by emergency
measures; manual labourers were employed on public
works, chiefly the improvement of roads at a wage lower than
the market rates. Meanwhile a violent quarrel took place
between the Social Democrats and the middle-class employers over the regulations for unemployment relief,
particularly as to whether it should be paid during the wage
disputes which had become common as a result of deflation.
Unemployment figures reached their maximum in 1922, but
then began to fall, and at the same time the Swedish crown
reached its former parity with gold. With business improving
all over the world, Sweden likewise recovered rapidly and
entered a new period of prosperity.

Foreign policy was overshadowed by domestic problems
in the years after the war. The general outlook was exemplified in the provisional decree, in 1919–20, for partial disarmament. In 1920, after a lively discussion, Sweden joined
the League of Nations, and she soon had an opportunity of
proving her faith in the new order of international law by
accepting the League's decision on the Åland islands.
The Ålanders had wished to be reunited with Sweden and

the matter had provoked heated discussion, but in 1921 the decision went in Finland's favour.

During these tense eight years, democracy had been fully established with remarkably little turmoil. And although the process took longer than it had done in Norway and Denmark, it was unusually complete. Interest in public affairs, which had earlier found expression in the great popular movements, could now find its outlet in political life. Indeed Sweden, having once been a country of popular movements, was becoming one of large-scale organizations.

The Labour movement, for example, had organized itself within the framework of the trade unions. Marxist ideas were no longer prominent in the party's programme, and though a committee was appointed in 1920 to discuss socialization, it had no appreciable results. The workers' movement in Sweden was beginning to assume a 'negotiating', moderate reformist character, which was due in large measure to the personality and influence of Branting. The temperance movement, meanwhile, rallied enthusiastically round a prohibition motion; a referendum in 1922 produced a small majority against it, however, and since then the question has been in abeyance. This movement, too, has tended to become more and more organized, and a sign of the times can be found in temperance legislation and control of the sale of alcohol initiated during the war. The religious movements also went through a period of organization, though a more revivalist outlook became apparent in new currents of opinion, particularly in the Pentecostal movement. It is characteristic that the popular movement which really established itself during this period, the Co-operative Association, was from the start a highly organized concern. It grew tremendously both during the war and in the critical years just after; between 1910 and the end of 1922 the membership increased from 68,000 to as many as 254,450, and the Association was beginning to hold an influential position in society.

All in all, then, the shifting, colourful, and subjective manifestations of the popular movements were being superseded by the stable and far-sighted directives of the great organizations, whose developments, incidentally, coincided with the final triumph of democracy.

# XXXVIII

# Between the Wars
## 1923-1939

By 1930 Sweden's economic recovery since the mid-twenties from the severe post-war depression could be described as her 'second period of greatness'. The words convey the extent to which gloom, with surprising rapidity, had been replaced by optimism. In view of the experience of the second half of the nineteenth century, it was only to be expected that Sweden would again be affected by world economic conditions and thus share in the international prosperity of the 1920's, but at the same time the country and its people themselves made no small contribution to this recovery.

One of the economic problems confronting industry in the early twenties arose from the eight-hour working day. Curiously enough, in spite of the shorter hours, wages had increased instead of being forced down; this was due to more rational organization, the widespread adoption of modern business methods, and ever-increasing mechanization. Swedish industrial output showed a steady rise during this period, and advances were made both in industry and in communications. Between 1913 and 1939 electric power was increased sixfold, a large number of power plants were built, and in the early twenties the main railways began to be electrified. Motor traffic was encouraged by the roadworks that had been initiated during the unemployment crisis at the end of the war; at the outbreak of war, there had been only a few thousand cars in Sweden, whereas by the end of the thirties there were nearly 249,000 motor vehicles of different kinds, of which the most important, perhaps, were the buses which helped to break down the isolation of the countryside, and the tractors, which brought benefits to agriculture. Since about 1910 the bicycle had also contributed largely to the linking up of remote communities. No more railroads were being built, apart from the new lines in Norrland; but the merchant navy was expanded, and many motor vessels were constructed on modern lines: in 1905 the gross tonnage of Swedish shipping totalled rather over 940,000, whereas in 1939 the figure was about 1,620,000. A beginning was also made in air transport. Meanwhile industry continued to advance along familiar lines. The manufacture of paper pulp was extremely important and was stimulated by improvements in forestry. Products of the rapidly expanding engineering industry provided an increasing proportion of Sweden's exports, and the various goods produced by, for example, the Electrolux Co. entered the world market. There were no great innovations in industry; nevertheless there was a considerable demand for Swedish goods, and more than before the 1914–18 War were sent to countries outside Europe. Moreover, in the 1920's Sweden, who had for so long been dependent on foreign capital, started to export her own. As the booms of the twenties became more marked, the country appeared to be a model of economic well-being and unemployment was reduced to comparatively small proportions.

There is room here to give no more than a chronological survey of the main political and economic events between the wars, and particularly the fundamental effects of the world situation on Swedish history – the historian has neither the necessary detachment nor the material to do more.

In April 1923, once the peace crisis receded and unemployment began to fall, Branting's government resigned. Its resignation was brought about by the First Chamber's rejection of its proposal to extend unemployment relief to those workers who had been drawn into labour disputes. Branting was succeeded by E. Trygger at the head of a Conservative ministry, which was specifically described as a 'democratic national government' – an indication of the way in which the right had been forced to change its character after the revision of the constitution. It had done this on the lines laid down by Lindman during the 1918 *Riksdag* debate: 'Henceforth we must, more than formerly, look for guarantees for a peaceful development in the people themselves, whereas, previously, security has been found in political institutions.'

Branting's government had resigned after a combined attack from Conservatives and Liberals, as neither party held a majority on its own. Nevertheless, a coalition government failed to materialize. The right had only 62 seats in the Second Chamber, whereas the Social Democrats had 93. As a result, the formation of the government in the spring of 1923 introduced into Sweden what has been called parliamentary government by minority, and this now prevailed for more than ten years. Trygger's government remained in office until the autumn of 1924, and thus saw the beginnings of the economic recovery: for it was in that year that production first attained its pre-war level. The government did not tackle any big issues in economic or social policy; its primary concern was to solve the vexed question of defence, which had been put on a provisional basis in 1919, pending the opportunity to arrive at a compromise solution. Trygger's government presented its proposal at the 1924 *Riksdag*; with certain modifications, it maintained as many as possible of the important and necessary innovations of the 1914 defence scheme. However, the proposals were thrown out by the Social Democrats and the Liberals on the grounds that they were too costly and too comprehensive – an attitude which was clearly influenced by the earnest hope of a peaceful world order based on international co-operation; and as the situation was virtually unchanged by the Second Chamber elections in the autumn, Trygger resigned.

During these years, two changes had taken place in the party alignments. To begin with the Liberals split in 1923 into two groups comprising those who stood for teetotalism and had their roots in the country districts and small communities, and a smaller group who adhered to the old-fashioned 'intelligentsia' Liberalism of the large towns, and who took the defence question more seriously than did their former colleagues. The first of these two groups, the *Folkfrisinnade*, had 35 seats in the Second Chamber in 1924, whereas the second group who retained the name of 'Liberals' held only 6. Secondly, the Left Wing Socialists rejoined their original party in 1923, thereby strengthening the position of the Social Democrats; the extreme left wing was now exclusively confined to the Communists, who remained more or less faithful to the Third International, and in 1924 these were themselves split into two sections.

On Trygger's resignation it was again Branting's turn to form a government, with Östen Undén as Foreign Minister. When the Premier died in February 1925 he was succeeded by Rickard Sandler, and on F. V. Thorsson's death shortly afterwards Ernst Wigforss became Minister of Finance. A new generation of Social Democrat politicians now came to the fore. Sandler, Undén, and Wigforss belonged to the academic group, while the workers' movement and journalism were represented chiefly by Per Albin Hansson, who still held the post of Minister of Defence that he had held in the first two Branting ministries. The government's first task was to arrive at a solution of the defence problem acceptable to a majority in the *Riksdag*. This was achieved in 1925 when extensive disarmament was decided upon with the approval of the Social Democrats, the *Folkfrisinnade*, and a few Liberals. Although it had the merit of setting up an air arm and held out the prospect of completing the naval expansion on a smaller scale, this was an ominous decision, and the support given to such a wholesale reduction can only be explained by the hopes that Sweden attached to the League of Nations.

Despite the continued improvement in the economic situation, there was still some unemployment. Several serious labour disputes had occurred during the last few years, relations between employee and employer were often strained, and it was on this conflict, which was linked with the continued but rather uncertain adjustment of industry to new conditions, that political affairs were next concentrated. The old question of unemployment relief in labour disputes was again brought up at the 1926 *Riksdag*; and in June, after sharp disagreements between the Social Democrats and the non-Socialist, 'bourgeois' parties, Sandler's government was defeated. Underlying the party differences on this issue was the clash of two legal doctrines, both of which had been conceived some decades earlier.

The Social Democrats were overthrown by a parliamentary manœuvre on the part of the leader of the *Folkfrisinnade*, Carl Ekman, who had made a career in the temperance movement and journalism. The procedure of the *Riksdag*, and especially the work of party members in committee, offered plenty of scope for a middle party under strong leadership, and Ekman made the most of it, both now and on other occasions. There was therefore every reason for asking him to form the new government. Swedish minority government was thus exemplified in its most extreme form: after the 1924 elections the *Folkfrisinnade* had only 29 members in the Second Chamber and the Liberals who joined them in office only 4. It was the key position of these parties between the Conservatives and the Social Democrats that had given them their influence. Ekman now drew the majorities for his various projects from diverse sources. In the 1927 school reform he was backed by the *Folkfrisinnade*, the Social Democrats and the Farmers, and on other occasions by quite different combinations. In 1928, for example, it was with the support of all 'bourgeois' parties and in face of strong Social Democrat opposition that he put through an important law (covering wages, hours, and conditions) on collective agreements and their validity, and on a special Industrial Court to deal with the legal aspect of labour disputes.

In the autumn elections to the Second Chamber in 1928 the Conservatives increased their seats from 65 to 73, and the Farmers from 23 to 27; the Liberals' position was weakened and the Social Democrats lost 15 seats, 4 of them to the Communists; this result, which was not unexpected, was doubtless due to the widespread alarm caused by a Social Democrat motion for increasing death duties at the preceding *Riksdag*. The government's position was relatively weakened as a result of this marked shift of strength, especially as the Liberals were no longer willing to support the *Folkfrisinnade*. Ekman resigned and a ministry was formed by Arvid Lindman, who unquestionably had a large personal share in transforming the right into a more popular Conservative party; Trygger became Foreign Minister.

Towards the end of the 1920's the general satisfaction, one might say self-satisfaction, over Sweden's successful economic recovery was disturbed by a discordant element affecting the future of Swedish agriculture. Notwithstanding a diminution in the number of people employed on the land, agricultural output had risen in recent years. This was due not least to the work of plant-breeding experts, chiefly H. Nilsson-Ehle; and as a result of experiments at Svalöv and Weibullsholm, seeds had been developed that were specially suited to the Swedish climate and Swedish conditions generally. It was not long before the acute world agricultural crisis had repercussions in Sweden. The farmers demanded assistance and Lindman's government undertook to solve the problem. At the 1930 *Riksdag* it put through measures for the support of dairy-farming, and sugar beet-growing was also assisted, if not in the manner suggested by the government. The latter proposed further that grain tariffs should be raised and that the flour mills should use a compulsory admixture of a certain quota of home-grown grain, a step which would greatly help the arable farmers. Though this last proposal was approved, the proposal to raise grain tariffs was rejected by the left wing parties, and the government thereupon resigned in June. Ekman, who had been largely responsible for this manœuvre, as well as previous ones, was commissioned to form a new ministry. His basis of support, however, was now even narrower, since the Liberals refused to co-operate, and his own party, the *Folkfrisinnade*, only held 28 seats in the Second Chamber. Nevertheless, he succeeded in formulating the final measures for assisting grain production, as usual in the form of a compromise; the tariff proposals were rejected, but the compulsory admixture of home-grown grain was introduced.

The general economic depression, which had begun in America in 1929, reached Sweden in 1931, provoking an industrial as well as an agricultural crisis, and in the autumn, Sweden, following England's example, again went off the gold standard. The crisis reached its climax in 1932, and in the spring of that year the Swedish financier Ivar Kreuger committed suicide. Industry suffered a severe setback and dairy farming, too, was affected by a steep fall in prices. There was again great unemployment and the slump was followed by bitter labour disputes. In mid-May 1931 a disturbance broke out in Ådalen in Norrland, where strikers attacked and maltreated a group of strike-breakers, and when the troops, who had been summoned to the spot, fired on the demonstrating strikers, lives were lost. Though this was perhaps the exception that proved the rule, and Swedish conflicts, political and otherwise, of the last few decades had been generally marked by restraint, this episode made a deep impression and caused much anxiety. No unanimity had yet been achieved either as to the form that unemployment relief was to take or on the question of further assistance to agriculture, especially dairy-farming, to aid which a scheme for controlling the price of milk had been introduced in 1932. Meanwhile the political situation remained fluid and unemployment figures rose; at the end of the year they exceeded 160,000. In the summer of 1932 the discovery that Ekman had accepted money from Kreuger led to a painful reckoning. Ekman was forced to resign: the Minister of Finance, F. Hamrin, took his place, only to resign with his government after the autumn elections, in which great gains were made by the Social Democrats and the Farmers (14 and 9 new seats respectively), while the Conservatives lost 15 seats and the *Frisinnade* 8. The two Communist groups now had a total of 8.

The dividing-line of Swedish politics in the years between the wars fell during the next *Riksdag*. After the elections P. A. Hansson formed a Social Democrat ministry in October 1932, with Sandler as Foreign Minister and Wigforss as Minister of Finance. At the 1933 *Riksdag*, Hansson presented an extensive programme designed to deal with the crisis; public works were to be undertaken by workers paid at market rates, agriculture was to receive more assistance, and an attempt was to be made by a bold financial policy to overcome the depression and pave the way for new recovery. At first there seemed small chance of unanimity on the necessary steps to be taken, until a sensational agreement on the main lines of the programme was reached between the Social Democrats and the Farmers' Union. Relief works were to be carried out according to the normal conditions in the open market – the old form of unemployment relief being maintained on a smaller scale – and the existing support to agriculture was not only to be continued but actually supplemented by a large number of new measures relating to the various branches of agriculture; these were worked out in more detail during 1934. This relief policy, which led to a tighter control of foreign trade, was financed by loans and increased taxes.

It was the parties representing the social groups most directly hit by the crisis, therefore, who now tried to find a compromise solution. Representatives of the other social classes could not upset their majority, although the unexpected coalition between Farmers and Socialists aroused strong opposition. Labour disputes in the building industry

prevented the immediate implementation of the programme;
nevertheless the government was now in a very strong position, which was reinforced by favourable developments in
the world economy. During the next few years the crisis
slackened, especially in industry, and in 1936 there was a
rapid fall in unemployment figures, which at the end of 1933
had risen to 185,000.

In the spring of 1936 the Social Democrats were formally
defeated on a proposal for remodelling the old age pension
scheme according to local costs of living. A short-lived
Farmers' Union government followed, but the strong position of the Social Democrats was confirmed in the autumn
elections when they gained a working majority with 112
seats out of 230; the Farmers' Union lost only one of its
former 37 seats, whereas the Conservatives, by losing 12,
were reduced to 44; the *Frisinnade* and the Liberals, who had
reunited in the People's party (*Folkpartiet*) in 1934, held
27 seats, as against their previous figure of 25. When the
new government was formed under P. A. Hansson, the
alliance between Social Democrats and Farmers was manifested in a coalition; the leader of the Farmers' Union
became Minister of Agriculture and three other members of
the party also became Ministers. In contrast to the period of
minority government, this combination resulted in a strong
government, which, under the banner of *folkhemmet* (lit.
home of the people), vigorously carried out the policy
demanded by the Welfare State.

It was clear that during these years party politics had lost
many of their sharp distinctions. This trend was particularly
apparent in the transformation of the Social Democrats into
a reformist party which virtually discarded the orthodox
Marxist views and instead adopted a typically Swedish
outlook. In a corresponding fashion, the Conservatives had
become a modern, nation-wide party, which frequently
revealed its concern for social questions and its sympathy
with 'liberal' economics. In the centre were the Liberal

groups which had carried over some of the old traditions from the turn of the century, though these had had to be modified after the original demands had been satisfied and new ones had emerged. The policy of the Farmers' Union, which had been rapidly incorporated in the Swedish party tradition, was determined solely by the interests of the social group it represented. The Communists played only a small part in politics and the occasional Nazi-inspired trends found no acceptance. This general levelling-out of differences has helped to reduce party strife, or rather has made it vary with each topic as it has arisen. Principles no longer formed the subject of lengthy debates; at the same time, the useful everyday work continued; and since the 1920's a large number of important reforms have been carried out after careful preparation and in an atmosphere of peaceful compromise. The object of social policy has not been merely to underpin, but to forestall and build up.

Though the nature of the educational reform of 1927 had provoked a certain amount of discussion, there was virtual agreement as to its basic aims: to provide a democratic school system. In 1929 came a lunacy law, and a law to extend the State accident insurance of occupational diseases. In 1934 voluntary unemployment insurance, partly supported by the State, was introduced; in 1935 and 1937 the old age pension scheme was reformed, and in 1938 came holidays with pay and the organization of a national dental service. A great reform of judicial procedure was also begun and completed later. The highways were taken over by the State in 1942–3; and in the course of years a large number of private railways have been nationalized. All this time labour disputes were under continuous investigation. It had become clear that their effect on production was often disastrous and that the results of a dispute were never in reasonable proportion to its cost. Realizing this, the disputants began to appreciate each other's point of view, especially during the exceptional international conditions of the thirties. The Industrial Court, which was created after fierce debate in 1928, introduced a new and interesting legal procedure and has acquired a powerful reputation. Collective agreements have become the general practice, and in 1940 no less than a million workers were involved. The problem of the rights of third parties in labour disputes has also been investigated and discussed, and in 1938 the famous Saltsjöbaden negotiations between the respective organizations of employers and employees culminated in an agreement for averting unnecessary conflicts. The State arbitrators have helped to discover a procedure for the peaceable settlement of differences, while a *modus vivendi* has been found between the once incompatible legal conceptions involved in these disputes.

During this period Sweden was increasingly influenced by the course of world politics. For a long time she was a loyal and independent member of the League of Nations, though this entailed a departure from the neutral line she had followed in the 1914–18 War. As the international situation became more complex at the beginning of the 1930's Swedish interest in foreign affairs increased, bringing with it an appreciation of the danger of her position. This soon had its effect on her attitude to defence, which from the outset had provoked strong and apparently irreconcilable opinions. In 1930 a new inquiry was initiated and its results were submitted in 1935, a few months before Sweden joined in the sanctions against Italy after the invasion of Abyssinia. The Social Democrats on the committee then proposed that some features of the defence system should be modernized and at the same time that the army should be cut down; the opposition on the other hand recommended expansion. Gradually, however – prompted no doubt by the world crisis that was brewing and by the altered conditions in Central Europe – agreement was reached on some of the points at issue. The Social Democrats reluctantly forsook their wholly negative attitude towards defence and in 1936, while the Great Powers were feverishly rearming, a compromise scheme for the reorganization of the army was accepted. It concentrated on the technical modernization of the different arms, and the infantry's normal period of training was fixed at 175 days. It was not long, however, before opinion received a further stimulus; and after Hitler's march into Austria, the Swedish Premier told the *Riksdag* that he had decided on the immediate strengthening of the defences. This was continued in 1939. At the same time Sweden adopted an increasingly cautious attitude to the League of Nations, and in 1938 it was announced by the Foreign Minister Sandler that Sweden reserved the right to remain neutral. But negotiations were already under way to incorporate this policy into a larger Scandinavian framework; in 1938, for example, a preliminary plan was drawn up for Finno-Swedish co-operation in defence of the neutrality of the unfortified Åland islands. The coming war between the great powers was already casting its shadow over Scandinavia.

Swedish society had changed considerably in the twenty years since 1918, as also had the individuals who composed it. Industry progressed, while the percentage of those engaged in agriculture sank still further. Urbanization proceeded equally rapidly; in 1900 21·5 per cent. of the population were living in towns, whereas in 1940 the figure was 37 per cent. But most striking, perhaps, were the reorganization of communications, the modernization of building and interior decoration, and the imposing public buildings which are now to be found even in small towns. Clothing was revolutionized by the ready-made garments and footwear manufactured by the new industries, and parallel with this came an improvement in the conditions and amenities of everyday life.

The Free Church, Labour, and Temperance movements of the turn of the century and the co-operative and educational organizations of the 1910's were now joined by the

economic and political associations of farmers and the rural
youth movements. The farmers' associations played a
significant part in the practical implementation of the policy
of assisting agriculture. The youth movements, political and
otherwise, are an interesting feature of present-day rural
life, and their organizations, which are modelled on those of
their older counterparts, are very active. The black-coated
worker also has his association. The older popular movements
have continued to consolidate, and it has been estimated
that every third Swede belongs to an organization. The
trade unions were estimated at the end of the 1930's to
include nearly a million men and women, the Free Church
organizations about 400,000, and the different Temperance
societies had about 300,000 members, including their youth
organizations. The membership of the Co-operative Association passed the half-million mark at the beginning of the
1930's, and the various agricultural associations soon had
many thousands of members. Besides those offered by the
big organizations, further educational facilities have been
provided by the Folk High Schools, correspondence schools,
the press, films, and broadcasting. And, generally speaking,
the new opportunities have been embraced by all sections of
Swedish society in a strong spirit of idealism, even if the new
forms took some time for assimilation. Intellectual activities
as a whole have been vigorously pursued. Literature and
art have flourished and have reflected in an interesting
manner the vicissitudes of the times; and a new generation
of writers, vying with one another in their presentation of
different ideals and currents of thought, have appeared
from all social classes and all parts of the country. University
education is now far from being considered, as formerly, a
prerequisite of authorship. A new group of leaders has
emerged in both the popular movements and the large-scale
organizations, and a new type of career man, quite free of
the academic and bureaucratic stamp of earlier ages, has
arisen, exemplified by Carl Ekman, P. A. Hansson, and the

farmers who have made their mark in politics. Much new ground has been covered by scientific research, chiefly in the natural sciences, medicine, and technology, while the ecumenical theories propounded by Archbishop Nathan Söderblom have had considerable influence on ecclesiastical development both inside and outside Sweden.

Such was Sweden at the end of the 1930's when, not without reason, she was described by foreigners as the land of the middle way. She had undergone a tremendous transformation, yet in spite of all the political conflicts, it had taken place quietly and with restraint. 'Poor Sweden', as she was called in the nineteenth century, had become in the course of barely a hundred years 'rich Sweden'. Motor traffic had welded the country into a firmer unit than ever before; remote villages were equipped with electric light, telephones, and wireless; and everyone had access to medical and hospital treatment and to education. The idea of poor relief had been superseded by that of national insurance, and a new outlook on social problems was developing. A great deal had been achieved, and few, if any, mourned the good old days.

Much of this advance had taken place during the last twenty years, and by the end of the 1930's the Swedes had shown what they could do in peace-time, despite the disturbance caused by depressions. But the political horizon was darkening, and the tension was increased by Germany's invasion of Czechoslovakia in 1939. Sweden rejected a German proposal for a pact of non-aggression and indicated, by intensifying her negotiations with other Scandinavian countries, that she intended to remain neutral in future conflicts. Soviet opposition, however, prevented the attempts at Finno-Swedish co-operation in the summer of 1939, and in August the European situation was fundamentally altered by the pact between Russia and Germany. The cataclysm was now imminent. The question was whether Sweden had sufficient resources to see her safely through the years to come.

# XXXIX

# The Second World War and After
## 1940-1952

When news of Germany's invasion of Poland reached
Sweden during the morning of 1st September 1939, it did not
come as a surprise. The country was partly, though by no
means completely, prepared for a new war and precautions
of various kinds had been taken in the last few years. As a
result of the speed-up in rearmament since 1938, vigorous
diplomatic activity (particularly with regard to the other
Scandinavian countries), the resumption of a declared policy
of neutrality, and, above all, the deliberate adoption in the
previous ten years of a self-supporting economic policy
designed to support home production and accumulate stocks
of necessary imports, Sweden was now better equipped than
she had been in 1914; she was also more experienced and
more united – and she had need to be.

At the outbreak of war, Sweden, in agreement with the
rest of Scandinavia, issued a declaration of neutrality; and
the next few months were marked by assiduous attempts to
consolidate Scandinavian solidarity. The leading spokesman
was the Foreign Minister, Sandler, and in October 1939 the
negotiations culminated in a public meeting in Stockholm
of the Kings of Denmark, Norway, and Sweden, and the
President of Finland. The Russian advances in the Baltic
States and the pressure on Finland soon showed where the
immediate danger lay. At the October meeting Sweden
refused to follow up earlier plans to send troops to the Åland
islands, but held out prospects of non-military aid; and
Sweden, Norway, and Denmark also endeavoured to give
Finland diplomatic support. But without success; on 30th
November came the Soviet attack. A Scandinavian union
against attack from any quarter would undoubtedly have

found public support; but there was little or nothing to build on and, as yet, little material with which to build.

The Russian attack had a tremendous effect on Swedish opinion, and demands for direct and immediate help to Finland came from many quarters. But the government thought otherwise; to them, intervention against Germany's ally involved too great a risk of their being drawn into the war of the Great Powers. In December, the government became a coalition, in which the Conservatives and the Liberals had two representatives each. The Foreign Minister resigned and was succeeded by a professional diplomat, C. Günther. Though there was thus no direct intervention in the war, the government decided to give as much material assistance and relief as possible to Finland, a policy that was accompanied by an unusual degree of popular enthusiasm. Volunteers from all over the country, from all classes and from most of the political parties, went to the war, while nearly 85,000 rifles, nearly 600 machine-guns, about 300 field-guns, and vast quantities of ammunition were placed at Finland's disposal, as well as millions of pounds' worth of gifts and credits. Nevertheless, in February 1940 Sweden rejected a Finnish appeal for intervention; and in March she withheld her permission from the allies, notably England, to send troops to Finland through Sweden. Immediately afterwards, peace was concluded between Russia and Finland – an outcome which Sweden, too, regarded as a humiliation.

The next important turning-point for Sweden – the German occupation of Denmark and invasion of Norway – occurred on 9th April. Though Sweden had been apprised of Germany's plans of attack, she was ill-prepared and could do nothing. In this critical situation, the government proclaimed complete Swedish neutrality; and after a heroic fight with insufficient means, to which little was contributed by a poorly equipped Anglo-French relief expedition, Norway was forced to surrender. While fighting was in process, the Swedish government rejected German demands for the transit of troops through the country, though she allowed medical supplies to be sent to Northern Norway under supervision. Just before midsummer 1940, however, when hostilities in Norway had ceased, the Swedish government were constrained to sanction the running of leave and supply trains across Swedish territory along the west coast railway to Norway, as well as to allow the transport of munitions and a limited number of troops on Swedish Norrland railways between different parts of northern Norway. This decision, which was not published till 5th July, was doubtless dictated by the awkward strategic position in which Sweden found herself after 9th April, together with the unpreparedness of the Swedish defences, despite the forced pace of rearmament after the outbreak of war. No doubt the government and army staff considered that under these circumstances the rejection of the German demands would render war inevitable – with Sweden's defeat a foregone conclusion. If the events of 9th April had stirred up indignation, grief and bitterness, and led to the widespread conviction that Sweden should fight in support of Norway, the reaction after the transit decision was no less strong. Just as the Winter War of 1939 provoked a popular movement on behalf of the Finns so now there was a similar movement in support of Norway. The hopes of Scandinavian solidarity raised in 1939 had received another severe setback; and it was felt all the more regrettable that Sweden and Finland had failed to achieve a defensive alliance in 1940–1. The prospect was black for both Sweden and Scandinavia, and a great responsibility rested on the government and the people, including not least the military conscripts charged with guarding the frontiers.

Germany's occupation of the western Scandinavian countries and the renewed Russian pressure on Finland, which became more and more open in the summer of 1940, had again altered Sweden's strategic position. As on similar previous occasions, the latter had both political and economic

3¹

aspects. On 9th April Sweden became more cut off from Western Europe and the rest of the world than at any time during the First World War, and the question of supplies became acute. Foreign trade had already suffered badly from the German mines and U-boats; and during the first six months of the war over thirty Swedish vessels had been lost. After 9th April the situation became much worse. About half the Swedish merchant navy lay outside the blockade brought about by the German occupation, and half inside. Approximately 600,000 tons of shipping, unable to return to Sweden, were leased to Great Britain and the United States. The ships that remained in Swedish waters were used primarily for trade with the Scandinavian countries and Germany, and it was from Germany that Sweden received a large proportion of her imports, including artificial manures, coal and coke, forged iron, such industrial goods as were necessary for the expansion of Sweden's defence, and synthetic rubber; in return for them, Sweden supplied Germany with iron ore, wood pulp and other timber products, together with certain industrial products. There were many goods, however, that could not be obtained from Germany; and one of the government's main tasks, specially after 9th April, was to draw up a carefully balanced scheme for distributing supplies within the country. In this they had the advantage of the existing stocks and the increased production of the previous decades.

Rationing, which had only been introduced quite late in the First World War, was regarded as of immediate importance in the Second, and a system was instituted in the first year. A Ministry of Food was set up in 1939 and emergency measures were administered with some success by a series of commissions. Rationing alone was not enough, however; positive steps were required as well. This time, Swedish industry and agriculture very quickly adapted themselves to the crisis: various goods that had previously had to be imported were now manufactured at home and a number of successful substitutes were produced. Swedish raw materials were used to make combustible oil, light metal, and fertilizers; cellulose from wood helped to replace shrinking supplies of woollen fabrics and fodder, and the entire civilian motor traffic was run on generator gas units, charcoal, or wood. The extensive electrification now proved of signal value. Agriculture, to which so much attention had been devoted during the thirties, at first appeared to break down; though this was the fault not of the farmers but of the weather. For two consecutive years the crops were so bad that the harvests of 1940 and 1941 yielded only two-thirds of the normal. The fodder harvests were also poor and a large number of cattle had to be slaughtered, which had a serious effect on meat supplies, though milk remained plentiful and unrationed. Just as beet crops had been developed during the first war in order to satisfy the demand for sugar, so now vegetable oil crops were encouraged during the second. All in all, the situation was met by adjustments in the nation's economy; and the association of employers, workers, and farmers also contributed to the task of organization, which was one of the most complicated aspects of the problem.

But this was still not enough; and the Swedish government therefore took a step which, even if not a very heroic one, was greatly to benefit the ordinary citizen and to lead to increased supplies. During 1940 the belligerents gave permission for Swedish ships, under certain complicated conditions, to carry various cargoes between Sweden and other countries. In 1941 these safe-conduct vessels brought in 12 per cent. of the country's imports, and in 1942 the figure rose to 20 per cent.; and although at times the system was forced to a standstill, it was regularly established again in the spring of 1943. By this means important additions were made to the stocks of, for example, skins and leather, wool and cotton, vegetable and mineral oils, concentrated foods, coffee and tobacco, not to mention grain when the bread supply was threatened by bad harvests at home.

Besides the question of supplies, the government was closely concerned with defence during these critical years. A deep sense of humiliation had been felt during the Winter War in Finland and the German invasion of Denmark and Norway, but there was now added to it the increasing conviction that the nation must work doubly hard so as to be in readiness for any eventuality, and be better able to hold her own in the future. Complete agreement was soon reached on the controversial matter of defence; and the nation responded to an appeal on the part of the government for large loans by raising, between 1940 and 1942, the considerable sum of nearly 2½ milliard crowns in three instalments – a practical and rare proof of united purpose and, incidentally, of good incomes. The new army organization – the five-year defence plan – was presented at the 1942 *Riksdag* and immediately approved, and work on it was then initiated at full speed. Swedish men between the ages of 20 and 47 became liable for military service, the period of training was fixed at 450 days, and the best of the conscripts were given an extra year's or six months' training to qualify them for the officers' or non-commissioned officers' corps. Aircraft and tanks were developed; all types of arms were modernized; and both the coastal defences and the navy were enlarged. A large part of industry was turned over to the manufacture of munitions; there was already an excellent cannon and ammunition factory in Bofors, besides a well-organized shipbuilding industry which could build and fit out warships; but new factories were developed or old ones converted. The situation necessitated long periods of military service for all age groups liable to conscription, and the effective care of their families during their absence – a responsible and difficult task – was successfully undertaken by social legislation. A Home Guard was set up and organized, the women formed voluntary services, and air-raid precautions were also organized. The defence of the country was of the first importance to all.

Various measures were taken to check inflation. A State Commission was set up to control prices, and wages were regulated according to the cost of living. Agreement was reached on ceiling prices and wages at the end of 1942, after the big national organizations had played a decisive part in the preparatory negotiations with the government.

Though the nation was agreed on defence and on economic and political questions, and there was little or no division of sympathies as there had been in the First World War, two matters in particular provoked considerable dispute. First came public utterances on foreign policy. The government considered that the outspokenness of certain newspapers and authors was likely to jeopardize Sweden's good relations with foreign powers, and they therefore put forward certain censorship measures to apply in time of war or threat of war. These were accepted in 1941, though only after heated debates, and they caused little satisfaction in the Swedish press. The second issue, which arose from Sweden's neutrality policy, concerned the concessions that had been made to Germany in the summer of 1940. Criticism increased as the German policy towards Norway became apparent, and in some areas – on the west coast, for example – there was strong opposition to the transit agreements. Nevertheless, this did not prevent Sweden from making still more concessions to Germany.

The third great change in the international situation which directly concerned Sweden was Germany's attack on the Soviet Union in the early summer of 1941. Again, the Swedish government were constrained to make a concession to Hitler, and a division of German troops was allowed to pass from Norway to Finland through Swedish territory. It was, as the Premier put it, 'a once and for all concession', and other such demands were refused. The defensive preparations proceeded rapidly, and in the New Year of 1943, the fourth year of the war, the army chiefs and the government publicly declared that 'every statement implying that resistance is to be abandoned is false.' On 5th August 1943 came the news that the transit agreements with Germany were to be withdrawn in the course of the month. The improvement in the international situation during the previous few months had had an immediate effect on Sweden's position, and the feeling of relief was universal.

Soon afterwards Denmark, like Norway and Finland before her, became the centre of interest. The resistance movement in Denmark had steadily intensified its opposition to the German occupation troops, and at the end of August 1943 Germany proclaimed a state of emergency in the country. At the same time the persecution of the Danish Jews was begun and during the late summer and the autumn they began to flee over the Sound to Sweden. In the war years – up to 1945 – Sweden opened her doors to more than 36,000 Norwegian refugees, and now she received over 15,000 Danes. Nor was this all. When Finland withdrew from the war and made a truce with the Soviet Union in 1944, the German troops stationed in Finland returned to northern Norway, ravaging as they went. Thousands of Finns fled with cattle and belongings over the northern frontier into Sweden, though they were subsequently able to return to their own country.

It was much more difficult to give any help to those beyond Sweden's western frontier, where neither expression of opinion nor diplomatic measures made any impression. This applied, for example, to the deportation of Norwegian students to Germany in the autumn of 1943. It was possible, however, to send some material help to Denmark and Norway; with the tacit agreement of the authorities, the resistance movements in these two countries had been supported in Sweden, where Danish and Norwegian police forces were being trained for service after the war. Greater opportunities for intervening arose during the very last phase of the war. In the spring of 1945 Count Folke Bernadotte, who was assassinated in 1948 while acting as mediator in

Palestine, negotiated with Himmler for the liberation of prisoners in the German concentration camps, and managed to ensure that a number of them, mainly Scandinavians, were transferred to Sweden. Never before had the country contained so many foreigners: in the spring of 1945 they totalled nearly 100,000.

During the war discussion and criticism had been focused on foreign policy. On the whole, the coalition government expressed the outlook common to the various parties, though there were always dissentients who demanded direct intervention in support of Sweden's neighbours. After December 1939 the composition of the government had altered. In 1944 Professor G. Bagge gave up his position as leader of the Conservatives and also withdrew from the government; his successor as leader of the party, the landowner F. Domö, was already a minister. In the same year the new leader of the People's party, B. Ohlin – like Bagge, a professor of political economy – became a member of the government, and the coalition thus retained its general character until the end of the war. It was replaced by an entirely new government in the summer of 1945, however, when an exclusively Social Democrat ministry was formed by P. A. Hansson. The elections to the Second Chamber in 1944 had paved the way for this move. It is true that the Social Democrats had lost the absolute majority they had held in 1940, but they still held exactly half of the seats – 115 out of 230. At the 1944 elections the Conservatives had obtained 39 seats, the Farmers' Party 35, the People's Party 26, and the Communists 15. The 1945 government contained several of the younger generation of Social Democrats, including Tage Erlander as Minister of Education.

The policy of the next few years was dominated by projects of a planned economy, which involved carrying out the nationalization programme of the Social Democrats. Though all parties were agreed in principle on the social welfare policy, there was disagreement as to its scope and the rate at which the reforms could be implemented. In 1947, for example, there was a great deal of dispute over the revision of taxation, the main sufferers from which were those with large incomes and property. At the same time, there were a number of innovations: the Old Age Pension scheme was further improved in 1948, and the system of sick benefits reorganized; furthermore, extensive State planning and modernization of agriculture were decided on in 1947, and have duly been put into effect. The effectiveness of this social policy, however, depended on the abolition of the traditional local-government divisions and the creation of more efficient large-scale local-government organs. Many aspects of the reforms still require a more centralized organization; the scope of the administration is being rapidly widened, and a number of new government departments are in process of development. After considerable discussion, an educational reform, of which the most important provision was for a compulsory school attendance of nine years, was approved in principle at the 1950 *Riksdag*.

Though the supply situation was satisfactory after the war, rationing was either retained or reintroduced, partly in accordance with Sweden's commercial policy and also to enable her to share more fully in the work of international rehabilitation; until 1949 meat, coffee, and sugar were still on the ration; but by 1950, only coffee remained, and it was freed that year. The general economic situation, however, has not been wholly satisfactory. Though there has been practically no unemployment, inflationary tendencies could not be prevented even by far-reaching State control; more-over, imports have been restricted by the extensive regulation of foreign trade necessitated by the foreign exchange position.

Foreign policy was at first dominated by the question of whether Sweden should join the United Nations. This she did in 1946, and in the same year she made a comprehensive trade agreement with the Soviet Union which provided for exports to the value of a milliard crowns, largely on credit.

The next burning question, on which opinion was partly influenced by the Communist revolution in Prague, was that of membership in the Atlantic Pact. Lengthy negotiations took place with Denmark and Norway during 1948 and 1949, designed to produce a joint solution of the defence problem, a step which was made vitally necessary by Scandinavia's position between the Eastern and Western Power blocs. Failing an alliance with any one of the Great Power groups, however, a Scandinavian league proved impracticable. Norway and Denmark joined the Atlantic Pact, while the Swedish government again proclaimed Sweden's neutrality. The question provoked fierce debate, and an alliance with the Western Powers was strongly advocated in certain sections of the Swedish press; on the whole, however, opinion appears to have been in favour of the neutrality policy. In the meantime, the expansion and even the modernization of the defence system has been the subject of investigation and debate.

The 1948 elections to the Second Chamber showed certain changes in the position of the parties. The Social Democrats obtained 112 seats, the People's Party showed a marked rise with 57 (+31), the Conservatives 23 (−16), the Farmers' Party 30 (−5), the Communists 8 (−7). In the autumn of 1946 the party in power underwent an important change on the death of its leader, P. A. Hansson, who was succeeded by Tage Erlander. And in 1949 came the resignation of the Minister of Finance, Ernst Wigforss. In September 1951 a coalition was formed between the Social Democrats and the Farmers' Party, four of whose members became ministers. In the elections to the Second Chamber in the following year the Social Democrats obtained 110 seats (−2), the People's Party 58 (+1), the Conservatives 31 (+8), the Farmers' Party 26 (−4), and the Communists 5 (−3). The coalition remained in power.

In 1950 King Gustav V died at the age of ninety-two, and was succeeded by his son Gustav VI Adolf (b. 1882).

The events of the last few years naturally cannot be regarded as history in the real sense, and much less can they be analysed on broad lines. The listing of the most important facts and the dominating questions must suffice. It would probably be true to say, however, that public opinion is now more concerned with questions of foreign policy than was the case in the years before the Second World War, although these are frequently overshadowed by the concrete problems which affect more directly the interests and livelihood of the private citizen.

# Index